ASTROLOGY YOUR PLACE AMONG THE STARS

ASTROLOGY YOUR PLACE AMONG THE STARS

BY

EVANGELINE ADAMS

GYAN

Published by

Gyan Publishing House
5, Ansari Road
Daryaganj, New Delhi-110002
Phone: 011-47034999, 9811692060
E-mail: books@gyanbooks.com

Distribution Network
gyanbooks.com
India, USA, Canada, UK, Australia

ISBN: 978-93-6280-571-3 (PB)
First Published, 1930

2nd Impression 2024

Printed at: Gyan Press, Delhi.

ASTROLOGY YOUR PLACE AMONG THE STARS
Author: EVANGELINE ADAMS

ASTROLOGY
YOUR PLACE AMONG THE STARS

By

EVANGELINE ADAMS

AUTHOR OF "THE BOWL OF HEAVEN," AND "ASTROLOGY: YOUR PLACE IN THE SUN"

With One Hundred Horoscopes of Famous People

DODD, MEAD AND COMPANY
NEW YORK

FOREWORD

The aim of this book is to give to the public the benefit of the practical findings gleaned by the author through a lifetime of astrological study and human experience in the course of her consultations with hundreds of thousands of clients. These daily and intimate contacts and this extensive research have made possible the interpretations set forth in this volume, so cosmic and yet so human and personal.

No attempt has been made to cover the elementary facts or instructions necessary for drawing up a chart of the heavens, as this has adequately been covered from time to time in many text books on the science.

The Sun, Moon and Planets have been touched upon rather briefly, as a more exhaustive description of them and of the twelve signs in the zodiac can be found in "Astrology—Your Place in the Sun," published by Dodd, Mead & Co. in 1927. In this present volume, the effects of the Sun, Moon and Planets in their passage through the twelve signs of the zodiac have been stressed at great length, and numerous examples of well-known persons in different periods and walks of life have been given to illustrate their operation.

The positions of the Planets, Uranus, Saturn and Jupiter, from about 1850 and through the 20th century, have been tabulated so that the layman, with little or no knowledge of astrology, will be able to discover just when he will come under the chaotic and beneficent influences of Uranus, the adverse effects of Saturn, and the beneficent vibration of Jupiter. With this information in his possession, he will know when to guard his health, when to take advantage of opportunities, when to push forward and when to hold back,—in short, how best to make the most of his life.

There are also tabulations which follow the description of each Planet in the twelve signs, giving the sign position of the Planets from about 1850 on, thus enabling the reader to ascertain the sign in which his own planets were placed according to his date of birth.

The time has passed when it is necessary to present a brief for Astrology, as the latest findings of science prove conclusively that life is vibration and that man is under the influence of the whole universe. We know that the difference between light, color and sound is a matter of vibration; in like manner, the difference between Saturn, which represents the centripetal vibration, and Mars, the centrifugal, is a matter of vibration.

And so with all the Planets.

Not even Einstein's latest contributions to astral science affect this aspect and implication of the Theory of Gravitation; namely, that we are part of a world of mutual influence and that every particle of matter, a star or an atom, and every kind of being, is influenced by (and, in turn, influences) every other.

Therefore, it is desirable that each of us should know the "setting" of our particular world, at our birth and throughout life. To this knowledge of our status and our relationship with the Cosmos, Astrology affords a continuously helpful clue.

The Individual—meaning YOU—should summon to his service all the Power available. That means, in addition to what has already been suggested, the use of all possible psychic force. We live not merely in a physical, but, even more significantly, in a psychic world, to which we should be intimately and consciously related.

The conscious being—YOU, as a spiritual individuality—should draw upon The Subconscious and the Superconscious. Ponder the implied significance of the inspiring suggestion contained in Emerson's lines:

> "The passive master lent his hand
> To the vast Soul that o'er him planned."

That merely means: That, if YOU, mastering the technique of living, make yourself actively passive to all the vast complex of physical and psychical energy in the universe, you can multiply infinitely your power and your efficiency.

Enlightened self-interest, then, should move you to Page Your Fate, and make it serve you most effectively towards a creative career of power, wisdom, beauty, and joy.

INTRODUCTION

MAJOR-KEY TO ASTROLOGY

I

It has often been a source of bewilderment to the student that, with such small variations in the heavens, the variations should be so large on earth. Everybody has just as many signs and planets as everybody else; yet one man is a nobody and another is more than half divine. No study of aspects as such can explain the fact. They "work," more or less, when they are far from being exact; and, on the theory of probabilities, it would seem as if at least a third of the human race should be of noble calibre. As a fact, hardly one man in ten thousand leaves even a transient mark upon his generation. How is this? The problem has always baffled astrologers and encouraged their critics. In fact, few astrologers have fairly faced it.

II

What is the difference between an amœba and an elephant? The cells of which an elephant is composed are one and all not very dissimilar from the amœba. The difference is that one is varied and organized, a harmonious republic; the other remains single.

What is the difference, to go higher in the scale of evolution, between a monkey and a man? The answer is similar. It is not so much the size and weight of the brain that differ; some men with small brains have been the intellectual superiors of men with large brains. But if we take the brain of an ape and that of a man from their envelopes, a radical difference becomes immediately patent. The convolutions in the ape are few and simple; in the man they are many and complex.

There lies the great secret; the men who mould the destinies of humanity are the most evolved and therefore the most highly complex types. They are not men who have small interests here, and small functions there; they have built up every factor in their being into a single composite pattern. Often the manifestations of the complex will be widely divergent, on the surface, but this is only another symptom of the complexity. All this is explained by Astrology.

III

A glance at the horoscopes of the greatest men of whom we have record shows that, generally speaking, the planets form exact or very close aspects, and also—this is the important point—that all, or very nearly all, the planets are interwoven. Sometimes we find two or three complexes in a nativity, perhaps even four; and these have no close relation with one another. Such horoscopes are those of commonplace people. It is as if they had several strands in their nature which had not been properly interwoven. As a result, there are times when one is at work in its own feeble way; then it is forgotten, and another comes into operation. The lack of continuity is fatal to the performance of any constructive work. If such a person should acquire fame, it is the result of some action suddenly conceived and executed, or because of an apparent accident. A few examples of great horoscopes will make these points certain.

Shakespeare, to begin with, has all nine planets in a single complex. Five of them are in aspect within three degrees, and only one is more than ten degrees from the very farthest.

Dante may be said to have two complexes, one of five planets, all within six degrees; another of four, all within nine degrees; and one complex is only nine degrees from the other.

Michael Angelo has six planets within six degrees, with a seventh only four degrees, and an eighth only three degrees away.

Petrarch has six planets within six and a half degrees, and the other three within ten degrees.

Sir Richard Burton has five planets within five degrees and the other four within seven degrees.

Bismarck has seven planets within ten degrees, the other two within four degrees.

Edison has six within eleven degrees; the others within eight degrees.

Shelley has five within eight degrees; three within two and a half degrees, and the other only six degrees from a conjunction with one of the larger complex.

Zola has all nine within eleven degrees; Copernicus, eight within the same limit.

Goethe has two distinct complexes, one of six planets, within thirteen degrees, the other of three within seven degrees.

Napoleon has six within ten degrees, three within three and a half degrees, and the one is but eight degrees from the other.

Newton has three within one and a half degrees, three within five and a half degrees, and three within seven degrees.

Balzac has four within nine degrees, five within ten degrees, and the two complexes are related within seven degrees.

Wagner has five within five degrees, three within six degrees, and the last only five degrees away.

Baudelaire has two complexes within ten degrees, one of five planets and the other of four.

Pasteur has six planets within six and a half degrees, two within three degrees, and the Moon, which stands aloof, is by far the least important of the host of heaven.

Swinburne has six planets within five degrees, the rest within one and a quarter degrees.

If we had chosen to include minor aspects, such as forty-five degrees and one hundred and thirty-five degrees, or the quincunx and sesquiquadrate an even stronger case could have been made out; but it is undesirable to introduce too much subtlety into an argument of this sort; we prefer to base it only upon obvious and patent facts.

IV

In the investigation of any nativity, it is quite useless to content oneself, as is too frequently done, with the consideration of planets in pairs. These will give details of the native, it is true; but it is the complex which decides on what scale these details are to be interpreted. Zola had Saturn trine to Mercury, which made him great in construction. But had not this aspect been merely part of a mighty complex, it would have made him a good merchant, a clever lawyer, or something comparatively common.

Shelley's conjunction of Mars and Jupiter is very differently effective from that aspect in the horoscope of the late J. P. Morgan. Why? Because they form parts of complexes of quite opposite natures. The mere fact that one is in Leo and the other in Libra would not account for the difference. And here it is that we must emphasize the necessity of looking not only for the complex, but for the key to it.

Two men might have identical aspects and yet be utterly different just because in one case the Lord of the Ascendant was Mars and in the other Venus. It is not always easy to divine the secret pivot on which a complex swings. The Lord of the Ascendant is usually the cardinal point, but if there be several planets or even one very strong planet rising, he may be overwhelmed by them or it and his place in heaven, as it were, usurped. And it is of the utmost importance that this fundamental planet be detected with accuracy; for it makes all the difference in the world whether we regard the other planets as modifying Saturn or Jupiter. If the native be a Saturnian at heart, the trine of Jupiter will favor his selfish plans; if a Jupiterian, the trine of Saturn will restrict and balance his enthusiasms. The conjunction of the Sun and Venus which made Shelley so glorious an incarnation of Light and Beauty would hardly have acted in that way had Scorpio, not Sagittarius, been his ascendant. It is the Lord, Jupiter, culminating in conjunction with Mars and Neptune, that determines the disposition, and the superiority of the Sun in Leo to Venus that made effective the manifestation of that disposition in the heart through art; had those planets been influenced by Pisces, for example, it would have shown itself in some soft shadowy way.

Enough has been said for a preliminary account of this matter; in the course of these pages we shall pile Pelion upon Ossa, and Ossa upon Olympus, in demonstration of this secret of the Astrological Complex.

CONTENTS

VENUS SYMBOLICALLY CONSIDERED

MARS SYMBOLICALLY CONSIDERED

JUPITER SYMBOLICALLY CONSIDERED

SATURN SYMBOLICALLY CONSIDERED

URANUS SYMBOLICALLY CONSIDERED

NEPTUNE SYMBOLICALLY CONSIDERED

ASTROLOGY

YOUR PLACE AMONG THE STARS

THE SUN SYMBOLICALLY CONSIDERED

HELIOS, Apollo, Sol, or the Sun, is the center and source of all things in our system. By him are all things, and in him all things subsist.

All the planets are children of the Sun, and in him all their qualities are harmonized and made perfect. There is nothing in them that is not in him; they are but specializations of one power, functions of one body, ministers of one king.

For the Sun is the image of God in the greater Universe, as Man is His image in the lesser.

It is, then, around the Sun that the true fables of all mythologies weave their magic dance. And their legend is ever the mystery which we have learnt in Christian symbol, the threefold mystery of Incarnation—Life, Death, Resurrection and Ascension. These five are one, and this is the history of every God, and every man.

Here is a great secret; if this were understood and valued, it would realize the dream of the adepts—the Brotherhood of Man. It is by virtue of this that Freemasonry has broken down the frontiers of nations, uniting all men in a simple and sublime sacrament that recalls the deepest truths of life to those who are apt to forget them in the frivolities of business, pleasure and ambition.

The Christian Church attempted the same work, and if orthodox religion is broken, it is because the Church insisted upon a literal interpretation of her mystery, confining to one time and place a tragedy as universal as the Cosmos.

For each one of us is the central figure of a drama divine and human. Each one of us has clothed immortal splendour in a veil of flesh, has doomed himself to suffer and to die in order to rise again and mount the heaven with ever-increasing joy and majesty. It is hard for us to realize why this formula must be fulfilled, why the nature of things is such that the incorruptible must feed on corruption, the immortal shroud itself in the cerecloth of mortality. Only when we consciously attain to the enjoyment of life as a sacrament, only when the universe is understood as being a vast replica of our own nature, do we accept the cross, and hail death as the culmination and prize of life.

For the Sun is preëminently Lord of Life and Death. From his glittering eye radiates the glory of life; then from his quiver he draws an arrow tipped with gold, and feathered from the eagle; he draws the string of his ivory bow to his shoulder; it twangs, and the life pours from the veins of the victim. Swift is he and glorious in his chariot, and the horses of Eternity gallop through the galaxies; to right and left he shoots, and misses never his mark. He hath given all, and he will take all back, that it may be made perfect.

Proud is he, and a spendthrift, but his wealth has no limit; bold and free, a prodigal lover; but his heart is great enough for all. He is the heir and viceregent of the Most High and Holy One that is hidden behind his intolerable brilliance. If our eyes could pierce the fiery gates of heaven, we might behold a vaster and more awesome form. Nor should the Sun arise without our meditating upon Him whose representative in matter he is, nor reach the zenith without our thrill of ecstasy in his triumph. At sunset let us pause, and partake of the grand and gloomy mystery of his crucifixion, and even at midnight let us in our silence call upon him, that being, descended into the darkness, who is the herald of our resurrection and ascension.

So also in the course of the Sun in the year, let us study the strange festivals of Egypt and of Chaldea, of Mexico, Peru, India, Persia, Tibet, Greece, Syria, Scandinavia, and Nineveh and Babylon of old. Let us trace their survival in the fasts and feasts of our own day, and, thereby understanding what we do, practise them with zeal and with intelligence.

In this way, we shall not only harmonize and perfect our natures, but thrill them with the rapture of illumination. We shall lose the petty personal consciousness that is the cause of our selfishness, and so of all our miseries and fears, of all our cruelty and our injustice; we shall regain the cosmic consciousness; we shall be once more one with all things, and the Universe will appear in its unsullied glory, freed from the veil of horror and darkness that our own imperfect light has seemed to cast upon its holy and adorable splendour.

Darkness is an infinitely rare phenomenon in the universe. Only on that side of a planet which is turned from its sun does even partial obscurity exist—and how that is recompensed by the aspect of the innumerable host of heaven! Only when clouds arise from the earth is that light hidden. It is not the Sun that is darkened; the veil is tied over our own eyes. It is for us to rise toward the Sun, beyond the cloudbank, and to bask in his glory. If we cannot do that, it is still our own fault; it is the grossness of our bodies, the attraction of the earth. "Set not your affections upon things of earth" but "Seek first the kingdom of God, and all these things shall be added unto you."

THE SUN

As the zodiacal signs form the basis of human temperament, so do the planets possess the magnetic forces which, playing upon that temperament, produce those countless modifications of which mankind is capable. They are the cosmic generators, as it were—the focus points of distinct types of electronic energy.

The four bodies whose influence and position have most to do with human character are the two luminaries, that is the Sun and the Moon, and the two minor planets, Mercury and Venus, whose orbits lie within that of the earth.

Experience shows us that these four react more directly upon the sensitive plate of man's being and have most to do with making him what he is. They have a modified effect upon events. The planets of the other orbits, while also affecting character in a measure, seem to modify it more in an evolutionary than a primary way.

Since prehistoric man stood in the primal jungle—his naked arms upraised in supplication to the morning light—man has worshipped the Sun. Not a plant grows, not a beast of the field nor a bird of the air, but lives in reference to and from the beneficence of the central orb. But for its light and power the very earth would cease to be. But for our continued baths in its warmth, we should become as sprouted potatoes in a cellar, white and lifeless. Not by any accident did the fire worshipper adore it, and the Greeks glorify it as Helios-Sol-Apollo, and with countless other names. He is "Sanso," the sun-god of India.

The individuality, indicated by the Sun, is to man's nature as the Sun to the Universe, its very formative force and center of life.

Thus in the correspondence between the Sun's position in the Universe, his passage through the Zodiac and his aspect to the planets revolving around him, we have the major measure of human nature and in each particular instance the primary major of that individuality. All other planetary aspects, positions and influences relate to these central and major aspects, positions and influences of the Sun in measure as the planets themselves relate to the Sun. There must be no confusion between what we mean as individuality, personality, temperament, mentality and character. Individuality is the thing we *feel* behind a handshake, behind our likes and dislikes, behind casual manners. Charm of manner is a matter of temperament and color. The swift come and go, the moods and habits are matters of personality. The ways of reacting, of speaking, frowning and smiling are matters of disposition.

A weak Sun (or individuality) in a horoscope implies a weak nature, no matter how many other strong factors are found, and vice versa, a strong Sun will carry a nativity far.

A strong Sun implies nobility of character, sturdiness of courage, dependability of action and integrity of purpose. It gives firmness to the nature and a strong sense of right and wrong. The Sun so endowed implies a sound mind and, unless other planets are unusually malefic, a strong and healthy body.

It is a splendid testimony for ultimate success because it so coordinates, so attunes the centers of the nature, so adjusts the attributes of individuality, that minor disturbances and humiliation tend to melt away with the years, leaving the simple fibre of a true nature.

An afflicted Sun is a strong testimony of individual limitation. The limitation may be one of character, of worth or of mental balance, of emotional capacity, of moral integrity, or of bodily health, in one, or may be in all of their ways, depending upon the type or the degree of malefic influences.

The Sun in the earthy signs gives excess of energy, increases pride and haughtiness and gives a headstrong individuality. In the airy signs it inclines to intellectual energy, to ability, social interest, arts and sciences. In the watery signs, a strong Sun gives great emotion, passion and sympathy, endowing great sex inclination, and capacity. In fiery signs, a strong Sun tends to power, ambition, leadership, gravity and dignity.

THE SUN IN THE SIGNS

THE Sun stands for the individuality, just as the Moon expresses the personality. It also governs the constitution and is the Life force and backbone of the whole system. Where the Sun is strong by position of aspects, it gives strength of character, a powerful will and a vigorous constitution, all of which contribute toward making the life successful. Where the Sun is weak, there is danger of short life or one broken by spells of illness or much misfortune.

In this volume, no consideration will be given to the significance of the decanates of the signs, as for example: Aries is subdivided into three sections of ten degrees each, ruled respectively by Mars, the Sun and Jupiter. These points, although important in the minute examination of the nativities of people with regard to whom it is possible to obtain exact data, are too exhaustive for consideration in a work of this kind.

It cannot be too strongly emphasized again that an analysis of the meaning of every factor in Astrology is dependent upon its relation to every other factor. For instance, the Sun in each sign has a certain definite influence which it invariably exerts, but that influence, thus exerted, is combined with every other influence of the Sun in its house position and in its aspects, as well as in reference to the ascending sign and other planetary positions and aspects. Thus, it is from the sum of the forces and not from each one of them separately judged, that an analysis is made.

The reader should remember, therefore, that to read the analysis of the Sun in the signs as it follows, as an analysis verbatim of the solar position in a nativity, to read it except as one of the forces of a nativity to be united, accentuated or modified by the other factors involved, is not scientific astrology and will not give a true interpretation. The statements true in themselves, must be united intellectually, in each particular nativity, with other particular factors of that nativity; and then, and only then, are the peculiarities of individual instances described.

SUN IN ARIES

In Aries the Sun is in his exaltation, very powerful and brilliant, with that first glow and exultation which is associated with the Spring. Aries, however, is under Mars as ruler, and this tends to bring out the arrows from the quiver of Apollo. In this sign, the Sun is sometimes apt to slay. Aries rules the head in man, and being also the beginning of the Zodiac, he tends to fill the mind of the native with extreme ambition to accomplish daringly original, yet practical, undertakings. Wilhelm I of Germany, and Bismarck, who built the German Empire from the ruins of the struggles of the Middle Ages and of the Napoleonic Wars, both had the Sun in this sign. So had Thiers, who restored the French Republic after the crash of Sedan and the flames of the Commune, and Gambetta who contributed so largely to the same work. It is frequently the case that the ideas of the native are considered impractical or impossible by those to whom he communicates them. It was fortunate for Bismarck that his King possessed the same Sun position, for it is characteristic of these people that, unless the vigorous energy which they manifest on the conception of their ideas shows an immediate result, their interest may wane and another idea of equal vehemence replace the first.

It is most necessary for the native to acquire patience and perseverance. The mind must be trained to continue in one channel and the dissipation of the forces of life must be guarded against with the utmost care. The native must not be content merely to imagine his career; also he must not shrink from the spade work which is essential to bring ideas to fruition.

The Aries constitution is rather finely balanced; it is powerful, yet delicate. There is a decided tendency to overwork the body, either intellectually or physically. There is, however, no danger of nervous over-strain. Aries people are generally lacking in the psychic and spiritual qualities. Dangers to the health are indicated by the planets involved, but fevers and apoplexy are principally to be feared; and the native may also suffer from headaches and other afflictions of that extremity of the body. The expression is usually commanding, sometimes even violent, and the countenance may at times be red, while there is a likelihood of some mole or birthmark on the face. In itself, this position of the Sun does not promise any great longevity. Diseases are likely to be aggravated by the disposition, which is usually careless and even contemptuous of the health; the appetites are sometimes excessive and the passions need control. Speaking generally, this is a better place for the Sun in a male nativity than in that of a female.

The following well known persons were also born with the Sun in the sign Aries:

Oliver Cromwell
John Burroughs
The late Senator Weeks
Houdini, Magician
General Gordon of England
King Albert of Belgium
King George of England
Hon. Charles E. Hughes
Mrs. Allan Leo
Nicholas Murray Butler
Ray Long
Frederick Collins
John Hays Hammond
Andrew Mellon
George F. Baker
The late Thomas Eugene Mitten
John W. Davis
James Branch Cabell
Prince Pierre Troubetskoy
"Bud" Fisher
Daniel Chester French
Elizabeth Goldsmith
Mary Pickford
Charlie Chaplin
Mary Miles Minter
Gloria Swanson
Margaret Anglin
Mr. McMorris

SUN IN TAURUS

THE natural sympathy between the Sun and Venus makes Taurus a happy habitation for the Sun. The earthy quality of the sign, moreover, tends to stabilize his influence, and its balanced nature lends still further dignity to the configuration. Taurus people are usually broad, sturdy and of iron constitution. Their vitality is great, but with a tendency to sluggishness; they are slow to start, but, once in motion, they gather momentum, and when well under way nothing will ever stop them. In a word, they are weighty, using that word in its full mechanical sense. The will is dominant and even obstinate and the persistence and tenacity of the native are never in doubt. General Grant is an excellent example of this position of the Sun.

Like other qualities, however, this tenacity may have its defects. The native is sometimes inclined to continue in a course which good judgment would see to be hopeless. Here we find in particular the devotees of lost causes. The reason for this is that Taurus being under Venus, the affections are strongly implicated. As a corollary, one may say that these people, though they can never be driven, may easily be led. They respond readily to appeals to their better feelings; at the same time to goad them is to rouse them to anger which may almost approximate madness.

The bull-nature is still further brought out by a certain placidity and domesticity in all cases where the more active qualities are not aroused. There is a great wealth of affection in this sign, which is frequently the aftermath of passion. In their love-affairs such people may begin with the vehemence of equinoctial gales, storm following storm. When this passes, the end comes not by breach or tragedy, but by the development of warm friendships. The disposition is thus ideal for marriage.

The mental activity of Taurus people is, as a rule, not great. Their original tendency is to be conservative, but if once convinced of the necessity of a revolutionary course, they will then pursue it to the bitter end. Even if on any point they seem radical, it is only accidental to the nature; on all fundamentals, they are reactionary. Consider Huxley, for example, the scientific side of his nature committed him to the advocacy of evolution, which was at that time misunderstood in England to imply belief in atheism, anarchy and free love. Yet his philosophical writings are based upon such comparatively early authors as Hume and Berkeley, while his political writings are the most steadily conservative that can be imagined.

The general inertia of the nature will cause the native to acquiesce in most of the conventionalities customary to his environment, not because he believes that they are right, (supposing him to be cross-examined on the subject) but because it would lead to trouble to ignore them. He would say frankly that he thought it did not matter very much what happened in so small a matter and that it was best "to let sleeping dogs lie."

People with the Sun in Taurus are usually very practical. They are not liable to be led away by idealism and dreams. One may quote Shakespeare as the most steady-going, sensible poet that ever lived. It is his extraordinary common sense which has so endeared him to the Anglo-Saxon. Spencer, too, has the Sun in this sign, and his philosophy was based upon objective facts. Hence, the name which he himself gave it, synthetic philosophy, as opposed to the analytic, which has held almost undisputed sway since the beginning of the science.

In the human anatomy, Taurus is said to rule the base of the brain, the neck and shoulders, and the throat. People with the Sun in this position are, to some extent, liable to disorders in one of these places, but, unless the Sun is badly afflicted, there is not the same danger of ill-health and of sudden death that we found in Aries, for while the Sun is not so brilliantly strong, he is more harmoniously placed and his rays fall more softly.

The following well known persons were also born with the Sun in the sign Taurus:

Alexander II of Russia
General Boulanger of France
Shakespeare
Balzac
Hon. Stephen A. Douglas
Harold F. McCormick
Cyrus H. McCormick
Cyril Maude

Lionel Barrymore
Effie Shannon
Roy Atwell
Jack Henderson
Norma Talmadge
Edwin Markham

SUN IN GEMINI

In Gemini the stability of the Sun is greatly diminished. The first principle of all mechanical efficiency is the fulcrum; a rigid base is necessary for every machine. An enormous proportion of the power developed for locomotion is wasted in hammering out a permanent way. If, therefore, the Sun, which is the fulcrum of the bodily machine, is in a movable, airy, mercurial sign, the working power of the engine is seriously diminished.

If Dante, Wagner, and Queen Victoria seem to be exceptions to this rule, it is because, in their cases, the Sun was still within a degree or two of Taurus and partakes very largely of his nature. In all these cases, too, it was well-aspected.

Speaking generally, people with the Sun in Gemini show a certain vagueness and irresponsibility, finding it hard to concentrate upon any subject or even to take any subject seriously. Even when their lives appear devoted to the prosecution of a particular object, it will seem as if there were no real basis in the nature corresponding to the observed effect. Their actions are prescribed by the mood of the moment, and they do things more because they are personally interested than with the idea of building up any important result for themselves. There is a great tendency to dissipate the force, and, owing to the dual nature of Gemini, such people are always happier when leading a double life. This expression is not used in any equivocal sense; it merely means that they are happiest when they have more than one dominant interest. They cannot stay, according to the expression, with their "noses to the grindstone." Permanent work makes them restless and uneasy in a very short space of time. "Variety is the spice of life" to them, and, especially when Venus and Mercury are both in the same sign, they often become "rolling stones," "Jacks-of-all-trades and masters of none," unless there is some extremely stabilizing influence from a steady-going planet like Jupiter or Saturn, more especially Saturn. Thomas Moore is an excellent example of the lighter talents given by the Sun in this sign, and the versatility of Bulwer-Lytton is also a manifest confirmation of this position.

Most of the force of the constitution and vitality of the native goes to nerve and intellect rather than to heart. We do not, as a rule, find people with warm dispositions having this position of the Sun. Albrecht Dürer, Bulwer-Lytton, Schumann, Strauss, are all examples of this. In the cases of Jay Gould and Nero, this coldness of disposition is even more marked.

Gemini rules not only the nerves but the ratiocinative part of the brain, as distinguished from the executive, which is under Aries, the sensory as opposed to the motor function. It also rules the hands and arms and, in particular, the lungs. The general sensitiveness of the nerves is, however, an excellent token of artistry. People with this position of the Sun are likely to hear more, to see more, than the average man. They are open to impressions, even the most delicate, and, where Mercury assists, are able to record them with exquisite fidelity. The intellectual qualities are, moreover, fine and strong. Their apprehension is based on knowledge; their memories are excellent, and they build up splendidly on existing foundations. There is, however, not likely to be any tremendous force of originality in the mind, unless Mercury holds aspects to Uranus or Neptune. The student will remark that even Dante was greatly indebted to Virgil on the one hand, and to the Patristic authors on the other.

Similarly, Wagner went entirely to existing tradition for his material, and a good third of the originality of his music is due to his exquisite sensibility in regard to sound, while his whole plan, particularly the cry of the leitmotif, is rationalistic and literary, rather than musical.

It is part of the Gemini nature to demand a change of scene and relaxation; exercise, sleep and fresh air are necessary to the health, which, however, will never be robust in the same way as we find it when the Sun is in such a sign as Taurus and Leo. The native is really too high-strung and, unless things go his way, he readily becomes depressed. It will be useless for him to endeavor to settle down in any fixed occupation. The best he can do is to try to take advantage, as far as possible, of the qualities of his defects and so to arrange his life that the sword does not too quickly wear out its scabbard.

The following well known persons were also born with the Sun in the sign Gemini:

Elbert Hubbard
Emerson
Robert M. LaFollette
Richard Mansfield
Walt Whitman
May Allison
Margaret de Alvarez
Elizabeth Marbury
John McCormick
Gene Tunney
Robert W. Chambers
William H. Woodin
Frances Alda
James Montgomery Flagg
Gilbert Emory
Queen Mary of England

SUN IN CANCER

In Cancer, the Sun finds a sign which is too watery and lunar to be altogether a happy habitation. Jupiter, exalted in this sign, blends some of his qualities with the solar rays, but, unless the Sun is well-dignified, the working is not altogether favorable; for, since it is Jupiter's luxuriousness that is brought out, the Sun in this sign tends to laxness of life, giving a disposition too contented and easy-going, and a disinclination to exercise energy. The disposition is apt to be idle; lassitude seems to be the rule of life, yet with this is associated what passes for tenacity of purpose. Such changes as take place are superficial and leave the temperament and purpose undisturbed, but there is little manifestation of any real vigor or energy. These remarks apply to undeveloped types. Where the influence of Jupiter, who is exalted in Cancer, enters strongly into the development of the native, we may find indomitable will and an extremely masterful disposition. Such types are fairly well represented by John Quincy Adams, Joseph Chamberlain, Cecil Rhodes, Lord Northcliffe and Mrs. Pankhurst.

A love of antiquity and of old, established things often manifests itself in the native, and he may take a deep interest in old books, paintings, bric-a-brac or in some such half-forgotten science as heraldry. The energetic type, on the other hand, occupies itself more exclusively with the affairs of the moment, and is apt to have a contempt for anything that is not entirely up-to-date.

Cancer rules the alimentary canal, as far as the bowels, which are under Virgo, and people with the Sun in this sign are often sufferers from indigestion, with functional troubles which may manifest in a hundred different forms, all of which can be traced to this original weakness, as occasionally caused by the implication of the pneumo-gastric nerve. The disposition of the native tends to confirm this threat against the health. The appetite is frequently both excessive and abnormal. Cancer being a watery sign, there is also a danger of over-indulgence in strong drink.

Especially when Venus is in the same sign, the sex appetite of the native is prone to be quite normal, and, being generally combined with strong affection and a placid disposition, this often makes for happiness in marriage.

This position of the Sun is not favorable to longevity. Children who come into the world about this time of the year seem not to get the necessary hardening, and the Moon, lady of the sign, being so easily influenced and so rapid in motion, evil directions come about, if not more frequently, yet at least with a much greater chance of shattering the citadel. This gives a natural explanation of the fact that in a list of hundreds of famous people, only a few isolated cases are found to have been born under the Sun's rays in Cancer. On the other hand, as the native of Cancer grows older, his constitution grows more robust and he stands a good chance of reaching a fairly good old age. This is bound to be so for the reason that the Sun, in time, progresses into the sign Leo.

The following well known persons were also born with the Sun in the sign Cancer:

Lord Kitchener
H. Rider Haggard
Mary Baker Eddy
Katherine Tingley
John Wanamaker
Dr. J. Frankel
Wallace Eddinger
Calvin Coolidge
Luis Cabrera
Walter Hampden
Cosmo Hamilton
Frank Crowninshield
John D. Rockefeller, Sr.
Frank Damrosch
Otis Skinner
John O'Hara Cosgrave
Dr. William James Mayo
Anne Morrow Lindbergh
Prince of Wales

SUN IN LEO

The Sun in Leo is his greatest strength, for Leo is his own house and his influence is not even complicated by the exaltation of any other planet therein. We find here the most enormous vitality and strength of constitution. We have examples of this in such grand old men as Petrarch, who died at seventy, but whose life was full of vigor; Colonel Olcott who died at over eighty; Tennyson, at eighty-three; Cardinal Gibbons, at eighty-three, and Franz Josef of Austria, at eighty-six. Blavatsky died at sixty, but her Sun is in opposition to Jupiter and Herschel, while Cancer was rising, a sign not predisposing to longevity. Napoleon, too, died at the age of fifty-two, but this is hardly a case of natural death, since the indigestion indicated by the presence of Saturn in Cancer in opposition to the Moon was aggravated to malignant disease by the cruel regimen imposed upon him by his captors. Shelley also had a magnificent constitution and a vitality as superabundant as that of the great conqueror; his life, too, was cut short by drowning.

People with the Sun in Leo are not only strong themselves, but shed forth this strength on others. It is emotionally the most magnetic of all the signs for the Sun; perhaps in consequence of this, the disposition is usually masterful and may possibly in some cases become almost tyrannical. There is immense generosity and nobility of feeling, but this again may sometimes degenerate into extravagance. The native is a tremendous worker, but anything in the nature of menial tasks revolts his soul, and while he is not ashamed to do anything of this kind when necessity calls or as an example to others, yet he will not do it as a matter of routine, while there is anyone else to do it for him. If he finds himself in a situation where people will not do for him what he thinks they ought to, he generally prefers to let the work go undone. The nature is excessively proud and incapable of meanness. Such persons must be trusted or they can do nothing. As long as they feel that they are in positions of authority and responsibility, they will kill themselves if necessary, in order to justify the confidence reposed in them. If forced into any other situation, they will despise their work and so neglect it.

The disposition of persons with the Sun in Leo is placable and not easily perturbed, but this advantage is gained by "preparedness." They give so forcibly the impression that they are ready for a fight that the peace is seldom in danger of being broken. When actually forced into combat, Leo people form the most determined opponents. They have taken to heart Shakespeare's advice:

> "Beware of entrance to a quarrel, but, being in,
> Bear't that the opposer may beware of thee."

Their only defect as fighters lies in their reckless courage. They expose themselves unnecessarily and they refuse to fight otherwise than fairly, however great may be the advantages offered. In victory they are magnanimous and in defeat unconquered.

People with this position of the Sun should always attend, as far as possible, to their own business, and not rely upon others to do it for them, or trust to correspondence (unless they happen to be born writers, because of good Mercury aspects) for their success depends almost entirely upon the magnetism of their personality. The ambition of these people is nearly always uncontrollable; however much they get, they will want far more, and this discontent may be the cause of much unhappiness. It is the mainspring of their success, but may also bring them to disaster, for they refuse to realize it when they come to a blank wall. They are consequently likely to waste their strength in attempting impossibilities. The same pride and masterfulness of which mention has been made makes it impossible to coerce the native, but he responds with extreme readiness to the slightest appeal to his better feelings, and he will often injure himself seriously rather than give anyone the chance of thinking that he has acted meanly, although such thought may be utterly unjust.

Leo rules the heart. The Sun in this position is very strong; it is because of his great power that the vitality is usually so tremendous, but when at the last, Apollo, lord of life and death, turns from the one to the other, it is at the heart that he will strike. Death is likely to come suddenly by some kind of stroke or by syncope. Where the Sun is over-excited by Mars, especially by squares and conjunctions, the tendency to diseases of the heart is greatly increased and may occur comparatively early in life. It may also lead to death in infancy through convulsions.

The following well known persons were also born with the Sun in the sign Leo:

Guy de Maupassant
Allan Leo
Boynton Moody
George B. McCutcheon
Raymond Poincaré
Herbert Hoover
Henry Ford
Stanley Baldwin
Mussolini

David Belasco
William Gillette
Julia Marlowe
Mary Anderson
Larz Anderson
George D. Pratt
Guthrie McClintic
Martha Hedman
Clare Eames
Ethel Barrymore
Mrs. Dorothy Caruso
Will Foster
Anne Morgan

SUN IN VIRGO

THE sign Virgo is almost as mercurial as that of Gemini, but, being of an earthy nature, it is rather the fixed than the volatile Mercury which it manifests. The natural coldness of Mercury is rather accentuated. The vitality is manifested upon the mental plane, but in a more practical way than was the case with Gemini. The ratiocinative power is strong and the sense of causality extremely so, but there is not the same tendency toward idealism as we saw with the sign of the Twins. Virgo is a practical sign; its native does not doubt the existence of spiritual planes, but the everyday facts of the world are apt to occupy his attention and prevent him from explorations into the unseen. The nature is just, but not oversympathetic. The native is apt to be retiring and somewhat solitary. There is a certain shyness in the disposition which prevents the native from showing himself as he is, and this often makes it difficult for him to acquire the confidence of others. Even where this reserve wears off superficially through social intercourse, it still exists beneath the surface, and the real native is at heart unapproachable, as is seen in observing Goethe, Maeterlinck, Tolstoi, and Herbert Asquith.

People with the Sun in Virgo are discriminative and keenly critical, but they are tactful and likely to keep their discoveries to themselves. They are accurate observers of detail, often very methodical, but, as a rule, have not the creative force necessary for successful generalization. The memory is excellent and retentive, but too apt to allow garnered facts to repose unused. The emotions are not easily aroused, nor easily quieted when aroused, but in no case do they play a great part in the disposition. There are few extremes in this sign. Generally even-balanced and cool-headed, the native makes few pretensions and works quietly and unobserved. But there is sometimes an inordinate pride in the intellectual ability, which may not be justified. Queen Elizabeth is a notable example of this intellectual vanity. The critical quality is a valuable mental attainment, but one is not in the first class unless he can construct originally.

Virgo rules the bowels and the sympathetic nervous system. The central nervous system of the human body is well symbolized by the caduceus of Mercury. The head of the wand is the cerebellum and the wings are the two halves of the cerebrum. The shaft is the spinal column and the snakes which surround it are the *nadi*, *ida*, and *pingala*, which surround the central *sushumna* in the Hindu anatomy. Thus, all mental and nervous forces in their most physical aspects are under Mercury. Many spinal complaints are, therefore, caused by afflictions of Virgo. Virgo also corresponds in man to the abdomen, ruling in this attribution the liver; the gall bladder and gall ducts; the spleen; pancreas and suprarenal capsules. The kidneys, acting as a filter, are under Libra. The remainder of the urinary apparatus is under Scorpio, which also rules the reproductive system. Capricornus is intimately connected with Scorpio and rules the muscular portion of the reproductive system, Scorpio being more concerned with the glands and their secretions. But an affliction of Virgo may lead to disease in any one of these parts sooner or later, through sympathetic response to any irritation of the spinal or glandular nerves. The Virgo native is greatly affected by worry and also by the magnetism of others, and care in diet is an extremely important factor in the preservation of his health.

The following well known persons were also born with the Sun in the sign Virgo:

W. J. Caldwell
Prince Albert (consort of Queen Victoria)
Melville E. Stone
General Pershing
Jane Addams
William H. Taft
Robert Benchley
Lynn Starling
Irene Fenwick
Charles Dana Gibson
Amelie Rives (Princess Troubetskoy)
Charles H. Sabin
Theodore Dreiser
Zona Gale
Rex Beach
Henrietta Crosman
H. L. Mencken
C. K. G. Billings
J. P. Morgan
Queen Wilhelmina of Holland

SUN IN LIBRA

Though the Sun is in his fall in Libra, the fact that this is a cardinal sign tends to restore his strength and on the whole the Venusian nature of the sign brings out more pleasing qualities than does the martial stimulus of Aries.

The disposition given by the Sun in Libra is extremely kind and sympathetic and the affection extraordinarily strong, but the sense of justice is extremely deep-rooted; and, if the native should feel that he is being abused or imposed upon, his indignation may make him seem cold and resentful. This same sense of justice seems to underlie every trait of the native. In religion, for example, he will not confine himself to any one system, but look for the best points in all and endeavor to strike a balance between them. Sometimes the delicacy of mental adjustment may be interpreted as indecision and, in undeveloped types, it may really amount to this weakness. It is certain that the native will not form snap judgments; he may prefer to suffer acutely himself rather than risk injustice to others. These people are also extremely sensitive in their feelings, and this makes them appear to some extent more dependent upon others than is the average person. They have an extremely powerful critical faculty, which, however, is sympathetic, and they are therefore generally appreciative. Their sense of harmony and proportion is admirable, and the native obtains the most intense pleasure from the contemplation of duty. Good examples of these qualities are found in Lord Roberts and Edward VI, both of whom have the Sun in this sign. Vulgarity revolts him and sometimes his disappointment in finding a suitable environment may bring out the Saturnian side of Libra and tend to make him try to live in a world of his own, or in some other way to be a recluse. Aspects of Uranus and Saturn to the Sun increase this possibility. Cornelius Agrippa has a sextile of Saturn to the Sun, and with Savonarola they are in far off conjunction.

In all matters involving accurate judgment, the native is at his best, but in practical matters he may be over-subtle. He may decline to believe a fact which is perfectly obvious to everybody else, just because it is thrust upon him.

The constitution is extremely sound, but does not manifest itself in strength or robustness. Endurance and the power of recuperation are its characteristics. The native will probably be of little good where sudden exertion is involved, but in the case of long-continued strain, he will outlast men apparently much stronger. Libra is preëminently the feminine sign, far more so than Taurus.

The principal part of the body ruled by Libra is the lumbar region, which of course includes the kidneys and affects materially the spine. With good aspects of the Sun, however, troubles with these parts are apt to be only functional, and it frequently happens that a delicate adolescence is followed by a life of perfect harmony and balance of health.

There is one singular trait of the disposition in Libra which is so remarkable as to deserve special mention. It is brought out very strongly when Venus or Mercury or both are also present in the sign. It is this, that the nature of the individual is neither decidedly male nor female, but partakes almost equally of both qualities. This will not necessarily manifest itself outwardly, though sometimes it seems to have a great effect in the moulding of the physical body.

The following well known persons were also born with the Sun in the sign Libra:

General French of England
Oscar Wilde
Lily Langtry
Frances Willard
Marshall Field
Charles Scribner
Edward D. Bok
Dr. John H. Finley
Ramsay MacDonald
Von Hindenburg
Thomas Fortune Ryan
Thomas W. Lamont
Wilton Lackeye
Arthur Hopkins
Alice Joyce
Eleanor Sears
Antonio Moreno
Ina Claire
Hereward Carrington

SUN IN SCORPIO

THE Sun in Scorpio, the house of death, is very strong, but the native is very likely to suffer violence. It is quite frequently found that people with this position suffer from diseases which bring them to a premature end, as for example Stevenson and Marie Bashkirtseff, or, when badly aspected, they may meet a violent death like Domitian, Marie Antoinette, President Garfield and Stanford White. This is physically the most magnetic sign in the Zodiac. There are three main types, classed respectively under eagle, serpent, and scorpion. But in every case, an extremely forceful and dominating personality is to be expected. With even the best types, the appearance is often somewhat austere. Tremendous will-power is evident in every line of the countenance, which is frequently what conventional people call ugly and occasionally this native bears scars. This rather formidable appearance is, however, frequently combined with a kindly disposition. However dark and forbidding may be the countenance, the nature has yet the fascination of the serpent.

The native is easily aroused to anger, and makes a most dangerous enemy, for he cannot be trusted to fight fair, as with Leo, but will take any means in his power to injure his antagonist; nor is he held back by any feeling of pity, but will go on to the bitter end. Occasionally, this is so pronounced as to cause actual defect in the fighting quality.

But it is doubtful if any sign in the Zodiac illustrates so markedly the contrast between the spiritually awakened soul and its opposite. Crafty and cunning, with intense passions and jealousies and with a vindictiveness which will wreak insatiable revenges, the Scorpio native becomes, under higher impulses, indefatigable in his desire to help mankind, and his coldness and insensibility to the sufferings of others is transmuted into devotion and self-sacrifice. The coolness of demeanor and stern sense of justice and integrity, together with uncontrollable desire for freedom, may degenerate into harshness, selfishness and discontent, or blossom into efficiency, sympathy and true generosity.

Where the Sun is fairly well aspected and Mars is free from affliction, the constitution is extraordinarily strong; the resisting power is greater than with any other sign. The native is capable of infinite hard work and is most dogged, persevering and tenacious in carrying out his plans. He does not, however, go at them like a bull at a gate. He is always exercising his intelligence to out-maneuver his opponent. Where Scorpio assumes the eagle type, the noblest qualities of Mars and the Sun are found combined, and there is a certain subtlety and intellectuality about them which come more from the nature of the sign itself than from either of the planets. There is no better sign in the Zodiac for commanding success, but this success nearly always comes through bitter fighting. There is a strong tendency to science and all other branches of life which demand the blending of the two qualities, energy and subtlety. Provided that the Sun is strengthened by some good aspects, it is as favorable a position as could be wished for him. At the same time, the student must never forget to expect something secret and sinister in the nature.

Scorpio rules the glands of the pelvis and, from its opposition to Taurus, often affects the corresponding parts in the neck and throat, but its most special signification is in connection with the organs of reproduction. Scorpio is particularly to be feared in the recurrence of Cancer after operations, for such secondary growths are usually glandular and such diseases are more dangerous than ordinary local afflictions of the reproductive organs.

The following well known persons were also born with the Sun in the sign Scorpio:

George Eliot
Theodore Roosevelt
Hetty Greene
Sarah Bernhardt
Eugene V. Debs
Anna Katherine Greene
Dr. E. H. Pratt
Margaret Mayo
Riccardo Martin
Maude Adams
George Gordon Battle
Viola Allen
Owen D. Young
William G. McAdoo
Nicholas Longworth
Ida M. Tarbell
John Philip Sousa
Marie Dressler
Henry Van Dyke
Alexander P. Moore
Samuel Insul
Jackie Coogan
Billy Sunday

SUN IN SAGITTARIUS

The Sun in Sagittarius is noble, refined, and forceful, but his influence may suffer through being too swift and sudden. The brilliancy conferred is sometimes fitful. The promise of youth remains unfulfilled. Occasionally, it may occur that it is fulfilled in some different way, it develops in some unexpected channel. Thus the qualities which brought Disraeli to the front were not at all those which confirmed him when he had arrived. The peculiar quality of high-strung and high-spirited character which this sign lends to the Sun is better shown by such people as Charles I, Swinburne, de Musset and Winston Churchill. William Blake's Sun was very much stabilized by the conjunction of Mercury and Jupiter.

The native of Sagittarius seems never to be altogether in repose, but always to be prepared to act. The temperament is exceedingly proud and the taste exquisitely refined. There is often a kind of wild shyness in these people, and they are sometimes rather difficult to deal with, because they seem so ready to spring away, and vanish into the forest glades. This impression is, however, to some extent illusory, for their nature is essentially true and trustworthy, but the thought of humiliation is maddening to them, and they suffer the most intense pain over trifles which, to less sensitive people, would cause hardly a moment's annoyance. They resent intensely any form of pressure, almost as much so as in Leo, but they are to be trusted to follow out their own aspirations in their own way. If they say they will do a thing, they will not go back on their word. The intuition of these people is extraordinarily good, and their mistakes often come from not following it. No matter what reason may say, they will err if they do not rather choose to act on instinct, for, in them, instinct is so strong that it can never be banished from the mind, and so acts as an inhibition when contradicted. Similarly, these people are never fortunate in taking the advice of others. They should trust their own initiative. Their greatest successes are obtained when sudden emergency arises. Opportunity is to them the keynote of success in life. They are naturally capable of extreme concentration, and cannot well do two things at once. They must finish what they are doing before starting anything else; if they once break off, they find it hard to resume.

There is some danger that they may go to extremes and those tasks which require patience and steady constructive force are distasteful to them.

The general health is good, although there is some liability to sudden attacks of nervous disorders, but the recuperative force is strong. An open-air life appeals naturally to the native and he is very fond of sports, especially those concerned with horses, dogs and forms of hunting. He is lithe and active, usually an excellent runner. The nature is free from any form of coarseness, and such things disgust even more than we found to be the case with Libra. This circumstance occasionally determines a rather peculiar attitude in regard to all the natural functions of life, and individuals with this position of the Sun are rarely normal in the sense in which ordinary people understand that word. There is a great desire to obtain the respect of others, and sometimes this may lead to a certain failure to live up to the best side of the character, for, to acquire or to retain the respect of unworthy persons, one must either be untrue to one's self or hypocritical. The personality is usually extremely magnetic, and its bold, free, dashing character and great brilliance often inspire the profoundest devotion.

Sagittarius rules the hips and thighs in particular, but all the tendons of the muscular system in general. It has also some connection with the motor impulses of the nervous system; the diseases of this sign are therefore sciatica, gout, hip disease, and some other forms of lameness. However, more octogenarians are born with the Sun in Sagittarius than in any other sign.

The following well known persons were also born with the Sun in the sign Sagittarius:

Samuel Clemens (Mark Twain)
Edith Cavell
Bishop Fallows
Reginald Vanderbilt
Queen Alexandra of England
Lillian Russell
Minnie Maddern Fiske
Harry Payne Whitney
Harold G. Villard

Newton D. Baker
William Durant
Thomas Coleman DuPont
Dr. Alexander Lambert
Arthur Brisbane
Fay Bainter
Louden Charlton
Marion Davies
Sally Farnham
Doris Keane
Helen Mencken
E. H. Sothern
Lou Tellegen
Lillian Westcott Hale

SUN IN CAPRICORN

The Sun is in some respects stronger in Capricorn than in any other sign, except Leo. He enters it at his annual re-birth, his resurrection from the dead, and it is therefore a new beginning to his force. The earthy, Saturnian, and Martial natures of the sign bring out the force of the Sun in the direction of practical energy. The capacity for hard work is the first characteristic which we observe in the Capricornus native. It is to be seen in such tremendous workers as Edward VII, Pasteur, Gladstone, Wallace, Sir Isaac Pitman, and Sir Isaac Newton. The leaping nature of the goat and the cardinal character of the sign also give the most tremendous power of initiative, a quality illustrated well enough by the people already mentioned. The character is extremely noble and self-respect is one of its strongest qualities. It is to be remembered that the natural mundane position of Capricornus in the Zodiac is the Mid-heaven. The Saturnian influence of the sign gives caution, prudence and thrift, as well as great solidity and strength of moral character. The native is very serious in disposition, with a strong sense of duty. These qualities may sometimes be exaggerated and become faults. Steadiness, foresight, trustworthiness, fidelity, and conscientiousness are nearly always present. In estimating the action of the Sun, due regard must, of course, be given to any afflictions, especially those by Mars or Uranus. Alexander VI had few of the qualities previously mentioned, but his Sun is squared by Uranus.

The constitution is usually of iron, capable of undergoing any degree of hardship, with great resisting power against disease. It is, therefore, next to Leo and Sagittarius, one of the best of all the signs for longevity. Capricornus governs the joints, particularly those of the knees, and has a general association with the bony system. The chief danger to the native's health is in rheumatism and in the tendency to over-indulgence in the appetites. He eats greedily of hot or spicy food, preferring it to any other. The Saturnian tendency to melancholia is also a dangerous element in this position of the Sun. Occasionally the morbidity of appetite leads, from the creation of an abnormal thirst, to similar indiscretions in regard to liquor. This, however, must be taken as a secondary and derived condition. The fact that the worst drunkards are often found to have the Sun in Capricorn comes largely from the mental or physical depression caused by Saturn.

The following well known persons were also born with the Sun in the sign Capricorn:

Duke of Clarence of England
Carmen Sylva (Queen of Roumania)
General Joffre of France
Woodrow Wilson
General Carranza of Mexico
Admiral George Dewey
Perry Belmont
Rudolph Spreckels
Frank B. Kellogg
Mrs. Calvin Coolidge
Carter Glass
Christopher Grant LaFarge
Rudyard Kipling
Josef Hoffman
David Starr Jordan
Sir Johnston Forbes-Robertson
Henry E. Dixey

P. R. S. DuPont
Augustus Thomas
Harry Gordon Selfridge
Edward Nicander
Eva LeGallienne
Carl Jorn
Madame Lina Cavalieri
Herbert Brennon

SUN IN AQUARIUS

Aquarius represents humanity progressing by the aid which it gives to others. The woman is Isis Unveiled; she pours forth science, progress, nobility of thought and conduct, the wisdom of the stars, giving freely to others, while she herself is refreshed and renewed by that life-giving stream.

Before the discovery of Uranus in the eighteenth century, Saturn was supposed to rule Aquarius, but it is now quite apparent that Uranus is its lord, a domination which easily explains its signification of "the future." In the consideration of the personal appearance under the discussion of the rising sign, we have noticed the peculiar and sometimes rather disconcerting look of the eyes of the native, as though the knowledge behind them were almost uncanny to the average person. The constitution is generally strong, though liable to sudden attacks of illness, which usually affect the nerves, or arise from some obscure cause, thus showing the Uranian influence, but his temperate habits of life are generally a good safeguard against danger from these tendencies. The disposition is kind and generous; the Aquarian cannot bear to see others suffer, and he will often make great sacrifices in order to relieve them. His judgment in practical things is not always sound, in the sense in which that term is usually employed, as his vision enables him to see too far ahead into the consequences to make his advice seem justified at the moment. What he says comes true, but often only after many vicissitudes. He judges on first principles and bed-rock facts, and the influence of these, though always finally determinative, may often be masked for a time by all kinds of accidents. To the average mind, therefore, the Aquarian often appears a dreamer, for he lays his plans so far ahead that he himself may never live to see them executed. Perhaps the most notable figure whose Sun is in Aquarius is Abraham Lincoln; other examples are found in Ruskin, Byron, Havelock Ellis, and Adelina Patti. A typical expression of the gospel of Aquarius is given by Thomas Paine, whose Sun is in this sign, in his exclamation: "Every man a brother, every woman a sister, the world my country, to do good my religion."

The Aquarian is inquiring by nature and very susceptible to the illumination of inspiration, but he has no disinclination caused by prejudice to accept any theory which has facts to support it. The "impossible" has been carefully erased from his dictionary. The mental poise is generally equable, and the sense of justice, as well as that of causality, is very strong. The Aquarian is superior to his environment; his surroundings do not limit him as they would most people. Disappointment does not turn him from any plan, once his mind is firmly made up to prosecute it. The intuition is abnormally strong, truth is recognized by the native with great ease; and in conjunction with this, frequently goes very remarkable psychic power.

The mental poise of the Aquarian is so remarkable that he makes an ideal consultant, whether in medicine, in law, or in other science. People naturally go to him for advice; even the insane may feel the steadying power of his influence and the self-mastery which goes with it. In spite of all this, the native is modest and unassuming, and his interest is not so much in himself as in his surroundings. It is this which makes him an admirable observer and successful in science.

The Aquarian does not quickly make friends, but once his confidence is given, there is never any doubt about his loyalty. He is not easily approached on the physical plane. His bonds of attachment are forged in the smithies of the soul and the mind. This, as in the case of Libra and Sagittarius, may lead to the formation of many very peculiar attachments. The circle of the native is never likely to be conventional. He is happiest when he feels that he is fulfilling his destiny of helping others.

Aquarius rules the calves of the leg, in particular, but it also refers to the vessels of the body which carry fluid of any kind, particularly the lymphatic system. There is danger of blood pressure in later years, and arterio-sclerosis is not uncommonly the cause of the native's death. Because the preponderant influence of its ruler Uranus is upon the higher planes of mental and spiritual activity, the greatest danger to the health of the native is apt to come through neglect of the physical attributes of the body. He is disinclined to take physical exercise but is overactive mentally. His deep subjective knowledge, however, will not allow him to abuse his body, even though he may be unmindful of it and consequently it is seldom that his general health is seriously impaired.

The following well known persons were also born with the Sun in the sign Aquarius:

Abraham Lincoln
Robert Burns
Sir Henry Irving
Mrs. Katherine Craig
Victor Herbert
Bert Reese
Colonel George Harvey
George Randolph Chester
Jean Adrienne Jusserand
Thomas A. Edison
Olive Fremstad
Charles M. Schwab
Edward Sheldon
John Barrymore
Colonel Charles A. Lindbergh
Antonio Scotti
Pierre Lorillard
John D. Rockefeller, Jr.
Franklin D. Roosevelt
Elihu P. Root
Louis C. Tiffany
Philip A. S. Franklin
Fritz Kreisler
Rev. Wm. D. Guthrie
George Jean Nathan

James F. Fargo
William Faversham
Frederick R. Coudert
William Allen White
Sinclair Lewis
Gatti-Cassazza
Maxine Elliott
Francis Wilson

SUN IN PISCES

THE influence of Pisces upon the Sun does not make specially for strength, except in the last decanate, which is ruled by Mars. Otherwise, there is a certain softness and placidity which diminish the vitality. The Pisces type is extraordinarily psychic, more so than is the case with that of any other sign, but this manifests itself in an entirely passive way. The native depends upon intuition and impressions generally, and the active qualities of the soul which make the great mystic are rarely present. Rudolph Steiner is fortunate enough to have aspects of Uranus, Saturn and Mars, which increase his practical power. Picus de Mirandola is a more typical example of this sign. Unless the dignities of the planets concerned in this matter are extremely good, the native may suffer from illusions and be led constantly astray. There is in him a notable lack of correlation in practical details, and he is apt to leave things at loose ends. His constructive power being psychic does not exactly translate itself into the objective. In spite of this, however, there is a great deal of practical good sense in the composition, but sometimes the native will be accused of hypocrisy, owing to the extreme contrast between the idealism expressed and the course of action undertaken, and people not similarly constituted may take it into their heads to "read them a lesson." The native is inclined to self-indulgence in emotional experience, and this in the undeveloped type very often takes the form of the abuse of alcoholic liquors or even occasionally of noxious drugs. This is partly due to the watery nature of the sign, and its ruler, Neptune, and partly to the soft and seductive influence of Venus, who is exalted in the sign, and to its connection with the Moon.

There is a good deal of discontent in this sign, naturally caused by such conflict between the aspirations and the expression of the life. This often manifests itself in restlessness and in inattentiveness, and in attaching far too much importance to trifles, the least of which often appears to them highly significant. Even in external manner, the native, though seemingly calm upon the surface, is full of tremor within, like the sea. The native is very fond of others and may be so solicitous as to their well-being that the result will often be trying to the recipient of his extreme devotion.

The constitution is, generally speaking, not particularly robust; the general health is good, but there is a lack of power to resist disease. The native is more susceptible than in almost any other sign. Michael Angelo and Sir Richard Burton had magnificent constitutions, but the Sun being in the last decanate of Pisces, the influence of Mars is able to correct the general weakness.

In the human body, Pisces rules primarily the feet, but his action extends throughout the whole body, over the lymph and all watery secretions of an excretory character, such as mucus. The principal diseases characteristic of this sign are œdema, ascitis, and dropsies in general. Another very common disease associated with Pisces is gout. In the consideration of Pisces as a rising sign, there is also danger of tuberculosis if the system is allowed to become depleted.

The following well known persons were also born with the Sun in the sign Pisces:

George Washington
Grover Cleveland
Victor Hugo
Ludwig II of Bavaria
Brander Mathews
William Jennings Bryan
William Dean Howells
Henry W. Savage
Enrico Caruso
Amelia Bingham
Rose Coghlan

Edward Stotesbury
Adolph S. Ochs
Margaret Deland
Percy A. Rockefeller
Isabel Irving
George H. Swift
Joseph E. Otis
Thomas Hastings
Oswald G. Villard
Van Hoogstraaten
Robert W. Goelet
Geraldine Farrar
Penrhyn Stanlaws
Mary Garden

PERIODS WHEN THE SUN WILL BE AFFLICTED BY URANUS

The Sun is the one heavenly body whose position is practically the same at the same time in the year of any year. Consequently, in this volume it is the only sphere that we have considered in making predictions regarding the future. In order that the effects of Uranus on the Sun may be fairly closely computed, the Sun has been divided into three sections, of ten degrees each. This makes the calculations as given within what is known as "orbs" and therefore sufficiently close to an aspect to make its effects distinctly felt. The periods when Uranus will form an aspect to the Sun are tabulated and will be found at the end of each sign. All aspects of Uranus are very important as it takes eighty-four years for the planet to make a revolution of the zodiac and the unfriendly aspects tabulated here will not be repeated for another twenty-one years.

Whenever the unconventional, revolutionary Uranus is unfriendly to the Sun, it always marks an epoch in the life. This planet is the herald of all movements which are in advance of the times and causes worn-out customs and obsolete beliefs to be cast aside. In the individual life, it tends to make one over-express oneself and has a very upsetting effect upon the nervous system, often causing high blood pressure, and giving rise to disorders obscure in origin, and difficult for the ordinary physician to diagnose or cure. A simple diet, plenty of sleep and fresh air, and congenial souls for companions will do more than medicine toward establishing equilibrium and overcoming the disorganizing influence of Uranus. It largely depends upon the intelligence used in handling this dominant force as to whether it will give Bolshevik tendencies or simply force issues, to do unpopular things, or to try to accomplish the impossible.

While under the influence of Uranus, schemers and unscrupulous promoters will often bring to the attention "get-rich-quick" propositions. Even if their motives be friendly, they may be self-deceived and their advice unreliable. This planet causes one to be at crossroads, and the decision made while under its sway will very materially affect the future. It should be realized that lack of harmony, restlessness, discontent and dissatisfaction with existing conditions will be largely due to a craving for new experience and for greater opportunities for self-expression. It will be most unwise to set the personal will against the Universal Will; one should rather make the most of the opportunities which Fate presents, and should not be surprised if one *almost* attains many things which, at the last moment, escape one.

This combination often causes sudden deaths, separations, and broken friendships, either in family or business life. One should listen to the inner promptings, make only necessary decisions, and, when order is again established, a higher plane of consciousness will be reached and it will be possible to use the added power with increased intelligence. Consequently, one should have no fear of any change or experience which comes about naturally during an affliction of Uranus to the Sun.

To unmarried women, it often brings temptation, either from married men or from those who are utterly unworthy. It is not a favorable vibration under which to become engaged or to marry. Married women are usually worried over the husband's affairs or frequently suffer a separation from the husband, because of misunderstandings, sudden death or divorce.

The greatest self-control in all matters must be exercised when under the influence of this erratic planet.

Children passing through this affliction will naturally feel its effects more through what happens to the parents, particularly the father, or in the family, although it tends to make them contrary and to bring to the fore characteristics which have hitherto not been expressed. It will cause a child to suddenly feel very mature, and the greatest sympathy and understanding should be exercised, for if children who are under this affliction imagine that they are being forced to do things simply because others arbitrarily desire it, they will display a rebellious spirit. Children of their own age will not interest them at such periods, and they may be fascinated by older people, and temporarily feel very much out of tune with their own family. Everything should be done to help them to keep their poise and be happy, as Uranus tends to intensify the whole being. Should there be an epidemic of any of the children's diseases, particularly those affecting the nervous system, these children should be protected most carefully and removed from the neighborhood, if it is at all possible.

It is well to bear in mind that Uranus is an exhilarating, quickening and original force which, if utilized constructively, can bring the most soul-stirring and mundane experiences; but if it is allowed to be unrestrained, or is not wisely guided, it can then bring the most devastating results. Its influence is always far-reaching, and it therefore behooves all who are under it, temporarily, to realize the importance of its effect and to try to maintain harmony within themselves, even though everything about them may be chaotic and difficult to control.

When the Sun is in Aries and temporarily afflicted by Uranus, there will be a tendency towards too great enthusiasm and impatience of all prescribed methods. Unless moderation and practicality are exercised, there will be danger of over-taxing the nervous and psychic powers and this may result in queer or neuralgic pains in the head and face, and sympathetically the stomach and kidneys. A change of scene or associates, as well as outdoor exercise, plenty of sleep, and a simple diet, will do much to keep the health normal and to restore mental and physical equilibrium.

Those born from March 21st to April 1st will be strongly under the influence of the epoch-making, revolutionary planet Uranus, during the following periods:

1929—From January through May, again from October through December
1930—During first two months
1948—From September through November
1949—From June through December
1950—Entire year
1951—From January through June
1968—October, November and December
1969—Entire year
1970—From January through October
1971—June and July
1988—From March through June, and again in December
1989—Entire year
1990—Entire year

Those born from April 1st to 11th will be strongly under the influence of the epoch-making, revolutionary planet Uranus, during the following periods:

1929—From June through September
1930—From March through December
1931—Entire year
1932—First four months
1933—January
1951—From July through December
1952—Entire year
1953—From January through July
1954—March, April and May
1970—November and December
1971—From January through May, again from August through December
1972—From January through October
1973—June and July
1991—Entire year
1992—Entire year
1993—January, again from August through November

Those born from April 11th to 21st will be strongly under the influence of the epoch-making, revolutionary planet Uranus, during the following periods:

1932—From May through December
1933—From February through December
1934—From January through May, also November and December
1935—From January through March
1953—From August through December
1954—January, February, and from June through December
1955—From January through August
1956—From March through May
1972—November and December
1973—From January through May, again August through December
1974—From January through November
1975—June, July and August
1993—From February through July, again in December
1994—Entire year
1995—From January through March and from July through December
1996—January

When the Sun is in Taurus and temporarily afflicted by Uranus, every effort should be made to be relaxed and composed physically and mentally. There may be a tendency to indulge in excessive gratification of the senses, and those who are under this affliction must try not to allow their determined, stubborn will to drive them too hard, if they hope to avoid suffering from nervous cough, headache at the base of the brain, and general nervous debility; and sympathetically they may suffer from irregular heart action, neuralgic pains in the generative organs, cramps in the calves, and creepy sensations in the skin. They should strive to be adaptable and take things as they come day by day, as this will be a great safeguard against ill-health or the most baneful effects of the affliction of Uranus.

Those born from April 21st to May 1st will be strongly under the influence of the epoch-making, revolutionary planet Uranus, during the following periods:

1934—From June through October
1935—From April through December
1936—Entire year
1937—From January through April
1955—From September through December
1956—January, February, and from June, through December
1957—From January through September
1958—From February through June
1974—December
1975—From January through May, again from September through December
1976—From January through November
1977—From June through September
1995—From April through June
1996—From February through December
1997—Entire year
1998—January, February, and from September through December

Those born from May 1st to 11th, will be strongly under the influence of the epoch-making, revolutionary planet Uranus, during the following periods:

1937—From May through December
1938—Entire year
1939—From January through June and again in December
1940—From January through March
1957—From October through December
1958—January, and again from July through December
1959—From January through September
1960—From February through July
1976—December
1977—From January through May, again from October through December

1978—Entire year
1979—From May through October
1998—From March through August
1999—Entire year
2000—From January through March, and from August through December
2001—January

Those born from May 11th to 21st, will be strongly under the influence of the epoch-making, revolutionary planet Uranus, during the following periods:

1939—From July through November
1940—From April through December
1941—From January through July, also November and December
1942—From January through May
1959—From October through December
1960—January, again from August through December
1961—From January through October
1962—From February through July
1979—From January through April, also November and December
1980—Entire year
1981—January, again from May through November
2000—From April through July
2001—From February through December

When the Sun is in Gemini and temporarily afflicted by Uranus, every effort should be made to avoid restlessness, to cultivate contentment and to give the entire attention to one thing at a time. Otherwise, those people who are under this affliction are likely to become depleted nervously and, if they disregard Nature's warnings, in time they will suffer from a nervous breakdown. One of the first signs of such a condition would be insomnia, neuritis or rheumatism, which might affect the hands, arms or shoulders, and sympathetically colic in the intestines, nervous sciatica, lumbago, nervous gout, and neuralgic pains in the feet or toes. Under this affliction, variety of occupation and pleasure is as essential to the well-being, as plenty of sleep and exercise in the fresh air.

Those born from May 21st to June 1st will be strongly under the influence of the epoch-making, revolutionary planet Uranus, during the following periods:

1941—From August through October
1942—From June through December
1943—Entire year
1944—From January through June
1945—February and March
1961—November and December
1962—January, again from August through December
1963—From January through November
1964—From February through August
1981—February, March, April, and December
1982—Entire year
1983—Entire year

Those born from June 1st to 11th will be strongly under the influence of the epoch-making, revolutionary planet Uranus, during the following periods:

1944—From July through December
1945—January, again from April through December
1946—From January through July
1947—From January through April
1963—December
1964—January, and again from September through December
1965—Entire year
1966—From February through September
1984—Entire year
1985—Entire year
1986—From August through October

Those born from June 11th to 22nd will be strongly under the influence of the epoch-making, revolutionary planet Uranus, during the following periods:

1946—From August through December
1947—From May through December
1948—From January through August, also December
1949—From January through May
1966—January, again from October through December
1967—Entire year
1968—From January through September
1986—From January through July, also November and December
1987—Entire year
1988—January and February, also from July through November

When the Sun is in Cancer and temporarily afflicted by Uranus, the appetite is likely to be very capricious, and in order to stimulate it, food must be very daintily prepared, if possible, and variety and frequent changes of diet be taken. If subjected to nervous emotion or shock, those who are under this affliction are likely to suffer from nervous dyspepsia. When physically exhausted or mentally agitated, an excess of acid is thrown into the stomach. In extreme cases of such distress, immediate relief may be experienced by using a small quantity of bicarbonate of soda, together with a large quantity of lukewarm water and by emptying the stomach by induced regurgitation. Neglect of acidity could result in ulcers of the stomach. Sympathetically, these people could suffer from neuralgic pains in the kidneys, (and ovaries in a woman), nervous headaches, and pains in the knees. Cancer has much influence on the solar-plexus; therefore, when Uranus is afflicting the Sun in this sign, it makes one very intuitive and susceptible to psychic influences. Repeated disregard of the intuitions or giving way to false fears or apprehensions could result in obsessions.

Those born from June 22nd to July 1st will be strongly under the influence of the epoch-making, revolutionary planet Uranus, during the following periods:

1929—From January through May, also from October through December
1930—During first two months
1948—From September through November

1949—From June through December
1950—Entire year
1951—From January through June
1968—October, November, December
1969—Entire year
1970—From January through October
1971—June and July
1988—From March through June, also December
1989—Entire year
1990—Entire year

Those born from July 1st to 11th, will be strongly under the influence of the epoch-making, revolutionary planet Uranus, during the following periods:

1929—From June through September
1930—From March through December
1931—Entire year
1932—First four months
1933—January
1951—From July through December
1952—Entire year
1953—From January through July
1954—March, April and May
1970—November and December
1971—From January through May, from August through December
1972—From January through October
1973—June and July
1991—Entire year
1992—Entire year
1993—January, again from August through November

Those born from July 11th to 22nd, will be strongly under the influence of the epoch-making, revolutionary planet Uranus, during the following periods:

1932—From May through December

1933—From February through December
1934—From January through May, also November and December
1935—From January through March
1953—From August through December
1954—January, February, and from June through December
1955—From January through August
1956—From March through May
1972—November and December
1973—From January through May, and from August through December
1974—From January through November
1975—June, July and August
1993—From February through July, again in December
1994—Entire year
1995—From January through March, and from July through December
1996—January

When the Sun is in Leo and temporarily afflicted by Uranus, an effort should be made to avoid being over-ambitious and over-enthusiastic. If those who are under this affliction allow themselves to become run down, or in case of nervous shock, they may suffer from an intermittent or erratic heart. If, however, they do not overtax this organ by undue strain of the psychic forces, they need have no serious trouble. Should they suffer from a pain in the back, this will usually be a warning that they are becoming exhausted physically, and they should try and have a change of environment or associates. Sympathetically, these people may suffer from irritation of the throat, nervous pains in the generative organs, swollen ankles, cramps in the calves and supersensitiveness of the skin.

Those born from July 22nd to August 1st will be strongly under the influence of the epoch-making, revolutionary planet Uranus, during the following periods:

1934—From June through October
1935—From April through December
1936—Entire year

1937—From January through April
1955—From September through December
1956—January, February, and from June through December
1957—From January through September
1958—From February through June
1974—December
1975—From January through May, again September through December
1976—From January through November
1977—From June through September
1995—From April through June
1996—From February through December
1997—Entire year
1998—January and February, again from September through December

Those born from August 1st to 12th, will be strongly under the influence of the epoch-making, revolutionary planet Uranus, during the following periods:

1937—From May through December
1938—Entire year
1939—From January through June, again in December
1940—From January through March
1957—From October through December
1958—January, and from July through December
1959—From January through September
1960—From February through July
1976—December
1977—From January through May, and from October through December
1978—Entire year
1979—From May through October
1998—From March through August
1999—Entire year
2000—From January through March, and from August through December
2001—January

Those born from August 12th to 23rd, will be strongly under the influence of the epoch-making, revolutionary planet Uranus, during the following periods:

1939—From July through November
1940—From April through December
1941—From January through July, also November and December
1942—From January through May
1959—From October through December
1960—January, also from August through December
1961—From January through October
1962—From February through July
1979—From January through April, also November and December
1980—Entire year
1981—January, also from May through November
2000—From April through July
2001—From February through December

When the Sun is in Virgo and temporarily afflicted by Uranus, every effort should be made to avoid being over-critical and too fastidious by those who are under this affliction. They should also avoid being too sarcastic or too analytical. When they are run down or forced to associate with those who get on their nerves, or, in case of any great nervous shock, they may suffer from queer sensations in the abdomen or from colic. They should be careful of the water they drink, particularly when abroad, and of the vegetables they eat, if they chance to be in the Orient. Sympathetically, these people could suffer from insomnia and neuritis in shoulders, arms and hands, nervous sciatica or lumbago, nervous gout and neuralgic pains in feet or toes. Ruptures or strains should be guarded against.

Those born from August 23rd to September 3rd will be strongly under the influence of the epoch-making, revolutionary planet Uranus, during the following periods:

1941—From August through October
1942—From June through December

1943—Entire year
1944—From January through June
1945—February and March
1961—November and December
1962—January, again from August through December
1963—From January through November
1964—From February through August
1981—February, March, April, and December
1982—Entire year
1983—Entire year

Those born from September 3rd to 12th, will be strongly under the influence of the epoch-making, revolutionary planet Uranus, during the following periods:

1944—From July through December
1945—January, and from April through December
1946—From January through July
1947—From January through April
1963—December
1964—January, again from September through December
1965—Entire year
1966—From February through September
1984—Entire year
1985—Entire year
1986—From August through October

Those born from September 12th to 23rd, will be strongly under the influence of the epoch-making, revolutionary planet Uranus, during the following periods:

1946—From August through December
1947—From May through December
1948—From January through August, also December
1949—From January through May
1966—January, again from October through December
1967—Entire year
1968—From January through September

1986—From January through July, also November and December
1987—Entire year
1988—January and February, also from July through November

When the Sun is in Libra and temporarily afflicted by Uranus, it will be necessary for those who are under this affliction to avoid supersensitiveness and being too esthetic or emotional. If obliged to associate with people whose magnetic aura is not sympathetic with their own, this would have a harmful effect on their psychic nervous system. If they happen to have an uncongenial marriage partner, then the incompatibility would upset their psychic condition in an alarming manner during this affliction. If run down, or in case of nervous shock, these people may suffer from pains difficult to describe. They may receive the quickest relief from a complete rest and through associating with congenial people and by being in happy surroundings. In case of strain, the back, particularly the lower part, and the kidneys, (as well as the ovaries in a woman), are most likely to suffer. These people should avoid violent exercises and guard against falls, for any unusual physical strain is likely to aggravate a tendency to floating kidney or suppression of urine. Sympathetically, they may suffer from neuralgic pains in the head, nervous indigestion, and pains in the knees.

Those born from September 23rd to October 3rd will be strongly under the influence of the epoch-making, revolutionary planet Uranus during the following periods:

1929—From January through May, also from October through December
1930—During first two months
1948—From September through November
1949—From June through December
1950—Entire year
1951—From January through June
1968—October, November and December
1969—Entire year
1970—From January through October
1971—June and July

1988—From March through June, also December
1989—Entire year
1990—Entire year

Those born from October 3rd to 13th, will be strongly under the influence of the epoch-making, revolutionary planet Uranus, during the following periods:

1929—From June through September
1930—From March through December
1931—Entire year
1932—During first four months
1933—January
1951—From July through December
1952—Entire year
1953—From January through July
1954—March, April and May
1970—November and December
1971—January through May, again from August through December
1972—From January through October
1973—June and July
1991—Entire year
1992—Entire year
1993—January, and from August through November

Those born from October 13th to 23rd, will be strongly under the influence of the epoch-making, revolutionary planet Uranus, during the following periods:

1932—From May through December
1933—From February through December
1934—From January through May, also November and December
1935—January through March
1953—From August through December
1954—January, February, and from June through December
1955—From January through August
1956—From March through May

1972—November and December
1973—From January through May, again from August through December
1974—From January through November
1975—June, July and August
1993—From February through July, and again in December
1994—Entire year
1995—From January through March, again from July through December
1996—January

When the Sun is in Scorpio and temporarily afflicted by Uranus, every effort should be made by those who are under its affliction to avoid being too bohemian, too self-centered, too passionate, and too anarchistic. It is most necessary that they have a normal outlet for their emotions, otherwise their sex lure may cause them to have temptations which, if indulged in to extremes, will injure their health and cause criticism that might injure their business interests. When Uranus is afflicting their Sun, they are likely to suffer from spasmodic action of the bladder and from neuralgic pains in the uterus (with a woman). Sympathetically, they could suffer from nervous coughs, irregular heart action, pains in the calves, and creepy sensations in the skin.

Those born from October 23rd to November 2nd will be strongly under the influence of the epoch-making, revolutionary planet Uranus, during the following periods:

1934—From June through October
1935—From April through December
1936—Entire year
1937—From January through April
1955—From September through December
1956—January, February, and from June through December
1957—From January through September
1958—From February through June
1974—December
1975—From January through May, again from September through December

1976—From January through November
1977—From June through September
1995—From April through June
1996—From February through December
1997—Entire year
1998—January and February, again from September through December

Those born from November 2nd to 12th, will be strongly under the influence of the epoch-making, revolutionary planet Uranus, during the following periods:

1937—From May through December
1938—Entire year
1939—From January through June again in December
1940—From January through March
1957—From October through December
1958—January, again from July through December
1959—From January through September
1960—From February through July
1976—December
1977—From January through May, again from October through December
1978—Entire year
1979—From May through October
1998—From March through August
1999—Entire year
2000—From January through March, again from August through December
2001—January

Those born from November 12th to 22nd, will be strongly under the influence of the epoch-making, revolutionary planet Uranus, during the following periods:

1939—From July through November
1940—From April through December

1941—From January through July, also November and December
1942—From January through May
1959—From October through December
1960—January, and again from August through December
1961—From January through October
1962—From February through July
1979—From January through April, also November and December
1980—Entire year
1981—January, again from May through November
2000—From April through July
2001—From February through December

When the Sun is in Sagittarius and temporarily afflicted by Uranus, it would be well for those who are under this affliction to avoid being fanatical on religious subjects, or going to extremes in any direction. Should a balance not be maintained between the psychic and physical, they may suffer from nervous sciatica, lumbago, or some form of rheumatism, and sympathetically from insomnia, neuritis of shoulders, arms and hands; also from colic of the intestines, nervous gout, neuralgic pains in the feet, particularly the toes. If, however, they keep normal and do not disregard Nature's warnings, there is no reason why they should feel as many ill-effects through the affliction of Uranus as is the case with the Sun in Scorpio. The affliction will have much more bearing on other departments of the life, than on health. It may stimulate the humanitarian, intuitive, prophetic, scientific and philosophical qualities and work out to their advantage, provided they avoid going to extremes.

Those born from November 22nd to December 2nd will be strongly under the influence of the epoch-making, revolutionary planet Uranus, during the following periods:

1941—From August through October
1942—From June through December
1943—Entire year
1944—From January through June
1945—February and March

1961—November and December
1962—January, again from August through December
1963—From January through November
1964—From February through August
1981—February, March, April and December
1982—Entire year
1983—Entire year

Those born from December 2nd to 12th, will be strongly under the influence of the epoch-making, revolutionary planet Uranus, during the following periods:

1944—From July through December
1945—January, and again from April through December
1946—From January through July
1947—From January through April
1963—December
1964—January, and again from September through December
1965—Entire year
1966—From February through September
1984—Entire year
1985—Entire year
1986—From August through October

Those born from December 12th to 21st, will be strongly under the influence of the epoch-making, revolutionary planet Uranus, during the following periods:

1946—From August through December
1947—From May through December
1948—From January through August, also December
1949—From January through May
1966—January, and again from October through December
1967—Entire year
1968—From January through September
1986—From January through July, also November and December
1987—Entire year
1988—January and February, also from July through November

When the Sun is in Capricorn and temporarily afflicted by Uranus, it will be necessary for those who are under this affliction to avoid too great extremes in mental reactions and to select a balanced diet, otherwise they are likely to have a craving for liquor or condiments and to suffer from digestive disorders, troubles with the knees, and sympathetically from nervous headaches, spasmodic pains in the kidneys of both sexes (and the ovaries in the case of women). Those who are under the affliction of Uranus should realize that their extremes of mood are largely due to the influence of this erratic planet, that they will soon pass, and that they must not take themselves or life too seriously, or exaggerate the importance of fancied slights or impositions.

Those born from December 21st to January 1st will be strongly under the influence of the epoch-making, revolutionary planet Uranus, during the following periods:

1929—From January through May, and again from October through December
1930—During first two months
1948—From September through November
1949—From June through December
1950—Entire year
1951—From January through June
1968—October, November, and December
1969—Entire year
1970—From January through October
1971—June and July
1988—From March through June, and again in December
1989—Entire year
1990—Entire year

Those born from January 1st to 10th, will be strongly under the influence of the epoch-making, revolutionary planet Uranus, during the following periods:

1929—From June through September
1930—From March through December
1931—Entire year
1932—During first four months

1933—January
1951—Last half of year
1952—Entire year
1953—From January through July
1954—March, April, May
1970—November and December
1971—From January through May, again from August through December
1972—From January through October
1973—June and July
1991—Entire year
1992—Entire year
1993—January, and again from August through November

Those born from January 10th to 20th, will be strongly under the influence of the epoch-making, revolutionary planet Uranus, during the following periods:

1932—From May through December
1933—From February through December
1934—From January through May, also November and December
1935—From January through March
1953—From August through December
1954—January, February, and from June through December
1955—From January through August
1956—From March through May
1972—November and December
1973—From January through May, again from August through December
1974—From January through November
1975—June, July and August
1993—From February through July, and again in December
1994—Entire year
1995—From January through March, and again from July through December
1996—January

When the Sun is in Aquarius and temporarily afflicted by Uranus, there will be less danger of those who are under this affliction feeling any ill effects from it, because of the extraordinary poise given by Aquarius. They are likely to so govern their lives as to avoid the indiscretions which are frequently responsible for much ill-health. Any physical disorders which overtake them when under the affliction of Uranus may be largely due to being forced to associate with those they naturally dislike or to live in an environment which is distasteful to them. Fortunately, they have the ability to detect at once whether or not they would be congenial with those who cross their path. When out of balance physically, they could suffer from swollen ankles, cramps in the calves, varicose veins and creepy sensations of the skin, and sympathetically from irregular heart action, nervous irritation in the throat, and neuralgic pains in the organs of generation.

Those born from January 20th to 30th, will be strongly under the influence of the epoch-making, revolutionary planet Uranus, during the following periods:

1934—From June through October
1935—From April through December
1936—Entire year
1937—From January through April
1955—From September through December
1956—January, February, and from June through December
1957—From January through September
1958—From February through June
1974—December
1975—From January through May, again from September through December
1976—From January through November
1977—From June through September
1995—From April through June
1996—From February through December
1997—Entire year
1998—January and February, again from September through December

Those born from January 30th to February 9th, will be strongly under the influence of the epoch-making, revolutionary planet Uranus, during the following periods:

1937—From May through December
1938—Entire year
1939—From January through June, and again in December
1940—From January through March
1957—From October through December
1958—January, and again from July through December
1959—From January through September
1960—From February through July
1976—December
1977—From January through May, and again from October through December
1978—Entire year
1979—From May through October
1998—From March through August
1999—Entire year
2000—From January through March, and again from August through December
2001—January

Those born from February 9th to 19th, will be strongly under the influence of the epoch-making, revolutionary planet Uranus, during the following periods:

1939—From July through November
1940—From April through December
1941—From January through July, also November and December
1942—From January through May
1959—From October through December
1960—January, and again from August through December
1961—From January through October
1962—From February through July
1979—From January through April, also November and December
1980—Entire year
1981—January, and again from May through November

2000—From April through July
2001—From February through December

When the Sun is in Pisces and temporarily afflicted by Uranus those who are under its affliction should avoid doing anything which upsets them psychically, as it takes only a trifle to disturb their nervous system and to cause them to suffer from imaginary ailments. When under this planet, they are likely to be thrown out of balance physically or psychically and to suffer from nervous tumors, gout, neuralgic pains in the feet, particularly the toes, and from a dropsical condition; sympathetically they may suffer from colic in the intestines, short breath, nervous pains in the hips and thighs, and lumbago. The tendency for those born with the Sun in Pisces to waste their nervous force and not to coordinate or concentrate on some one matter at a time, will be very much exaggerated during an affliction of Uranus to the Sun, and it will require the greatest will-power and self-control if the force is to be directed and controlled.

Those born from February 19th to March 1st, will be strongly under the influence of the epoch-making, revolutionary planet Uranus, during the following periods:

1941—From August through October
1942—From June through December
1943—Entire year
1944—From January through June
1945—February and March
1961—November and December
1962—January, and again from August through December
1963—From January through November
1964—From February through August
1981—February, March, April and December
1982—Entire year
1983—Entire year

Those born from March 1st to 10th, will be strongly under the influence of the epoch-making, revolutionary planet Uranus, during the following periods:

1944—From July through December

1945—January, and again from April through December
1946—From January through July
1947—From January through April
1963—December
1964—January, and again from September through December
1965—Entire year
1966—From February through September
1984—Entire year
1985—Entire year
1986—From August through October

Those born from March 10th to 21st, will be strongly under the influence of the epoch-making, revolutionary planet Uranus, during the following periods:

1946—From August through December
1947—From May through December
1948—From January through August, also December
1949—From January through May
1966—January, and again from October through December
1967—Entire year
1968—From January through September
1986—From January through July, also November and December
1987—Entire year
1988—January and February, also from July through November

PERIODS WHEN THE SUN WILL BE BENEFICENTLY ASPECTED BY URANUS

The Sun is the one heavenly body whose position is practically the same at the same time in the year of any year. Consequently, in this volume it is the only sphere that we have considered in making predictions regarding the future. In order that the effects of the friendly aspect of Uranus on the Sun may be fairly closely computed, the Sun has been divided into three sections, of ten degrees each. This makes the calculations as given, within what is known as "orbs," and therefore sufficiently close to an aspect to make its effects distinctly felt. The periods when Uranus will be in friendly aspect to the Sun are tabulated and will be found at the end of each sign. All aspects of Uranus are very important, as it takes eighty-four years for the planet to make a revolution of the zodiac, and it forms a friendly aspect about once in every fourteen years.

Whenever the unconventional, revolutionary Uranus is in friendly aspect to the Sun, it has a very powerful influence for good and is very far reaching in its effects. Just as Uranus being unfriendly to the Sun stirs one's nature to the depths, but with danger of going to extremes and working much as does a cyclone—i. e. tears down in order to rebuild—the friendly or harmonious vibration of Uranus enables one to build without first destroying. It causes one's sympathies to be broadened, adds efficiency, and the whole nature is harmoniously attuned to the highest pitch attainable up to this time. Those enjoying a friendly aspect of Uranus to the Sun should feel a sense of power, and awakened energy which will give them a conviction of success that will be felt by others and which will help them to put over whatever they undertake. These will be the most propitious times for having dealings with people of unusual and highly original ability, and with those who are in power, especially if involved in public affairs or in important movements connected with the community. The friendly aspect of Uranus to the Sun often brings unexpected opportunities of a high order from unusual sources or from strangers, and frequently out of a clear sky.

When under this aspect, the single woman should set her stage and do everything within her power to place herself under the most favorable conditions for meeting the type of man she would desire to marry. She should not take too lightly any opportunities for meeting men or for benefitting through them while under this aspect, for although she will experience other favorable vibrations from time to time, this particular aspect, as stated above, will not occur again for another fourteen years. Remember to "choose not alone a proper mate, but proper time to marry."

The married woman can expect increased success for her husband, as well as for herself, if she has any interests apart from the home. If she leads a purely domestic life, then she may have the desire to launch out into an enterprise of her own, because of her increased urge for self-expression. This may manifest itself simply in the desire to build a new home or to make improvements in her surroundings. If by any chance her husband is in politics or connected with any philanthropic or communal movements, she should do everything in her power to encourage him and aid him in this direction, realizing that efforts made under these vibrations stand a much better chance of meeting with success than will be the case again for many years.

Both men and women will not only be in harmony with their better selves, but also in more sympathetic relation with all those who touch their lives at these particular periods. They should cultivate friends they may chance to meet, as they are likely to prove fortunate through being in a position of influence or power or because they have a desire to do so. Unless already satisfactorily placed in life, these would be very constructive and fortunate periods for embarking on any new undertakings and for enlarging one's activities already under way, as well as for finding one's niche in the Universe. One should not, however, set one's will against the Universal Will, but try to realize as never before, the power of an intelligent non-resistance. One should feel that any changes which come about naturally are for one's ultimate good, but one should not force issues against what seems to be the natural order of things.

In the case of children, the benefits experienced when under the constructive aspect of Uranus are naturally more likely to be felt through the family, especially the father, or some other man intimately connected in the destiny. Such a man may meet with rapid or unexpected advancement or have some unusual honor bestowed upon him. Children will experience quite remarkable interior development and, in spite of the fact of their youth, they will be filled, as never before, with a desire to express themselves and to work things out in their own way. They should be encouraged in originality, provided with the opportunity to enjoy their own pleasures in their own way, and be allowed all possible freedom, as under this aspect they will just naturally be wise in their decisions. They must be made to understand, however, that there is no royal road to either wisdom or success and they should be taught that all Fate can do is to bring opportunity and it is for them to make wise use of it.

When the Sun is in Aries and temporarily beneficently aspected by Uranus, any original qualities which the person born under this sign may possess will be stimulated. Those who are feeling its effect may have a greater urge for doing pioneer work and for breaking down limitations within themselves (but in a constructive way) than will be the case again for another fourteen years.

Those born from March 21st to April 1st will be strongly under the beneficent influence of Uranus during the following periods:

1941—From August through October
1942—From June through December
1943—The entire year
1944—From January through June
1945—February and March
1955—From September through December
1956—January and February and from June through December
1957—From January through September
1958—From February through June
1981—February, March, April and December
1982—The entire year
1983—The entire year
1995—April, May and June
1996—From February through December
1997—The entire year
1998—January and February and from September through December

Those born from April 1st to 11th will be strongly under the beneficent influence of Uranus during the following periods:

1944—From July through December
1945—January and from April through December
1946—From January through July
1947—From January through April
1957—October, November and December
1958—January and from July through December
1959—From January through September
1960—From February through July
1984—The entire year
1985—The entire year

1986—August, September and October
1998—From March through August
1999—The entire year
2000—January, February and March and August through December
2001—January

Those born from April 11th to the 21st will be strongly under the beneficent influcnce of Uranus during the following periods:

1946—From August through December
1947—From May through December
1948—From January through August, also December
1949—From January through May
1959—October, November and December
1960—January and from August through December
1961—From January through October
1962—From February through July
1986—From January through July, also November and December
1987—The entire year
1988—January and February and from July through November
2000—From April through July
2001—From February through December

When the Sun is in Taurus and temporarily beneficently aspected by Uranus, the constructive qualities which the sign implies will be stimulated. Those who are feeling its effects will find it less difficult to coöperate with others and to bend their dominant will to that of the Universe. In consequence, tasks which they have hitherto found it impossible to complete, will seem to be accomplished with greater ease.

Those born from April 21st to May 1st will be strongly under the beneficent influence of Uranus during the following periods:

1948—From September through November
1949—From June through December
1950—The entire year

1951—From January through June
1961—November and December
1962—January and from August through December
1963—From January through November
1964—From February through August
1988—From March through June, also December
1989—The entire year
1990—The entire year

Those born from May 1st to 11th will be strongly under the beneficent influence of Uranus during the following periods:

1951—From July through December
1952—The entire year
1953—From January through July
1954—March, April and May
1963—December
1964—January and from September through December
1965—The entire year
1966—From February through September
1991—The entire year
1992—The entire year
1993—January and from August through November

Those born from May 11th to the 22nd will be strongly under the beneficent influence of Uranus during the following periods:

1953—From August through December
1954—January and February and from June through December
1955—From January through August
1956—March, April and May
1966—January and October, November and December
1967—The entire year
1968—From January through September
1993—From February through July, also December
1994—The entire year
1995—From January through March and from July through December
1996—January

When the Sun is in Gemini and temporarily beneficently aspected by Uranus, any original qualities which the person born under this sign may possess will be stimulated. The versatility given by Gemini will be more readily directed in some one channel when under this aspect, and there will be less dissatisfaction with existing conditions and more constructive work likely to be accomplished and with less effort.

Those born from May 21st to June 1st will be strongly under the beneficent influence of Uranus during the following periods:

1929—From January through May, also October, November and December
1930—January and February
1955—From September through December
1956—January and February and from June through December
1957—From January through September
1958—From February through June
1968—October, November and December
1969—The entire year
1970—From January through October
1971—June and July
1995—From April through June
1996—From February through December
1997—The entire year
1998—January and February and from September through December

Those born from June 1st to the 11th will be strongly under the beneficent influence of Uranus during the following periods:

1929—From June through September
1930—From March through December
1931—The entire year
1932—From January through April
1933—January
1957—October, November and December
1958—January and from July through December
1959—From January through September
1960—From February through July

1970—November and December
1971—From January through May and from August through December
1972—From January through October
1973—June and July
1998—From March through August
1999—The entire year
2000—January, February and March and from August through December
2001—January

Those born from June 11th to the 22nd will be strongly under the beneficent influence of Uranus during the following periods:

1932—From May through December
1933—From February through December
1934—From January through May, also November and December
1935—From January through March
1959—October, November and December
1960—January and from August through December
1961—From January through October
1962—From February through July
1972—November and December
1973—From January through May and from August through December
1974—From January through November
1975—June, July and August
2000—From April through July
2001—From February through December

When the Sun is in Cancer and temporarily beneficently aspected by Uranus, the subjective qualities of the sign Cancer will be stimulated and in a constructive manner. Those who are feeling its effects may have a broader outlook on life and because of this become less conventional and less wedded to old customs and beliefs. They may become more impersonal and less sensitive, and consequently accomplish more in their own field and be a greater comfort to their friends and associates.

Those born from June 22nd to July 1st will be strongly under the beneficent influence of Uranus during the following periods:

1934—From June through October
1935—From April through December
1936—The entire year
1937—From January through April
1961—November and December
1962—January and from August through December
1963—From January through November
1964—From February through August
1974—December
1975—From January through May, and from September through December
1976—From January through November
1977—From June through September

Those born from July 1st to the 11th will be strongly under the beneficent influence of Uranus during the following periods:

1937—From May through December
1938—The entire year
1939—From January through June, also December
1940—From January through March
1963—December
1964—January, and from September through December
1965—The entire year
1966—From February through September
1976—December
1977—From January through May, also October, November and December
1978—The entire year
1979—From May through October

Those born from July 11th to the 22nd will be strongly under the beneficent influence of Uranus during the following periods:

1939—From July through November

1940—From April through December
1941—From January through July, also November and December
1942—From January through May
1966—January, October, November and December
1967—The entire year
1968—From January through September
1979—From January through April, also November and December
1980—The entire year
1981—January and from May through November

When the Sun is in Leo and temporarily beneficently aspected by Uranus, any executive qualities which the sign Leo implies will be enhanced. Those who are feeling its effects will find it possible at these times to carry to a successful conclusion ambitions which they have long cherished but hitherto found difficult or even impossible of accomplishment. Even the tendency to be too dictatorial which is one of the faults of the Leo type will not be resented, as at these periods the person born under Leo will be more diplomatic and less offensive in his manner of approach.

Those born from July 22nd to August 1st will be strongly under the beneficent influence of Uranus during the following periods:

1929—From January through May, also October, November and December
1930—January and February
1941—From August through October
1942—From June through December
1943—The entire year
1944—From January through June
1945—February and March
1968—October, November and December
1969—The entire year
1970—From January through October
1971—June and July
1981—From February through April, also December
1982—The entire year

1983—The entire year

Those born from August 1st to the 12th will be strongly under the beneficent influence of Uranus during the following periods:

1929—From June through September
1930—From March through December
1931—The entire year
1932—From January through April
1933—January
1944—From July through December
1945—January and from April through December
1946—From January through July
1947—From January through April
1970—November and December
1971—From January through May and from August through December
1972—From January through October
1973—June and July
1984—The entire year
1985—The entire year
1986—From August through October

Those born from August 12th to the 23rd will be strongly under the beneficent influence of Uranus during the following periods:

1932—From May through December
1933—From February through December
1934—From January through May, also November and December
1935—From January through March
1946—From August through December
1947—From May through December
1948—From January through August, also December
1949—From January through May
1972—November and December
1973—From January through May, also from August through December

1974—From January through November
1975—June, July and August
1986—From January through July, also November and December
1987—The entire year
1988—January and February and from July through November

When the Sun is in Virgo and temporarily beneficently aspected by Uranus, the most desirable qualities which the sign Virgo implies will be stimulated. Those who are inclined to be too analytical and too critical will, temporarily at least, be more sympathetic, more tolerant and less offensive to those who look upon them as purists. If their work is along mental lines, then the influence of Uranus will make them more original and more romantic. If engaged in manufacturing, building or mining, then they may have brought to their attention schemes for developing large properties, for merging huge enterprises and for opening up the natural resources of the country.

Those born from August 23rd to September 3rd will be strongly under the beneficent influence of Uranus during the following periods:

1934—From June through October
1935—From April through December
1936—The entire year
1937—From January through April
1948—September, October and November
1949—From June through December
1950—The entire year
1951—From January through June
1974—December
1975—From January through May and from September through December
1976—From January through November
1977—From June through September
1988—From March through June, also December
1989—The entire year
1990—The entire year

Those born from September 3rd to the 12th will be strongly under the beneficent influence of Uranus during the following periods:

1937—From May through December
1938—The entire year
1939—From January through June, also December
1940—January, February and March
1951—From July through December
1952—The entire year
1953—From January through July
1954—March, April and May
1976—December
1977—From January through May, also October, November and December
1978—The entire year
1979—From May through October
1991—The entire year
1992—The entire year
1993—January and from August through November

Those born from September 12th to the 23rd will be strongly under the beneficent influence of Uranus during the following periods:

1939—From July through November
1940—From April through December
1941—From January through July, also November and December
1942—From January through May
1953—From August through December
1954—January and February and from June through December
1955—From January through August
1956—From March through May
1979—From January through April, also November and December
1980—The entire year
1981—January, and from May through November
1993—From February through July, also December

1994—The entire year
1995—January, February and March and from July through December
1996—January

When the Sun is in Libra and temporarily beneficently aspected by Uranus, the equitable qualities which the sign Libra implies will be stimulated. It all depends upon the type of endeavor, whether it be professional, technical or artistic, as to how the Libra type who will be under this influence, will be benefitted by it. In any case, the more nearly universal he can make his interests, the greater will be his chances for getting the most from these vibrations.

Those born from September 23rd to October 3rd will be strongly under the beneficent influence of Uranus during the following periods:

1941—From August through October
1942—From June through December
1943—The entire year
1944—From January through June
1945—February and March
1955—From September through December
1956—January and February also from June through December
1957—From January through September
1958—From February through June
1981—From February through April, also December
1982—The entire year
1983—The entire year
1995—April, May and June
1996—From February through December
1997—The entire year
1998—January and February and from September through December

Those born from October 3rd to the 13th will be strongly under the beneficent influence of Uranus during the following periods:

1944—From July through December
1945—January and from April through December

1946—From January through July
1947—From January through April
1957—October, November and December
1958—January and from July through December
1959—From January through September
1960—From February through July
1984—The entire year
1985—The entire year
1986—From August through October
1998—From March through August
1999—The entire year
2000—From January through March and from August through December
2001—January

Those born from October 13th to the 23rd will be strongly under the beneficent influence of Uranus during the following periods:

1946—From August through December
1947—From May through December
1948—From January through August, also December
1949—From January through May
1959—October, November and December
1960—January and from August through December
1961—From January through October
1962—From February through July
1986—From January through July, also November and December
1987—The entire year
1988—January and February and from July through November
2000—From April through July
2001—From February through December

When the Sun is in Scorpio and temporarily beneficently aspected by Uranus, the less desirable qualities of this sign will temporarily be held in abeyance and the more impersonal and unselfish qualities will be stimulated. Surgeons, chemists, executives and inventors will be particularly inspired to do better work when under this influence of Uranus. All those born under Scorpio will feel a greater urge for constructive accomplishment and will meet with more ready success at these periods.

Those born from October 23rd to November 2nd will be strongly under the beneficent influence of Uranus during the following periods:

1948—September, October and November
1949—From June through December
1950—The entire year
1951—From January through June
1961—November and December
1962—January and from August through December
1963—From January through November
1964—From February through August
1988—From March through June, also December
1989—The entire year
1990—The entire year

Those born from November 2nd to the 12th will be strongly under the beneficent influence of Uranus during the following periods:

1951—From July through December
1952—The entire year
1953—From January through July
1954—March, April and May
1963—December
1964—January and from September through December
1965—The entire year
1966—From February through September
1991—The entire year
1992—The entire year
1993—January and from August through November

Those born from November 12th to the 22nd will be strongly under the beneficent influence of Uranus during the following periods:

1953—From August through December
1954—January and February and from June through December
1955—From January through August
1956—March, April and May
1966—January, also October, November and December
1967—The entire year
1968—From January through September
1993—From February through July, also December
1994—The entire year
1995—From January through March and from July through December
1996—January

When the Sun is in Sagittarius and temporarily beneficently aspected by Uranus, the more generous and prophetic qualities which this sign implies will be augmented. While at all times those who are born strongly under the influence of this sign are generally actuated by high motives and attracted to large enterprises, when they come under a friendly Uranus aspect they will be fired with a desire to do greater things and Fate will seem to assist them to this end. In some cases this may come about through the influence of powerful people and at other times because there will seem to be no obstacles, delays or other annoying conditions to beset the path.

Those born from November 22nd to December 2nd will be strongly under the beneficent influence of Uranus during the following periods:

1929—From January through May, also October, November and December
1930—January and February
1955—From September through December
1956—January and February and from June through December
1957—From January through September
1958—From February through June
1968—October, November and December
1969—The entire year
1970—From January through October
1971—June and July

1995—April, May and June
1996—From February through December
1997—The entire year
1998—January and February and from September through December

Those born from December 2nd to the 12th will be strongly under the beneficent influence of Uranus during the following periods:

1929—From June through September
1930—From March through December
1931—The entire year
1932—From January through April
1933—January
1957—October, November and December
1958—January and from July through December
1959—From January through September
1960—From February through July
1970—November and December
1971—From January through May and from August through December
1972—From January through October
1973—June and July
1998—From March through August
1999—The entire year
2000—From January through March and from August through December
2001—January

Those born from December 12th to the 21st will be strongly under the beneficent influence of Uranus during the following periods:

1932—From May through December
1933—From February through December
1934—From January through May, also November and December
1935—From January through March
1959—October, November and December

1960—January and from August through December
1961—From January through October
1962—From February through July
1972—November and December
1973—From January through May and from August through December
1974—From January through November
1975—June, July and August
2001—From April through July
2001—From February through December

When the Sun is in Capricorn and temporarily beneficently aspected by Uranus, the tendency to be too serious and too easily depressed or discouraged will be modified. The greater vision and broader outlook on life given at these times will assist them in carrying out their ambitions. The danger of the Capricorn type to become too greatly immersed in detail and to allow their scope to become too limited will be lessened, as Uranus will be a liberating influence, which will bring unusual opportunities, particularly through strangers or unexpected sources.

Those born from December 21st to January 1st will be strongly under the beneficent influence of Uranus during the following periods:

1934—From June through October
1935—From April through December
1936—The entire year
1937—From January through April
1961—November and December
1962—January and from August through December
1963—From January through November
1964—From February through August
1974—December
1975—From January through May and from September through December
1976—From January through November
1977—From June through September

Those born from January 1st to the 10th will be strongly under the beneficent influence of Uranus during the following periods:

1937—From May through December
1938—The entire year
1939—From January through June, also December
1940—From January through March
1963—December
1964—January and from September through December
1965—The entire year
1966—From February through September
1976—December
1977—From January through May, also October, November and December
1978—The entire year
1979—From May through October

Those born from January 10th to the 20th will be strongly under the beneficent influence of Uranus during the following periods:

1939—From July through November
1940—From April through December
1941—From January through July, also November and December
1942—From January through May
1966—January, October, November and December
1967—The entire year
1968—From January through September
1979—From January through April, also November and December
1980—The entire year
1981—January and from May through November

When the Sun is in Aquarius and temporarily beneficently aspected by Uranus, the humanitarian and philanthropic qualities which the sign Aquarius implies will be stimulated. Aquarius being a very impersonal sign and Uranus an impersonal planet, those who are enjoying this aspect should be enabled to do some of their best work. They will just naturally attract projects of an original and unusual character connected with scientific, religious or inventive research. It is under these influences that they will be inspired to originate and assist in blazing new trails.

Those born from January 20th to the 30th will be strongly under the beneficent influence of Uranus during the following periods:

1929—From January through May, also October, November and December
1930—January and February
1941—From August through October
1942—From June through December
1943—The entire year
1944—From January through June
1945—February and March
1968—October, November and December
1969—The entire year
1970—From January through October
1971—June and July
1981—From February through April, also December
1982—The entire year
1983—The entire year

Those born from January 30th to February 9th will be strongly under the beneficent influence of Uranus during the following periods:

1929—From June through September
1930—From March through December
1931—The entire year
1932—From January through April
1933—January
1944—From July through December
1945—January and from April through December
1946—From January through July
1947—From January through April
1970—November and December
1971—From January through May and from August through December

1972—From January through October
1973—June and July
1984—The entire year
1985—The entire year
1986—From August through October

Those born from February 9th to the 19th will be strongly under the beneficent influence of Uranus during the following periods:

1932—From May through December
1933—From February through December
1934—From January through May, also November and December
1935—From January through March
1946—From August through December
1947—From May through December
1948—From January through August, also December
1949—From January through May
1972—November and December
1973—From January through May and from August through December
1974—From January through November
1975—June, July and August
1986—From January through July, also November and December
1987—The entire year
1988—January and February and from July through November

When the Sun is in Pisces and temporarily beneficently aspected by Uranus, the altruistic qualities which the sign Pisces implies will be stimulated. Because of the tendency of the Pisces type to be unduly modest, they may be in danger of neglecting to take full advantage of these periods. They should leave no stone unturned to try to take advantage of all their opportunities, even though they may seem to be something beyond their wildest dreams.

Those born from February 19th to March 1st will be strongly under the beneficent influence of Uranus during the following periods:

1934—From June through October
1935—From April through December
1936—The entire year
1937—From January through April
1948—September, October and November
1949—From June through December
1950—The entire year
1951—From January through June
1974—December
1975—From January through May and from September through December
1976—From January through November
1977—From June through September
1988—From March through June, also December
1989—The entire year
1990—The entire year

Those born from March 1st to the 10th will be strongly under the beneficent influence of Uranus during the following periods:

1937—From May through December
1938—The entire year
1939—From January through June, also December
1940—From January through March
1951—From July through December
1952—The entire year
1953—From January through July
1954—March, April and May
1976—December
1977—From January through May, also October, November and December
1978—The entire year
1979—From May through October
1991—The entire year
1992—The entire year
1993—January and from August through November

Those born from March 10th to the 21st will be strongly under the beneficent influence of Uranus during the following periods:

1939—From July through November
1940—From April through December
1941—From January through July, also November and December
1942—From January through May
1953—From August through December
1954—January and February and from June through December
1955—From January through August
1956—March, April and May
1979—From January through April, also November and December
1980—The entire year
1981—January and from May through November
1993—From February through July, also December
1994—The entire year
1995—From January through March and from July through December
1996—January

PERIODS WHEN THE SUN WILL BE AFFLICTED BY SATURN

The Sun is the one heavenly body whose position is practically the same at the same time in the year of any year. Consequently, in this volume it is the only sphere that we have considered in making predictions regarding the future. In order that the effects of Saturn on the Sun may be fairly closely computed, the Sun has been divided into three sections of ten degrees each. This makes the calculations as given within what is known as "orbs" and therefore sufficiently close to an aspect to make its effects distinctly felt. The periods when Saturn will form an aspect to the Sun are tabulated and will be found at the end of each sign. Saturn forms an unfriendly aspect to the Sun every seven years. This is treated of below.

Whenever the cold, phlegmatic Saturn is unfriendly to the Sun, the excretory functions become sluggish, it has a very debilitating effect upon the health and anæmia can be easily induced. Those temporarily under Saturn will be susceptible to diseases which may be prevalent or to troubles to which they may be naturally subject.

It tends to make them look and feel older and to be less magnetic and have less influence over others than will be the case again for about seven years.

Anything which has a tendency to cause mental depression should be avoided, so far as possible, and it would be well to try to associate with people who have a cheering influence over the spirits and to avoid worrying over imaginary troubles, or implanting fixed ideas in the mind.

Saturn also has a very depressing influence over business and the domestic and social life. It may be difficult to maintain harmony and, while under Saturn, such people should guard against being too skeptical or analytical and should give their friends and associates as much freedom as possible and not criticise their actions or misjudge their motives; otherwise friendships may be broken and many misunderstandings result. They should be diplomatic and in every way avoid inviting criticism and being blamed for things for which they are not responsible. Elderly people connected with them should give more attention than usual to their health, as Saturn frequently brings about a death.

Women cannot be too discreet as to the men in whom they place confidence; single women are likely to attract men who are married or those who for some other reason are unworthy of their confidence or incapable of benefitting them, and who will bring only sorrow or disappointment. To the married women this aspect often brings temporary estrangement, through lack of sympathy or magnetism, or anxiety over the husband's health or business. They should do everything in their power to avoid having a depressing effect on their partners, whether in a domestic or business way, and they should not count too much on any new men who cross their paths; they will not prove to be permanent influences and may have a disrupting effect on the life.

Both men and women would do well not to make changes unless forced to do so; any urge to expand or change their business activities or the personnel of their organizations should not be encouraged, unless looked into very carefully. They should make sure of the integrity of those with whom they negotiate and the practicality of the enterprise. In order to accomplish satisfactory results, more effort than usual is necessary when under the influence of

Saturn; it is better at such a time to give attention to routine matters and the finishing up of undertakings already under way than to select such periods for initiating new schemes or enterprises. Conditions which may have been dormant are often brought to the surface, and events which have happened in the past and presumably been forgotten frequently come to light and with unpleasant results.

Whenever under the influence of Saturn, it is well to take things very much as they come, live one day at a time and go along the line of intelligent non-resistance. By refusing to force issues one will come out much better in the long run. On the other hand, if one insists on putting through things at any cost, one is likely to make bad matters worse and be in danger of making very unwise moves, pushing aside opportunities and failing to embrace things which are worth while.

Children passing through this affliction will very naturally feel its influence most through conditions in the home or from what happens to the parents, particularly to the father. It will have a depressing effect on their own health, causing anæmia, and will make them susceptible to any children's diseases which may be prevalent at the time or which come as the result of debility. They may temporarily take on a rather serious mental attitude or seem very old for their age. The greatest patience should be exercised by those who have them in charge and everything should be done to keep them cheerful and to make them philosophical. Under this aspect a child is often blamed for circumstances for which he is not responsible. The father or any man who is playing an important part in the destiny may temporarily suffer in health or business.

Through Saturn's vibration, the balance is thrown out, especially through the system becoming depleted physically, as well as by causing the mental attitude to be pessimistic, suspicious or melancholy. While Saturn is a severe disciplinarian, great benefit can come through his influence, provided philosophy, patience and tolerance are exercised. The experiences which come when Saturn is in power can either broaden the horizon, break down limitations and give one a better understanding of life, or they can cause one to become embittered, suspicious and skeptical of one's friends and of life. It is up to the individual, therefore, to realize that all we can take out of life is the wisdom gained through experience, and not fear anything, as it will all work out for good in the end.

When the Sun is in Aries and temporarily afflicted by Saturn, everything should be done to prevent catarrh, for should colds in the head or throat be neglected, deafness may result later in life. Sympathetically, troubles with the kidneys in both sexes (and ovaries in a woman), as well as digestive disorders which, if not corrected, could lead to rheumatism could also be easily aggravated. It will be necessary to be careful in the selection of the diet, avoiding too many sweets or rich food, and to eliminate as much as possible through the skin and intestines, thereby avoiding overtaxing the kidneys. In case of headache, the trouble may be caused by eyestrain, if it does not come because of a disordered stomach.

Those born from March 21st to April 1st will be afflicted by the depressing, restricting planet Saturn during the following periods:

1929—April, May and December
1930—January and February and from July through November
1937—From May through October
1938—From February through April
1944—From July through September, also December
1945—From January through May
1950—December
1951—From January through March and from September through November
1952—From May through July
1959—From February through December
1960—January
1967—April, May and from October through December
1968—January and February
1973—From August through December
1974—May, June and July
1980—October, November and December
1981—From January through August
1988—From March through June, also November and December
1989—January and February and from August through October
1996—From May through December
1997—From January through March

Those born from April 1st to the 11th will be afflicted by the depressing, restricting planet Saturn during the following periods:

1930—From March through June, also December
1931—January, February and from August through November
1938—From May through December
1939—From January through March
1944—October and November
1945—From June through August
1946—From March through May
1951—December
1952—From January through April and from August through October
1960—From February through December
1961—January
1967—From June through September
1968—March, April, May and December
1969—January
1974—From August through December
1975—From January through June
1981—September, October, November and December
1982—From April through August
1989—From March through July, also November and December
1990—January and February
1997—From April through July, also from September through December
1998—From January through March

Those born from April 11th to the 21st will be afflicted by the depressing, restricting planet Saturn during the following periods:

1931—From March through July, also December
1932—January, February, September, October and November
1939—April, May, June, October, November and December
1940—January, February and March
1945—September, October, November and December
1946—January, February, June and July
1952—November and December

1953—From January through October
1961—February, March and April and from June through December
1968—From June through November
1969—February, March and April
1975—July, August and September
1976—From February through June
1982—From January through March also September through November
1983—June, July and August
1990—From March through December
1991—January
1997—August
1998—April, May, June, November and December
1999—January, February and March

When the Sun is in Taurus and temporarily afflicted by Saturn, the results are likely to be more lasting and more depressing physically, mentally and mundanely, than when in Aries. As Taurus rules the neck and throat, and sympathetically the heart, bladder and organs of generation, diseases affecting these parts may develop when under the affliction of Saturn, particularly tonsilitis, glandular swellings upon the neck, and diphtheria. It is necessary that during an affliction of Saturn to the Sun one should not give way to temper or be too stubborn; too much self-indulgence in eating or drinking should be avoided. The greatest discretion should be exercised in selecting associates and pleasures, as venereal diseases can be more easily contracted when under an affliction of Saturn to the Sun when it is in Taurus.

Those born from April 21st to May 1st will be afflicted by the depressing, restricting planet Saturn during the following periods:

1932—From March through August, also December
1933—January and February
1939—July, August and September
1940—April, May, June and December
1941—January and February
1946—From August through December

1947—From January through July
1953—November and December
1954—From January through October
1961—May
1962—From January through April and from August through December
1969—From May through December
1970—From January through April
1975—October, November and December
1976—January, July and August
1977—April
1982—December
1983—From January through May, also September, October and November
1991—From February through December
1992—January
1998—From July through October
1999—April and May
2000—January

Those born from May 1st to the 11th will be afflicted by the depressing, restricting planet Saturn during the following periods:

1933—From March through December
1934—January and February
1940—From July through November
1941—March, April and May
1947—August, September and October
1948—From February through June
1954—November and December
1955—January and from May through October
1962—May, June and July
1963—From January through March and from September through December
1970—From May through July, also November and December
1971—January, February and March
1976—From September through December

1977—From January through March and from May through August
1983—December
1984—From January through November
1992—From February through December
1993—January
1999—From June through December
2000—From February through May

Those born from May 11th to the 22nd will be afflicted by the depressing, restricting planet Saturn during the following periods:

1934—From March through December
1935—January and February
1941—From June through December
1942—From January through May
1947—November and December
1948—January, July, August and September
1949—May
1955—From February through April, also November and December
1956—January and from June through October
1963—From April through August
1964—From January through March, also October through December
1970—From August through October
1971—April, May and June
1972—January, February and March
1977—From September through November
1978—From January through July
1984—December
1985—From January through November
1993—From February through May and from August through December
1994—January
2000—From June through August, also November and December
2001—From January through April

When the Sun is in Gemini and temporarily afflicted by Saturn, every effort should be made to guard against indulging in vain fears, giving way to restlessness or indecision, for in this mental sign Saturn is apt to depress mentally and to distort the imagination, as well as to render one prone to fixed ideas. Anything which would bring about tenseness is detrimental to the health. Sleep and fresh air are very essential. As Gemini rules the arms, hands, shoulders, lungs, including tracheæ and bronchial tubes, thymus gland, upper ribs, capillaries, and sympathetically the feet, thighs, intestines and nervous system, diseases affecting these parts will be easily aggravated under an affliction of Saturn. It will be necessary not to neglect any symptoms which might lead to bronchitis, pulmonary consumption, nervous afflictions, pneumonia, pleurisy, impure blood or anæmia. Those born under Gemini should always try to avoid mental depression when under Saturn, as the state of the health is largely dependent upon the mental attitude. Associate as little as possible with people who bring to the surface this worrying, over-serious side of the nature.

Those born from May 21st to June 1st will be afflicted by the depressing, restricting planet Saturn during the following periods:

1935—March, April and May and from August through December
1936—January and February
1942—June, July and December
1943—From January through April
1948—October, November and December
1949—From January through April and from June through September
1956—From February through May, also November and December
1957—January and from July through September
1964—From April through September
1965—From January through March
1971—From July through December
1972—April and May
1977—December
1978—August, September and October

1979—From March through June
1985—December
1986—From January through November
1993—June and July
1994—From February through April and from September through December
1995—January
2000—September and October
2001—From May through July

Those born from June 1st to the 11th will be afflicted by the depressing, restricting planet Saturn during the following periods:

1935—June and July
1936—March, April and May and from September through December
1937—January
1942—From August through November
1943—May, June and July
1949—October, November and December
1950—From January through August
1957—From February through June, also October, November and December
1958—August and September
1965—From April through December
1966—January, February and March
1972—June, July, August, November and December
1973—From January through May
1978—November and December
1979—January, February, July, August and September
1986—December
1987—January, February and from June through November
1994—From May through August
1995—From February through April, also November and December
1996—January
2001—From August through December

Those born from June 11th to the 22nd will be afflicted by the depressing, restricting planet Saturn during the following periods:

1929—From January through March and from June through November
1936—June, July and August
1937—From February through April, also November and December
1938—January
1943—From August through December
1944—From January through June
1950—From September through November
1951—From April through August
1958—From January through July, also October, November and December
1959—January
1966—From April through December
1967—January, February and March
1972—September and October
1973—June and July
1974—From January through April
1979—October, November and December
1980—From January through September
1987—March, April, May and December
1988—January and February and from July through October
1995—From May through October
1996—February, March and April

When the Sun is in Cancer and temporarily afflicted by Saturn, everything should be done to overcome sensitiveness as well as a tendency to be distrustful of the motives of others. As Cancer rules the stomach, breast, lacteals, chest cavities, solar plexus, pancreas, epigastric region, diaphragm, and upper lobes of liver, and sympathetically the head, kidneys and knees, diseases affecting these parts will be easily aggravated under an affliction of Saturn. It will be necessary not to neglect any symptoms which might lead to digestive ailments, dropsy, loose coughs, cancer, dipsomania, tumors, ovarian trouble, asthma, kidney trouble, flatulency and nervous exhaustion.

Those born from June 22nd to July 1st will be afflicted by the depressing, restricting planet Saturn during the following periods:

1929—April, May and December
1930—January, February and from July through November
1937—From May through October
1938—From February through April
1944—July, August, September and December
1945—From January through May
1950—December
1951—January, February and March, also from September through November
1952—From May through July
1959—From February through December
1960—January
1967—April, May and from October through December
1968—January and February
1973—From August through December
1974—May, June and July
1980—October, November and December
1981—From January through August
1988—From March through June, also November and December
1989—January and February and from August through October
1996—From May through December
1997—From January through March

Those born from July 1st to the 11th will be afflicted by the depressing, restricting planet Saturn during the following periods:

1930—From March through June, also December
1931—January, February and from August through November
1938—From May through December
1939—From January through March
1944—October and November
1945—From June through August
1946—From March through May
1951—December
1952—From January through April and from August through October
1960—From February through December

1961—January
1967—From June through September
1968—March, April, May, and December
1969—January
1974—From August through December
1975—From January through June
1981—September, October, November and December
1982—From April through August
1989—From March through July, also November and December
1990—January and February
1997—From April through July and from September through December
1998—From January through March

Those born from July 11th to the 22nd will be afflicted by the depressing, restricting planet Saturn during the following periods:

1931—From March through July, also December
1932—January, February, September, October and November
1939—April, May, June, October, November and December
1940—January, February and March
1945—September, October, November and December
1946—January, February, June and July
1952—November and December
1953—From January through October
1961—February, March and April and from June through December
1968—From June through November
1969—February, March and April
1975—July, August and September
1976—From February through June
1982—From January through March, also September through November
1983—June, July and August
1990—From March through December
1991—January
1997—August
1998—April, May, June, November and December
1999—January, February and March

When the Sun is in Leo and temporarily afflicted by Saturn, every effort should be made to maintain an optimistic outlook on life and to avoid grieving over disappointments and losses. As Leo rules the heart and back, and sympathetically the throat and organs of generation, diseases affecting these parts will be easily aggravated during an affliction of Saturn to the Sun. It will be necessary not to neglect any symptoms which might lead to affections of the heart, particularly angina pectoris, palpitation, poor circulation, fevers, spinal meningitis, locomotor ataxia, or fainting spells. Worry should be avoided, as it has a very depressing effect on the action of the heart. Coal-tar preparations should not be taken, as drugs that depress the heart are much more injurious than those which have an exhilarating effect. Extreme exposure to the Sun should be avoided during an affliction of Saturn, as it might cause sunstroke.

Those born from July 22nd to August 1st will be afflicted by the depressing, restricting planet Saturn during the following periods:

1932—From March through August, also December
1933—January and February
1939—July, August and September
1940—April, May, June and December
1941—January and February
1946—From August through December
1947—From January through July
1953—November and December
1954—From January through October
1961—May
1962—From January through April and from August through December
1969—From May through December
1970—From January through April
1975—October, November and December
1976—January, July and August
1977—April
1982—December
1983—From January through May, also September, October and November

1991—From February through December
1992—January
1998—From July through October
1999—April and May
2000—January

Those born from August 1st to 12th will be afflicted by the depressing, restricting planet Saturn during the following periods:

1933—From March through December
1934—January and February
1940—From July through November
1941—March, April and May
1947—August, September and October
1948—From February through June
1954—November and December
1955—January and from May through October
1962—May, June and July
1963—January, February and March and from September through December
1970—From May through July, also November and December
1971—January, February and March
1976—From September through December
1977—From January through March and from May through August
1983—December
1984—From January through November
1992—From February through December
1993—January
1999—From June through December
2000—From February through May

Those born from August 12th to the 23rd will be afflicted by the depressing, restricting planet Saturn during the following periods:

1934—From March through December
1935—January and February
1941—From June through December

1942—From January through May
1947—November and December
1948—January, July, August and September
1949—May
1955—From February through April, also November and December
1956—January and from June through October
1963—From April through August
1964—From January through March, also October through December
1970—August, September and October
1971—From April through June
1972—From January through March
1977—From September through November
1978—From January through July
1984—December
1985—From January through November
1993—From February through May and from August through December
1994—January
2000—June, July, August, November and December
2001—From January through April

When the Sun is in Virgo and temporarily afflicted by Saturn, everything should be done to avoid being too critical; generosity and optimism should be encouraged. As Virgo rules the liver, the intestines, alimentary canal, abdominal cavity and its membranes, and duodenum, and sympathetically the hands and feet, the lungs and nervous system, diseases affecting these parts will be easily aggravated during an affliction of Saturn to the Sun. It will be necessary not to neglect any symptoms which might lead to afflictions of the intestines and digestive tract, cholera, peritonitis, malnutrition, typhoid fever, appendicitis, intestinal paralysis and maladies obscure in origin. The germs which have an affinity for and thrive in the intestines cause mental depression, and this may account for the fact that all dyspeptics are pessimists. Mental depression, especially when there is no definite cause, usually indicates a sluggish liver or constipation. While under Saturn one should get as much sleep and exercise in the fresh air as possible.

Those born from August 23rd to September 3rd will be afflicted by the depressing, restricting planet Saturn during the following periods:

1935—March, April and May and from August through December
1936—January and February
1942—June, July and December
1943—From January through April
1948—October, November and December
1949—From January through April, also from June through September
1956—From February through May, also November and December
1957—January, July, August and September
1964—From April through September
1965—January, February and March
1971—From July through December
1972—April and May
1977—December
1978—August, September and October
1979—From March through June
1985—December
1986—From January through November
1993—June and July
1994—From February through April and from September through December
1995—January
2000—September and October
2001—May, June and July

Those born from September 3rd to the 12th will be afflicted by the depressing, restricting planet Saturn during the following periods:

1935—June and July
1936—From March through May and from September through December

1937—January
1942—From August through November
1943—May, June and July
1949—October, November and December
1950—From January through August
1957—From February through June, also October, November and December
1958—August and September
1965—From April through December
1966—January, February and March
1972—June, July, August, November and December
1973—From January through May
1978—November and December
1979—January, February, July, August and September
1986—December
1987—January, February, and from June through November
1994—From May through August
1995—From February through April, also November and December
1996—January
2001—From August through December

Those born from September 12th to the 23rd will be afflicted by the depressing, restricting planet Saturn during the following periods:

1929—From January through March and from June through November
1936—From June through August
1937—From February through April, also November and December
1938—January
1943—From August through December
1944—From January through June
1950—From September through November
1951—From April through August
1958—From January through July, also October, November and December

1959—January
1966—From April through December
1967—January, February and March
1972—September and October
1973—June and July
1974—From January through April
1979—October, November and December
1980—From January through September
1987—March, April, May and December
1988—January and February and from July through October
1995—From May through October
1996—February, March and April

When the Sun is in Libra and temporarily afflicted by Saturn, it is very necessary that elimination should be stimulated through the skin and intestines in order that the kidneys, which serve as a filter and refiner for the purification of the blood, are not overtaxed. As Libra rules the kidneys, ovaries in a woman, adrenals, loins, lumbar vertebræ, and the skin in general, and sympathetically the head, stomach and knees, diseases affecting these parts will be easily aggravated during an affliction of Saturn to the Sun. It will be necessary not to neglect any symptoms which might lead to Bright's disease, all forms of kidney trouble, spinal trouble, lumbago, and diabetes. People born strongly under the influence of Libra are easily thrown out of balance physically as well as emotionally, but yield very readily to treatment and easily regain their equilibrium.

Those born from September 23rd to October 3rd will be afflicted by the depressing, restricting planet Saturn during the following periods:

1929—April, May and December
1930—January and February and from July through November
1937—From May through October
1938—From February through April
1944—From July through September and December
1945—From January through May
1950—December

1951—From January through March and from September through November
1952—From May through July
1959—From February through December
1960—January
1967—April, May and from October through December
1968—January and February
1973—From August through December
1974—May, June and July
1980—October, November and December
1981—From January through August
1988—From March through June, also November and December
1989—January and February and from August through October
1996—From May through December
1997—From January through March

Those born from October 3rd to the 13th will be afflicted by the depressing, restricting planet Saturn during the following periods:

1930—From March through June, also December
1931—January and February and August through November
1938—From May through December
1939—From January through March
1944—October and November
1945—From June through August
1946—From March through May
1951—December
1952—From January through April and from August through October
1960—From February through December
1961—January
1967—From June through September
1968—March through May, and December
1969—January
1974—From August through December
1975—From January through June

1981—September, October, November and December
1982—From April through August
1989—From March through July, also November and December
1990—January and February
1997—From April through July and from September through December
1998—From January through March

Those born from October 13th to the 23rd will be afflicted by the depressing, restricting planet Saturn during the following periods:

1931—From March through July, also December
1932—January, February, September, October and November
1939—April, May, June, October, November and December
1940—January, February and March
1945—September, October, November and December
1946—January, February, June and July
1952—November and December
1953—From January through October
1961—From February through April and from June through December
1968—From June through November
1969—February, March and April
1975—July, August and September
1976—From February through June
1982—January through March and September through November
1983—June, July and August
1990—From March through December
1991—January
1997—August
1998—April, May, June, November and December
1999—January, February and March

When the Sun is in Scorpio and temporarily afflicted by Saturn, every effort should be made to avoid being too tense and too fault finding. As Scorpio rules the generative organs, the bladder and rectum, and sympathetically the throat, heart, back, blood and circulation, diseases affecting these parts will be easily aggravated during an affliction of Saturn to the Sun. It will be necessary not to neglect any symptoms which might lead to ruptures, hemorrhoids, fistulas, scurvy, diseases of the generative system in general, venereal diseases, ulcers, toxic complaints, nasal catarrh and strictures. With older men trouble with the prostate gland must be guarded against. Pregnant women with the Sun in Scorpio may find childbirth more difficult than usual during an affliction of Saturn to the Sun, and may even find it advisable to resort to a Cæsarian operation.

Those born from October 23rd to November 2nd will be afflicted by the depressing, restricting planet Saturn during the following periods:

1932—From March through August, also December
1933—January and February
1939—July, August and September
1940—April, May, June and December
1941—January and February
1946—From August through December
1947—From January through July
1953—November and December
1954—From January through October
1961—May
1962—From January through April and from August through December
1969—From May through December
1970—From January through April
1975—October, November and December
1976—January, July and August
1977—April
1982—December
1983—From January through May and from September through November
1991—From February through December
1992—January
1998—From July through October
1999—April and May

2000—January

Those born from November 2nd to the 12th will be afflicted by the depressing, restricting planet Saturn during the following periods:

1933—From March through December
1934—January and February
1940—From July through November
1941—March, April and May
1947—August, September and October
1948—From February through June
1954—November and December
1955—January and from May through October
1962—May, June and July
1963—From January through March and from September through December
1970—From May through July, also November and December
1971—January, February and March
1976—From September through December
1977—From January through March and from May through August
1983—December
1984—From January through November
1992—From February through December
1993—January
1999—From June through December
2000—From February through May

Those born from November 12th to the 22nd will be afflicted by the depressing, restricting planet Saturn during the following periods:

1934—From March through December
1935—January and February
1941—From June through December
1942—From January through May
1947—November and December
1948—January, July, August and September

1949—May
1955—From February through April, also November and December
1956—January and from June through October
1963—From April through August
1964—From January through March, also October through December
1970—August, September and October
1971—From April through June
1972—From January through March
1977—From September through November
1978—From January through July
1984—December
1985—From January through November
1993—From February through May and from August through December
1994—January
2000—From June through August, also November and December
2001—From January through April

When the Sun is in Sagittarius and temporarily afflicted by Saturn, there will be less danger of depressing effects from the affliction than is the case when the Sun is in any of the other signs. As Sagittarius rules the hips and thighs, and sympathetically the nervous system, intestines, hands, and feet, diseases affecting these parts will be easily aggravated during an affliction of Saturn to the Sun. It will be necessary not to neglect any symptoms which might lead to rheumatism, gout, sciatica, locomotor ataxia, some forms of paralysis, and dislocation of hip joints. If exposed to cold weather, the small of the back and hips should be well protected, as these are susceptible parts and are easily chilled when Saturn is unfriendly to the Sun in Sagittarius.

Those born from November 22nd to December 2nd will be afflicted by the depressing, restricting planet Saturn during the following periods:

1935—From March through May and from August through December

1936—January and February
1942—June, July and December
1943—From January through April
1948—October, November and December
1949—From January through April and from June through September
1956—From February through May, also November and December
1957—January and from July through September
1964—From April through September
1965—January, February and March
1971—From July through December
1972—April and May
1977—December
1978—From August through October
1979—From March through June
1985—December
1986—From January through November
1993—June and July
1994—From February through April and from September through December
1995—January
2000—September and October
2001—From May through July

Those born from December 2nd to the 12th will be afflicted by the depressing, restricting planet Saturn during the following periods:

1935—June and July
1936—From March through May and from September through December
1937—January
1942—From August through November
1943—May, June and July
1949—October, November and December
1950—From January through August
1957—From February through June and from October through December

1958—August and September
1965—From April through December
1966—From January through March
1972—From June through August, also November and December
1973—From January through May
1978—November and December
1979—January and February and from July through September
1986—December
1987—January, February and from June through November
1994—From May through August
1995—From February through April, also November and December
1996—January
2001—From August through December

Those born from December 12th to the 22nd will be afflicted by the depressing, restricting planet Saturn during the following periods:

1929—From January through March and June through November
1936—From June through August
1937—From February through April, also November and December
1938—January
1943—From August through December
1944—From January through June
1950—From September through November
1951—From April through August
1958—From January through July and from October through December
1959—January
1966—From April through December
1967—From January through March
1972—September and October
1973—June and July
1974—From January through April

1979—October, November and December
1980—From January through September
1987—March, April, May and December
1988—January and February and from July through October
1995—From May through October
1996—From February through April

When the Sun is in Capricorn and temporarily afflicted by Saturn, every effort should be made to overcome a tendency to melancholia and dread of the future. As Capricorn rules the skeleton, particularly the knees, outer epidermis, and sympathetically the head, kidneys, and stomach, diseases affecting these parts will be easily aggravated during an affliction of Saturn to the Sun. It will be necessary not to neglect any symptoms which might lead to skin diseases, articular rheumatism, hysteria, cramps, erysipelas, ankylosis and synovitis. Dwelling upon troubles, real or imaginary, is likely to bring on nervous dyspepsia. Very few sweets or too concentrated foods should be eaten, and plenty of water should be taken between meals.

Those born from December 22nd to January 1st will be afflicted by the depressing, restricting planet Saturn during the following periods:

1929—April, May and December
1930—January and February and from July through November
1937—From May through October
1938—From February through April
1944—From July through September and December
1945—From January through May
1950—December
1951—From January through March and from September through November
1952—From May through July
1959—From February through December
1960—January
1967—April, May and from October through December
1968—January and February
1973—From August through December

1974—May, June and July
1980—October, November and December
1981—From January through August
1988—From March through June, also November and December
1989—January and February and from August through October
1996—From May through December
1997—From January through March

Those born from January 1st to the 10th will be afflicted by the depressing, restricting planet Saturn during the following periods:

1930—From March through June, also December
1931—January and February and from August through November
1938—From May through December
1939—From January through March
1944—October and November
1945—From June through August
1946—From March through May
1951—December
1952—From January through April and from August through October
1960—From February through December
1961—January
1967—From June through September
1968—March through May, and December
1969—January
1974—From August through December
1975—From January through June
1981—September, October, November and December
1982—From April through August
1989—From March through July, also November and December
1990—January and February
1997—From April through July and from September through December
1998—From January through March

Those born from January 10th to the 20th will be afflicted by the depressing, restricting planet Saturn during the following periods:

1931—From March through July, also December
1932—January, February, September, October and November
1939—April, May, June, October, November and December
1940—January, February and March
1945—September, October, November and December
1946—January, February, June and July
1952—November and December
1953—From January through October
1961—From February through April and from June through December
1968—From June through November
1969—February, March and April
1975—July, August and September
1976—From February through June
1982—January through March and September through November
1983—June, July and August
1990—From March through December
1991—January
1997—August
1998—April, May, June, November and December
1999—January, February and March

When the Sun is in Aquarius and temporarily afflicted by Saturn, strict attention should be given to elimination, and any signs of blood poisoning not be neglected. As Aquarius rules the calves, ankles, teeth, blood, and circulation, and sympathetically the throat, heart, back, and organs of generation, diseases affecting these parts will be easily aggravated during an affliction of Saturn to the Sun. It will be necessary not to neglect any symptoms which might lead to anæmia, cramps, heart weaknesses, spasmodic and nervous diseases, varicose veins and infected teeth. The ankles may become swollen and easily turned.

Those born from January 20th to the 30th will be afflicted by the depressing, restricting planet Saturn during the following periods:

1932—From March through August, also December
1933—January and February
1939—July, August and September
1940—April, May, June and December
1941—January and February
1946—From August through December
1947—From January through July
1953—November and December
1954—From January through October
1961—May
1962—From January through April and from August through December
1969—From May through December
1970—From January through April
1975—From October through December
1976—January, July and August
1977—April
1982—December
1983—From January through May and from September through November
1991—From February through December
1992—January
1998—From July through October
1999—April and May
2000—January

Those born from January 30th to February 9th will be afflicted by the depressing, restricting planet Saturn during the following periods:

1933—From March through December
1934—January and February
1940—From July through November
1941—March, April and May
1947—August, September and October
1948—From February through June
1954—November and December
1955—January, and from May through October

1962—May, June and July
1963—From January through March and from September through December
1970—From May through July, also November and December
1971—From January through March
1976—From September through December
1977—From January through March and from May through August
1983—December
1984—From January through November
1992—From February through December
1993—January
1999—From June through December
2000—From February through May

Those born from February 9th to the 19th will be afflicted by the depressing, restricting planet Saturn during the following periods:

1934—From March through December
1935—January and February
1941—From June through December
1942—From January through May
1947—November and December
1948—January and from July through September
1949—May
1955—From February through April, also November and December
1956—January and from June through October
1963—From April through August
1964—From January through March and from October through December
1970—From August through October
1971—From April through June
1972—January, February and March
1977—From September through November
1978—From January through July
1984—December

1985—From January through November
1993—From February through May and from August through December
1994—January
2000—From June through August, also November and December
2001—From January through April

When the Sun is in Pisces and temporarily afflicted by Saturn, every precaution should be taken to avoid going to excesses of any kind, as abuse of Nature could very easily result in a nervous breakdown. As Pisces rules the feet, especially the bones and muscles of the toes, the lungs, and sympathetically the intestines, thighs and nervous system, diseases affecting these parts will be easily aggravated during an affliction of Saturn to the Sun. It will be necessary not to neglect any symptoms which might lead to colds, tumors, tuberculosis, liver troubles and anæmia. Serious colds or bowel trouble may follow carelessness in getting the feet wet or in the care of these members, since so much elimination of the body passes through the pores of the feet in perspiration.

Those born from February 19th to March 1st will be afflicted by the depressing, restricting planet Saturn during the following periods:

1935—From March through May and from August through December
1936—January and February
1942—June, July and December
1943—From January through April
1948—October, November and December
1949—From January through April and from June through September
1956—From February through May, also November and December
1957—January and from July through September
1964—From April through September
1965—From January through March
1971—From July through December

1972—April and May
1977—December
1978—August, September and October
1979—From March through June
1985—December
1986—From January through November
1993—June and July
1994—February, March and April and from September through December
1995—January
2000—September and October
2001—May, June and July

Those born from March 1st to the 10th will be afflicted by the depressing, restricting planet Saturn during the following periods:

1935—June and July
1936—From March through May and from September through December
1937—January
1942—From August through November
1943—May, June and July
1949—From October through December
1950—From January through August
1957—From February through June and from October through December
1958—August and September
1965—From April through December
1966—From January through March
1972—From June through August, also November and December
1973—From January through May
1978—November and December
1979—January and February and from July through September
1986—December
1987—January, February, and from June through November
1994—From May through August

1995—From February through April, also November and December
1996—January
2001—From August through December

Those born from March 10th to the 21st will be afflicted by the depressing, restricting planet Saturn during the following periods:

1929—From January through March and June through November
1936—From June through August
1937—From February through April, also November and December
1938—January
1943—From August through December
1944—From January through June
1950—From September through November
1951—From April through August
1958—From January through July and from October through December
1959—January
1966—From April through December
1967—January, February and March
1972—September and October
1973—June and July
1974—From January through April
1979—October, November and December
1980—From January through September
1987—March, April, May and December
1988—January and February and from July through October
1995—From May through October
1996—February, March and April

PERIODS WHEN THE SUN WILL BE BENEFICENTLY ASPECTED BY JUPITER

THE Sun is the one heavenly body whose position is practically the same at the same time in the year of any year. Consequently, in this volume it is the only sphere that we have considered in making predictions regarding the future.

In order that the effects of Jupiter on the Sun may be fairly closely computed, the Sun has been divided into three sections of ten degrees each. This makes the calculations as given within what is known as "orbs" and therefore sufficiently close to an aspect to make its effects distinctly felt. The periods when Jupiter will form an aspect to the Sun are tabulated and will be found at the end of each sign. Jupiter forms a friendly aspect to the Sun every four years. This is treated of below.

Whenever the beneficent planet Jupiter, known as the "Greater Fortune," is in friendly aspect to the Sun, it causes one's "personal stock" to rise, and gives greater personal confidence in one's ability; a desire for self-improvement is stirred and one may safely take advantage of business opportunities which may come about naturally. It causes one to be more optimistic and more nearly universal in one's attitude toward life; this will add to one's efficiency and those who are temporarily under its influence will be more alert to recognize opportunities. Because of their keener discernment and better judgment, long-cherished hopes are more likely to be fulfilled. Unless an advance in position or salary comes about of itself, it would be well to do everything within reason to seek promotion at these periods.

New friends and new interests will be attracted and even routine work will go more smoothly. If opposition is met with at every turn, then it may be taken for granted that lack of wisdom has been exercised in the choice of activity, and instead of doggedly persisting, one should make the most of what happens naturally. It is most essential to realize that anything which may happen without any effort on one's part may prove a connecting link to greater things in the future, even though what happens may seem unimportant at the time.

In the case of single women, they should do everything within their power to place themselves under the most favorable conditions for having more influence over old friends in whom they may already be interested, or from whom they may have temporarily been estranged, as well as for meeting new men who are in a position to benefit them. It would be well also for them to remember what Shakespeare says:

> "Costly thy habit as thy purse can buy,
> But not express'd in fancy; rich, not gaudy;
> For the apparel oft proclaims the man."

For instance, a woman spending the summer at Bretton Woods, recognized as being the resort for the most exclusive and wealthy set, or spending the winter at The Breakers at Palm Beach, would certainly stand a better chance of meeting men who would benefit her than she would by spending these seasons in a small Main Street town.

Married women can anticipate better health and business conditions for the husband, or for the men who intimately touch their lives, either in a social or business way. These periods would be favorable for wives to encourage their husbands, and to inspire them to do greater things than hitherto.

Both men and women will be in more harmony with themselves and the Universe, and their relations with people and their influence over them should be most pleasant and fortunate. The beneficent influence of Jupiter causes people to attract the best, not only from the Universe and those with whom they are associated, but also causes them to get more nutriment out of their food and, in consequence, it is very necessary that they watch their diet, unless they desire to put on flesh.

The influence of Jupiter will also assist them in gaining recognition in their work, or, if they are connected with politics, these periods would be favorable for allowing their constituents to name them as candidates for office, as they stand an excellent chance of winning the election. Just as one should never allow himself to be a candidate for any important office when Uranus is unfriendly to his Sun (for defeat inevitably follows), just the opposite is likely to happen when Jupiter is friendly to the Sun. As examples, our late President Roosevelt had Uranus unfriendly to his Sun when he was defeated by Woodrow Wilson; his son, Theodore Roosevelt had this aspect when he ran for Governor of New York and was defeated, and Al Smith, too, was under the influence of

Uranus when he was defeated in the Presidential campaign of 1928.

Even though there may be adverse aspects operating in one's chart during a friendly aspect of Jupiter to the Sun, (but this, of course, can only be ascertained by having a complete reading of the horoscope by an efficient astrologer) this will have a very modifying influence and bring directly or indirectly good conditions out of what may appear to be adversity. For instance, Saturn afflicting the Sun might indicate a death and the fact that Jupiter was friendly at the same time might indicate that there would either be an inheritance, or that death might bring release from responsibility.

When Jupiter is beneficently aspecting the Sun in the horoscopes of children, this will have a beneficial effect on their health; it sometimes indicates the arrival of a new baby brother, and further indicates that the family, particularly the father, may enjoy improved conditions, both as regards health and general prosperity.

This friendly aspect of Jupiter to the Sun occurs once in every four years, and the way it operates depends very largely upon one's age, sphere in life, and one's ability for grasping opportunities, and conditions surrounding one at the time. With the boy or girl, it frequently brings honors when they are students and, in any event, they stand remarkably well with their instructors and classmates.

When the Sun is in Aries and temporarily beneficently aspected by Jupiter, the best qualities which the sign Aries implies will be stimulated to greater activity. Those who are feeling its effects may enjoy more than ever making plans and doing pioneer work. If they are holding managerial positions or are at the head of any important undertakings, then these would be propitious periods for enlarging their enterprises or for trying to merge them with others of a similar character. There may be a tendency for their added enthusiasm and confidence to cause them to take an attitude which may stir the resentment of those less executive or fortunate than themselves. It is most essential that these people should not allow themselves to put on too much flesh or to become too full-blooded, as the danger of apoplexy is especially to be avoided in the case of people born with the Sun in Aries, when Jupiter is in friendly relation. An excess of anything even though good, can prove a detriment.

Those born from March 21st to April 1st will be strongly under the beneficent influence of the "Greater Fortune" Jupiter during the following periods:

1931—August
1935—December
1939—From June through November
1940—January and February
1943—July and August
1947—November and December
1951—May and June, again from October through December
1952—January
1954—November and December
1955—July
1959—March, April, and November
1963—April and May
1966—From October through December
1967—January, June and July
1971—From February through June, October and November
1975—April
1978—From October through December
1979—January, February, March, and May and June
1983—January, February, again from May through October
1987—March and April
1990—September and October
1991—From February through June
1995—January, July, August and September
1999—March

Those born from April 1st to 11th will be under the beneficent influence of the "Greater Fortune" Jupiter during the following periods:

1931—September and October
1932—From February through June
1936—January and February, again from July through October

1940—March
1943—September
1944—April and May
1948—January and August
1951—From July through September
1952—February and March
1955—August and September
1959—December
1960—January
1963—From June through December
1964—January and February
1967—August
1971—December
1975—May, June, November and December
1976—January
1979—July and August
1983—March, April, November and December
1987—May
1990—November and December
1991—January and again July
1995—From February through June, again October and November
1999—April and May

Those born from April 11th to 21st will be under the beneficent influence of the "Greater Fortune" Jupiter during the following periods:

1931—November and December
1932—January, July and August
1936—From March through June, and again November
1940—April and May
1943—From October through December
1944—From January through March, and June and July
1948—From February through July, and from September through November
1952—April
1955—October and November
1956—From February through July

1960—February, and from July through October
1964—March and April
1967—September and October
1968—From April through June
1972—January, February, August and September
1975—From July through October
1976—February and March
1979—September
1984—January
1987—June, July, and from October through December
1988—January, February and March
1991—August and September
1995—December
1999—June, November and December
2000—January and February

When the Sun is in Taurus and temporarily beneficently aspected by Jupiter, the best qualities which the sign Taurus implies will be stimulated to greater activity. Because of the added success and power which Jupiter may temporarily bring, those born with the Sun in Taurus may find it necessary to exercise greater self-control than usual in order to avoid going to excesses in the gratification of their generosity and in their inordinate love for eating and drinking.

People born from April 21st to May 1st will be strongly under the beneficent influence of the "Greater Fortune" Jupiter during the following periods:

1932—September
1936—December
1937—January
1940—June and December
1941—January and February
1944—August and September
1948—December
1952—May and June
1955—December
1956—January and August

1960—From March through June, again November and December
1964—May
1967—November and December
1968—From January through March, again July and August
1972—From March through July, again October and November
1976—April and May
1979—From October through December
1980—From January through July
1984—February and March, again from July through November
1987—August and September
1988—April
1991—October and November
1992—From March through June
1996—January, February, September and October
1999—From July through October
2000—March

Those born from May 1st to 11th will be under the beneficent influence of the "Greater Fortune" Jupiter during the following periods:

1932—October and November
1933—From March through July
1937—From February, September and October
1940—From July through November
1941—March and April
1944—October
1945—May and June
1949—January and February
1952—July, August, November and December
1953—January, February and March
1956—September and October
1961—January
1964—June, July and December
1965—January and February
1968—September
1972—December

1973—January
1976—June
1980—August and September
1984—April, May, June and December
1988—May
1991—December
1992—January, February, July and August
1996—From March through August, again November and December
2000—April and May

Those born from May 11th to 22nd will be under the beneficent influence of the "Greater Fortune" Jupiter during the following periods:

1932—December
1933—January, February, August and September
1937—From March through August, and November and December
1941—May
1944—November and December
1945—From January through April, again July and August
1949—March and April, and from August through November
1952—September and October
1953—April and May
1956—November and December
1957—From March through August
1961—February, March, September and October
1964—From August through November
1965—March and April
1968—October and November
1969—May, June and July
1973—February
1976—July, August, November and December
1977—From January through March
1980—October
1985—January and February
1988—June and July

1989—January, February and March
1992—September and October
1997—January
2000—June

When the Sun is in Gemini and temporarily beneficently aspected by Jupiter, the best qualities which the sign Gemini implies will be stimulated to great activity. New schemes of diversified characters may just naturally present themselves, but it should be borne in mind that the one danger to those with the Gemini temperament is to have too many interests; consequently, they may not make the most of the periods when Jupiter is friendly to their Sun, because of scattering their forces.

Those born from May 21st to June 1st will be under the beneficent influence of the "Greater Fortune" Jupiter during the following periods:

1929—July
1930—January, February and March
1933—October
1938—January
1941—June and July
1945—September and October
1949—From May through July, again in December
1950—January
1953—June
1957—January, February and September
1961—From April through August, again November and December
1965—May and June
1968—December
1969—From January through April, again August and September
1973—March, April, and from August through December
1976—September and October
1977—April and May
1980—November and December
1981—January, and from March through August

1985—March, and from September through November
1988—From August through December
1989—April
1992—November and December
1993—From April through August
1997—February and March
2000—July, August, again in December
2001—From January through April

Those born from June 1st to 11th will be under the beneficent influence of the "Greater Fortune" Jupiter during the following periods:

1929—From August through December
1930—April and May
1933—November and December
1934—From April through August
1938—February and March
1941—August, September and December
1942—From January through April
1945—November
1946—June and July
1950—February
1953—July and August
1954—January, February and March
1957—October and November
1962—January and February
1965—July
1969—October
1973—May, June and July
1974—January
1977—June
1981—February, September and October
1985—From April through August, again in December
1986—January
1989—May and June
1993—January, February, March and September
1997—April, and from August through December

2000—From September through November
2001—May

Those born from June 11th to 22nd will be under the beneficent influence of the "Greater Fortune" Jupiter during the following periods:

1930—June
1934—January, February, March, September and October
1938—April, May, and from September through December
1941—October and November
1942—May and June
1945—December
1946—From January through May, August and September
1950—March, April, October and November
1953—From September through December
1954—April and May
1957—December
1958—January, and from April through September
1962—March
1965—August, September and December
1966—From January through May
1969—November and December
1970—June, July and August
1974—February and March
1977—July and August
1978—February, March and April
1981—November
1986—February
1989—July
1993—October and November
1997—May, June and July
1998—January and February
2001—June and July

When the Sun is in Cancer and temporarily beneficently aspected by Jupiter, the best qualities which the sign Cancer implies will be stimulated to greater activity. Those who are feeling its effects may enjoy even more than usual entertaining their friends, making constructive plans for the future welfare of their family, engaging in communal interests for the benefit of the masses, and in salvaging an enterprise which is on the rocks or in organizing new enterprises. The expansive influence of Jupiter on the Cancer temperament will give them a broader outlook on life, and consequently they will be less sensitive, more impersonal, and more liberal in their attitude toward the conventions.

Those born from June 22nd to July 1st will be under the beneficent influence of the "Greater Fortune" Jupiter during the following periods:

1930—July and August
1934—November
1938—From June through August
1939—January and February
1942—July
1946—October and November
1950—From May through September, again in December
1951—January
1954—June and July
1958—February, March and October
1962—April, May, and from September through December
1963—January
1965—October and November
1966—June
1970—From January through May, again September and October
1974—April, November and December
1977—From September through December
1978—January, May and June
1981—December
1982—January, February, and from April through September
1986—March and April
1989—August, September, again in December
1990—From January through May
1993—December
1994—January, and from May through August

1998—March
2001—August

Those born from July 1st to the 11th will be under the beneficent influence of the "Greater Fortune" Jupiter during the following periods:

1930—September and October
1931—From January through May
1934—December
1935—January, again from May through September
1939—March
1942—August and September
1943—From February through May
1946—December
1947—July and August
1951—February and March
1954—August
1958—November and December
1962—From June through August
1963—February
1966—July and August
1970—November
1974—From May through October
1975—January
1978—July
1982—March, October and November
1986—May, again from October through December
1987—January
1989—October and November
1990—June
1994—February, March, April, September and October
1998—April, November and December
2001—From September through December

Those born from July 11th to the 22nd will be under the beneficent influence of the "Greater Fortune" Jupiter during the following periods:

1930—November and December
1931—June and July
1935—February, March, April, October and November
1939—April, May and December
1942—October, November and December
1943—January and June
1947—From January through June, again September and October
1951—April
1954—September and October
1955—From January through June
1959—January, February, again from May through October
1963—March
1966—September
1967—From February through May
1970—December
1971—January, July, August and September
1975—February and March
1978—August and September
1979—April
1982—December
1986—From June through September
1987—February
1990—July and August
1994—November and December
1998—From May through October
1999—January and February

When the Sun is in Leo and temporarily beneficently aspected by Jupiter, the constructive qualities which the sign Leo implies will be stimulated to greater activity. Those who are feeling its effects may enjoy more than ever exercising their executive ability and directing the work of large bodies of people. As Jupiter always tends to stimulate self-expression, there may be a tendency for those born under the sign Leo to become too self-expressive, and they may be looked upon as being too dictatorial. Putting on flesh or allowing the blood to become too rich are the dangers of a friendly aspect of Jupiter with the Sun in Leo, and this may cause the heart to be overworked and sometimes causes sudden heart seizures.

Those born from July 22nd to August 1st will be strongly under the beneficent influence of the "Greater Fortune," Jupiter during the following periods:

1931—August
1935—December
1939—From June through November
1940—January and February
1943—July and August
1947—November and December
1951—May and June, again from October through December
1952—January
1954—November and December
1955—July
1959—March, April, and November
1963—April and May
1966—From October through December
1967—January, June and July
1971—From February through June, October and November
1975—April
1978—From October through December
1979—From January through March, and May and June
1983—January and February, again from May through October
1987—March and April
1990—September and October
1991—From February through June
1995—January, July, August and September
1999—March

Those born from August 1st to 12th will be strongly under the beneficent influence of the "Greater Fortune" Jupiter, during the following periods:

1931—September and October
1932—From February through June
1936—January and February, again from July through October
1940—March

1943—September
1944—April and May
1948—January and August
1951—From July through Setember
1952—February and March
1955—August and September
1959—December
1960—January
1963—From June through December
1964—January and February
1967—August
1971—December
1975—May, June, November and December
1976—January
1979—July and August
1983—March, April, November and December
1987—May
1990—November and December
1991—January and July
1995—From February through June, again October and November
1999—April and May

Those born from August 12th to 23rd will be strongly under the beneficent influence of the "Greater Fortune" Jupiter during the following periods:

1931—November and December
1932—January, July and August
1936—From March through June, and again in November
1940—April and May
1943—From October through December
1944—From January through March, again June and July
1948—From February through July, and September and November
1952—April
1955—October and November

1956—From February through July
1960—February, again from July through October
1964—March and April
1967—September and October
1968—From April through June
1972—January, February, August and September
1975—From July through October
1976—February and March
1979—September
1984—January
1987—June, July, and from October through December
1988—January, February and March
1991—August and September
1995—December
1999—June, and November and December
2000—January and February

When the Sun is in Virgo and temporarily beneficently aspected by Jupiter, the constructive qualities which the sign Virgo implies will be stimulated to greater activity. Jupiter's influence, even though only temporary, stimulates sympathy and benevolence, so those born under the Sun in Virgo will be less critical and less analytical. If they are of a literary turn of mind, then their work will be broader in sympathy and less purely intellectual. They will get more joy in the expenditure of money both for themselves and others.

Those born from August 23rd to September 3rd will be strongly under the beneficent influence of the "Greater Fortune" Jupiter during the following periods:

1932—September
1936—December
1937—January
1940—June and December
1941—January and February
1944—August and September
1948—December

1952—May and June
1955—December
1956—January and August
1960—From March through June, again November and December
1964—May
1967—November and December
1968—From January through March, again July and August
1972—From March through July, again October and November
1976—April and May
1979—From October through December
1980—From January through July
1984—February and March, again from July through November
1987—August and September
1988—April
1991—October and November
1992—From March through June
1996—January, February, September and October
1999—From July through October
2000—March

Those born from September 3rd to 12th will be under the beneficent influence of the "Greater Fortune" Jupiter, during the following periods:

1932—October and November
1933—From March through July
1937—February, September and October
1940—From July through November
1941—March and April
1944—October
1945—May and June
1949—January and February
1952—July, August, November and December
1953—January, February and March
1956—September and October

1961—January
1964—June, July and December
1965—January and February
1968—September
1972—December
1973—January
1976—June
1980—August and September
1984—April, May, June and December
1988—May
1991—December
1992—January, February, July and August
1996—From March through August, November and December
2000—April and May

Those born from September 12th to 23rd will be under the beneficent influence of the "Greater Fortune" Jupiter, during the following periods:

1932—December
1933—January, February, August and September
1937—From March through August, November and December
1941—May
1944—November and December
1945—From January through April, July and August
1949—March, April, and from August through November
1952—September and October
1953—April and May
1956—November and December
1957—From March through August
1961—February, March, September and October
1964—From August through November
1965—March and April
1968—October and November
1969—May, June and July
1973—February
1976—July, August, November and December

1977—From January through March
1980—October
1985—January and February
1988—June and July
1989—January, February and March
1992—September and October
1997—January
2000—June

When the Sun is in Libra and temporarily beneficently aspected by Jupiter, the constructive qualities which the sign Libra implies will be stimulated to greater activity. While the sign Libra tends to make those born under its influence fair and just under all circumstances, when Jupiter throws its beneficent ray on it, they are inclined to be even more desirous of doing the right thing in all their dealings with those about them. If those born under Libra have been forced into the commercial world or into doing some type of work which is not entirely congenial, then, during a friendly aspect of Jupiter to their Sun will be a propitious time for trying to make a change of work, or if this is not practical, for taking up a congenial hobby or avocation.

Those born from September 23rd to October 3rd will be under the beneficent influence of the "Greater Fortune" Jupiter during the following periods:

1929—July
1930—January, February and March
1933—October
1938—January
1941—June and July
1945—September and October
1949—From May through July, again in December
1950—January
1953—June
1957—January, February and September
1961—From April through August, again November and December
1965—May and June

1968—December
1969—From January through April, again August and September
1973—March, April, again from August through December
1976—September and October
1977—April and May
1980—November and December
1981—January, and from March through August
1985—March, and from September through November
1988—From August through December
1989—April
1992—November and December
1993—From April through August
1997—February and March
2000—July, August and December
2001—From January through April

Those born from October 3rd to 13th will be under the beneficent influence of the "Greater Fortune" Jupiter during the following periods:

1929—From August through December
1930—April and May
1933—November and December
1934—From April through August
1938—February and March
1941—August, September and December
1942—From January through April
1945—November
1946—June and July
1950—February
1953—July and August
1954—January, February and March
1957—October and November
1962—January and February
1965—July
1969—October
1973—May, June and July

1974—January
1977—June
1981—February, September and October
1985—From April through August, again in December
1986—January
1989—May and June
1993—January, February, March and September
1997—April, and from August through December
2000—From September through November
2001—May

Those born from October 13th to 23rd will be under the beneficent influence of the "Greater Fortune" Jupiter during the following periods:

1930—June
1934—From January through March, again September and October
1938—April, May, and from September through December
1941—October and November
1942—May and June
1945—December
1946—From January through May, August and September
1950—March, April, October and November
1953—From September through December
1954—April and May
1957—December
1958—January, and from April through September
1962—March
1965—August, September and December
1966—From January through May
1969—November and December
1970—From June through August
1974—February and March
1977—July and August
1978—From February through April
1981—November
1986—February

1989—July
1993—October and November
1997—From May through July
1998—January and February
2001—June and July

When the Sun is in Scorpio and temporarily beneficently aspected by Jupiter, the best qualities which the sign Scorpio implies will be stimulated to greater activity. Those who are responding to this influence may be less selfish, less personal, and more tolerant in their attitude toward those with whom they are thrown in a domestic, social, or business way. During the operation of this aspect, the ambition, whether it be for power in the financial, artistic, or social world, is enhanced and the chances are greater for meeting with success with greater ease.

Those born from October 23rd to November 2nd will be under the beneficent influence of the "Greater Fortune" Jupiter during the following periods:

1930—July and August
1934—November
1938—From June through August
1939—January and February
1942—July
1946—October and November
1950—From May through September, again in December
1951—January
1954—June and July
1958—February, March, and October
1962—April, May, and from September through December
1963—January
1965—October and November
1966—June
1970—From January through May, again September and October
1974—April, November and December
1977—From September through December
1978—January, May and June

1981—December
1982—January, February, and from April through September
1986—March and April
1989—August, September and December
1990—From January through May
1993—December
1994—January, and from May through August
1998—March
2001—August

Those born from November 2nd to 12th will be under the beneficent influence of the "Greater Fortune" Jupiter during the following periods:

1930—September and October
1931—From January through May
1934—December
1935—January, again from May through September
1939—March
1942—August and September
1943—From February through May
1946—December
1947—July and August
1951—February and March
1954—August
1958—November and December
1962—From June through August
1963—February
1966—July and August
1970—November
1974—From May through October
1975—January
1978—July
1982—March, October and November
1986—May, again from October through December
1987—January
1989—October and November
1990—June

1994—From February through April, again September and October
1998—April, November and December
2001—From September through December

Those born from November 12th to 22nd will be under the beneficent influence of the "Greater Fortune" Jupiter during the following periods:

1930—November and December
1931—June and July
1935—From Feburary through April, again October and November
1939—April, May and December
1942—From October through December
1943—January and June
1947—From January through June, again September and October
1951—April
1954—September and October
1955—From January through June
1959—January, February, and from May through October
1963—March
1966—September
1967—From February through May
1970—December
1971—January, and from July through September
1975—February and March
1978—August and September
1979—April
1982—December
1986—From June through September
1987—February
1990—July and August
1994—November and December
1998—From May through October
1999—January and February

When the Sun is in Sagittarius and temporarily beneficently aspected by Jupiter, the best qualities which the sign Sagittarius implies will be stimulated to greater activity. While Jupiter's influence is always important, its aspect to the Sun in Sagittarius is even more pronounced, for the reason that both the sign Sagittarius and the planet Jupiter tend to give qualities savoring of the "good Samaritan." To those in projects of a philanthropic and religious character, these periods will be favorable for making plans, for trying to get the coöperation of others, and for enlarging their activities generally. Under this aspect, one frequently benefits through an inheritance or because people of influence, wealth, and power extend their friendship and assistance.

Those born from November 22nd to December 2nd will be strongly under the beneficent influence of the "Greater Fortune" Jupiter, during the following periods:

1931—August
1935—December
1939—From June through November
1940—January and February
1943—July and August
1947—November and December
1951—May and June, again from October through December
1952—January
1954—November and December
1955—July
1959—March, April, and November
1963—April and May
1966—From October through December
1967—January, June and July
1971—From February through June, October and November
1975—April
1978—From October through December
1979—From January through March, May and June
1983—January, February, and from May through October
1987—March and April
1990—September and October
1991—From February through June

1995—January, July, August and September
1999—March

Those born from December 2nd to 12th will be strongly under the beneficent influence of the "Greater Fortune" Jupiter during the following periods:

1931—September and October
1932—From February through June
1936—January and February, again from July through October
1940—March
1943—September
1944—April and May
1948—January and August
1951—From July through September
1952—February and March
1955—August and September
1959—December
1960—January
1963—From June through December
1964—January and February
1967—August
1971—December
1975—May, June, November and December
1976—January
1979—July and August
1983—March, April, November and December
1987—May
1990—November and December
1991—January and July
1995—From February through June, again October and November
1999—April and May

Those born from December 12th to the 21st will be strongly under the beneficent influence of the "Greater Fortune" Jupiter during the following periods:

1931—November and December
1932—January, July and August
1936—From March through June, and again November
1940—April and May
1943—From October through December
1944—From January through March, again June and July
1948—From February through July, and September through November
1952—April
1955—October and November
1956—From February through July
1960—February, and from July through October
1964—March and April
1967—September and October
1968—From April through June
1972—January, February, August, and September
1975—From July through October
1976—February and March
1979—September
1984—January
1987—June, July, and from October through December
1988—January, February and March
1991—August and September
1995—December
1999—June, and November and December
2000—January and February

When the Sun is in Capricorn and temporarily beneficently aspected by Jupiter, the good qualities which the sign Capricorn implies will be stimulated to greater activity. The expansiveness of Jupiter is particularly beneficial to the restricted and overcautious tendencies of this sign. It, therefore, behooves those born under Capricorn who come under this aspect to make the most of these periods. They will be more optimistic and hopeful and they will have greater vision; in fact, because of their broader outlook on life and confidence in themselves and the Universe, they will be more magnetic and their efforts will be attended by greater success.

Those born from December 21st to January 1st will be strongly under the beneficent influence of the "Greater Fortune" Jupiter during the following periods:

1932—September
1936—December
1937—January
1940—June and December
1941—January and February
1944—August and September
1948—December
1952—May and June
1955—December
1956—January and August
1960—From March through June, again November and December
1964—May
1967—November and December
1968—From January through March, again July and August
1972—From March through July, again October and November
1976—April and May
1979—From October through December
1980—From January through July
1984—February and March, again from July through November
1987—August and September
1988—April
1991—October and November
1992—From March through June
1996—January, February, September and October
1999—From July through October
2000—March

Those born from January 1st to 10th will be under the beneficent influence of the "Greater Fortune" Jupiter, during the following periods:

1932—October and November
1933—From March through July
1937—February, September and October
1940—From July through November

1941—March and April
1944—October
1945—May and June
1949—January and February
1952—July, August, November and December
1953—January, February and March
1956—September and October
1961—January
1964—June, July, and December
1965—January and February
1968—September
1972—December
1973—January
1976—June
1980—August and September
1984—April, May, June and December
1988—May
1991—December
1992—January, February, July and August
1996—From March through August, again November and December
2000—April and May

Those born from January 10th to 20th will be under the beneficent influence of the "Greater Fortune" Jupiter, during the following periods:

1932—December
1933—January, February, August and September
1937—From March through August, November and December
1941—May
1944—November and December
1945—From January through April, and July and August
1949—March, April, and from August through November
1952—September and October
1953—April and May
1956—November and December
1957—From March through August
1961—February, March, September and October

1964—From August through November
1965—March and April
1968—October and November
1969—May, June and July
1973—February
1976—July, August, November and December
1977—From January through March
1980—October
1985—January and February
1988—June and July
1989—January, February and March
1992—September and October
1997—January
2000—June

When the Sun is in Aquarius and temporarily beneficently aspected by Jupiter, the best qualities which the sign Aquarius implies will be stimulated to greater activity. Aquarius being the most humanitarian and impersonal sign in the Zodiac, and Jupiter being the "Preserver" and the so-called connecting link between the Infinite and the Finite, those born under this sign, and who have Jupiter temporarily aspecting it, are likely to be inspired to work toward the betterment of their fellow men. At these times the plans they have visualized stand a better chance of being carried through to completion with less effort; consequently, they should take advantage of these periods. This applies not only to their projects intended to benefit others, but also to their personal affairs as well. The Aquarian, perhaps more than the average human being, realizes the truth of the following words: "Help thy brother's boat across, and lo! thine own shall reach the shore."

Those born from January 20th to 30th will be under the beneficent influence of the "Greater Fortune" Jupiter, during the following periods:

1929—July
1930—January, February and March
1933—October
1938—January
1941—June and July

1945—September and October
1949—From May through July, again in December
1950—January
1953—June
1957—January, February and September
1961—From April through August, again November and December
1965—May and June
1968—December
1969—From January through April, again August and September
1973—March, April, again from August through December
1976—September and October
1977—April and May
1980—November and December
1981—January, and from March through August
1985—March, and from September through November
1988—From August through December
1989—April
1992—November and December
1993—From April through August
1997—February and March
2000—July, August and December
2001—From January through April

Those born from January 30th to February 9th will be under the beneficent influence of the "Greater Fortune" Jupiter during the following periods:

1929—From August through December
1930—April and May
1933—November and December
1934—From April through August
1938—February and March
1941—August, September and December
1942—From January through April
1945—November
1946—June and July

1950—February
1953—July and August
1954—January, February and March
1957—October and November
1962—January and February
1965—July
1969—October
1973—May, June and July
1974—January
1977—June
1981—February, September and October
1985—From April through August, again in December
1986—January
1989—May and June
1993—January, February, March and September
1997—April, and from August through December
2000—From September through November
2001—May

Those born from February 9th to 19th will be under the beneficent influence of the "Greater Fortune" Jupiter during the following periods:

1930—June
1934—From January through March, again September and October
1938—April, May, and from September through December
1941—October and November
1942—May and June
1945—December
1946—From January through May, August and September
1950—March, April, October and November
1953—From September through December
1954—April and May
1957—December
1958—January, and from April through September
1962—March
1965—August, September and December

1966—From January through May
1969—November and December
1970—From June through August
1974—February and March
1977—July and August
1978—From February through April
1981—November
1986—February
1989—July
1993—October and November
1997—From May through July
1998—January and February
2001—June and July

When the Sun is in Pisces and temporarily beneficently aspected by Jupiter, the best qualities which the sign Pisces implies will be stimulated to greater activity. Pisces causes one to be so adaptable, so unselfish and generous, that Jupiter temporarily aspecting it will augment these qualities to a dangerous degree. Too much even of good is no longer constructive, so it would be well for those born under this sign at these times to remember that "self-preservation is the first law of nature" and to use these advantageous periods to help themselves as well as others. The new people who happen to cross the path or the opportunities which come about naturally should be looked upon more earnestly, realizing that they may have more significance than appears on the surface.

Those born from February 19th to March 1st will be under the beneficent influence of the "Greater Fortune" Jupiter during the following periods:

1930—July and August
1934—November
1938—From June through August
1939—January and February
1942—July
1946—October and November
1950—From May through September, again in December
1951—January

1954—June and July
1958—February, March and October
1962—April, May, and from September through December
1963—January
1965—October and November
1966—June
1970—From January through May, again September and October
1974—April, November and December
1977—From September through December
1978—January, May and June
1981—December
1982—January, February, and from April through September
1986—March and April
1989—August, September and December
1990—From January through May
1993—December
1994—January, and from May through August
1998—March
2001—August

Those born from March 1st to 10th will be under the beneficent influence of the "Greater Fortune" Jupiter during the following periods:

1930—September and October
1931—From January through May
1934—December
1935—January, and from May through September
1939—March
1942—August and September
1943—From February through May
1946—December
1947—July and August
1951—February and March
1954—August
1958—November and December
1962—From June through August

1963—February
1966—July and August
1970—November
1974—From May through October
1975—January
1978—July
1982—March, October and November
1986—May, again from October through December
1987—January
1989—October and November
1990—June
1994—From February through April, again September and October
1998—April, November and December
2001—From September through December

Those born from March 10th to 21st will be under the beneficent influence of the "Greater Fortune" Jupiter during the following periods:

1930—November and December
1931—June and July
1935—From February through April, again October and November
1939—April, May and December
1942—From October through December
1943—January and June
1947—From January through June, again September and October
1951—April
1954—September and October
1955—From January through June
1959—January, February, and from May through October
1963—March
1966—September
1967—From February through May
1970—December
1971—January, and from July through September

1975—February and March
1978—August and September
1979—April
1982—December
1986—From June through September
1987—February
1990—July and August
1994—November and December
1998—From May through October
1999—January and February

THE MOON SYMBOLICALLY CONSIDERED

SELENE, or Diana, or Luna, is the twin sister of the Sun. She is complete woman, in all phases, untouched by male caresses.

The Moon in her increase is the child, innocent and receptive, smiling above the sunset; nightly we see her grow, nearer and nearer to her triumph over darkness, queen of heaven! It is this Moon that gleams so phantastically yet so candescent, a motive repeated again and again in the hymns of every poet. Keats was a mere nympholept to the Moon, like his own Endymion. In the pages of Swinburne, her lustre lamps fitfully his verse. Baudelaire, one of the greatest of all poets, seems rather of the moon than of the earth. The Indian lyrists chant her beauty in unnumbered songs, and the priests of all nations have done worship to her on hidden altars. She has been incorporated in all religions as the symbol of woman at her highest.

Yet she is also huntress like her brother Apollo; she is to be seen in dim woods with her maidens and her hounds. Woe to him who, not being utterly chaste, surprises her! Her arrows are barbed with silver as his with gold; and if his are dipped in death, so are hers poisoned with madness. Restlessness, hunger for the unattainable, seeking after strange pleasures, such are some of the lesser signs of moon-infatuation.

It is noticeable how small a section of poetic attention is given to the gracious childhood of the Moon. For at first she is asleep in the arms of the Sun, and almost before we are aware she springs to fullness.

But glorious is that fullness. She is now Sophia, the Virgin Wisdom of the Father. It is she that appears in the gloom of the threshold, and leads us into the Temple. She is our pure aspiration to things high and holy, the triple cord that binds us to the stainless unity beyond all. She is the veil upon the sanctuary, the mist of tears before the eyes of the penitent. She is sorrow, and pure love that burns up sorrow! She is the lustral water, and the mystic bearer of the Holy Grail. It is she who will clothe us about with all purity and all perfection; it is she who will give us to drink in the House of the Father.

Gaze upon her splendour, gaze not only with your eyes but with your heart; follow her in dreams with such strength that dream becomes reality. For the Moon is in heaven what the sea is upon earth; and what that is, only they know who truly love the sea.

For so do we gain life most, when most absolutely we surrender it; the goal of our existence is not on earth. Life is but an ordeal; let us manfully pass through it; but whatever its rewards may be, it is not on earth but in heaven that we come to the understanding of ourselves. That is the End of the Quest.

THE MOON

It is by no accident that the Moon is the only one of the heavenly bodies which revolves around the earth. In the nativity, the Moon is not really part of the character in the same way that the planets are; she is however, of extreme importance, because she represents the sensorium.

The Moon has, by far, the most powerful influence on destiny, although its influence is not so direct; it never produces clear, traceable events in life, as do the major planets. Its effect, however, is steady, permanent and active at all times, because the Moon is the ruler of environment.

Our destiny comes first of all out of our environment, and viewed from this standpoint, the Moon is most important. As an illustration, suppose we find the Moon greatly afflicted in the nativity of a male, and so placed as to affect the first four years of his life in his mother relations, and later to affect his marriage relations.

He will be in danger the first four years of receiving from his mother what might be called the "Œdipus complex"; in other words, he may get such a violent modification of his character because of an abnormal attachment to his mother that he becomes a timid, repressed character, lacking initiative and personal force. As the result of this repression of the self, a whole line of unfortunate, malefic events will inevitably follow in his life. A man having received such a restricting complex is seldom happily married, is rarely, if ever, happy in social relations; the results upon his destiny are here clearly marked.

It is from this point of view that we have traced the various spheres of human interest and activity which follow the force of the Moon's position as it may affect personal initiative, money matters, business, success, marriage, friends, and so on. This is because of its modifying force upon the most intimate and personal qualities of the life, and its effect upon the instinctive plane or subconscious mind of the human being.

One has only to look at an ephermeris to see that the Moon is afflicted by one planet or another almost every day of the week. Some afflictions will naturally be more serious than others, but the way to consider the problem is to recognize that, in the majority of horoscopes, there is affliction at one time or another, and that it is a rare and happy circumstance when none of them are serious enough to prevent the full maturing of the good aspects.

We may now proceed to consider in more detail the action of the Moon. Her aspects will naturally show the particular development of sense instruction which will occur in the native. Thus, for example, the opposition of the Sun usually means romance, but frustrated by circumstances over which the native has little or no control; the rays of the Sun falling full upon the disc of the Moon thrill her with all the glow and warmth of creative life. A trine of Jupiter, on the other hand, will cause the senses of the native to be impressed strongly by the qualities of Jupiter. As an illustration, imagine a man born with a very strong combination of Saturn and Mars, giving him great selfishness and great executive power. Let him have also a trine of Jupiter and the Moon, and we have at first sight, a rather contradictory situation. But the harmony is easy to find. Such a person will be impressed by altruistic subjects like religion, and, therefore, religious channels will be those through which his selfishness and power can best operate. We may, therefore, find him develop into an ambitious and intriguing ecclesiastic. It is by the consideration of the many different aspects that the astrologer is able to determine the facts of any given case with such wonderful accuracy. It is probably fair to say that any serious affliction of the Moon dulls the acuteness of at least one of the senses. Philip Bourke-Marston's blindness was evidently caused by the approaching opposition of Saturn and exact opposition of Uranus. Byron's clubfoot may have been due to the conjunction of the Moon, rising below Mars, square to Neptune and probably assisted by a conjunction of Saturn and Venus close to the cusp of Pisces. Probably the conjunction of the Moon and Mars, and squared by Uranus, had something to do with Edison's deafness, though the affliction of Jupiter by Saturn, which planets are square, is a contributory cause. Perhaps, however, it will be more exact to say that the affliction of the Moon enabled the affliction of Jupiter to manifest itself in this form. As a general rule, a single minor affliction produces only minor consequences. There is analogy for this theory in other branches of science. In chemistry, for example, even such highly exothermic reactions as the combination of hydrogen and chlorine, or ammonia and carbonic acid gas cannot take place without the presence of some third body. If these gases are prepared in a state of absolute chemical dryness and purity, you can pass the electric spark through them indefinitely without causing their combustion.

It seems possible, therefore, that in many nativities where we see a threat which does not materialize or a promise which is not fulfilled, the cause is due to the absence of a starting impulse. The rifle may be loaded, but unless the trigger be pulled, there will be no explosion. In determining, therefore, whether any given configuration of the heavens will or will not produce its result, we must look to some other point apparently unconnected with it. Imagine, for example, a case of a man from whose horoscope we should expect death by drowning. The position which shows us this does not show us whether he will be forgotten in his tub by his nurse or be shipwrecked at eighty. It is possible that the fatal direction or transits may not occur for a very long time, while in another case, it may be in operation within a few hours of birth.

Many of these remarks have been in the nature of a digression, yet, if properly considered, they would be seen to have a bearing upon the limitations and aptitudes imposed by the position and aspects of the Moon.

THE MOON IN THE SIGNS

THE Moon has to do largely with personality, just as the Sun has to do with individuality. The signs in which the Moon is placed describe the type of the personality. It shows the variety and quality just as the Sun shows the type and quality of the individuality. As the personality is the intimate and more immediate expression of the temperament and measures the quality and power of sense impression, and therefore the scope and precision of the mental forces, it indirectly determines what we might call the fluid of being. Moreover, as both mental and emotional forces depend first upon sense impression, and since personality is that singular union of the mental and the emotional, it follows that the Moon's position is the focal point wherein sense, mind, and emotion meet in the formation of character.

The Moon largely determines the kind of life and activity with which the average human being meets life day by day. Excellent illustrations of this are found throughout history; in fact, there is really no exception or contradiction to this rule. Robespierre, for instance, with his Moon in Aries, gave his life to political revolution and to civil war. Shakespeare, on the other hand, with his Moon in Taurus, although gifted with a marvellously brilliant mind, never felt willing to write purely original plays, but conservatively preferred to develop already established dramas, and to instil into them his practical though dramatic vision of the everyday. Kipling, with his Moon in Gemini turned early to letters and has had a distinctly journalistic quality throughout his poetry and prose. A man like Theodore Roosevelt, though he became President, is known best of all for his influence toward national conservatism and a development of home life, which mental tendencies are perfectly illustrated by his Moon in Cancer. Asquith, on the other hand, with his Moon in Leo, was the typical fixed politician, the natural ruler, while Cleo de Merode, with her Moon in Virgo made, so far as herself was concerned, a commercial success of the loose moral tendencies shown in the rest of her nature. Maeterlinck, with his Moon in Libra, has given his whole life to the furtherance of beauty, poetry, and the drama, while Ex-Kaiser Wilhelm, with his Moon in Scorpio was possessed of that type of personal egotism and martial love of war (the mailed fist) which the Moon in Scorpio so loves. Huxley, with the Moon in Sagittarius, is a perfect picture of the clear, scientific mentality and the like interest of this position, while Bismarck, the subtle, reserved, covetous politician, exactly expresses the Moon in Capricorn. Henry Ford with his Moon in Aquarius, where it is so wonderfully placed, shows all the humanitarian instincts of this splendid position, while Lily Langtry, with her Moon in Pisces, expressed all the idealistic, dramatic and somewhat weakly emotional tendency of the position.

Indeed, we may say that the average person is largely judged in life by the sign position of his Moon, and that this position may even act as a completely qualifying influence, if evil aspects interfere, and thus bring out some of the lower phases of the sign influence. We have thousands of instances, in astrological record, of such complete modification of the personality through the Moon position that the whole life was totally wrecked; and it is not difficult to see why this should be so, for, if the Moon primarily governs the Sensorium, that is, the sight, hearing, smell, taste, and touch, it necessarily is sufficiently strong absolutely to dominate the man. If we remember that all knowledge, all information, all preference, all judgment, come into the man first of all through the use of his senses, that the sight, hearing, smell, taste and touch are the mental mouth, without which the rational stomach can receive no food, we can understand why the Moon can completely block a life development.

Among famous figures showing such a complete modification of the life, we have that of Savonarola, whose Moon in Capricorn, evilly aspected in the tenth, was certainly his ultimate undoing. It gave him that tense, religious egotism and moral repressiveness which ended his life at the stake. George the III, on the other hand, with his Moon in Capricorn, in the sixth house, evilly aspected by planets in the ninth house, dealing with the mind, had senses which became so twisted as to produce absolute madness most of his days.

We might go on indefinitely, bringing similar instances where the mere position of the Moon, reacting in such a way as to congest the Sensorium, either ruined or made the whole figure. Huxley's position of the Moon in Sagittarius, on the other hand, was a tremendous factor in his scientific success. He was really made by this position.

Lastly, we must remember that the Moon, being a luminary, that is, one of the lights, has a tremendous influence over the eyes, particularly the left in man and right in woman, and when placed in signs that react upon vision and evilly aspected, has much to do with blindness. We should always look to see where the Moon is placed in estimating any affliction of this kind.

Finally, it would be well to remember that the Moon, which rules over Cancer, being watery in influence, usually enters into all cases of drowning, either through a discordant position or through evil aspects. Few, if any, cases of drowning are on record where the Moon is exalted and in no way afflicted. The Moon governing the public also has much to do with those types of death that are of a public order, and here again its sign position is important. It will be seen, therefore, that the Moon is more sensitive to its sign than the Sun or any of the planets.

We now turn to a totally different subject. The astrological quality of the Moon determines the character of the women who are thrown into the life of the native. Even in such special cases as the mother and the wife, where they are signified by particular houses, the Moon has still some effect. But more especially, it refers to those women with whom the native becomes acquainted either in a social or business way. It will immediately be objected that everyone who lives to a reasonable age meets hundreds of women, no two of whom are alike; and this is, of course, perfectly true. The objection is, notwithstanding, untenable. In the first place, the Moon can hardly be held to refer to mere casual acquaintances, but only to such women as have some marked effect upon the life of the native, or are naturally attracted to him. Yet it is still frequent for anyone to be intimately associated with a dozen different types; nevertheless there will be disuniformity in that diversity, that, in so far as they touched him, they will resemble one another. For example, in the case of a man who has the Moon in Pisces, practically all the women with whom he is closely associated will be very emotional, romantic, poetical, affectionate, unselfish and solicitous for his welfare. Now, in the case of a man with Aries rising and Mars very strong, this condition might be unfortunate for him; he might be pestered to death by their attentions. It is only where his own nature responds naturally to such people that he will consider himself lucky. As a rule, however, there is this great safeguard against too much trouble arising from such a cause, that those women who have the most influence upon the life of the native have very often their own Moon in his rising sign or on his Sun, or otherwise sympathetic with his nativity; the so-called law of natural affinity has, in nine cases out of ten, an astrological basis of a quite obvious kind. For example, it may occur in the case of a great and beautiful passion that the Sun of one may be in the exact place of the Moon with the other. It is for such reasons that astrological investigation of the horoscopes of both parties become so enormously important where marriage is contemplated. One may have two machines, each of which goes splendidly by itself, but if they are connected and fail to synchronize, the result is the breakdown of both.

The Moon being so easily influenced by every other force, it is of prime importance to investigate everything that may, by any possibility, react upon her. She is more sensitive to the influence of the signs of the Zodiac than the planets. One might imagine two children born exactly twenty-four hours apart whose horoscopes would be, to all intents and purposes identical, except for the Moon, and this one change might produce the most significant differences in the two lives, owing to the Moon having moved, say from Taurus into Gemini.

Not only do the signs themselves affect the Moon tremendously, but also their subdivisions into the decanates. This refinement, however, is too subtle to treat of in this volume.

THE MOON IN ARIES

Aries is not at all sympathetic to the Moon, he being the most active, hot, and fiery of the signs, and she, the most passive, cold, and watery of the planets. It gives great brilliancy, acuteness, and susceptibility to the senses, but they are always on a terribly fine edge, so that extreme nervousness is likely to result. This may show itself in an extraordinarily quick temper, almost amounting to snappiness. Alexander VI, Henry VIII, Robespierre, Swinburne, and Lord Northcliffe are all very good examples of this trait, which arose, not from any fault of temper or bad disposition in the ordinary sense, but from the intense over-strain upon them by the too great activity of the nerves which communicated impressions. In the case of women, where the life also is ruled by the Moon, we get an excellent example in George Sand. The directness and vividness of the sensations usually lead to great mental independence and activity; mental reaction takes place very rapidly. It is very difficult for persons with this position to doubt the evidence of their senses; and, unless some other aspects tend to diminish the executive power or to delay the operation of the judgment, the native will be so convinced as to the accuracy of whatever is presented to him that he will act immediately without consideration. For the same reason, the native is apt to resent authority and to be disinclined to listen to advice. There is a strong tendency to accept all ideas which are presented to one as merely emotional and to leave them thus; as if the mind were naturally attracted to Berkeleyan idealism. In consequence of this, and of the swift, almost automatic operation of action and reaction, the native is sometimes credited with originality, but this gift is often a defect, since it usually implies contradictions in thought, arising from a lack of reflection and correlation of the various trains of thought. Thus, for example, we see Swinburne reading a paragraph in the newspapers about the wrongs of somebody in Russia and flashing into print with a violent sonnet against the Czar or perhaps against kings in general. In the same way, Henry VIII would dismiss a trusted minister, perhaps send him to the block, in what was little better than a fit of temper.

Such people, however, are generally fortunate when they are in the exercise of professions where quick decision is everything to success, and where hesitation, however necessary to calm judgment, means failure. The position obtained by Lord Northcliff in English journalism is evidently due, in great measure, to possession of this quality. His rashness may have led him into follies, but they did not matter, because everything was forgotten in the excitement of the next moment. This quickness to respond to impression is obviously likely to lead to the exhibition of qualities precisely contrary to those which are described as fidelity and domesticity. Every new fancy makes its full impression at once, and then passes, leaving little trace.

When the Moon is in Aries, the women in the life of the native are brilliant, passionate, headstrong, and impractical. They are very often intellectual and capable of immense initiative. As a general rule, in the case of a man, he will find it very difficult to control them, and, for the most part, his association with them will be short-lived, terminating more often than not, in quarrel. Where the Moon is well-aspected, they may be of the greatest use to him in his career. There is, however, no great promise of anything like enduring constancy on the part of the man.

We find Alexander VI, and others whom we have mentioned above, flitting from flower to flower like butterflies; Henry VIII even carried this tendency into matrimony; but in not one of these cases do we find any woman in the life who exercised a permanent influence of a truly domestic character.

Mothers having children with the Moon in Aries must strive to be practical and avoid being too ambitious for them, allowing them to use their own judgment in selecting their playmates and amusements, and later in life, in deciding on their own career.

The following well known persons were also born with the Moon in the sign Aries.

E. H. Sothern
Gifford Pinchot
Victor D. Brenner
Maude Adams
Bishop Greer
Henry George
John Drew

Emile Coué
Booth Tarkington
Oliver Wendell Holmes
Harriet Beecher Stowe

Note 1—The remarks regarding the mother's attitude toward the child will naturally suggest the query: "How about the mother who has a large family of children, as their Moon, in each case, will probably be in a different sign?" Every mother realizes that although she loves each child equally well, she inevitably plays a different role or takes a different attitude toward each individual child; this is largely determined by the position of the Moon in its sign position, and is also further modified by the aspects of the Moon. Then, too, the horoscope of one child may be sympathetic to the horoscope of the mother and little or no friction exists between them; while the horoscope of another child may be entirely antagonistic towards the mother's planets and, in consequence, everything the child does irritates her and she finds it next to impossible to be impartial or tolerant in her attitude. It behooves the mother, therefore, to have the horoscopes of her children and to make a serious study of them, thereby enabling her to understand their natures and how to develop their most constructive qualities.

Note 2—As the Moon takes only twenty-eight days to pass through the twelve signs of the zodiac, it moves so rapidly that to note the sign in which it is placed would fill a volume of itself; consequently, the only way to ascertain the position of the Moon in each reader's individual chart, if he is unfamiliar with Raphael's Ephemerides, is to have a map of his chart drawn which will give him the position not only of the Moon, but also of the Sun and the seven planets.

THE MOON IN TAURUS

The Moon in Taurus is in her exaltation; the sign tends to bring out the quiet and reflective side of the Moon and at the same time to steady her changeful nature. It is one of the best signs in which she can be found.

People with the Moon in this sign hold to their impressions with extreme obstinacy; they react slowly, but with great vigor. They are almost as uncritical as the Moon in Aries type, but for totally different reasons. They remember accurately and tenaciously and they mould their actions for a long period on the original die. If any fact is communicated to them of a startling character, they manifest no excitement or distress. It sinks slowly into the mind, but instead of being held there for a long period without transmutation into motion, as we shall find happens when the Moon is in Cancer, a slow but purposeful decision with regard to that fact is undertaken, and, unless executive power be entirely wanting, owing to some affliction of Mars, action follows, steady, purposeful, and relentless. It is very difficult to make such people change their minds. You cannot make a person with the Moon in Aries change his mind, because, before you speak to him, he has already acted on his impression and forgotten about it; but with Taurus the case is different. His action has been taken and, however foolish and wrong you may prove it to be, it is his action and he goes on with it.

When the Moon is in Aries, the best developed of the senses is usually sight; in Taurus, taste and touch are probably more important to the native. These people strongly resent interference with their ideas. They are so solidly impressed with what comes to them that they welcome only ideas which naturally cohere with the general temperament. This, of course, tends to make the nature rather conservative and conventional.

Shakespeare had this position of the Moon, and, in spite of his astounding genius, he gave little expression to new ideas; he expressed the accepted sentiments of his times with extreme power and beauty, but he seemed incapable of seeing anything wrong with the social system of his period. The same is true of Rossetti and Chatterton, each of whom, in his different way, gave mediævalism a new dress, without changing its features. The same conventional attitude is found in Dumas, in Joseph Chamberlain, in Arthur Balfour, and in President Garfield. Although Joseph Chamberlain was at first a radical, radicalism was conventional in Birmingham, which he represented. In the House of Commons, he drifted to conservatism of a very steady kind. It is not likely that any man with the Moon in this sign will break away from the fundamental principles in which he was brought up. As an apparent exception we have the case of Swedenborg; but here Uranus is within one degree of a conjunction of the Moon, the most upsetting circumstance that could possibly occur, Uranus being preëminently the planet of explosion. Yet even Swedenborg was not much more revolutionary than Virgil or Dante with regard to his ideas of Heaven and Hell; it was merely that he took them rather more seriously, a point of view that would naturally arise from the trine of Jupiter to that conjunction. There is no such breaking away from orthodoxy, if one considers the matter philosophically, as in the case of even such a reformer as John Wesley. Where the native is a woman, so that the Moon refers also to the life itself, her presence in this sign still further increases the obstinacy of the character as is evident in the case of Queen Elizabeth.

The women who influence the native will be domestic, faithful, and of strong, enduring passion. Even an artist like Rossetti had the love of a truly devoted wife. It does not follow, however, that the relations will always be fortunate. Rossetti's wife died early. The curse of Shakespeare's life was Mary Fitton, but here again obstinacy was in itself the cause of the trouble; she treated him badly, but she could not leave him alone. In the case of Queen Elizabeth, we also find this curious clinging tendency; and though Mary, Queen of Scots, had no Taurus in her disposition with regard to her male acquaintances, she had Taurus rising, and acted in an entirely Taurus manner toward her rival.

The dominion exercised upon the native by the women with whom he or she is associated will always be due to this characteristic; they will always apply steady pressure, though it may often be only that their fidelity appeals to the native and makes it impossible for him to get rid of them.

Mothers having children with the Moon in Taurus must not try to dominate their lives to such an extent as to rob them of their individuality, thus forcing them to turn to others for sympathy and understanding. Even though they may be most practical and devoted, they can easily arouse the stubbornness and antagonism of their children having the Moon in this sign.

The following well known persons were also born with the Moon in the sign Taurus.

Harrison Fisher
Norma Talmadge
Julia Marlowe
Clarence Mackey
Henry Ward Beecher

THE MOON IN GEMINI

Gemini tends to accentuate the restlessness of the Moon, but it also develops the mental qualities and, where the native is engaged in an intellectual pursuit, the situation is not unfavorable. We see great mental activity in Dürer, Pasteur, and Bernard Shaw, all of whom had this position. There is certainly a strong tendency to diminish the enjoyment of the senses, which are valued chiefly on account of the information which they give, and are, comparatively speaking, unconnected with the pleasures of the native. It is evident in the above three cases that this is so, but the effect is still more easy to remark in Alfred Tennyson, in whose poetry a certain lack of robustness indicates that the senses communicated rather with the reason or intellect than with the personality. This position is certainly an advantage in that kind of investigation where the presence of passion may act as an interference, but it is far from good where knowledge of and sympathy with humanity are required. Such a type of inhumanity is evident in the case of Ludwig II, of Bavaria.

The native is extraordinarily quick to receive impressions and to judge them with great accuracy, but there is not much depth in such judgment, and we find constantly that people with the Moon in this sign change their minds more readily than when she is in any other. The native is quick and eager to learn, but the part of the brain which attends to these matters seems rather disconnected with the deeper functions of the soul. There is a great readiness to communicate information acquired, and sometimes the native is over-loquacious. The critical faculty is good, though superficial, and there is not sufficient power to bring any given opinion into due relation with general experience. The inability to digest his observations is likely to cause the native to seek variety. If he reads a book, he partially assimilates it and throws it aside. He is likely to be unable to ruminate upon it and develop its ideas within himself, and he is consequently in need immediately of some new mental stimulus. This may find expression in love of travel, or, especially when the Moon is in the fifth house, in love of pleasure. In the absence of constant change, the nervous system may be very distressed. It seems to be rather a disadvantage for the Moon in Gemini to be strengthened by aspects. She is not sufficiently well-placed here to make it desirable for her to be too strong. Pasteur, for example, has no close aspect of any kind to his Moon. The relation of the senses to the soul is thus indicated by the Moon's position in the sign, but the other phases of the character are not absorbed into this in such a way as to hurt them.

This position of the Moon is much better in the case of women, the vitality being indicated by Luna; for the lack of ordinary feminine qualities often makes for success. Queen Victoria, Frances Willard, and Patti were saved by this position of the Moon from having their careers interrupted by too great insistence upon domestic matters or love-affairs. They were able to concentrate upon the mental side of their work. It is, of course, not a desirable position for any woman who looks forward to a normal, domestic life; for the woman with the Moon in Gemini must have strong intellectual interests, else the Gemini qualities appear in mere childishness, frivolity, and inconstancy.

The women with whom the native is intimately associated will either be mainly intellectual companions or they will be rather shallow and unreliable. It is, therefore, very important for the native to choose his or her female friends for brains, rather than for beauty. If he finds his affections seriously engaged, he may look for disappointment. People with this sign as the lodge of the Moon have usually a very delicate and accurate sense of smell and an exceptionally good ear for music; the other senses may not be so strongly developed. Madame Patti, Ludwig II of Bavaria, and Bernard Shaw are singularly good examples of this fact. There is also to be observed in them a very quick and delicate reaction to minute impression, which may sometimes seem to the observer like intuition, but is really operated in quite a different manner and should, by no means, be confounded with it.

Mothers who have children with the Moon in Gemini should strive to be more maternal in their attitude toward them and not allow their versatility and many interests to interfere with the personal attention which such children require. Otherwise, they may become too indifferent to their mother and the home influence.

The following well known persons were also born with the Moon in the sign Gemini.

John Philip Sousa
John D. Rockerfeller, Sr.
William C. de Mille
Henry Carmichael
Bliss Carman
Mussolini
Robert Mantell
George H. Lorimer
James H. Hyslop
Rudyard Kipling

THE MOON IN CANCER

The Moon in Cancer is in her own house and she is stronger in this sign than in any other of the Zodiac. Its receptivity, placidity, and sensuousness are in complete harmony with her nature, and the Moon being dignified in the sign also tends to make her disposition less changeable, while the influence of Jupiter, who is exalted in the sign, takes away something of her coldness.

The senses of the native reflect with extreme accuracy the impressions presented to them. They sink into the mind and dissolve completely in it; the mind takes their mould with exquisite delicacy, but there is one drawback, in that, as a rule, there is little tendency to act upon the information they received. The mind is not idle, but rather meditative. Reaction is slow and uncertain. As a rule, the native lacks the intense energy which we associate with great creative genius, unless there are other indications in the horoscope; and these have to be pretty strong to overcome what may be called the contentment of the mind to remain passive. In the case of Sir Isaac Newton, we have a sextile of Mars to supply energy, and he is decidedly the most creative of the people on our list. But, even in his case, we observe the extreme thoroughness of reflection necessary to him before he began to give out again in a new form his deductions from the facts which he had absorbed. Baudelaire is another great creative genius, but his Moon is trined by Mercury, and yet this reflective quality of the mind is apparent, in the extraordinary repose of such writings as the "Little Poems in Prose."

It follows, more or less, that the native will not go out of his way to obtain mental pabulum. This state of contentment with such impressions as come naturally to it may reveal itself as love of home and parents. There is usually a great deal of natural affection of the placid order; even the passion of love is likely to be gentle, peaceful, and perhaps romantic, when the Moon is in this sign. While the mind is not restless, it is very sensitive to impressions, though not at all in the way which we observed in the case of Gemini. There is no desire to acquire, merely a readiness to do so. One must be careful not to seek to upset the minds of people with this position, even for their own good. They will merely dislike you for doing so. It occasionally happens that the mind is psychic or mediumistic, but in any case the memory may be considered good. Blake is a first-rate example of the Moon in this sign at her best.

The position is not really so good for women as for men. It makes them too passive, too easily influenced by those with whom they come in contact. Nell Gwyn is a notable example of this disposition.

The women with whom the native will come in close contact will be extremely warm-hearted and affectionate, sometimes maternal and sometimes romantic. Their affection will be enduring, and it may even be somewhat cloying. With bad aspects, the native may be seriously injured by the character of the women in his or her life. Byron, for example, with a retrograde Uranus in close conjunction with his Moon, was almost destroyed by women. It is probable, at all events, that they will be somewhat conventional and exacting, demanding more from the native than he will bestow upon them.

Mothers having children with the Moon in Cancer must avoid being so devoted and conventional in their attitude toward them as to make them too selfish or too dependent on the home influences. Many boys with the Moon so placed suffer from the "Œdipus complex" and later remain bachelors, or do not marry until after the mother's death.

The following well known persons were also born with the Moon in the sign Cancer.

Von Hindenburg
Hugo Stinnes

Lee Shubert
Theodore Roosevelt
General Ballington Booth
Ethel Barrymore
Samuel Gompers
"Bud" Fisher
Geraldine Farrar
John O'Hara Cosgrave
Will Levington Comfort
Edith Cavell
President Lowell of Harvard

THE MOON IN LEO

LEO has an admirable effect on the Moon, the sign of the Sun linking her with the source of her life. Its influence tends to diminish both her coldness and her instability, and also redeems her from that darkness which is one of her drawbacks. While stronger in Cancer, where she is almost unmodified, the Moon is really better in Leo because her own nature is so imperfect that modification of some kind is necessary before we can consider her entirely excellent. With regard to the senses of people with the Moon in Leo, generally speaking, the sight is the best developed, but all the other senses should be thoroughly well balanced and healthy. A certain degree, however, of interest and even of affection for any subject must exist before the senses can give true and full communication. Unless the heart is in some way implicated, impressions do not easily reach the mind of the native. As a rule, for example, they have little curiosity, even scientific curiosity, but where the native is anxious to learn, he learns quickly and accurately, though his knowledge is always tinctured, to some extent, by his belief and emotions. It is extremely hard to convince a person with this position of the Moon, against his will; but when ready to receive impressions, no one apprehends them more quickly.

Where the Moon also indicates the personality, as in the case of women, or when Cancer is on the cusp of the Ascendant, the indication is particularly strong. The native is then very solar in character, positive, assertive, self-indulgent, noble, generous, and self-sacrificing, physically vital and robust, and mentally strong and decisive. There will also be great confidence born of the conviction that one is, as it were, a medium of the forces from beyond. This will naturally bring about initiative, capacity for leadership, and a hopeful and determined attitude toward life. The native is independent, and almost fanatically fond of freedom in the best sense of the word. He will refuse to recognize limitation; in some cases this will prove a disadvantage, as he may be inclined to dash his head against a brick wall. A fine example of this temperament is Anna Kingsford. The position does not seem nearly so favorable for a man, in whom it tends to produce a certain amount of conceit. The impressions that come to him will be rather inflated with a sense of his own vitality. They are not properly criticized and they expand, in his mind, unduly, sometimes even to a degree of megalomania. We all recognize a certain floridity with an over-valuing of little things in the characters of Oscar Wilde, James II, Louis XVI, Disraeli, and Abbas Effendi, which may be put down to this position. These remarks apply, to some extent, even to men who have Cancer rising, but they do not at all refer to women, who are usually as modest as they are excellent in all other ways.

The women in the life of the native will probably be the best of all influences to him, as they will be solar, and of the character described in speaking of women who have the Moon in Leo.

Mothers having children with the Moon in this sign will find it very difficult to avoid being too dictatorial in their attitude toward them; as a general rule, however, their influence on them will be excellent in a mental and spiritual way, even though they may not stress their physical and material needs, preferring to have the latter attended to by some one else.

The following well known persons were also born with the Moon in the sign Leo:

Henry Watterson
Luther Burbank
P. T. Barnum
Eleanor Gates
Gandhi

Daniel Chester French
Ralph Waldo Emerson
Gelett Burgess
Jack London
J. J. Hill

THE MOON IN VIRGO

THE general influence of the sign Virgo upon the Moon is to accentuate her coldness and to develop the mental qualities very much as in the case of Gemini, but the restlessness of that sign is replaced by a great steadiness and whole-hearted practicality. There is usually a good deal of materiality akin to pragmatism in the general tendency of the mind. The native does not, as a rule, value knowledge for its own sake, but, immediately on acquiring it, asks how it may be used. This is even the case in so intensely intellectual an individual as Immanuel Kant, who, although employed in the deepest and most abstract problem of metaphysics, never failed to remember that his conclusions were but the necessary basis for an ethical and religious system. We have, on the other hand, in this sign, many examples of the most eminent and practical minds: Alexander the Great, Edward VII, Paul Kruger, Lord Brougham, Cromwell, the late J. Pierpont Morgan, Winston Churchill, and Sainte Beuve being all good examples of the way in which the acquisitions of the mind are immediately put to service. It should be observed that Kant's Moon was very powerfully dignified by the trine of an exact conjunction of the Sun and Mercury, and another trine of Saturn. These aspects obviously tend to increase the abstract power. This point is further exemplified by a consideration of the Moon of Tolstoi, whose mind was decidedly lacking in practicality. Mercury and the Moon are only two degrees from conjunction, Mercury in his own house being evidently stronger than the Moon. Therefore, the influence of Mercury gives an additional touch of his nature to the Moon, thus causing her to act more as if she were in Gemini than in Virgo.

The native is very fastidious with regard to his impressions, analyzing and criticizing them with extreme care. He is genuinely anxious to acquire knowledge, but entertains strong prejudices. He has, however, a keen sense of truth, and is, generally speaking, ready to face facts.

Women born with the Moon in this sign are usually coldblooded and ambitious, as was the case with Cleo de Merode. There is a certain lack of romantic sentiment, a calculating cleverness in their attitude toward men, which is repugnant to the average emotional man. Such women are generally good in the practical affairs of managing the home, but they are not likely to contribute very largely to its happiness. The women who influence them are usually very clever or intellectual and are rarely jealous of them.

The women associated with men who have the Moon in this sign will, as a rule, be rather of this same type. Generally speaking, their influence upon the man will not be very strong in a sentimental way, although they may admire their practicality and common sense.

Mothers having children with the Moon in Virgo should endeavor to be more affectionate or personal in their attitude toward them; they may display efficiency and common sense in their dealings with such children, but are inclined to call attention to faults which may later in life develop into virtues.

The following well known persons were also born with the Moon in the sign Virgo:

Senator Borah
Stanley Baldwin
Ralph Waldo Trine
The late J. P. Morgan
Robert Lorraine
Charles E. Hughes
William Randolph Hearst

THE MOON IN LIBRA

Libra being the house of Venus, her influence upon the Moon is to increase the æsthetic perceptions. The indications of the senses are principally valued on account of their reference to beauty, though, of course, a serious affliction of the Moon can entirely destroy this.

Jay Gould, for example, has Saturn in conjunction retrograde, and Venus square, utterly killing the Venus or beauty sense. The presence of Saturn in the sign of his exaltation, obviously brings out the Saturnian qualities of Libra, while the square of Venus destroys her influence therein; consequently, all that remains to Libra is the faculty of cold judgment, which of course, he possessed in an extremely high degree.

The quality of balanced judgment is quite universally manifest in Libra. With the Moon in this position, the senses report to the mind with unusual accuracy, and facts are criticized with great acumen. The matter is occasionally likely to rest there, for the airiness of the sign inhibits practicality. In many cases, the native remains in the contemplation of knowledge without turning it to immediate account. He builds up great ideas, but finds it difficult to execute them. A fine example of the critical judgment combined with considerable æsthetic perception is shown by Gladstone and Burton. Both acquired most extraordinary stores of knowledge and both put it forth in a most voluminous manner, but the great creative faculty was not equally well-developed. Gladstone's writings were far inferior to his power of moving men as a speaker. Burton's writings are of a high order, but they do not possess that indescribable quality which we find in the greatest of masters. This defect is, of course, not to be wholly ascribed to the position of the Moon. Very characteristic, too, of the position, is its power to give the native a sense of what may be called unearthly beauty, as in the cases of Chopin and Maeterlinck.

Of women with the Moon in Libra, we have three examples, Mme. Blavatsky, Marie Antoinette and Marie Bashkirtseff. In the first case, the Moon is particularly strong, being the lady of the Ascendant, and she is further dignified by a close trine of Uranus. The position in Libra indicates the keenness of her critical perception. The same power of introspection is shown by Marie Bashkirtseff, but here Mars is lord of the Ascendant and trining the Moon, instead of Uranus, as in the case of the Russian adept. The quality of her criticism of life throws an excellent light upon the distinctions between Mars and Uranus. Marie Antoinette has the Moon extremely powerful, Cancer being the rising sign, but afflicted by a close square of Saturn. In this case, one may consider the influence of Libra, which is on the cusp of the fifth house, unusually strong.

The women with whom the native is intimately associated are likely to be distinguished, impersonal, delicate, refined, and subtly passionate. There is usually a danger of their exercising too strong an influence upon the life of the native, whether man or woman. Cardinal signs have an extraordinary power in determining the general horoscope, and unless the man's own important planets are equally strong, it is possible that women may sway his judgment to an undesirable extent. These women are not nearly as "good" in the old-fashioned, motherly sense of the word, as Cancer or Leo women. They are more attractive, more brilliant, but do not have the same solid qualities. Of course, they may be expected to possess talent, frequently artistic, and to live their own individual life even after marriage. This is not altogether a fortunate circumstance for the average man, who may either be henpecked or find his marriage little better than a new leaf of bachelorhood.

Mothers having children who have the Moon in Libra should do everything to inspire in them a feeling of pride and admiration; otherwise, regardless of the mother's devotion, such children can easily become indifferent and be attracted to other women who possess more charm or beauty.

The following well known persons were also born with the Moon in the sign Libra.

Gloria Swanson
William O. Stoddard
Richard Watson Gilder
William Faversham
Otto Kahn

THE MOON IN SCORPIO

The Moon is in her fall in Scorpio, never a good position for her. Scorpio brings out the watery and sensuous side of the Moon, but tends to make her extremely positive and impassioned. People with this position are naturally hedonists, regarding the senses as vehicles of pleasure rather than of knowledge. These qualities, of course, may be overbalanced by aspects, as in the case of Herbert Spencer, whose Moon has the opposition of the Sun and a square of Mars. The interference of these planets eliminates the laxity of the sign, thereby allowing its scientific qualities freer scope. Thomas Moore, and Louis XVI, are, however, good examples of the hedonistic nature of the position. When, however, Scorpio tends to science, its effect is truly admirable, more so, perhaps, than any other sign. The senses are preternaturally acute and the powers of observation almost unlimited. The mind, too, reacts steadily, neither too quickly nor too slowly, to its impressions, and, unless there is some contrary indication in the horoscope, great will-power is indicated; for so strongly do the ideas presented take hold of the mind that it cannot rest in the mere acquisition of knowledge, but must construct, organize, and give out to the world what it has received.

One cannot say, however, that Scorpio is an altogether happy position for the Moon, for the tendency to sensuality is undoubtedly very great. This is especially dangerous in women born with this position. This sign influences the Moon in this respect more powerfully than it does Venus. Not only do we find a danger of sexual irregularity or excess, but a strong predisposition to indulgence in liquor.

The women with whom the native is associated are apt to be very strongly sexed, self-willed, and somewhat unscrupulous in attaining their ends. They may be deceitful and treacherous; this, of course, applies to bad cases only. But where the Moon of the native is well-dignified, he will meet the better type of Scorpio woman, courageous, ambitious, enterprising, and endowed with executive power. In spite of these facts, it does not necessarily follow that women will play a very important part in the life of the native. Scorpio is the weakest sign as well as the strongest. There is an element of corruption in it, unless well-dignified, which makes it sometimes practically void of influence or extremely limited and intermittent in its operation. One may consequently expect rather extreme cases; in the case of a man with this position, one may be utterly ruined by women, another will pass through life almost entirely uninfluenced by them.

Mothers having children who have the Moon in Scorpio should guard against allowing their ambition for them to overshadow their tender emotions. They should avoid influencing such children to such an extent as to interfere with any latent talent or natural inclination in choosing a career.

The following well known persons were also born with the Moon in Scorpio.

Alex. Agassiz
Charles H. Sabin
Charles G. Dawes
Henry Van Dyke
William Gillette

THE MOON IN SAGITTARIUS

Sagittarius, by its keeness, seems to have the tendency to reduce the Moon to the clear, cold sparkle of a star. Almost all the femininity in her is taken away. There is no passive acquiesence in the information conveyed by the senses. The prophetic or inspirational sense is keen, more so than when the Moon is in any other sign. There is hardly any plasticity in the attitude of the native to life. The impressions are admirably focussed—the picture presented to the mind is entirely without blurring, perfectly sharp and well-defined. The mind has consequently to deal with clearer images than when the Moon is in any other sign, and therefore one most important element, in the formation of judgment, is quite perfect, and the judgment is almost preternaturally acute. We find the coldest and clearest intelligences with this position of the Moon. This fact almost leads us to think that the main cause of mental obfuscation may be original defective presentation of the non-ego to the ego through a fault in what one may call the lens. The student will note the extraordinary clearness and concentration of the mental vision of such men of science as Copernicus, Huxley, Alfred Russell Wallace, and Davy, of a philosopher like Sir William Hamilton, and of novelists like Balzac, Victor Hugo, and one may even add, Dickens. If the observation of humanity is, to some extent, in this last case somewhat distorted by his whimsical method of portraiture, so that his creations appear like caricatures, the reason is that Neptune was in direct conjunction with the Moon. In the political world, we have an excellent example of singularly clear and simple vision in the case of John Bright. The minds of people with the Moon in this sign appear to resent any confusion of issues, and are always afraid of being cheated by the introduction of facts which are foreign to the subjects under discussion. The extreme breadth of vision in Balzac may be set down to the close square of Uranus to the Moon, which enlarges the outlook and makes it more vital. In the case of the men of science mentioned above, one must note the limitation of their work. Much of the success which they obtained was due to their faculty of attending to one thing at a time. This made them, in some way, a little narrow and one-sided, as compared with universal geniuses like Newton. To produce a man like Newton, one would have to combine a Huxley and a Hamilton. The reaction of the mind to the senses, when the Moon is in this sign, is extremely quick and keen, but the reflective qualities are usually not great, unless developed by favorable aspects of the major planets.

Women born with this position of the Moon will have very much the same quality as they would have were Sagittarius rising.

The women who come closely into the life of the native will be of a high type, delicate, refined, yet keenly passionate and, at the same time, almost too ethereal to satisfy the tastes of the average man. There will also be difficulty in holding them. Gentle and timid as deer, the slightest sound alarms them and they may dash off into the depths of the woodland. They are not domestic, unless from a sense of duty, but they make admirable companions, particularly in outdoor sports. The native will be able to amuse himself with them, but may find it difficult to make them practical.

Women having the Moon in this sign will attract high-minded, religious and admirable women, and seldom suffer, if at all, from their jealousy or enmity, unless, of course, their Moon is badly aspected.

Mothers having children with the Moon in Sagittarius may give too much thought to their spiritual and mental needs at the expense of their emotional requirements. They should strive to display more affection and sympathy toward such children.

The following well known persons were also born with the Moon in the sign Sagittarius.

Dr. John D. Quackenbos
James O'Neil
Gutzon Borglum
Admiral George Dewey
Spencer Trask
Hudson Maxim
Frederick MacMonnies
Ramsey MacDonald
Thomas W. Lamont
Charles Hayden

THE MOON IN CAPRICORNUS

CAPRICORNUS is, on the whole, a very bad position for the Moon, for here she is in her detriment and the whole nature of Capricornus is unsympathetic. Almost the worst feature of the Moon is her coldness, and this Capricornus accentuates. The senses of people with the Moon in this sign are not likely to be particularly acute. The mental response to impression is rather quick, angry, and antagonistic, yet there is an extreme keenness to receive information. Where the Moon is well-dignified, this may be of very happy augury. Edison's Moon, for example, with the conjunction of Mars to energize it, the sextile of Saturn and Venus to soften and steady it, indicates the quick mental reaction, the power to seize opportunity, and to solve problems in a flash, which has been responsible for the greater part of his success. In this faculty of unusual quickness of judgment, the power of sudden and correct decision, he has a rival in Napoleon. Here Saturn and Mercury are again in aspect to the Moon.

Bismarck also has a sextile of Mercury, a semi-sextile of Saturn, a trine of Venus, a square of the Sun and Jupiter, and a semi-sextile of Uranus, all of which aspects may be taken as greatly strengthening and solidifying the mental reaction. We often find, however, illusions of sense, sometimes so serious as almost to justify ascribing their cause to what is called obsession. We have no reason to doubt the good faith of Joseph Smith any more than we have reason to believe that what he said was true. He may, therefore, have been a deluded, but not a false teacher. On referring to his nativity, we find the Moon on the cusp of the eleventh house, squared by a conjunction of Uranus and Saturn. The sextile of Neptune would naturally give a whimsical turn to the delusion and hence we find extravagant stories about Scriptures written upon golden plates. It is usually a case of definite obsession that we find with the Moon in Capricornus, differing from her nature in Pisces, where we get a different kind of dream-world, the romantic sphere of the poet and the mystic. In Capricornus, the Moon often gives a tendency in persons of the average type to intoxication, always in the nature of obsession. This tendency to obsession is certainly the most characteristic of all the qualities of the Moon in Capricornus. Even in the best cases, people with this position tend to have the idea fixed. Bismarck, Napoleon, and Savonarola are obvious examples. In their cases, the fixed idea was very much in tune with the general purpose of the life, and so was not an affliction, but in a case like that of George III, who had Uranus in conjunction with his Moon and Mars square, there could be no result but madness.

Mary, Queen of Scots, and George Eliot, both had somewhat of a morbid strain, and it is evident that neither of them possessed the disposition to make any man permanently happy. The position of their Moon is to be held, for the most part, responsible for this. There is also in women an evident tendency to brood, and brooding is often a condition antecedent to obsession.

The women with whom the native will probably be associated may possess excellent practical qualities, but they will be apt to be exacting and capricious, sometimes exceedingly cold and unsympathetic, or, if not cold, they may have a callous quality which is almost worse than coldness. They will, however, in all probability be thoroughly reliable, and possess a strong sense of moral responsibility. They will also be patient, and generally speaking, faithful, but the callousness of their disposition will hardly be conducive to the happiness of the men whose lives they influence. If the reader will run his eye back over the people mentioned as having the Moon in this sign, and add the names of Isaac Pitman, Cicero, and Edward VI, he will notice that in none of these cases have women played a really important part in the life, for sympathy is the true foundation of influence.

Women having the Moon in this sign attract women who are not in sympathy with them. They are more likely to benefit their women friends than to receive benefit from them.

Mothers having children with the Moon in Capricorn will be naturally efficient and practical regarding their physical and material needs; unless they can be proud of such children, however, they will seldom give them the love and sympathy which the children will naturally crave.

The following well known persons were also born with the Moon in the sign Capricorn.

George F. Baker
Reginald de Koven
Percival Lowell

THE MOON IN AQUARIUS

AQUARIUS has, on the whole, a very favorable effect upon the Moon. It represents her at her very best. The touch of coldness and inhumanity is no longer there. The sterility and instability are taken away. The indications afforded by the senses are admirable; not only are they accurate, but their effect upon the mind is altogether what it should be. There is the scientific attitude, but there is also the human interest. There is no error either toward emotionalism or sentimentality or rationalism. The reaction is strong and neither too swift nor too slow. We may take as the best examples of this position of the Moon, Dante and Wagner. Here we find, almost equally in both cases, the religious instinct, the humanitarian instinct, the sex instinct and the scientific instinct all admirably developed and not one of them over-developed. Both were familiar with the science of their period, but neither became an extremist. Both followed the religious average of their period, but without undue fanaticism on the one hand or skepticism on the other. People with this position are always likely to be somewhat in advance of their contemporaries, but this advance will be of an all-round character—not distorted or even one-sided. This is a very rare and perfect circumstance. The majority of so-called advanced thinkers have merely a disproportion of over-development on some one line, but people with the Moon in Aquarius are so well-balanced that it is rare for them to upset their contemporaries by an extravagance of views. This universality of interest nearly always tends to make the native a charming companion, whose conversation is always well worth listening to. It is difficult for the native to be satisfied with any one individual; his sympathies move in too many channels. He may, therefore, give more pleasure to his friends than they to him.

This sign is not altogether so fortunate as the home of the Moon in the case of a woman. She becomes almost too Aquarian, and even a good quality can be overdone. There will probably be some lack of heart, unless there is a corresponding correction, as for example the Sun in Cancer or Leo.

The women in the native's life will be much above the average, loyal, broad-minded, intelligent, and while, to some extent, idealistic, they will indubitably prove of the greatest practical assistance to the native, whether man or woman, particularly if his career lies in some such direction as is indicated by the sign itself.

Mothers having children with the Moon in Aquarius are likely to play the part of a chum and companion with them, but they should avoid being too indulgent or unselfish in their attitude toward them.

The following well known persons were also born with the Moon in the sign Aquarius:

Elbert Hubbard
Sir Ernest Shackleton
Maude McCarthy
Joseph Pulitzer
Adolph Ochs
General Goethals
Mary Baker Eddy
Frank H. Dodd
Walter Damrosch
Andrew Carnegie
Joe Cannon

Louisa M. Alcott
Clarence Darrow
Henry Ford.

THE MOON IN PISCES

The Moon and Pisces are peculiarly sympathetic. Taken by itself, there is great danger that the person with this position may receive totally false impressions through the senses. There is an excessive tendency to optimism and romanticism; Don Quixote must have had the Moon in Pisces. Among real people we find it in the horoscopes of Shelley, Goethe, Petrarch, and Stevenson. This position accounts for their extraordinary refusal to accept things as they are. The outside world came to them through such colored glasses that everything appeared bathed in a luminous mist.

The reader will note, however, that, of these persons, Goethe alone had also the scientific attitude, the sense of realism; and Goethe's greatness really consists in his ability to blend these totally opposite qualities of the mind. The explanation is that, in his case, Saturn was square to Uranus, the latter planet being in the third house; a square of Saturn and Mercury would have done equally well. But unless there be some such compensation, we do not find any power of realizing the facts of life with accuracy. The skeptical quality is absent. Cardinal Gibbons, for example, could not entertain any objection to his faith. Mabel Collins, similarly accepting the main theosophic theory, weaves happy dreams. We do not find in her any philosophical interest in its tenets.

Similarly, people like Sir Henry Wood and Rosa Bonheur take the masterpieces of great artists—in the one case Wagner, in the other the creator of that horse "whose neck God clothed with thunder"—and interpret them very nicely, very correctly, but with absolute lack of any analytical or critical faculty. The great artist is always a great realist, however romantic he may be, and however idealistic, for beauty is but the garment of truth; and if there is no truth behind apparent beauty, be sure that your eyes have once more deceived you. Now, the tendency of Pisces is always to present things in symbolic form. The veil between the gross and the subtle world is but a spider's web, so far as Pisces is concerned. This is what makes the sign so astoundingly psychic.

A great deal will depend upon the dignity of the Moon. If she has such good aspects as Mars trine or sextile to make her active, or if a favorable ray from Uranus or the Sun fall upon her, then she gives true vision. If she is afflicted, especially by Saturn, Neptune, Uranus, Mars, or Jupiter, she is likely to bring the most diseased fancies to birth and to harbor the grossest illusions. In fact Pisces may be either the best or the worst of all the places of the Moon, but, in view of what we have said, it appears that the tendency to illusion is so strong that, taken by itself, the position is not a good one in a world where capacity to look facts in the face is the principal asset of the masters of life. People can get into far more trouble through believing the best about everything than through believing the worst. A pleasant surprise can do no harm; an unpleasant one may upset one completely.

One of the most dangerous features of this position of the Moon is that the need to see everything through rose-tinted spectacles often drives the native to indulgence in drink or drugs, which temporarily renews the illusion that everything is beautiful. Any aspect of Neptune to the Moon will naturally accentuate this tendency. It must never be forgotten how closely allied are the temperamental qualities of Neptune and Pisces.

Women with the Moon in this sign fill the above description even more closely than do men. It makes their romanticism and, to a certain extent, their other-worldliness, extraordinarily strong. Sometimes, like Lily Langtry, they are able to turn these qualities to great advantage. In her case, though Neptune was in conjunction with the Moon, the sextile of Uranus and the square of Saturn gave her balance. Without these aspects, she might have been so self-sacrificing, generous, and passive, that she would have been the prey of every unscrupulous person with whom she came in touch.

The women with whom the native is closely associated will be, as a rule, highly emotional, extremely unselfish, romantic, voluptuous, passionate, and sometimes dreamy. They take love to the highest planes and have the power of making themselves appear of extravagant value in the eyes of the native. In the case of a man they will thus enable him to gain pleasure and happiness from their affection, but as a general rule, they will not be of much help to him in his career. In a general way, the woman devotes herself to the man so completely that she has little care for anything in the world but his devotion. She may be, however, extremely useful to him by romantically inspiring him and making him happy.

Mothers having children who have the Moon in Pisces must avoid being so unselfish and "soft" in their attitude toward them as to unconsciously develop their weakest points and to undermine their character and their will-power.

The following well known persons were also born with the Moon in the sign Pisces:

Dr. Felix Adler
Oscar Hammerstein
Cardinal Gibbons
Frank Damrosch
Richard Carle
A. G. Trent
Augustus Thomas
John Burroughs
Richard Le Gallienne

MERCURY SYMBOLICALLY CONSIDERED

Hermes, or Mercury, is the winged and vital intelligence of God. He is the wisdom of the Creator, the Logos or Word by whom all things came into being.

Hermes is swifter than the lightning, for he is thought itself, wherein the lightning lives. The divine consciousness is free from time and space, which are merely the conditions whereby we perceive the limited, and so Hermes, being the thought of Deity, transcends all such bonds. All objects of thought are bounded, but not thought itself. To Hermes the poet has addressed his lyre; and rightly, for Hermes is the inventor of the lyre and all music, as well as of all science and art. He is the master also of magic, and the patron of all those who seek after God by solitude and meditation.

Mercury is the god of playful trickery; he appears "as a boy mischievous and lovely," for, not having acquired that sense of responsibility which comes with the development of the sex-instinct, his cleverness is without serious purpose. As he grows, it turns to evil, and he becomes a thief and a liar; or to good, and he becomes the man of science, the keen intellectual investigator. But so elusive is this god that even pure intellect needs to be tempered by holier forces, or it is cold and evil. And it must be steadied, or its influence may be destructive as the lightning.

Mercury delights to strike and pass; the attention must be riveted, the intellect chained to lofty purpose, before permanent results can be achieved. Of all the powers that can befriend him, Jupiter is the best, even as a boy is best in the hands of a wise and truly religious teacher. He must not be entirely abandoned to the gaiety of Venus or to the changeability of the Moon. Mars may make him unreliable and irritable. The Sun is too near his own nature to be wholly a good companion; Saturn must be indeed kindly and wise if youth is not to acquire the pessimism of age.

So Mercury is the most fascinating of the planets; he is a riddle to which new answers constantly are given; he is subtle and ambiguous, soft of speech and vivid of smile. Even his worst pranks move the Gods to laughter! Only when hardened in evil does he become the apache of the planets.

The lesson of Mercury is education. By right schooling and discipline, intellect, which is by nature non-moral, may be developed under noble auspices to create new worlds of thought. Intellect can solve the secrets of the stars, tame lightning, and give it to the children for a toy, discover the treasures of the ocean, force even philosophy to disclose her brows, rear the colossus, civilization, in the harbor of mankind—in a word, work every wonder. But this intellect is also capable of things wholly worthless, of dangerous exploits leading to disaster. It can inspire a skeptic to the ruin of religion, destroy a social system with false logic, uproot an empire, and dismay humanity. So seductive is the sophistical appeal to reason that man's pride in his mind often blinds him to the lessons of experience. There is no metal but iron that quicksilver will not corrode; and only firmness and moral courage can resist the plausibilities of the demagogue.

The mind is primarily a sword; it is easy to destroy the fabric of society, because its foundations are compromise and convention. The world is admittedly false and evil; it never corresponds with our *a priori* ideas of it.

Destructive criticism is the principal function of the Devil. Satan is "the accuser of the brethren"; and it is fortunate that the great Judge of all the earth is not only just, but merciful.

But, above all, Mercury is he that standeth upon the threshold of the House of Heaven; he is the Messenger of the Gods. For as by intellect we are raised above the beasts, so it is our link with Deity. Only, it is not for us to be active, but to be passive. Let us listen to Nature in all her manifold mysteries, and especially in Art, for that which is not in the storm of the lightning or the earthquake, but in the still small voice. Let our intellect be illuminated by the great Light that is beyond it but let us receive humbly that which may be given us by the grace of the Omniscient. Let us indeed inquire ardently, with all the labor of which we are capable, into all things; but let us also remember the last words of the greatest philosopher—"All things end in mystery." Let us realize that Absolute Truth resides beyond the reach of mortal mind, beyond the limitations of Time and Space, and that, were we wise as Solomon, this would still be true of us, that "the wisdom of this world is foolishness with God." So it is the supreme achievement of the mind to recognize its own incapacity, and bow before the fact. "These things are hidden from the wise and prudent and revealed unto babes." What is the issue? To become as little children; "for of such is the Kingdom of God."

MERCURY IN THE SIGNS

MERCURY is the most truly sensitive of all the planets. Venus and the Moon are more easily affected, it is true, but for them a better term is "impressionable." Mercury is the adolescent; he responds to every impression like the weather-vane, which is a very different thing from the reception and reflection of every impression. In slightly different language, Mercury is not modified by the signs as are the more passive planets; rather each excites him to give a special expression of opinion. Mercury is, as we know, the mind; and while the contents of the mind are determined by the food of the mind, yet different minds deal quite differently with identical foods. It has been said (by Browning, was it not?) that thousands of people before Newton saw apples fall from trees, but their only impulse was to eat them.

The proper and best influence upon Mercury is Saturn, and without his steadying hand to hold him in tutorship to a profounder wisdom, Mercury may be frivolous and vain. It is only when Mercury is overpowered by Venus that the mental qualities become subservient and slavish, so that one may say of the native "he has no mind of his own." There is, however, always the safeguard of the proximity of the Sun, especially when the conjunction is not too close.

We must urge upon the student to regard carefully the aspects to this planet, but not to accept them as operative unless very close. At the same time whatever aspects may exist will not alter the essential character of Mercury, as determined by the sign in which he is placed. It is further to be observed that the close juxtaposition of the Sun and Mercury makes the quality of the latter, as a rule, practically that of the Sun himself. This is, of course, only natural since there is a closer connection between the man and his mind than there is (for example) between him and his will. The exceptions will be, of course, when Mercury is at his farthest from the Sun and in a sign of opposite nature. But the main point to remember is the delicate sensitiveness of the mental ruler, and the fact that such impressions as are made on him are not like seals upon wax, but like the rise and fall of the column of quicksilver at every change in the atmosphere.

MERCURY IN ARIES

In Aries, Mercury is strong and impetuous. The native is usually a creature of impulse, taking up ideas with enthusiasm, but unable to concentrate upon them for any length of time. He is often witty, inventive, vigorous in execution, a capable administrator or governor, though apt to be dictatorial and impatient of opposition and still more so of delay. He is liable to fits of passion, and when Mercury is afflicted, especially by Uranus, he may be subject to persistent and acute headache, neuralgia, and, in bad cases, intermittent mania or epilepsy.

But where Mercury is well dignified, this position is altogether admirable for sheer brilliancy of mind. Shakespeare, Zola, Sir Richard Burton, J. M. W. Turner, Tschaikowsky, Daudet, and Swinburne all had their Mercury in Aries. In science we find Copernicus, in military affairs General Grant, and in the modern world of finance the late J. Pierpont Morgan. One may also remark on the fact that Madame Steinheil was similarly favored, and collate it with what has been said elsewhere with regard to her career.

The following well known persons were also born with Mercury in the sign Aries:

William Shakespeare
Emile Zola
Sir Richard Burton
The late J. P. Morgan
Joseph Pulitzer
Elihu P. Root
Dr. John Duncan Quackenbos
Palmer Cox
"Bud" Fisher
Senator Weeks (Secretary of War)
Dr. Percy Stickney Grant
Chauncey M. Depew
Charlie Chaplin
John Burroughs
John B. Herreshoff

For the benefit of those who are not in possession of Raphael's Ephemeris, or who are not able to interpret the symbols contained therein, the years when Mercury is in the sign Aries are as follows:

From	March	9th	through	May	14th	1840
	March	3d	"	March	20th	1841
	April	18th	"	May	8th	1841
	April	14th	"	April	30th	1842
	April	8th	"	April	22d	1843
	March	30th	"	April	13th	1844

From	March	22d	through	April	5th	1845
	March	14th	"	March	31st	1846
	April	18th	"	May	16th	1846
	March	6th	"	May	13th	1847
	April	16th	"	May	5th	1848
	April	11th	"	April	27th	1849
	April	4th	"	April	18th	1850
	March	27th	"	April	10th	1851
	March	18th	"	April	2d	1852
	March	10th	"	May	15th	1853
	March	3d	"	March	26th	1854
	April	17th	"	May	9th	1854
	April	15th	"	May	2d	1855
	April	8th	"	April	23d	1856
	March	31st	"	April	14th	1857
	March	23d	"	April	6th	1858
	March	15th	"	March	31st	1859
	April	25th	"	May	15th	1859
	March	6th	"	May	13th	1860
	March	3d	"	March	9th	1861
	April	17th	"	May	6th	1861
	April	12th	"	April	28th	1862
	April	5th	"	April	20th	1863
	March	28th	"	April	10th	1864
	March	19th	"	April	3d	1865
	March	11th	"	May	16th	1866
	March	4th	"	April	3d	1867
	April	16th	"	May	11th	1867
	April	15th	"	May	2d	1868
	April	9th	"	April	24th	1869
	April	2d	"	April	16th	1870
	March	25th	"	April	8th	1871
	March	16th	"	March	31st	1872
	May	4th	"	May	12th	1872
	March	8th	"	May	14th	1873
	March	3d	"	March	16th	1874
	April	18th	"	May	7th	1874
	April	14th	"	April	30th	1875

From			through			
From	April	6th	through	April	20th	1876
	March	29th	"	April	12th	1877
	March	21st	"	April	4th	1878
	March	13th	"	April	1st	1879
	April	13th	"	May	16th	1879
	March	5th	"	May	11th	1880
	April	16th	"	May	4th	1881
	April	10th	"	April	26th	1882
	April	3d	"	April	17th	1883
	March	25th	"	April	8th	1884
	March	17th	"	April	1st	1885
	March	9th	"	May	15th	1886
	March	3d	"	March	22d	1887
	April	18th	"	May	9th	1887
	April	14th	"	April	30th	1888
	April	7th	"	April	22d	1889
	March	31st	"	April	13th	1890
	March	22d	"	April	5th	1891
	March	13th	"	March	30th	1892
	April	20th	"	May	15th	1892
	March	6th	"	May	12th	1893
	April	17th	"	May	5th	1894
	April	12th	"	April	27th	1895
	April	4th	"	April	18th	1896
	March	27th	"	April	9th	1897
	March	19th	"	April	2d	1898
	March	11th	"	May	15th	1899
	March	4th	"	March	29th	1900
	April	17th	"	May	10th	1900
	April	16th	"	May	3d	1901
	April	9th	"	April	24th	1902
	April	2d	"	April	16th	1903
	March	24th	"	April	7th	1904
	March	16th	"	April	1st	1905
	April	29th	"	May	15th	1905
	March	8th	"	May	14th	1906
	March	4th	"	March	13th	1907
	April	18th	"	May	8th	1907

From	April	13th	through	April	29th	1908
	April	6th	"	April	20th	1909
	March	29th	"	April	12th	1910
	March	21st	"	April	4th	1911
	March	12th	"	May	16th	1912
	March	5th	"	April	7th	1913
	April	14th	"	May	11th	1913
	April	17th	"	May	4th	1914
	April	11th	"	April	26th	1915
	April	2d	"	April	16th	1916
	March	25th	"	April	8th	1917
	March	17th	"	April	2d	1918
	March	9th	"	May	15th	1919
	March	3d	"	March	19th	1920
	April	18th	"	May	8th	1920
	April	14th	"	April	30th	1921
	April	7th	"	April	22th	1922
	March	31st	"	April	14th	1923
	March	22d	"	April	5th	1924
	March	14th	"	April	1st	1925
	April	16th	"	May	16th	1925
	March	6th	"	May	12th	1926
	April	18th	"	May	5th	1927
	April	11th	"	April	26th	1928
	April	4th	"	April	18th	1929

MERCURY IN TAURUS

In Taurus, Mercury is the very antithesis of himself in Aries. The mind of the native is slow, patient, solid and constructive, and often obstinate. He may have a great intellect, but often may learn more from travel and experience than from books. There is, however, frequently some tendency to mental inertia, and this nearly always expresses itself as conservatism. Such minds resist new ideas. Consider Queen Victoria, the most successful reactionary of the nineteenth century. She came to a throne already tottering beneath the blows of the French Revolution, and of such thinkers as Shelley, and she smothered Republicanism by "fighting the fight of sit-down" until at her Jubilee she was more firmly seated than any Tudor!

Huxley, too, for all his brilliancy and originality was in some ways as conservative as his Queen. In science he never jumped at conclusions; he was, perhaps, the most cautious and profound thinker, both in science and in philosophy, that England had produced. Similar qualities, not so well-dignified, are visible in General Boulanger and George V. In them there is some hanging back noticeable; hesitation just where dash was wanted! For constructive obstinacy in politics we should look rather to Cromwell, who was, of course, a far more absolute monarch than the weak king whom he replaced.

And when Mercury in Taurus is constructive, he is very constructive indeed, as is exemplified in Kant, Wagner and Balzac.

There is never any doubt about the solidity and worth of the intellect of people with this position; how it may work out to advantage or disadvantage depends almost entirely upon the aspects.

The following well known persons were born with Mercury in the sign Taurus:

Queen Victoria
Wagner
Joseph G. Cannon
Beauregard
Rudolph Valentino
Oscar Hammerstein
Daniel Chester French
Clarence Darrow
Alan Dale
William Randolph Hearst

For the benefit of those who are not in possession of Raphael's Ephemeris, or who are not able to interpret the symbols contained therein, the years when Mercury is in the signs Taurus are as follows:

From	May	15th	through	June	1st	1840
	May	9th	"	May	23d	1841
	May	1st	"	May	15th	1842

From	April	23rd	through	May	6th	1843
	April	14th	"	April	29th	1844
	April	6th	"	June	12th	1845
	April	1st	"	April	17th	1846
	May	17th	"	June	6th	1846
	May	14th	"	May	29th	1847
	May	6th	"	May	19th	1848
	April	28th	"	May	11th	1849
	April	19th	"	May	3d	1850
	April	11th	"	April	30th	1851
	May	20th	"	June	13th	1851
	April	3d	"	June	9th	1852
	May	16th	"	June	2d	1853
	May	10th	"	May	25th	1854
	May	3d	"	May	16th	1855
	April	24th	"	May	7th	1856
	April	15th	"	April	30th	1857
	April	7th	"	June	13th	1858
	April	1st	"	April	24th	1859
	May	16th	"	June	7th	1859
	May	14th	"	May	29th	1860
	May	7th	"	May	21st	1861
	April	29th	"	May	12th	1862
	April	21st	"	May	4th	1863
	April	11th	"	April	28th	1864
	May	28th	"	June	11th	1864
	April	4th	"	June	11th	1865
	May	17th	"	June	4th	1866
	May	12th	"	May	26th	1867
	May	3d	"	May	17th	1868
	April	25th	"	May	8th	1869
	April	17th	"	May	1st	1870
	April	9th	"	June	13th	1871
	April	1st	"	May	3d	1872
	May	13th	"	June	7th	1872
	May	15th	"	May	31st	1873
	May	8th	"	May	22d	1874
	May	1st	"	May	14th	1875

From April	21st	through	May	5th	1876
April	13th	"	April	29th	1877
April	5th	"	June	12th	1878
April	2d	"	April	12th	1879
May	17th	"	June	5th	1879
May	12th	"	May	27th	1880
May	5th	"	May	18th	1881
April	27th	"	May	10th	1882
April	18th	"	May	2d	1883
April	9th	"	April	30th	1884
May	13th	"	June	13th	1884
April	2d	"	June	9th	1885
May	16th	"	June	1st	1886
May	10th	"	May	24th	1887
May	1st	"	May	14th	1888
April	23d	"	May	6th	1889
April	14th	"	April	30th	1890
April	6th	"	June	13th	1891
March	31st	"	April	19th	1892
May	16th	"	June	5th	1892
May	13th	"	May	28th	1893
May	6th	"	May	20th	1894
April	28th	"	May	11th	1895
April	19th	"	May	3d	1896
April	10th	"	April	29th	1897
May	22d	"	June	12th	1897
April	3d	"	June	10th	1898
May	16th	"	June	3d	1899
May	11th	"	May	25th	1900
May	4th	"	May	17th	1901
April	25th	"	May	9th	1902
April	17th	"	May	2d	1903
April	8th	"	June	13th	1904
April	2d	"	April	28th	1905
May	16th	"	June	8th	1905
May	15th	"	May	31st	1906
May	9th	"	May	22d	1907
April	30th	"	May	13th	1908

From April	21st	through	May	5th	1909
April	13th	"	April	30th	1910
June	2d	"	June	11th	1910
April	5th	"	June	12th	1911
May	17th	"	June	4th	1912
May	12th	"	May	27th	1913
May	5th	"	May	18th	1914
April	27th	"	May	10th	1915
April	17th	"	May	2d	1916
April	9th	"	June	14th	1917
April	3d	"	June	9th	1918
May	16th	"	June	1st	1919
May	9th	"	May	23d	1920
May	1st	"	May	14th	1921
April	23d	"	May	6th	1922
April	15th	"	April	30th	1923
April	6th	"	June	12th	1924
April	2d	"	April	15th	1925
May	17th	"	June	6th	1925
May	13th	"	May	29th	1926
May	6th	"	May	20th	1927
April	27th	"	May	10th	1928
April	19th	"	May	3d	1929

MERCURY IN GEMINI

In Gemini Mercury is in his own house, but although quite as strong as one would expect, it is his airy changeful side that is most accentuated. There is danger of over-development of the mind at the expense of the vital forces, of living too wholly on the mental plane, of restlessness and anxiety and overwork, which errors may culminate in nervous breakdown. Ill aspects of Neptune, the Moon, and Uranus confirm this threat.

The mind of such people is often singularly lucid, but intellectually, rather than instinctively or intuitively. They rationalize admirably, but nearly always neglect more important considerations. Their logical processes are perfect, but they are apt to generalize from insufficient data, or to omit some cardinal fact in their premises. They are often, therefore, regarded as silly, though never as stupid. Their superficial rapidity of mind often makes them good public speakers or journalists, for rapidity is an essential mental qualification in these professions, and their facility in logical process without rigid insistence upon precedent fact makes them successful lawyers.

They possess great versatility; often too much, sometimes lacking steadiness and application. They are easily influenced by their environment; a slight matter starts them off on a new trail. Where the hearing is good, they make fine linguists, but, unless Mercury is fortified by good aspects of the heavier planets, not especially adapted for any of the deeper modes of thought. Albert Dürer and Dante are the greatest names upon our list, and in both cases Mercury is greatly steadied and helped by Saturn and Uranus. In the second rank we find George Sand, Thomas Hardy, and Bulwer-Lytton. Richard Strauss, whose Mercury is in the last degree of Taurus and therefore blends the influences of both signs, may perhaps be worthy of the first-class. But more characteristic of Gemini is the coldly intellectual quality of mind shown by George III, Robespierre, Brigham Young, Jay Gould, and Abbas Effendi. There is something colorless and bloodless about the manner of thought of all these people, which puts them in a class apart. Yet more typical of the purely mental and superficial character of this position of Mercury is George Bidder, the "Lightning Calculator." The mind in such a case is as merely a machine as if it were made of metal; and this is the essentially mental quality, and the occasion of St. Paul's remark, "The carnal mind is enmity against God."

The following well known persons were born with Mercury in the sign Gemini:

Colonel George W. Goethals
P. T. Barnum
Emerson
Charles Hayden
Captain George W. Walrond
James Stillman
Harriet Beecher Stowe

For the benefit of those who are not in possession of Raphael's Ephemeris, or who are not able to interpret the symbols contained therein, the years when Mercury is in the sign Gemini, are as follows:

From	June	2d	through	June	14th	1840
	May	24th	"	June	6th	1841
	May	16th	"	May	30th	1842
	May	7th	"	May	30th	1843
	June	14th	"	July	13th	1843
	April	30th	"	July	7th	1844
	June	13th	"	June	29th	1845
	June	7th	"	June	20th	1846
	May	30th	"	June	12th	1847
	May	20th	"	June	3d	1848
	May	12th	"	May	28th	1849
	May	4th	"	July	11th	1850
	May	1st	"	May	19th	1851
	June	14th	"	July	4th	1851
	June	10th	"	June	25th	1852
	June	3d	"	June	16th	1853
	May	26th	"	June	8th	1854
	May	17th	"	May	31st	1855
	May	8th	"	May	27th	1856
	June	22d	"	July	12th	1856
	May	1st	"	July	8th	1857
	June	14th	"	June	30th	1858
	June	8th	"	June	22d	1859
	May	30th	"	June	12th	1860
	May	22d	"	June	4th	1861
	May	13th	"	May	29th	1862
	May	5th	"	July	12th	1863
	April	29th	"	May	27th	1864
	June	12th	"	July	4th	1864
	June	12th	"	June	26th	1865
	June	5th	"	June	18th	1866
	May	27th	"	June	9th	1867
	May	18th	"	June	1st	1868

From	May	9th	through	May	27th	1869
	July	2d	"	July	10th	1869
	May	2d	"	July	9th	1870
	June	14th	"	July	2d	1871
	June	8th	"	June	22d	1872
	June	1st	"	June	14th	1873
	May	23d	"	June	5th	1874
	May	15th	"	May	30th	1875
	May	6th	"	July	12th	1876
	April	30th	"	July	6th	1877
	June	13th	"	June	28th	1878
	June	6th	"	June	19th	1879
	May	28th	"	June	10th	1880
	May	19th	"	June	2d	1881
	May	11th	"	May	28th	1882
	May	3d	"	July	10th	1883
	May	1st	"	May	12th	1884
	June	14th	"	July	2d	1884
	June	10th	"	June	24th	1885
	June	2d	"	June	15th	1886
	May	25th	"	June	7th	1887
	May	15th	"	May	30th	1888
	May	7th	"	May	28th	1889
	June	16th	"	July	12th	1889
	May	1st	"	July	7th	1890
	June	14th	"	June	29th	1891
	June	6th	"	June	20th	1892
	May	29th	"	June	11th	1893
	May	21st	"	June	3d	1894
	May	12th	"	May	28th	1895
	May	4th	"	July	10th	1896
	April	30th	"	May	21st	1897
	June	13th	"	July	4th	1897
	June	11th	"	June	25th	1898
	June	4th	"	June	17th	1899
	May	26th	"	June	8th	1900
	May	18th	"	June	1st	1901
	May	10th	"	May	28th	1902

From June 26th	through	July	12th	1902
May 3d	"	July	10th	1903
June 14th	"	July	1st	1904
June 9th	"	June	22d	1905
June 1st	"	June	14th	1906
May 23d	"	June	6th	1907
May 14th	"	May	29th	1908
May 6th	"	July	12th	1909
May 1st	"	June	1st	1910
June 12th	"	July	6th	1910
June 13th	"	June	28th	1911
June 5th	"	June	18th	1912
May 28th	"	June	10th	1913
May 19th	"	June	2d	1914
May 11th	"	May	28th	1915
May 3d	"	July	10th	1916
June 15th	"	July	2d	1917
June 10th	"	June	24th	1918
June 2d	"	June	15th	1919
May 24th	"	June	6th	1920
May 15th	"	May	30th	1921
May 7th	"	May	31st	1922
June 11th	"	July	13th	1922
May 1st	"	July	8th	1923
June 13th	"	June	29th	1924
June 7th	"	June	20th	1925
May 30th	"	June	11th	1926
May 21st	"	June	4th	1927
May 11th	"	May	28th	1928
May 4th	"	July	11th	1929

MERCURY IN CANCER

So receptive a sign as Cancer is not wholly suitable to Mercury, who easily "loses himself," one fluid in another, so to speak. The result is often seen in poor memory, particularly in old age, although, if the planet be well dignified, the mind may be singularly retentive, particularly in the matter of history. In fact, the tendency is often to assimilate precedent, and rather to refer to antiquity than to reason upon actualities. It is good for such persons as may be occupied in what may be called the by ways of life. Dealers in antiquities, bibliophiles, bookworms, and to a less extent, lawyers, may find some advantage in this position.

There is in all cases a decided lack of the sense of actuality, and, above all, of originality. Yet the intuition is often exceedingly good; such people may know, without being told, and without knowing how they know. The understanding is usually excellent, and the sympathy is easily excited. On the other hand, where these people dislike, the feeling is intense; they cannot endure the company of those who are not in harmony with them. Yet, although sensitive, they are more tolerant than the average person. The contrast in this respect with people who have Mercury in Scorpio is singularly well marked; for the latter, although they may deem it politic to conceal their contempt for inferior minds, keep inwardly the most extraordinary bitterness. Mercury in Cancer is really tolerant; its natives have the sense that opinions are, after all, not of supreme importance. They are, too, not always aware of their own defect of memory and lack of logic. Here one must pause, confronted by the fact that the most marvelous memory in the world, that of "Datas," and the most powerful rationalizing mind of modern times, that of Bernard Shaw, both came under Mercury in Cancer. But the Mercury of "Datas" has Venus in exact conjunction, and his memory is purely detached and self-sufficient, and exclusively historical. He remembers dates, and dates only; and he remembers them in a mechanical manner, absolutely, and not because of their relation to other matters. This is in fact the precise type of memory indicated above as characteristic of this position. The case of Bernard Shaw is explained by the exact trine of Neptune to Mercury, which gives him his extraordinary faculty of detecting the falsity of conventional thought.

It may also be mentioned that the effect of Cancer is to make Mercury sway to the purely passive side. The mind is unusually impressionable, and though the inscriptions thereupon be "writ in water," yet for the moment they sway the native. There is little real stability in the mind, and yet it falls easily into habit, which may be obstinate if subjected for long periods to a single stress. The position inclines to mental idleness, and any powerful will can easily obtain dominion over the mind of the native by appealing to the senses rather than by argument, which arouses obstinate resistance. All this being peculiarly contrary to the best attributes of mind, we must regard Cancer as one of the less fortunate positions for Mercury.

The following well known persons were born with Mercury in the sign Cancer:

Alexander Dumas
Lord Tennyson
George Bernard Shaw
Robert Schumann
Henry Ward Beecher
Mark Benson
John O'Hara Cosgrave
William Gillette
Harrison Grey Fiske
Harrison Fisher
John D. Rockefeller, Sr.
Calvin Coolidge
George M. Cohan
Booth Tarkington
Elbert Hubbard

For the benefit of those who are not in possession of Raphael's Ephemeris, or who are not able to interpret the symbols contained therein, the years when Mercury is in Cancer, are as follows:

From	June	15th	through	June	30th	1840
	June	7th	"	June	25th	1841
	August	6th	"	August	8th	1841
	May	31st	"	August	7th	1842
	May	31st	"	June	13th	1843
	July	14th	"	July	31st	1843
	July	8th	"	July	21st	1844
	June	30th	"	July	13th	1845

From	June	21st	through	July	5th	1846
	June	13th	"	June	28th	1847
	June	4th	"	June	26th	1848
	July	15th	"	August	10th	1848
	May	29th	"	August	4th	1849
	July	12th	"	July	27th	1850
	July	5th	"	July	18th	1851
	June	26th	"	July	9th	1852
	June	17th	"	July	1st	1853
	June	9th	"	June	26th	1854
	June	1st	"	August	9th	1855
	May	28th	"	June	21st	1856
	July	13th	"	July	31st	1856
	July	9th	"	July	23d	1857
	July	1st	"	July	14th	1858
	June	23d	"	July	6th	1859
	June	13th	"	June	28th	1860
	June	5th	"	June	25th	1861
	July	23d	"	August	11th	1861
	May	30th	"	August	5th	1862
	July	13th	"	July	28th	1863
	July	5th	"	July	19th	1864
	June	27th	"	July	10th	1865
	June	19th	"	July	3d	1866
	June	10th	"	June	27th	1867
	June	2d	"	August	9th	1868
	May	28th	"	July	1st	1869
	July	11th	"	August	2d	1869
	July	10th	"	July	24th	1870
	July	3d	"	July	16th	1871
	June	23d	"	July	7th	1872
	June	15th	"	June	30th	1873
	June	6th	"	June	25th	1874
	July	30th	"	August	10th	1874
	May	31st	"	August	7th	1875
	July	13th	"	July	29th	1876
	July	7th	"	July	20th	1877
	June	29th	"	July	12th	1878

From June	20th	through	July	4th	1879
June	11th	"	June	27th	1880
June	3d	"	June	28th	1881
July	10th	"	August	10th	1881
May	29th	"	August	3d	1882
July	11th	"	July	26th	1883
July	3d	"	July	16th	1884
June	25th	"	July	8th	1885
June	16th	"	July	1st	1886
June	8th	"	June	26th	1887
May	31st	"	August	7th	1888
May	29th	"	June	15th	1889
July	13th	"	July	30th	1889
July	8th	"	July	22d	1890
June	30th	"	July	13th	1891
June	21st	"	July	4th	1892
June	12th	"	June	28th	1893
June	4th	"	June	26th	1894
July	18th	"	August	10th	1894
May	29th	"	August	5th	1895
July	11th	"	July	26th	1896
July	5th	"	July	18th	1897
June	26th	"	July	10th	1898
June	18th	"	July	2d	1899
June	9th	"	June	26th	1900
June	2d	"	August	9th	1901
May	29th	"	June	25th	1902
July	13th	"	August	2d	1902
July	11th	"	July	25th	1903
July	2d	"	July	15th	1904
June	23d	"	July	7th	1905
June	15th	"	June	30th	1906
June	7th	"	June	26th	1907
July	27th	"	August	12th	1907
May	30th	"	August	6th	1908
July	13th	"	July	29th	1909
July	7th	"	July	21st	1910
June	29th	"	July	12th	1911

From						
From June	19th	through	July	3d	1912
June	11th	"	June	27th	1913
June	3d	"	August	10th	1914
May	29th	"	August	3d	1915
July	11th	"	July	25th	1916
July	3d	"	July	17th	1917
June	25th	"	July	8th	1918
June	16th	"	July	1st	1919
June	7th	"	June	26th	1920
August	3d	"	August	9th	1920
May	31st	"	August	7th	1921
June	1st	"	June	10th	1922
July	14th	"	July	31st	1922
July	9th	"	July	22d	1923
June	30th	"	July	13th	1924
June	21st	"	July	5th	1925
June	12th	"	June	28th	1926
June	5th	"	June	28th	1927
July	14th	"	August	11th	1927
May	29th	"	August	4th	1928
July	12th	"	July	27th	1929

MERCURY IN LEO

THE steady glow of Leo has an altogether admirable effect on the shy, silvery Mercury. As "the adolescent" among the planets, the solar influence is just what he needs "to make a man of him." In other language, it may be said that this position adds heart to brain; and brain without heart is the essence of all mischief—the intellectuality of Mephistopheles. There are, of course, certain dangers, notably a tendency to pride and anger, sometimes to bombast and boastfulness. Ambition, too, is a common quality; but ambition is a virtue unless it is ill-regulated. Since the Sun is more frequently than not in the same sign as Mercury, in this particular case it follows that, as lord of Leo, he is generally stronger than his satellite, and this tends still further to steady him.

Taking a comprehensive view, one may affirm that this is one of the best possible positions for Mercury. As we have noticed in dealing with other planets, it is not always well for them to be too strongly reinforced in their own essential qualities. Mercury in mercurial signs may prove too mercurial, just as Mars in martial signs is often over-martial. Every planet needs balance, and the lesser planets need it more than the greater. Accordingly, we discover this position of Mercury in the nativities of some of the greatest of mankind. Who more admirably illustrates greatness of heart and brain than Cardinal Gibbons, in our own times? Or if we must choose a rival, in these qualities, what of Cecil Rhodes? Looking backward we have yet greater names and in each case we shall note this remarkable balancing of the highest intelligence by the human touch, this harmonious union of the perceptive and the emotional qualities. This it is that made Cicero orator as well as essayist, and this that colored the intellectuality of Petrarch with the ray of love. Here, too, must we look for the condition that brought the genius of Goethe and of Napoleon into sympathetic touch with their lesser fellows; and it is this same tempering of perspicacity with the "human element" that made Lord Northcliffe the greatest journalist of his period in England.

Virgo may lend Mercury more acuteness, Aquarius more lofty passion; but Leo is the fitting place for the mental ruler of the "man of the people."

The following well known persons were born with Mercury in the sign Leo:

Lord Northcliffe
Cecil Rhodes
Cardinal Gibbons
Henry Ford
David Belasco
Stanley Baldwin
Ralph Waldo Trine
Mary Baker Eddy

For the benefit of those who are not in possession of Raphael's Ephemeris, or who are not able to interpret the symbols contained therein, the years when Mercury is in the sign Leo are as follows:

From July	1st	through	September	7th	1840
June	26th	"	August	5th	1841
August	9th	"	August	31st	1841
August	8th	"	August	23d	1842
August	1st	"	August	15th	1843
July	22d	"	August	6th	1844
July	14th	"	July	30th	1845
July	6th	"	July	25th	1846
August	29th	"	September	10th	1846
June	29th	"	September	5th	1847
June	27th	"	July	14th	1848
August	11th	"	August	27th	1848
August	5th	"	August	19th	1849
July	28th	"	August	11th	1850
July	19th	"	August	3d	1851
July	10th	"	July	27th	1852
July	2d	"	July	26th	1853
August	12th	"	September	8th	1853
June	27th	"	September	1st	1854
August	10th	"	August	24th	1855
August	1st	"	August	15th	1856
July	24th	"	August	7th	1857
July	15th	"	July	31st	1858
July	7th	"	July	26th	1859
September	5th	"	September	9th	1859
June	29th	"	September	5th	1860
June	26th	"	July	22d	1861
August	12th	"	August	29th	1861
August	6th	"	August	20th	1862
July	29th	"	August	12th	1863
July	20th	"	August	4th	1864
July	11th	"	July	28th	1865
July	4th	"	July	25th	1866
August	19th	"	September	9th	1866
June	28th	"	September	3d	1867
August	10th	"	August	25th	1868
August	3d	"	August	17th	1869
July	25th	"	August	9th	1870

From	July	17th	through	August	1st	1871
	July	8th	"	July	26th	1872
	July	1st	"	September	7th	1873
	June	26th	"	July	29th	1874
	August	11th	"	August	30th	1874
	August	8th	"	August	22d	1875
	July	30th	"	August	13th	1876
	July	21st	"	August	5th	1877
	July	13th	"	July	29th	1878
	July	5th	"	July	25th	1879
	August	25th	"	September	10th	1879
	June	28th	"	September	3d	1880
	June	29th	"	July	9th	1881
	August	11th	"	August	26th	1881
	August	4th	"	August	18th	1882
	July	27th	"	August	10th	1883
	July	17th	"	August	2d	1884
	July	9th	"	July	27th	1885
	July	2d	"	July	28th	1886
	August	7th	"	September	8th	1886
	June	27th	"	September	1st	1887
	August	8th	"	August	22d	1888
	July	31st	"	August	14th	1889
	July	23d	"	August	6th	1890
	July	14th	"	July	30th	1891
	July	5th	"	July	25th	1892
	August	30th	"	September	9th	1892
	June	29th	"	September	5th	1893
	June	27th	"	July	17th	1894
	August	11th	"	August	28th	1894
	August	6th	"	August	20th	1895
	July	27th	"	August	10th	1896
	July	19th	"	August	3d	1897
	July	11th	"	July	28th	1898
	July	3d	"	July	26th	1899
	August	15th	"	September	9th	1899
	June	27th	"	September	2d	1900
	August	10th	"	August	25th	1901

From August	3d	through	August	17th	1902
July	26th	"	August	9th	1903
July	16th	"	August	1st	1904
July	8th	"	July	26th	1905
July	1st	"	September	7th	1906
June	27th	"	July	26th	1907
August	13th	"	August	30th	1907
August	7th	"	August	21st	1908
July	30th	"	August	13th	1909
July	22d	"	August	5th	1910
July	13th	"	July	30th	1911
July	4th	"	July	25th	1912
August	21st	"	September	10th	1912
June	28th	"	September	3d	1913
August	11th	"	August	26th	1914
August	4th	"	August	18th	1915
July	26th	"	August	9th	1916
July	18th	"	August	2d	1917
July	9th	"	July	27th	1918
July	2d	"	September	8th	1919
June	27th	"	August	2d	1920
August	10th	"	August	31st	1920
August	8th	"	August	23d	1921
August	1st	"	August	14th	1922
July	23d	"	August	7th	1923
July	14th	"	July	30th	1924
July	6th	"	July	25th	1925
August	27th	"	September	10th	1925
June	29th	"	September	5th	1926
June	29th	"	July	13th	1927
August	12th	"	August	28th	1927
August	5th	"	August	19th	1928
July	28th	"	August	11th	1929

MERCURY IN VIRGO

In this sign Mercury is not only in his own house, but also in the the house of his exaltation, and it is natural to suppose that he will be stronger and more excellent here than anywhere else in the Zodiac. To a great extent this is the case. So far as Mercury is sufficient, he is admirable; and it is irrational to blame Mercury because he is not also Venus! Yet this is the danger: A native with Mercury so placed may be overwhelmed by this part of his character. Virgo, however, is much to be preferred to Gemini as a place for the mental ruler; the duplicity of the Twin-sign is avoided, and Virgo, being an earthy sign, tends to add stability to the planet.

The extreme development of intellect naturally causes a certain coldness and detachment; people thus endowed sometimes forget that this world is not altogether ruled by reason, but very largely by prejudice, emotion, and self-interest. They are, therefore, better fitted to deal with abstractions than with practical affairs; Leo is much better than Virgo for the man of the world. The great men are the true men, no doubt; but this is exactly why the great men are often never discovered until they have been dead for many years.

People with Mercury in Virgo are quick to learn; indeed they often learn so easily that they do not concentrate sufficiently to retain their acquired knowledge. They have excellent memories subject to exactly the same limitations. They are often fertile of fancy, make excellent linguists, and good orators. Their mind is well adapted for scientific inquiry and, if Mercury is strengthened by Saturnian wisdom, their attainment in Science may be really profound. They are clever in handicrafts, and should excel in scientific agriculture. The mind, too, is essentially honest. As lawyers they are not so sharp as those with Mercury in Gemini. There is much plasticity and receptiveness, moreover, in the mind; and they are easily influenced, especially by argument.

On the other hand, they are sharply critical, sometimes too much so, though this trait rarely takes so aggressive a form as when Mercury is in Scorpio. They are intolerant towards stupidity in others and cannot understand the point of view of "common sense," when it conflicts with their reasoned judgment. In a sense they are idealists as much as those who live in an emotional dream-world, and are just as fanatical, though in the opposite camp. They take "the world as it ought to be" (in their opinion) instead of the world as it is.

From this fault come the practical blunders of such really magnificent intellects as those of Anna Kingsford and Mme. Blavatsky. Shelley and Tolstoi had this same limitation. Each "proved conclusively" that a certain course of action was correct; and each was amazed that humanity remained unconvinced.

In pure philosophy this does not apply. Sir William Hamilton, dealing with the abstractions of metaphysics, was content to leave his work where he found it, on the intellectual plane. In politics, too, the coldness of perception often sets as an advantage. Witness: Franz Josef and Louis XIV. Both these monarchs were able to pursue a difficult policy with success because of their detachment from emotional considerations. Mr. Asquith, Cæsar Borgia, and Sadi Carnot may be cited as further examples. On the other hand, Louis XVI and Ludwig II of Bavaria failed from this identical course; they were not identified with politics in the same way as those just mentioned, and they lost their thrones and their lives from lack of interest.

It is to be noticed that every single one of these people could see only his own point of view, and rode roughshod over his opponents. There is much selfishness in intellectuality, and even where the heart is humanitarian, this lurks unsuspected by the native. Consider the pain given to the very objects of their devotion by Shelley and Tolstoi. A little human silliness and weakness would have been much more productive of human happiness! Man shall not live by syllogisms alone, even though each one be an ideal formula for the production of perfection.

The following well known persons were also born with Mercury in the sign Virgo:

Leo Tolstoi
Lord Roberts
H. H. Asquith
Maeterlinck
Blavatsky
Jane Addams
Lyman Abbott
Oliver Wendell Holmes
Kate Douglas Wiggin

Dr. Felix Adler
Nathan Haskell Dole
Charles G. Dawes

For the benefit of those who are not in possession of Raphael's Ephemeris, or who are not able to interpret the symbols contained therein, the years where Mercury is in Virgo are as follows:

From	September	8th	through	September	24th	1840
	September	1st	"	September	16th	1841
	August	24th	"	September	8th	1842
	August	16th	"	September	1st	1843
	August	7th	"	August	26th	1844
	October	5th	"	October	9th	1844
	July	31st	"	October	6th	1845
	July	26th	"	August	28th	1846
	September	11th	"	September	29th	1846
	September	6th	"	September	21st	1847
	August	28th	"	September	12th	1848
	August	20th	"	September	5th	1849
	August	12th	"	August	29th	1850
	August	4th	"	August	26th	1851
	September	21st	"	October	10th	1851
	July	28th	"	October	3d	1852
	July	27th	"	August	11th	1853
	September	9th	"	September	25th	1853
	September	2d	"	September	17th	1854
	August	25th	"	September	10th	1855
	August	16th	"	September	2d	1856
	August	8th	"	August	27th	1857
	August	1st	"	August	29th	1858
	September	4th	"	October	8th	1858
	July	27th	"	September	4th	1859
	September	10th	"	September	30th	1859
	September	6th	"	September	21st	1860
	August	30th	"	September	14th	1861
	August	21st	"	September	6th	1862
	August	13th	"	August	30th	1863

From	August	5th	through	August	25th	1864
	September	25th	"	October	10th	1864
	July	29th	"	October	4th	1865
	July	26th	"	August	18th	1866
	September	10th	"	September	27th	1866
	September	4th	"	September	19th	1867
	August	26th	"	September	10th	1868
	August	18th	"	September	3d	1869
	August	10th	"	August	28th	1870
	August	2d	"	August	26th	1871
	September	12th	"	October	9th	1871
	July	27th	"	October	1st	1872
	September	8th	"	September	23d	1873
	August	31st	"	September	15th	1874
	August	23d	"	September	8th	1875
	August	14th	"	August	31st	1876
	August	6th	"	August	26th	1877
	October	1st	"	October	10th	1877
	July	30th	"	October	5th	1878
	July	26th	"	August	24th	1879
	September	11th	"	September	28th	1879
	September	4th	"	September	19th	1880
	August	27th	"	September	11th	1881
	August	19th	"	September	4th	1882
	August	11th	"	August	29th	1883
	August	3d	"	August	25th	1884
	September	17th	"	October	9th	1884
	July	28th	"	October	2d	1885
	July	29th	"	August	6th	1886
	September	9th	"	September	24th	1886
	September	2d	"	September	17th	1887
	August	23d	"	September	8th	1888
	August	15th	"	September	1st	1889
	August	7th	"	August	26th	1890
	July	31st	"	October	7th	1891
	July	26th	"	August	29th	1892
	September	10th	"	September	29th	1892
	September	6th	"	September	21st	1893

From	August	29th	through	September	13th	1894
	August	21st	"	September	5th	1895
	August	11th	"	August	29th	1896
	August	4th	"	August	25th	1897
	September	22d	"	October	10th	1897
	July	29th	"	October	4th	1898
	July	27th	"	August	14th	1899
	September	10th	"	September	26th	1899
	September	3d	"	September	18th	1900
	August	26th	"	September	10th	1901
	August	18th	"	September	3d	1902
	August	10th	"	August	28th	1903
	August	2d	"	August	27th	1904
	September	8th	"	October	8th	1904
	July	27th	"	October	1st	1905
	September	8th	"	September	23d	1906
	August	31st	"	September	15th	1907
	August	22d	"	September	7th	1908
	August	14th	"	August	31st	1909
	August	6th	"	August	26th	1910
	September	29th	"	October	11th	1910
	July	31st	"	October	6th	1911
	July	26th	"	August	20th	1912
	September	11th	"	September	27th	1912
	September	4th	"	September	19th	1913
	August	27th	"	September	12th	1914
	August	19th	"	September	4th	1915
	August	10th	"	August	28th	1916
	August	3d	"	August	26th	1917
	September	15th	"	October	9th	1917
	July	28th	"	October	2d	1918
	September	9th	"	September	25th	1919
	September	1st	"	September	16th	1920
	August	24th	"	September	8th	1921
	August	15th	"	September	1st	1922
	August	8th	"	August	27th	1923
	October	5th	"	October	11th	1923
	July	31st	"	October	6th	1924

From					
From July	26th	through	August	26th	1925
September	11th	"	September	29th	1925
September	6th	"	September	21st	1926
August	29th	"	September	13th	1927
August	20th	"	September	5th	1928
August	12th	"	August	29th	1929

MERCURY IN LIBRA

The fine and delicate judgment given by Mercury in Libra is at once its virtue and its vice; for in practical matters rough-and-ready decision is often of more value than accuracy, and the insistence on the latter which this position gives, if exaggerated, means hesitation, vacillation, and delay. There is generally a quick intuitive flash of conviction followed by the attempt to weigh the decision logically, which is often dangerous. The better policy would be to train the mind to follow its intuitions. It is the old story of the ass who starved between two thistles because he could not decide which he would eat first. In matters where mind is the sole consideration, however, Libra is as good a sign as can be found for Mercury. The Venusian nature softens the metallic coldness of the Mercurial nature, and Saturn being exalted in Libra, there is an added element of wisdom which pure reason lacks. The real drawback is in the airy nature of the sign, which may give a certain looseness and even frivolity to the disposition of the mind. There is usually great ambition for intellectual accomplishments, but little inclination to labor to attain them. The mind easily becomes distracted; sometimes we may find the native "Jack of all trades, and master of none," as the saying goes.

Such people, too, have the defect common to the open mind; they form an opinion after long and careful study, and yet may abandon it at a moment's notice on quite inadequate grounds. The sensitive balance of the mind makes it very difficult to speak positively about such people without the fullest study of the whole horoscope. With this position we find the most varied accomplishments. Great mystics and artists like Coleridge, great lexicographers like Sir Richard Quain, great statesmen like Kruger, great lawyers like Lord Brougham, great theologians like Savonarola, great scholars like Erasmus, great philosophers like Cornelius Agrippa, great rulers like Queen Elizabeth, great actresses like Mrs. Langtry, great courtesans like Cleo de Mérode—all come under this possibility. One cannot tell merely from the position itself along what lines the mind may move, or even how it will work, as Mercury in this sign is more sensitive and pliable than in any other.

The position may, however, be called good; it is rare to find a thoroughly incompetent mentality with Mercury in this sign; such an event is unlikely to occur unless there be serious affliction. Unless, however, there are some good aspects to strengthen Mercury, the mind is likely to be shallow.

The following well known persons were also born with Mercury in the sign Libra:

Alfred Dreyfus
Lily Langtry
Whitelaw Reid
Spencer Trask
Christabel Pankhurst
Henry George
Eleanor Gates
Von Hindenburg
William O. Stoddard
David Graham Phillips
Edward W. Bok
MacMonnies
Ramsay MacDonald

For the benefit of those who are not in possession of Raphael's Ephemeris, or who are not able to interpret the symbol contained therein, the years when Mercury is in the sign Libra, are as follows:

From	September	25th	through	October	12th	1840
	September	17th	"	October	5th	1841
	September	9th	"	September	29th	1842
	September	2d	"	September	29th	1843
	October	7th	"	November	8th	1843
	August	27th	"	October	4th	1844
	October	10th	"	October	31st	1844

From	October	7th	through	October	24th	1845
	September	30th	"	October	16th	1846
	September	22d	"	October	9th	1847
	September	13th	"	October	1st	1848
	September	6th	"	September	27th	1849
	October	26th	"	November	10th	1849
	August	30th	"	November	5th	1850
	August	27th	"	September	20th	1851
	October	11th	"	October	29th	1851
	October	4th	"	October	20th	1852
	September	26th	"	October	13th	1853
	September	18th	"	October	6th	1854
	September	11th	"	September	30th	1855
	September	3d	"	September	26th	1856
	October	13th	"	November	8th	1856
	August	28th	"	November	2d	1857
	August	30th	"	September	3d	1858
	October	9th	"	October	25th	1858
	October	1st	"	October	18th	1859
	September	22d	"	October	9th	1860
	September	15th	"	October	3d	1861
	September	7th	"	September	27th	1862
	October	31st	"	November	11th	1862
	August	31st	"	November	6th	1863
	August	26th	"	September	24th	1864
	October	11th	"	October	29th	1864
	October	5th	"	October	22d	1865
	September	28th	"	October	14th	1866
	September	20th	"	October	7th	1867
	September	11th	"	September	30th	1868
	September	4th	"	September	26th	1869
	October	18th	"	November	9th	1869
	August	29th	"	November	3d	1870
	August	27th	"	September	11th	1871
	October	10th	"	October	27th	1871
	October	2d	"	October	18th	1872
	September	24th	"	October	11th	1873
	September	16th	"	October	4th	1874

From September	9th	through	September	28th	1875
November	6th	"	November	10th	1875
September	1st	"	November	6th	1876
August	27th	"	September	30th	1877
October	11th	"	October	31st	1877
October	6th	"	October	23d	1878
September	29th	"	October	16th	1879
September	20th	"	October	7th	1880
September	12th	"	October	1st	1881
September	5th	"	September	27th	1882
October	23d	"	November	10th	1882
August	30th	"	November	4th	1883
August	26th	"	September	16th	1884
October	10th	"	October	27th	1884
October	3d	"	October	19th	1885
September	25th	"	October	12th	1886
September	18th	"	October	5th	1887
September	9th	"	September	28th	1888
September	2nd	"	September	27th	1889
October	9th	"	November	8th	1889
August	27th	"	November	1st	1890
October	8th	"	October	24th	1891
September	30th	"	October	16th	1892
September	22d	"	October	9th	1893
September	14th	"	October	2d	1894
September	6th	"	September	27th	1895
October	28th	"	November	11th	1895
August	30th	"	November	4th	1896
August	26th	"	September	21st	1897
October	11th	"	October	28th	1897
October	5th	"	October	21st	1898
September	27th	"	October	13th	1899
September	19th	"	October	6th	1900
September	11th	"	September	30th	1901
September	4th	"	September	27th	1902
October	16th	"	November	10th	1902
August	29th	"	November	3d	1903
August	28th	"	September	7th	1904

From October	9th	through	October	26th	1904
October	2d	"	October	18th	1905
September	24th	"	October	11th	1906
September	16th	"	October	4th	1907
September	8th	"	September	28th	1908
November	2d	"	November	11th	1908
September	1st	"	November	7th	1909
August	27th	"	September	28th	1910
October	12th	"	October	31st	1910
October	7th	"	October	23d	1911
September	28th	"	October	15th	1912
September	20th	"	October	8th	1913
September	13th	"	October	1st	1914
September	5th	"	September	27th	1915
October	21st	"	November	11th	1915
August	29th	"	November	4th	1916
August	27th	"	September	14th	1917
October	10th	"	October	27th	1917
October	3d	"	October	20th	1918
September	26th	"	October	12th	1919
September	17th	"	October	4th	1920
September	9th	"	September	29th	1921
September	2d	"	September	30th	1922
October	5th	"	November	8th	1922
August	28th	"	October	4th	1923
October	12th	"	November	1st	1923
October	7th	"	October	24th	1924
September	30th	"	October	16th	1925
September	22d	"	October	9th	1926
September	14th	"	October	2d	1927
September	6th	"	September	27th	1928
October	25th	"	November	10th	1928
August	30th	"	November	5th	1929

MERCURY IN SCORPIO

In Scorpio Mercury is "quick and powerful, sharper than a two-edged sword." No other position so thoroughly accentuates the fierce acuteness of the mind. People with Mercury in this sign are far-seeing and clear-sighted; it is almost impossible to deceive them, but on the contrary they are often over-critical and sometimes incurably suspicious. The thought is bitter and eager, often vitriolic, and the word follows suit. They have an uncanny faculty of knowing exactly where to wound. They make admirable vivisectors on every plane, and they are usually quite unscrupulous in their methods and careless of what pain they may inflict. Furthermore, they are intensely secretive; they hate to commit themselves to any positive statement, but their capacity for insinuation and innuendo may well be described as infernal. They make the most dangerous enemies, and in some cases (though, fortunately, this is rare) there is something of the snake in their temperament, and they may turn suddenly and treacherously upon their antagonists. They make excellent secret-service men. They are capable of long continued dissimulation and, the imagination being exceedingly vivid, they are well fitted to deceive others. With all these qualities, goes an intense skepticism, an intolerance of the opinions of others whom they regard as inferior, and a supreme contempt for those who disagree with them. On the other hand, the secretive side of the sign may sometimes develop as mysticism or some profound interest in secret societies (particularly, of course, when Mercury is in the twelfth house) or in hidden and obscure matters of one sort or another. They have tremendous capacity for investigation and are quite ruthless in their methods. These qualities often coöperate to bring about success, and some of the most profound seekers into the mysteries of life have this position of Mercury.

This is exemplified in its highest and best form by William Blake, probably the most profound mystic that the English race has produced. The activity of mind and the love for secret subjects of thought are shown in the horoscope of Robert Louis Stevenson. The particular determinants of this matter are discussed more fully in another place.

Martin Luther exemplifies very clearly the critical, militant, destructive tone of the mind, conferred by this position. Truth, as he saw it, was his God, and he could see Europe plunged into every kind of horror, sooner than abandon a theological thesis which a mind of broader humanity might have considered trivial.

An example of the vigorous eloquence and keen critical instincts of this position manifesting in matters of less universal importance is given by John Bright, and of these same qualities in more intense form by Theodore Roosevelt and Winston Churchill. W. S. Gilbert, the greatest of the social satirists of the Victorian Age, has Mercury in this sign.

Something of the brilliancy and secretiveness, with a most unfortunate turn, not only for repartee, which made him enemies, but for obscure thoughts, which gave them their weapon against him, is shown in the nativity of Oscar Wilde.

The following well known persons were born with Mercury in the sign Scorpio:

Winston Churchill
Ex-President James A. Garfield
John Bright
William Blake
Oscar Wilde
Robert Louis Stevenson
Gandhi
Theodore Roosevelt
Eugene Debs
Andrew Carnegie
George H. Lorimer

For the benefit of those who are not in possession of Raphael's Ephemeris, or who are not able to interpret the symbols contained therein, the years when Mercury is in the sign Scorpio are as follows:

From	October	13th	through	November	1st	1840
	October	6th	"	October	29th	1841
	November	12th	"	December	10th	1841
	September	30th	"	December	4th	1842
	September	30th	"	October	6th	1843
	November	9th	"	November	27th	1843
	November	1st	"	November	19th	1844
	October	25th	"	November	12th	1845

From	October	17th	through	November	5th	1846
	October	10th	"	October	31st	1847
	November	29th	"	December	13th	1847
	October	2d	"	December	8th	1848
	September	28th	"	October	25th	1849
	November	11th	"	December	1st	1849
	November	6th	"	November	24th	1850
	October	30th	"	November	16th	1851
	October	21st	"	November	8th	1852
	October	14th	"	November	2d	1853
	October	7th	"	October	29th	1854
	November	17th	"	December	11th	1854
	October	1st	"	December	5th	1855
	September	27th	"	October	12th	1856
	November	9th	"	November	27th	1856
	November	3d	"	November	20th	1857
	October	26th	"	November	13th	1858
	October	19th	"	November	6th	1859
	October	10th	"	October	30th	1860
	December	3d	"	December	12th	1860
	October	4th	"	December	9th	1861
	September	28th	"	October	30th	1862
	November	12th	"	December	2d	1862
	November	7th	"	November	25th	1863
	October	30th	"	November	17th	1864
	October	23d	"	November	10th	1865
	October	15th	"	November	3d	1866
	October	8th	"	October	29th	1867
	November	22nd	"	December	12th	1867
	October	1st	"	December	6th	1868
	September	27th	"	October	17th	1869
	November	10th	"	November	29th	1869
	November	4th	"	November	22d	1870
	October	28th	"	November	14th	1871
	October	19th	"	November	6th	1872
	October	12th	"	October	31st	1873
	October	5th	"	October	30th	1874
	November	8th	"	December	10th	1874

From	September	29th	through	November	5th	1875
	November	11th	"	December	3d	1875
	November	7th	"	November	25th	1876
	November	1st	"	November	18th	1877
	October	24th	"	November	11th	1878
	October	17th	"	November	4th	1879
	October	8th	"	October	29th	1880
	November	25th	"	December	12th	1880
	October	2d	"	December	7th	1881
	September	28th	"	October	22d	1882
	November	11th	"	November	30th	1882
	November	5th	"	November	23d	1883
	October	28th	"	November	15th	1884
	October	20th	"	November	8th	1885
	October	13th	"	November	1st	1886
	October	6th	"	October	29th	1887
	November	14th	"	December	11th	1887
	September	29th	"	December	4th	1888
	September	28th	"	October	8th	1889
	November	9th	"	November	27th	1889
	November	2d	"	November	19th	1890
	October	25th	"	November	12th	1891
	October	17th	"	November	4th	1892
	October	10th	"	October	30th	1893
	November	30th	"	December	12th	1893
	October	3d	"	December	8th	1894
	September	28th	"	October	27th	1895
	November	12th	"	December	1st	1895
	November	5th	"	November	23d	1896
	October	29th	"	November	16th	1897
	October	22d	"	November	9th	1898
	October	14th	"	November	2d	1899
	October	7th	"	October	29th	1900
	November	19th	"	December	12th	1900
	October	1st	"	December	6th	1901
	September	28th	"	October	15th	1902
	November	11th	"	November	29th	1902
	November	4th	"	November	22d	1903

From	October	27th	through	November	14th	1904
	October	19th	"	November	7th	1905
	October	12th	"	November	1st	1906
	December	7th	"	December	12th	1906
	October	5th	"	December	10th	1907
	September	29th	"	November	1st	1908
	November	12th	"	December	3d	1908
	November	8th	"	November	26th	1909
	November	1st	"	November	18th	1910
	October	24th	"	November	11th	1911
	October	16th	"	November	4th	1912
	October	9th	"	October	30th	1913
	November	24th	"	December	12th	1913
	October	2d	"	December	7th	1914
	September	28th	"	October	20th	1915
	November	12th	"	November	30th	1915
	November	5th	"	November	22d	1916
	October	28th	"	November	15th	1917
	October	21st	"	November	8th	1918
	October	13th	"	November	2d	1919
	October	5th	"	October	30th	1920
	November	11th	"	December	10th	1920
	September	30th	"	December	4th	1921
	October	1st	"	October	4th	1922
	November	9th	"	November	27th	1922
	November	2d	"	November	20th	1923
	October	25th	"	November	11th	1924
	October	17th	"	November	5th	1925
	October	10th	"	October	30th	1926
	November	28th	"	December	13th	1926
	October	3d	"	December	8th	1927
	September	28th	"	October	24th	1928
	November	11th	"	December	1st	1928
	November	6th	"	November	23d	1929

MERCURY IN SAGITTARIUS

In considering Mercury in Sagittarius it should be remembered how brilliant and sudden is the effect of Sagittarius, but how lightning-like and transitory. The older astrologers, indeed, attributed even lightning rather to Aries, leaving only the rainbow for Sagittarius, as if the effect were not merely swift, but, to a certain degree, illusory. This, however, is only the case with a badly aspected Mercury. Too much importance should not be given to the fact that Mercury in this sign has always been considered in his detriment. For we have seen that this planet very easily becomes unbalanced and the Jupiterian influence of Sagittarius seems to act rather as the restraining hand of a father upon an impetuous and wayward child. Much, however, will always depend upon aspects.

The general qualities of this position are directness of thought and expression. People with Mercury thus placed usually speak without reflection—they tend to say whatever comes into their heads. They do not wound deliberately, like people with Mercury in Scorpio. It simply never occurs to them to think how their remarks may strike the hearer. The quality of their thoughts is similarly unripe. Their thoughts are like mushrooms or shooting stars. They are impatient; speak in haste and repent at leisure. They do not trouble to formulate a judgment, and what they say consequently partakes too often of the nature of the shallower form of epigram. This same absence of the reflective quality makes them extremely simple, honest and sincere (duplicity by its very nature involves the balancing of truth and falsehood), and if these people lie, they only do so on the spur of the moment. A long continued course of deception is entirely out of their power. It would, too, be repugnant to their nature.

Another difficulty caused by this position is that the thoughts are disconnected, and, though the native may promise with sincerity, or conceive undertakings with earnestness, he often has not the patience enabling him to make good. What he thinks and says, however, is sometimes remarkably, one might almost say irrationally, right. He may speak like an oracle, and his intuition is often so extraordinarily acute that it more than replaces the general weaknesses of the faculties of memory and of ratiocination. Another characteristic trait conferred by this position is a habit of interruption. No sooner do these people hear anything than a thought strikes them and they have to say it without a moment's delay.

The discontinuous and flitterbat quality of this type of mind is very well shown by the anarchist Vaillant, every one of whose thoughts was probably right in its way, but who was totally incapable of weighing one thought against another and of striking a balance. An almost equally bad example is Marie Bashkirtseff, who totally failed to understand the universe into which she was born, owing to a similar defect. Her diary is full of brilliant, bitter, satirical things, all of which are perfectly true in themselves and yet totally false because they are not balanced against the weight of general experience.

Another bright, brilliant, but brief and unbalanced mind was that of Thomas Chatterton, whose genius, had it been accompanied by a mind capable of patient labor, might have placed him in the small first circle of English poets. The case of Dr. Zamenhof is a good illustration. In Esperanto, he invented a language which is eminently convenient and easy to learn and has all the other advantages that a language should have. It has only one defect, which is that it really is not a language at all and nobody seems to wish to speak it.

To show this quality of incapacity for reflection in its most complete absurdity, we need only recall the remark of Marie Antoinette, who had Mercury in this position, and who, being offered some exquisite pastry by the leading confectioner of Paris, exclaimed, "The stupid people are always complaining that they can get no bread, but why do they not eat these delicious little cakes?" Another monarch almost equally silly and unfortunate with this position is Charles I, the inconstancy of whose domestic policy cost him his throne and his life.

Fortunately, however, this position does not always result in such sparkling imbecility. We have three quite great people in the world of art and literature with this position, Sir David Wilkie, Alfred de Musset, and Rudyard Kipling. The limitation is nevertheless still visible. Both the French and the English writers excel in short stories and poems, but neither has written great novels. Similarly, Sir David Wilkie, admirable painter as he was, never attained to the sustained execution of a great canvas. Another example is in the Mercury of Joan of Arc, though the planet's being in the 29th degree may have done something to steady matters. There is, however, little need for making this reservation, as her career was singularly fitful and she depended entirely upon inspiration.

The greatest exception to all that has been said is Sir Isaac Newton, but here Mercury is in the third house, with a sextile of Venus and a square of Saturn. Jupiter, lord of the third, is within six degrees of the conjunction of Saturn, and is exactly trined by Uranus, while the Sun, also in the third house, stands sextile to all three. The whole configuration is of the most extraordinary power, with every planet in heaven which tends to stability included in it, even Mars in Taurus assisting by making a near sextile with the Moon. With such great dignities the influence of the sign itself is reduced to a minimum. The fact that the Lord of the sign is in conjunction with Saturn tends to alter its very nature, and there is therefore no comparison with ordinary cases, where the action of Mercury is more or less isolated. In the horoscope of Marie Antoinette, Mercury is trine to Neptune, but square to Uranus which takes away all its more serious qualities. There is slight help from a semi-sextile of Venus and a sextile of Jupiter, but as has been well said, Mercury without Saturn is like an egg without salt.

The following well known persons were born with Mercury in the sign Sagittarius:

Felix Faure
George Eliot
Rudyard Kipling
Marie Bashkirtseff
Sir Isaac Newton
Edward VII
Hamilton Wright Mabie
Louisa M. Alcott
Henry Van Dyke
Agassiz
Bishop Fallows
President Lowell of Harvard

For the benefit of those who are not in possession of Raphael's Ephemeris, or who are not able to interpret the symbols therein, the years when Mercury is in Sagittarius are as follows:

From	January	1st	through	January	13th	1840
	November	2d	"	December	31st	1840
	January	1st	"	January	6th	1841
	October	30th	"	November	11th	1841
	December	11th	"	December	31st	1841
	December	5th	"	December	23rd	1842
	November	28th	"	December	16th	1843
	November	20th	"	December	8th	1844
	November	13th	"	December	2d	1845
	January	2d	"	January	13th	1846
	November	6th	"	December	31st	1846
	January	1st	"	January	10th	1847
	November	1st	"	November	28th	1847
	December	14th	"	December	31st	1847
	January	1st	"	January	4th	1848
	December	9th	"	December	27th	1848
	December	2d	"	December	20th	1849
	November	25th	"	December	13th	1850
	November	17th	"	December	6th	1851
	November	9th	"	November	30th	1852
	December	20th	"	December	31st	1852
	January	1st	"	January	13th	1853
	November	3d	"	December	31st	1853
	January	1st	"	January	8th	1854
	October	30th	"	November	16th	1854
	December	12th	"	December	31st	1854
	January	1st	"			1855
	December	6th	"	December	25th	1855
	November	28th	"	December	17th	1856
	November	21st	"	December	9th	1857
	November	14th	"	December	3d	1858
	January	9th	"	January	11th	1859
	November	7th	"	December	2d	1859
	December	7th	"	December	31st	1859
	January	1st	"	January	11th	1860
	October	31st	"	December	2d	1860
	December	13th	"	December	31st	1860
	January	1st	"	January	4th	1861

From	December	10th	through	December	29th	1861
	December	3d	"	December	21st	1862
	November	26th	"	December	14th	1863
	November	18th	"	December	6th	1864
	November	11th	"	December	1st	1865
	December	25th	"	December	31st	1865
	January	1st	"	January	13th	1866
	November	4th	"	December	31st	1866
	January	1st	"	January	9th	1867
	October	30th	"	November	21st	1867
	December	13th	"	December	31st	1867
	January	1st	"	January	2d	1868
	December	7th	"	December	25th	1868
	November	30th	"	December	18th	1869
	November	23d	"	December	11th	1870
	November	15th	"	December	4th	1871
	November	7th	"	November	30th	1872
	December	12th	"	December	31st	1872
	January	1st	"	January	11th	1873
	November	1st	"	December	31st	1873
	January	1st	"	January	6th	1874
	October	31st	"	November	7th	1874
	December	11th	"	December	30th	1874
	December	4th	"	December	23d	1875
	November	26th	"	December	14th	1876
	November	19th	"	December	7th	1877
	November	12th	"	December	2d	1878
	December	30th	"	December	31st	1878
	January	1st	"	January	13th	1879
	November	5th	"	December	31st	1879
	January	1st	"	January	10th	1880
	October	30th	"	November	24th	1880
	December	13th	"	December	31st	1880
	January	1st	"	January	3d	1881
	December	8th	"	December	26th	1881
	December	1st	"	December	19th	1882
	November	24th	"	December	12th	1883
	November	16th	"	December	4th	1884

From	November	9th	through	November	30th	1885
	December	17th	"	December	31st	1885
	January	1st	"	January	12th	1886
	November	2d	"	December	31st	1886
	January	1st	"	January	7th	1887
	October	30th	"	November	13th	1887
	December	12th	"	December	31st	1887
	December	5th	"	December	23d	1888
	November	28th	"	December	16th	1889
	November	20th	"	December	9th	1890
	November	13th	"	December	3d	1891
	January	4th	"	January	13th	1892
	November	5th	"	December	31st	1892
	January	1st	"	January	10th	1893
	October	31st	"	November	29th	1893
	December	13th	"	December	31st	1893
	January	1st	"	January	4th	1894
	December	9th	"	December	28th	1894
	December	2d	"	December	21st	1895
	November	24th	"	December	12th	1896
	November	17th	"	December	6th	1897
	November	10th	"	November	30th	1898
	December	22d	"	December	31st	1898
	January	1st	"	January	13th	1899
	November	3d	"	December	31st	1899
	January	1st	"	January	8th	1900
	October	30th	"	November	18th	1900
	December	13th	"	December	31st	1900
	January	1st	"	January	2d	1901
	December	7th	"	December	25th	1901
	November	30th	"	December	18th	1902
	November	23d	"	December	11th	1903
	November	15th	"	December	4th	1904
	November	8th	"	December	1st	1905
	December	10th	"	December	31st	1905
	January	1st	"	January	12th	1906
	November	2d	"	December	6th	1906
	December	13th	"	December	31st	1906

From	January	1st	through	January	6th	1907
	December	11th	"	December	30th	1907
	December	4th	"	December	22d	1908
	November	27th	"	December	15th	1909
	November	19th	"	December	8th	1910
	November	12th	"	December	2d	1911
	December	28th	"	December	31st	1911
	January	1st	"	January	14th	1912
	November	5th	"	December	31st	1912
	January	1st	"	January	9th	1913
	October	31st	"	November	23d	1913
	December	13th	"	December	31st	1913
	January	1st	"	January	3d	1914
	December	8th	"	December	27th	1914
	December	1st	"	December	19th	1915
	November	23d	"	December	11th	1916
	November	16th	"	December	5th	1917
	November	9th	"	December	1st	1918
	December	16th	"	December	31st	1918
	January	1st	"	January	13th	1919
	November	3d	"	December	31st	1919
	January	1st	"	January	7th	1920
	October	31st	"	November	10th	1920
	December	11th	"	December	30th	1920
	December	5th	"	December	23d	1921
	November	28th	"	December	16th	1922
	November	21st	"	December	9th	1923
	November	12th	"	December	2d	1924
	January	1st	"	January	13th	1925
	November	6th	"	December	31st	1925
	January	1st	"	January	10th	1926
	October	31st	"	November	27th	1926
	December	14th	"	December	31st	1926
	January	1st	"	January	4th	1927
	December	9th	"	December	28th	1927
	December	2d	"	December	20th	1928
	November	24th	"	December	13th	1929

MERCURY IN CAPRICORNUS

In Capricornus the admirable influence of Saturn upon Mercury is emphasized by the influence of Saturn's sign. Capricornus lends to Mercury the utmost gravity, dignity, steadfastness, earnestness, comprehensiveness, and power. The memory is usually splendid and the power of concentration is no less good than that of attention to detail. Sometimes these qualities may be over-emphasized. There is now and again a tendency to the lack of a sense of humor, and sometimes this operates as a serious defect. This is particularly true when the environment of the mind is unsuited to this disposition. People with Mercury in Capricornus may sometimes be a little like the skeleton at the feast. They are apt to be bores—they are incapable of frivolity, even at a picnic, and they are likely to be annoyed without cause at what they may think the shallowness of other people, though sometimes those people may merely be laughing at their misplaced seriousness. In youth, this position of Mercury gives what is called an "old head on young shoulders." There is some disposition to sullenness or sulking. The child seems to be rapt in its own thought; very likely it prefers solitude and does not care for play.

The mind is careful to examine closely any facts which may be presented to it, and it is inclined to suspicion, especially to the suspicion that other people are laughing at it. There is a very strong sense of causality and the reasoning powers generally are admirable. There is no tendency for the mind to waver, but it sometimes shifts violently from one idea to another or from one mood to another. There is very little real joyousness in the mind and the native is often the subject of quite unreasonable fear and liable to fits of depression which may end by endangering the reason. There being so much already of Saturn in the character of the sign itself, aspects of Saturn are sometimes to be feared, as likely to overwhelm altogether the natural elasticity. The unfriendly influence of Neptune and Uranus and even of Mars is equally dangerous. Conjunctions of the Sun may, however, be relied upon largely to counteract any such tendency.

It is very necessary for people with this position of Mercury to cultivate optimism. Good aspects of Venus are decidedly useful in making this possible. If they fail to conceal the general gravity of their disposition, they may find themselves unpopular with the majority of people. They should also be careful to avoid the expression of the often sardonic thought which is one of their characteristics, and they should not give utterance to the rebuke which is very ready on their tongue. These people are very censorious, stern and intolerant. Unless Mercury is well-aspected, they do not make sufficient allowance for the idiosyncracies of other people.

This type of mind is to be distinguished carefully from the critical type, such as we saw in Scorpio. Mercury in Capricornus is not at all critical—its aggressiveness is of a totally different character. The native always knows that he is right and nothing can persuade him of the contrary or even make him listen to arguments. Very often this temperament is associated with extremely narrow views of religion, and the fixity of the mind may not infrequently seem grossly tyrannical to those associated with the native. The attitude is very much that of the schoolmaster. Whenever such people are "dressed in a little brief authority," they are likely to become even more tyrannical than before. The position also develops an extreme degree of diplomacy which in many cases renders the native very clever in gaining his ends.

In the best cases, those in which the general horoscope indicates the possibilities of real greatness, the bad side of these qualities does not develop in such petty manner, and we have plenty of examples of really admirable characters with this position. In such cases, one must read only the nobler characteristics hitherto mentioned, and even these must be emphasized and expanded.

The founders of Christianity and of Mormonism were both born with this position of Mercury. It seems an admirable position for statesmen. The great protagonists of Victorian politics, Disraeli, and Gladstone, both had it. In Science we find this postion in the nativities of Pasteur, Davy, Alfred Russell Wallace, and Havelock Ellis; while literature is represented by Lord Byron, Dickens, Lewis Carroll, Sainte Beuve, and Ruskin. It will be particularly noticed how excellently capable of laborious, steady constructiveness were all these minds. Even in the case of Lewis Carroll, it must not be forgotten that his real life was that of a mathematician of a very high order.

These people should all be compared and contrasted with the list given under Mercury in Sagittarius. Note the entire difference in the capacity for continuous construction. The more scholarly type of soldier, the organizing general is also represented in this position by General Gordon. Special attention should be paid to the integrity of this man's mind. Wilhelm II may also be mentioned as an example of a patient, laborious thinker, and in the less exalted, yet truly noble field, we have Sir Isaac Pitman. The task that he set himself recalls that of Dr. Zamenhof previously mentioned under Sagittarius, and here again the contrast between the effect of the two signs is salient. Pitman was no visionary. Common sense was his long suit, and the results have been the practically universal adoption of his system of shorthand. By so far does patience exceed enthusiasm.

As examples of the depressing and constricting effects of this sign, we have Henry VI of England and Mary, Queen of Scots. Here there was evidently much incapacity to modify the mind to the exigencies of the situation. In comparing these two monarchs with the statesmen mentioned in previous paragraphs, one must consider the effect of the environment. There are situations in politics where it is decidedly better to be rigid and aggressive; in others, the only policy is to appear to yield.

The following well known persons were born with Mercury in the sign Capricorn:

Benjamin Disraeli
Lord Byron
William Gladstone
General Gordon
Charles Dickens
Lewis Carroll
Alfred Wallace
Sir Isaac Pitman
Louis Pasteur
John Ruskin
Havelock Ellis
Roy Howard
Arthur Brisbane

Stanley Hall
Horatio Dresser
Admiral Dewey
Will Levington Comfort
Edith Cavell
Augustus Thomas
Gelett Burgess
Hudson Maxim
Richard Le Gallienne
Woodrow Wilson

For the benefit of those who art not in possession of Raphael's Ephemeris, or who are not able to interpret the symbols contained therein, the years when Mercury is in the sign Capricorn are as follows:

From	January	14th	through	February	3d	1840
	January	7th	"	January	26th	1841
	January	1st	"	January	18th	1842
	December	24th	"	December	31st	1842
	January	1st	"	January	11th	1843
	December	17th	"	December	31st	1843
	January	1st	"	January	4th	1844
	February	9th	"	February	12th	1844
	December	9th	"	December	31st	1844
	January	1st	"	February	12th	1845
	December	3d	"	December	31st	1845
	January	1st	"			1846
	January	14th	"	February	6th	1846
	January	11th	"	January	31st	1847
	January	5th	"	January	23d	1848
	December	28th	"	December	31st	1848
	January	1st	"	January	15th	1849
	December	21st	"	December	31st	1849
	January	1st	"	January	7th	1850
	December	14th	"	December	31st	1850
	January	1st	"			1851
	January	24th	"	February	15th	1851
	December	7th	"	December	31st	1851

From	January	1st	through	February	11th	1852
	December	1st	"	December	19th	1852
	January	14th	"	February	3d	1853
	January	9th	"	January	27th	1854
	January	2d	"	January	20th	1855
	December	26th	"	December	31st	1855
	January	1st	"	January	12th	1856
	December	18th	"	December	31st	1856
	January	1st	"	January	4th	1857
	December	10th	"	December	31st	1857
	January	11th	"	February	13th	1858
	December	4th	"	December	31st	1858
	January	1st	"	January	8th	1859
	January	12th	"	February	8th	1859
	December	3d	"	December	6th	1859
	January	12th	"	February	1st	1860
	January	5th	"	January	24th	1861
	December	30th	"	December	31st	1861
	January	1st	"	January	16th	1862
	December	22d	"	December	31st	1862
	January	1st	"	January	9th	1863
	December	15th	"	December	31st	1863
	January	1st	"	January	2d	1864
	January	29th	"	February	15th	1864
	December	7th	"	December	31st	1864
	January	1st	"	February	11th	1865
	December	2d	"	December	24th	1865
	January	14th	"	February	5th	1866
	January	10th	"	January	28th	1867
	January	3d	"	January	21st	1868
	December	26th	"	December	31st	1868
	January	1st	"	January	13th	1869
	December	19th	"	December	31st	1869
	January	1st	"	January	5th	1870
	December	12th	"	December	31st	1870
	January	16th	"	February	14th	1871
	December	5th	"	December	31st	1871
	January	1st	"	February	9th	1872

From	December	1st	through	December	11th	1872
	January	12th	"	February	1st	1873
	January	7th	"	January	25th	1874
	December	31st	"			1874
	January	1st	"	January	17th	1875
	December	24th	"	December	31st	1875
	January	1st	"	January	10th	1876
	December	15th	"	December	31st	1876
	January	1st	"	January	2d	1877
	February	3d	"	February	13th	1877
	December	8th	"	December	31st	1877
	January	1st	"	February	12th	1878
	December	3d	"	December	29th	1878
	January	14th	"	February	6th	1879
	January	11th	"	January	30th	1880
	January	4th	"	January	21st	1881
	December	27th	"	December	31st	1881
	January	1st	"	January	14th	1882
	December	20th	"	December	31st	1882
	January	1st	"	January	7th	1883
	December	13th	"	December	31st	1883
	January	1st	"			1884
	January	21st	"	February	14th	1884
	December	5th	"	December	31st	1884
	January	1st	"	February	9th	1885
	December	1st	"	December	16th	1885
	January	13th	"	February	3d	1886
	January	8th	"	January	26th	1887
	January	1st	"	January	19th	1888
	December	24th	"	December	31st	1888
	January	1st	"	January	10th	1889
	December	17th	"	December	31st	1889
	January	1st	"	January	4th	1890
	December	10th	"	December	31st	1890
	January	1st	"			1891
	January	7th	"	February	13th	1891
	December	4th	"	December	31st	1891
	January	1st	"	January	3d	1892

From	January	14th	through	February	7th	1892
	January	11th	"	January	30th	1893
	January	5th	"	January	23d	1894
	December	29th	"	December	31st	1894
	January	1st	"	January	15th	1895
	December	22d	"	December	31st	1895
	January	1st	"	January	8th	1896
	December	13th	"	December	31st	1896
	January	1st	"			1897
	January	25th	"	February	14th	1897
	December	7th	"	December	31st	1897
	January	1st	"	February	10th	1898
	December	1st	"	December	21st	1898
	January	14th	"	February	4th	1899
	January	9th	"	January	28th	1900
	January	3d	"	January	20th	1901
	December	26th	"	December	31st	1901
	January	1st	"	January	13th	1902
	December	19th	"	December	31st	1902
	January	1st	"	January	6th	1903
	December	12th	"	December	31st	1903
	January	1st	"			1904
	January	14th	"	February	14th	1904
	December	5th	"	December	31st	1904
	January	1st	"	February	8th	1905
	December	2d	"	December	9th	1905
	January	13th	"	February	1st	1906
	January	7th	"	January	25th	1907
	December	31st	"			1907
	January	1st	"	January	18th	1908
	December	23d	"	December	31st	1908
	January	1st	"	January	9th	1909
	December	16th	"	December	31st	1909
	January	1st	"	January	3d	1910
	January	31st	"	February	15th	1910
	December	9th	"	December	31st	1910
	January	1st	"	February	12th	1911
	December	3d	"	December	27th	1911

From	January	15th	through	February	6th	1912
	January	10th	"	January	29th	1913
	January	4th	"	January	22d	1914
	December	28th	"	December	31st	1914
	January	1st	"	January	14th	1915
	December	20th	"	December	31st	1915
	January	1st	"	January	7th	1916
	December	12th	"	December	31st	1916
	January	1st	"			1917
	January	18th	"	February	14th	1917
	December	6th	"	December	31st	1917
	January	1st	"	February	9th	1918
	December	2d	"	December	15th	1918
	January	14th	"	February	3d	1919
	January	8th	"	January	27th	1920
	December	31st	"			1920
	January	1st	"	January	18th	1921
	December	24th	"	December	31st	1921
	January	1st	"	January	11th	1922
	December	17th	"	December	31st	1922
	January	1st	"	January	4th	1923
	February	7th	"	February	13th	1923
	December	10th	"	December	31st	1923
	January	1st	"	February	13th	1924
	December	3d	"	December	31st	1924
	January	14th	"	February	6th	1925
	January	11th	"	January	30th	1926
	January	5th	"	January	23d	1927
	December	29th	"	December	31st	1927
	January	1st	"	January	16th	1928
	December	21st	"	December	31st	1928
	January	1st	"	January	7th	1929
	December	14th	"	December	31st	1929

MERCURY IN AQUARIUS

In Aquarius we again find the influence of Saturn decidedly beneficial to Mercury. It is an even better position for the planet than

Capricornus, since Aquarius is also air, and does not fix the mind in such stubborness as the previous sign. We must also reflect upon the good influence of the sign itself. The mind of the native having this position of Mercury tends naturally to science and humanitarianism. Its interests are not so earth-bound and selfish. There is not quite the same faculty of steady application for this very reason. One must not expect any sign to combine all the virtues and exclude all the vices. But the faculty of concentration is admirable, and the mind is ingenious, resourceful, and logical, and that in a much better sense than we found with Capricornus. The logic of Capricornus is too rigid for application to practical affairs. It reigns supreme only in the exact sciences. The native loves truth for its own sake, but more in truth as a quality than in a mere collocation of facts. He understands Newman's outburst against Huxley, "As if evidence were the test of truth!"

It may be said here that there are two general types of minds among men, and this remark of Newman's is a very touchstone by which to recognize them. To one class, Newman's remark appears a triumphant refutation of academic precision and scholastic dullness. The other is absolutely bewildered by such a remark. He cannot conceive of any other test of truth than evidence. To him the sentence appears meaningless. And yet he may be subconsciously distressed by the mere existence of any man who can say such a thing. Now, we should not like to say definitely that Mercury in Aquarius would be violently partisan on either side. On the contrary, it is just these people who understand both positions and lean strongly to neither. The antithesis on this point would be Capricornus and Pisces—the former understanding nothing that could not be proved in Barbary, the other contemptuous of all such conventional sources of knowledge. This rule will be found practically invaluable.

The native with Mercury in Aquarius is a clever reasoner, but does not altogether disdain sophistry. He consequently makes a dangerous opponent in any argument, but he is amenable to reason and he often pronounces, for the sake of exercising his wits, propositions in which he does not seriously believe. He is usually a good judge of human nature, deriving his conclusions both from intuition and from experience. Where these conflict he is sometimes found at a loss.

The weak point of this sign is the absence of artistic impulse. Even where the power of visualization is great, its expression tends to be commonplace. Compare Swedenborg, who had this position, with Blake, whose Mercury was in Scorpio, the writings of both dealing with visions of a character decidedly similar.

This sign gives a very pronounced tendency to investigations into the occult, but on lines much less mystical than we found in Scorpio. Besides Swedenborg, we have Proclus, Picus de Mirandola, and Swami Vivekananda. All these possessed immense learning, a strong power of vision, and were accurate observers and devoted students, but not one of them possessed the power of imagination in its highest sense.

As common as the capacity for research into these subtler matters of the soul is that for practical invention. In this connection one need only mention the name of Edison.

The following well known persons were born with Mercury in the sign Aquarius:

Thomas Edison
Sir Henry J. Wood
Swedenborg
Algernon Blackwood
Wilson Barrett
Richard Watson Gilder
Dean Cornwell
Horace Greeley
Henry Watterson
George Washington
Luther Burbank
Harriet Stanton Black
Dr. William S. Bainbridge
Colonel George Harvey
Emile Coué
Jack London

For the benefit of those who are not in possession of Raphael's Ephemeris, or who are not able to interpret the symbols contained therein, the years when Mercury is in the sign Aquarius are as follows:

From	February	4th	through	February	21st	1840
	January	27th	"	February	12th	1841
	January	19th	"	February	5th	1842
	January	12th	"	January	31st	1843
	February	10th	"	March	17th	1843
	January	5th	"	February	8th	1844
	February	13th	"	March	11th	1844
	February	13th	"	March	4th	1845
	February	7th	"	February	25th	1846
	February	1st	"	February	17th	1847
	January	24th	"	February	9th	1848
	January	16th	"	February	1st	1849
	March	1st	"	March	17th	1849
	January	8th	"	March	15th	1850
	January	2d	"	January	23d	1851
	February	16th	"	March	9th	1851
	February	12th	"	March	1st	1852
	February	4th	"	February	21st	1853
	January	28th	"	February	13th	1854
	January	21st	"	February	6th	1855
	January	13th	"	January	31st	1856
	February	16th	"	March	17th	1856
	January	5th	"	March	12th	1857
	January	1st	"	January	10th	1858
	February	14th	"	March	6th	1858
	February	9th	"	February	26th	1859
	February	2d	"	February	18th	1860
	January	25th	"	February	10th	1861
	January	17th	"	February	3d	1862
	March	9th	"	March	14th	1862
	January	10th	"	March	16th	1863
	January	3d	"	January	28th	1864
	February	16th	"	March	9th	1864

From	February	12th	through	March	2d	1865
	February	6th	"	February	23d	1866
	January	29th	"	February	15th	1867
	January	22d	"	February	7th	1868
	January	14th	"	January	31st	1869
	February	20th	"	March	17th	1869
	January	6th	"	March	14th	1870
	January	1st	"	January	15th	1871
	February	15th	"	March	7th	1871
	February	10th	"	February	28th	1872
	February	2d	"	February	19th	1873
	January	26th	"	February	11th	1874
	January	18th	"	February	4th	1875
	January	11th	"	February	2d	1876
	February	6th	"	March	16th	1876
	January	3d	"	February	2d	1877
	February	14th	"	March	11th	1877
	February	13th	"	March	4th	1878
	February	7th	"	February	24th	1879
	January	31st	"	February	16th	1880
	January	22d	"	February	8th	1881
	January	15th	"	February	1st	1882
	February	26th	"	March	17th	1882
	January	8th	"	March	15th	1883
	January	2d	"	January	20th	1884
	February	15th	"	March	7th	1884
	February	10th	"	February	28th	1885
	February	4th	"	February	20th	1886
	January	27th	"	February	13th	1887
	January	20th	"	February	5th	1888
	January	11th	"	January	30th	1889
	February	12th	"	March	17th	1889
	January	5th	"	March	12th	1890
	January	2d	"	January	6th	1891
	February	14th	"	March	5th	1891
	February	8th	"	February	25th	1892
	January	31st	"	February	17th	1893
	January	24th	"	February	9th	1894

From	January	16th	through	February	2d	1895
	March	4th	"	March	16th	1895
	January	9th	"	March	15th	1896
	January	2d	"	January	24th	1897
	February	15th	"	March	9th	1897
	February	11th	"	March	1st	1898
	February	5th	"	February	22d	1899
	January	29th	"	February	14th	1900
	January	21st	"	February	6th	1901
	January	14th	"	February	1st	1902
	February	18th	"	March	18th	1902
	January	7th	"	March	14th	1903
	January	2d	"	January	13th	1904
	February	15th	"	March	6th	1904
	February	9th	"	February	27th	1905
	February	2d	"	February	19th	1906
	January	26th	"	February	11th	1907
	January	19th	"	February	4th	1908
	January	10th	"	March	16th	1909
	January	4th	"	January	30th	1910
	February	16th	"	March	11th	1910
	February	13th	"	March	4th	1911
	February	7th	"	February	24th	1912
	January	30th	"	February	15th	1913
	January	23d	"	February	8th	1914
	January	15th	"	February	1st	1915
	February	24th	"	March	18th	1915
	January	8th	"	March	14th	1916
	January	2d	"	January	17th	1917
	February	15th	"	March	8th	1917
	February	10th	"	February	28th	1918
	February	4th	"	February	21st	1919
	January	28th	"	February	13th	1920
	January	19th	"	February	4th	1921
	January	12th	"	February	1st	1922
	February	9th	"	March	17th	1922
	January	5th	"	February	6th	1923
	February	14th	"	March	12th	1923

From February	14th	through	March	4th	1924
February	7th	"	February	25th	1925
January	31st	"	February	17th	1926
January	24th	"	February	9th	1927
January	17th	"	February	2d	1928
February	29th	"	March	17th	1928
January	8th	"	March	15th	1929

MERCURY IN PISCES

Too much emphasis has been laid by astrologers on the fact that Mercury is in his fall and detriment in Pisces. It is true that there is very little which can be called scientific about the mind of any native with this position. The sharp edge of the reason is usually wanting, and there is a disposition to a curious kind of mental idleness, which, however, is not really a defect. It merely means that the mind plunges itself into a bath of reflection, only to emerge purified and strengthened. However, this type of mental operation is not at all understandable by the devotees of reason, pure and simple. Those people who boast that their brains are always clear and active and who measure their achievements by the amount of visible work which they put into them cannot understand such individuals as we are now discussing. One might go further and say that they do not understand the laws under which the creative instinct works, or even the ordinary laws of generation and growth, either in the vegetable or animal kingdom.

As a matter of fact, the minds of those born with Mercury in Pisces possess one very contradictory pair of qualities. They are intensely practical in matters of thought, and tend to accept the pragmatic philosophy; they may even be utilitarians or hedonists. At the same time, they set a high value upon the conclusions of theoretical reasoning; but it does not follow from this that they will act on these conclusions. There is a fund of strong common sense in their nature and, when it comes to the test, they will follow instinct in preference to reason. In its manifestation, the mental power is far from stable. There may be periods when the mind seems almost dormant. In reality, what is happening is that the subconsciousness has taken hold and wishes to operate without interference from the more active portions of the mind. The memory is extremely retentive and the power of reflection enormous. But there is always this psychic quality in their mental processes. They make statements, *ex cathedra*, for which they cannot give chapter and verse. They know, but they do not know how they know. To people of different types of mind this often gives the idea that their knowledge is unreliable, but experience proves that this is not the case.

Their conversation, as a general rule, is fluent and subtle, but they are decidedly dependent on their environment, and, if their society is uncongenial, they keep silent. Sometimes this trait is very exaggerated; acute dislike founded upon no tangible reason throws them into a sullen mood, from which it is almost impossible to extricate them. Whenever they find themselves in harmonious surroundings, the fault will be in the other direction. They will talk too much, and, if undeveloped, are rather inclined to be talebearers and revealers of secrets. This is not because of any malice in the disposition, but because they are incapable of appreciating the amount of mischief that an unguarded word may cause.

The psychic character of Pisces causes this sign to react upon the mind when Mercury is placed therein, not only by making it sensitive to subtle influences, but also by exposing it to all the disorders which they are apt to cause unless carefully balanced by strong common sense. The mind is not robust and vigorous in the way that we find when Mercury is in a more positive and virile sign. The forces which stir it have a different kind of strength. It is the rapier, not the broadsword. The result is that heavy and long-continued strain upon the mind brings about nervous break-downs in a way which could never happen with a person whose Mercury was in Aries or Virgo.

Pisces being ruled by Neptune, and Venus being exalted therein, and there being much sympathy both with Neptune and the Moon, it is natural that the artistic temperament should find a very full development in the mind. The tendency is to be romantic, perhaps, but this is not incompatible with extraordinary achievement. Naturally, in many cases, perhaps in most, the Sun will also be in Pisces, accentuating and steadying this disposition. One of the greatest romantic artists that ever lived, Victor Hugo, has this position of Mercury. Charles Baudelaire brings out more fully the intenser, more psychic, and less flamboyant qualities. Where Mercury refers to voice rather than thought, we have Adelina Patti. Here the quality of Mercury is adapted to the physical organs of speech. The romantic, subtle, and rather shy and retiring temperament of mind is shown by Dr. Rudolph Steiner, who, engaged as he was, in a work of world-wide importance, yet managed to remain quietly and modestly in retirement, neither seeking fame nor troubling himself about advertisement.

The following well known persons were born with Mercury in the sign Pisces:

W. B. Yeats
Victor Hugo
Rosa Bonheur
Ellen Terry
Charles Evans Hughes
Adolph Ochs
Henry W. Longfellow
Lee Shubert
Charles M. Schwab
John Hays Hammond
Bishop Greer
Henry Carmichael
Bliss Carman
Abraham Lincoln
Chester S. Lord
Otto Kahn

For the benefit of those who are not in possession of Raphael's Ephemeris, or who are not able to interpret the symbols contained therein, the years when Mercury is in the sign Pisces are as follows:

From	February	22d	through	March	8th	1840
	February	13th	"	March	2d	1841
	March	21st	"	April	17th	1841
	February	6th	"	April	13th	1842

From	February	1st	through	February	9th	1843
	March	18th	"	April	7th	1843
	March	12th	"	March	29th	1844
	March	5th	"	March	21st	1845
	February	26th	"	March	13th	1846
	February	18th	"	March	5th	1847
	February	10th	"	April	15th	1848
	February	2d	"	February	28th	1849
	March	18th	"	April	10th	1849
	March	16th	"	April	3d	1850
	March	10th	"	March	26th	1851
	March	2d	"	March	17th	1852
	February	22d	"	March	9th	1853
	February	14th	"	March	2d	1854
	March	27th	"	April	16th	1854
	February	7th	"	April	14th	1855
	February	1st	"	February	15th	1856
	March	18th	"	April	7th	1856
	March	13th	"	March	30th	1857
	March	7th	"	March	22d	1858
	February	27th	"	March	14th	1859
	February	19th	"	March	5th	1860
	February	11th	"	March	2d	1861
	March	10th	"	April	16th	1861
	February	4th	"	March	8th	1862
	March	15th	"	April	11th	1862
	March	17th	"	April	4th	1863
	March	10th	"	March	27th	1864
	March	3d	"	March	18th	1865
	February	24th	"	March	10th	1866
	February	16th	"	March	3d	1867
	April	4th	"	April	15th	1867
	February	8th	"	April	14th	1868
	February	1st	"	February	19th	1869
	March	18th	"	April	8th	1869
	March	15th	"	April	1st	1870
	March	8th	"	March	24th	1871
	February	29th	"	March	15th	1872

From	February	20th	through	March	7th	1873
	February	12th	"	March	2d	1874
	March	17th	"	April	17th	1874
	February	5th	"	April	13th	1875
	February	3d	"	February	5th	1876
	March	17th	"	April	5th	1876
	March	12th	"	March	28th	1877
	March	5th	"	March	20th	1878
	February	25th	"	March	12th	1879
	February	17th	"	March	4th	1880
	February	9th	"	April	15th	1881
	February	2nd	"	February	25th	1882
	March	18th	"	April	9th	1882
	March	16th	"	April	2nd	1883
	March	8th	"	March	24th	1884
	March	1st	"	March	16th	1885
	February	21st	"	March	8th	1886
	February	14th	"	March	2nd	1887
	March	23d	"	April	17th	1887
	February	6th	"	April	13th	1888
	January	31st	"	February	11th	1889
	March	18th	"	April	6th	1889
	March	13th	"	March	30th	1890
	March	6th	"	March	21st	1891
	February	26th	"	March	12th	1892
	February	18th	"	March	5th	1893
	February	10th	"	April	16th	1894
	February	3d	"	March	3d	1895
	March	17th	"	April	11th	1895
	March	16th	"	April	3d	1896
	March	10th	"	March	26th	1897
	March	2d	"	March	18th	1898
	February	23d	"	March	10th	1899
	February	15th	"	March	3d	1900
	March	30th	"	April	16th	1900
	February	7th	"	April	15th	1901
	February	2nd	"	February	17th	1902
	March	19th	"	April	8th	1902

From	March	15th	through	April	1st	1903
	March	7th	"	March	23d	1904
	February	28th	"	March	15th	1905
	February	20th	"	March	7th	1906
	February	12th	"	March	3d	1907
	March	14th	"	April	17th	1907
	February	5th	"	April	12th	1908
	March	17th	"	April	5th	1909
	March	12th	"	March	28th	1910
	March	5th	"	March	20th	1911
	February	25th	"	March	11th	1912
	February	16th	"	March	4th	1913
	April	8th	"	April	13th	1913
	February	9th	"	April	16th	1914
	February	2nd	"	February	23d	1915
	March	19th	"	April	10th	1915
	March	15th	"	April	1st	1916
	March	9th	"	March	24th	1917
	March	1st	"	March	16th	1918
	February	22d	"	March	8th	1919
	February	14th	"	March	2d	1920
	March	20th	"	April	17th	1920
	February	5th	"	April	13th	1921
	February	2d	"	February	8th	1922
	March	18th	"	April	6th	1922
	March	13th	"	March	30th	1923
	March	5th	"	March	21st	1924
	February	26th	"	March	13th	1925
	February	18th	"	March	5th	1926
	February	10th	"	April	17th	1927
	February	3rd	"	February	28th	1928
	March	18th	"	April	10th	1928
	March	16th	"	April	3d	1929

VENUS SYMBOLICALLY CONSIDERED

Aphrodite, or Venus, daughter of Jove, heavenly and earthly, Morning Star and Queen of Sunset, is Life, Art, Rapture; she is goddess beyond the human, she is Woman in fullness of human perfection.

Man reveals himself in Saturn, Jupiter, Mars and the Sun. Neptune expresses the masculine soul raised to a spiritual completeness that includes the highest feminine vibration. In Mercury sex is nascent. Uranus symbolizes the feminine soul so perfected that it includes the higher masculine vibration. Woman is expressed to us by Venus and by the Moon.

The Moon symbolizes the child-woman and the woman-form beyond its period of fruitfulness. Venus reveals the woman of complete physical function— Woman from fourteen to forty-five. Expressed by Venus she is Woman-fruitful, the fulfillment of Desire, the Vessel of life, the Mother, the Giver of physical form to spirit.

Venus represents the passive—the receptive. She receives—and she gives back in kind what she receives. She reflects and glorifies and represents that which possesses her. Under the rays of the Sun she warms to grace and beauty and bears him exquisite brood of life—fruitful earth beneath the widespread glow of his beams.

The rough caress of Mars may rouse her to passion, violence and fierce physical return; and to all his constructive powers she may give form in shapes of art—the sculptured marble, the wrought metal—the stately temple.

The noble influence of Jupiter makes the gracious matron of her, the glory of a household and of her husband.

Should she abandon herself to Saturn, all her beauty may turn to evil, or her love be sordid drudgery of service, bleak task of faithfulness and gray patience.

Uranus makes of her a witch—a siren—a vampire even, or, answering his higher demands, she is white flame of genius—inspiration her breath, art her crown of stars.

To Neptune she will masquerade, a flicker of illusion and fantasy, or she will run swift-foot and wide-eyed into the very fastnesses of his far kingdom—and make his visions real!

Mercury finds her wits as keen as his. With him to challenge, she turns flirt—even she may be mercenary and too cunning, or turn her gaieties into coin, or sell out her pretty ways and take to books and intellectualities.

Under the silver of the Moon, she comes into an austerity all her own. Here she is chaste wife—calm mother—housemaker; ordered are her footsteps and her glance is level.

All these phases of the Venus expression are beautiful—to each the heart of the artist responds, each is a string in that harp of life across which the Hand of the All-Father sweeps the music of his Eternal Pleasure.

And Venus calls to each of us. It is for us to set words to her call. Shall she be devil or the voice of our own perfection? She echoes us! Kundry is saved in Parsifal's redemption. Tannhäuser's loss is included in the damnation of his Venus.

Woman! Either in the form of that fearful image, Lilith, the demon queen, "drawing down with her hands little figures of men into Hell," or Woman the goddess, who blazes in the heavens, clothed with the Sun, the Moon her footstool, and crowned with the Zodiac —the planets clustered in her hands.

So Venus, ever herself, is always what she reflects—gaiety—mirth—and happy companionings are of her making. The arts are her handmaidens; music is for her dancing feet; scents delight her, and touch is hers—the fine touch of light upon her eyes, of sound at her lips, the light touch of caressing fingers and the hungry embrace of all-seeking love. Beauty, allurement, passion, graciousness all are hers, and if she be dragged down to the vices of all these—ours be the shame!

Virtue, domesticity, chastity are hers—and form and ceremony too. By whatever name the nations call her, down the ages—Isis, Astarte, Aphrodite, Halbor, Freya, Kali—her legends, her attributes, her images are all the same—Kwan-nan in China, Nephthys in Egypt. So it is later religion borrows her, and divine Motherhood, clasping her celestial Babe, smiles from Christian altars.

Thus let us gaze upon the face of her, be she called Venus or Madonna, with reverence and worship, invoking the power of love by the ritual of Purity.

VENUS IN THE SIGNS

It may, on first consideration appear somewhat difficult to differentiate between the action of Venus, the "lesser Fortune," and that of Jupiter, the "Greater Fortune." Both represent the expansive and altruistic spirit. But Venus is the handmaiden of the Sun and she is consequently attached to the vital force, even as Jupiter is more closely an emanation of Neptune, the other extreme of the system, the Soul. The altruism of Venus, therefore, means love in a quite conventional and often selfish or personal sense; her expansiveness is often mere amiability, possibly assumed in order to gain some end associated with the instinct of self-preservation; and, finally, Venus is altogether more material and, so to speak, fleshly, than Jupiter. But religion itself is psychically correlated with both sex and the drama, and the reader will note that Jupiter in certain signs—Scorpio for example—becomes intensely sexual in character. Venus in any sign has so much connotation or reference that it is very necessary to take into consideration not only the sign in which it is placed, but also its aspects to other planets before judging of its effects. But the importance of the impact of the different signs is very great. In fact, the more material a planet is, the more easily it is influenced. We see no such violent commotion in the vaster planets; Uranus in Aries is not so different from Uranus in Libra, but Venus in Gemini is utterly different from Venus in Scorpio. This is all as it should be, and is in consonance with Initiated Theory.

In dealing with Venus on the lines hitherto followed with the other planets, we are confronted with a difficulty peculiar to the nature of her own influence. It is easy to observe most of the effects of other planets in the life, character, and work of great men, but we know little of the inner details of their domestic and intimate relations.

Alexander the Great, may have beaten his wife, and Cromwell may have been a very clever and tactful father, but in the majority of those examples which have hitherto served us so well, we know little or nothing of the private life. And it is essentially, and first of all, the private life that Venus influences. She has, of course, other significances. In the horoscope of Emperor Franz Josef, the dominance of Venus implies that all his gains had to come through peaceful channels, that war could never serve his ends; and this was the case. Similarly, the powerfully placed and well aspected Venus of Czar Alexander II reacted on his policy, as well as on his character; but, as said before, these are exceptions. In many cases, we find stern conquerors with polite manners, and, conversely, weak statesmen who are autocratic in their homes.

There is also the question of the external and objective Venus. Most often its effect occurs in the petty matters; it is difficult to trace it in big affairs, for these come so much under Uranus and Jupiter that Venus takes but a secondary part in the determination of such events. The upshot of all these considerations is that one is compelled to rely on the observations of private research; and here the proof is not producible, both because the names of everyday natives could mean nothing to the general reader, and also because such details would be matters of a confidential nature, and, in a good many cases, unprintable. Even if specified, such an account would need verifications; while, in the case of people well known to every student of history, the facts speak for themselves and are convincing. The reader must, therefore, (to sum up the situation) be content to rely, to a certain extent, in this chapter, upon the authority of the author.

This caveat is uttered emphatically, in order to assure the reader that there is no confusion in the mind of the author with regard to what is clear and convincing evidence patent to the world, and what, though in reality no less reliable, rests upon proofs not thus obvious.

VENUS IN ARIES

Venus in this sign is in her fall, and the position is not fortunate, on the whole. There is evidence of the action of Mars in a certain rash impulsiveness in emotion, but the effect is rarely lasting or deep even at the moment. There is a strong tendency to be what the French call *cérébral*, and also to what is really coldness, though it may manifest itself in fiery sparks.

It is only necessary to study the writings of Baudelaire and Swinburne, to see the attitude taken towards love and art by both of them, to understand this position of Venus. There is fierceness and glitter, but it is the fire of the lightning rather than that of the hearth. Among women we see the same quality—modified in certain ways—in Mme. Steinheil and Queen Victoria. The former example needs no comment; the latter does. Victoria appeared a most domesticated person, but she was not; it was merely part of her ambitious policy to appear so.

In music one sees this fitful brilliancy of Venus represented by Tchaikovsky, and in literature by Bulwer-Lytton. The domestic affairs of the latter are well known, too well known, and show in life what he also expressed in his novels.

The tendency to lack stability is also manifest in Robespierre.

The trouble seems to be not that there is any lack of activity in Venus when she is in this sign, but that that activity is ill-directed. She is not really fickle, but appears to be so because of her idealism. Reality failing to respond to her mental conception, she becomes discontented. At the same time, it must be understood that no fulfillment of her desires, however nearly perfect, would satisfy her. It is in the contemplation of her wishes that she finds pleasure rather than in the enjoyment of them. She is extraordinarily imaginative; the merest hint excites her. She loves by sight, but touch disappoints her. When a person with this position of Venus discovers that Shelley quarreled with his wife or that Browning smoked a pipe or that Matthew Arnold wore whiskers, disappointment and disillusion follow. The poetry is spoiled for them, because it is not written by a creature who not only does not, and did not, but never could exist.

A remarkable example of the idealism of this position is afforded us by Abraham Lincoln, whose Venus trined his rising Neptune. This is an unsurpassable position for unfaltering devotion to an ideal. Lincoln was as conscious as any other man, as prescient as any seer could possibly have been, of what it meant in immediate agony to humanity to call for volunteers, as he did on that dramatic day which changed the whole history of these States. But his high purpose was not overwhelmed by his great sympathy for the temporary sufferings of humanity. To him, right was right, and must be supported, no matter what the cost. Had Neptune been in Capricornus, and Venus in Taurus, instead of in Sagittarius and Aries respectively, he would have thought far more of the material miseries which immediately threatened his country, and secession might have become an accomplished fact. It was his idealism which not only prevented the disruption of the Union, but implanted as a principle, which will never cease to be paramount in this country, to do the right thing no matter what the cost. One can readily understand how this attitude may be misinterpreted by the other party as lack of sympathy.

Venus in this sign is extraordinarily brilliant; she is the beauty of the sparks which are struck from the sword of Mars as he goes into battle, but she is robbed of all the importance which she has as tenderness and graciousness. She becomes the Amazon, panoplied and splendid, with no trace of the Hausfrau. Baudelaire and Swinburne both have this position, and she is buttressed by the most formidable aspects; yet she fails to flower with that voluptuous graciousness that we find, for example, in Michael Angelo who has her in Pisces. She is hard, brilliant, subtle, passionate, but not enduring and not inclined to please. She attacks and she repels, but all her operations are operations of assault and battery. She stirs to activity and quits. In women, this position is exceptionally unpleasant. She may be extraordinarily attractive but, even if she gratifies, will never satisfy. She excites and irritates, never calms and soothes. Even in art, one perceives clearly how unsatisfactory, from the point of view of Venus herself, so to speak, is this position for her. When Swinburne wrote "Dolores," he was trying to paint a picture of Venus in Libra or in Scorpio; he only succeeded in painting a Venus in Aries type.

We see the same thing in the writing of Baudelaire and the music of Tchaikovsky. It is always irritation without satisfaction; it is not Isis veiled, but Isis in armor. As indicated above, this position is very much better for men than it is for women, but it is good even for them only where Venus is a subsidiary figure, not only in the horoscope itself, but in the general character of the native. Where his general pursuit in life is of the character of Venus, it is bad, but it is not bad for such men as Lincoln and J. P. Morgan to have Venus under arms.

It may be of great value in the horoscope of any man of the more studious and serious sort not to have Venus flower too fully. We find her in this position in the horoscopes of such men as Emerson, Alexander Graham Bell, Dr. Quackenbos and the Hon. Stephen A. Douglas. Where, however, the native is an artist, the limitations may be regarded as troublesome. Thus we find Palmer Cox in art and Frank R. Stockton in literature somewhat lacking in the graciousness and floridity that seem appropriate to the artistic temperament. Occasionally, the effect of Venus in Aries is very bad indeed, implying heartlessness, and this will particularly apply when the general temperament is already mercurial. We class the position as a decided restriction upon Venus. She always fails to attain her full development, and whether this be good or bad for the native, in a general way, must depend upon considerations entirely foreign to her. It is evident, for example, that a great soldier will not be benefited by having Venus of equal importance with Mars, or a great man of science by having her stronger than Uranus, Saturn and Mercury. Consideration, such as the foregoing, must always be taken into account, in estimating the real value to the native of any particular position of any particular planet. Each description must be regarded as an isolated statement, merely one pawn in a complex position of many pieces.

The following are the names of well known persons who have Venus in the sign Aries:

Oscar Hammerstein
Palmer Cox
J. P. Morgan
Percival Lowell
Ralph Waldo Emerson
Emile Coué
Bessie Leo
Reginald de Koven
Bliss Carman
John Burroughs
Abraham Lincoln
Bulwer-Lytton
Queen Victoria
Algernon Swinburne

For the benefit of those who are not in possession of Raphael's Ephemeris, or who are not able to interpret the symbols contained therein, the years when Venus is in the sign Aries are as follows:

From	April	16th	through	May	10th	1840
	February	5th	"	March	3rd	1841
	March	18th	"	April	10th	1842
	April	30th	"	May	25th	1843
	February	17th	"	March	12th	1844
	April	2nd	"	April	25th	1845
	May	7th	"	June	4th	1846
	March	3rd	"	March	26th	1847
	April	16th	"	May	9th	1848
	February	4th	"	March	3rd	1849
	March	17th	"	April	10th	1850
	April	30th	"	May	24th	1851
	February	17th	"	March	11th	1852
	April	1st	"	April	24th	1853
	May	7th	"	June	4th	1854
	March	2nd	"	March	26th	1855
	April	15th	"	May	9th	1856
	February	4th	"	March	3rd	1857
	March	17th	"	April	9th	1858
	April	29th	"	May	24th	1859
	February	16th	"	March	11th	1860
	March	31st	"	April	24th	1861
	May	7th	"	June	4th	1862
	March	2nd	"	March	25th	1863
	April	15th	"	May	8th	1864
	February	4th	"	March	3rd	1865
	March	16th	"	April	8th	1866
	April	29th	"	May	23rd	1867
	February	16th	"	March	11th	1868
	March	31st	"	April	23rd	1869
	May	7th	"	June	3rd	1870
	March	1st	"	March	25th	1871
	April	14th	"	May	8th	1872
	February	3rd	"	March	3rd	1873
	March	16th	"	April	8th	1874
	April	28th	"	May	23rd	1875
	February	15th	"	March	10th	1876
	March	30th	"	April	23rd	1877

From	May	7th	through	June	3rd	1878
	March	1st	"	March	24th	1879
	April	14th	"	May	7th	1880
	February	3rd	"	March	3rd	1881
	March	15th	"	April	7th	1882
	April	28th	"	May	22nd	1883
	February	15th	"	March	10th	1884
	March	30th	"	April	22nd	1885
	May	7th	"	June	3rd	1886
	February	28th	"	March	24th	1887
	April	13th	"	May	7th	1888
	February	3rd	"	March	4th	1889
	March	15th	"	April	7th	1890
	April	27th	"	May	22nd	1891
	February	14th	"	March	9th	1892
	March	29th	"	April	22nd	1893
	May	6th	"	June	2nd	1894
	February	28th	"	March	23rd	1895
	April	13th	"	May	6th	1896
	February	2nd	"	March	4th	1897
	March	14th	"	April	6th	1898
	April	27th	"	May	21st	1899
	February	14th	"	March	10th	1900
	March	30th	"	April	22nd	1901
	May	7th	"	June	3rd	1902
	February	28th	"	March	23rd	1903
	April	13th	"	May	7th	1904
	February	3rd	"	March	5th	1905
	May	9th	"	May	27th	1905
	March	15th	"	April	7th	1906
	April	28th	"	May	22nd	1907
	February	14th	"	March	9th	1908
	March	29th	"	April	21st	1909
	May	7th	"	June	3rd	1910
	February	28th	"	March	23rd	1911
	April	13th	"	May	6th	1912
	February	3rd	"	March	6th	1913
	May	2nd	"	May	30th	1913

From	March	14th	through	April	6th	1914
	April	27th	"	May	21st	1915
	February	14th	"	March	9th	1916
	March	29th	"	April	21st	1917
	May	7th	"	June	2nd	1918
	February	27th	"	March	22nd	1919
	April	12th	"	May	6th	1920
	February	3rd	"	March	6th	1921
	April	26th	"	June	1st	1921
	March	13th	"	April	6th	1922
	April	27th	"	May	21st	1923
	February	13th	"	March	8th	1924
	March	28th	"	April	20th	1925
	May	7th	"	June	2nd	1926
	February	27th	"	March	22nd	1927
	April	12th	"	May	5th	1928
	February	3rd	"	March	7th	1929
	April	20th	"	June	2nd	1929

VENUS IN TAURUS

Venus in Taurus is in her own house and is therefore very strong; but the earthy quality of the sign has two effects which seem at first sight curiously incompatible. The action is drawn down to the physical plane—we shall find but rare examples of "ideal love" or "platonic affection" in people with this position—but also it is slow to start. People with Venus so placed, though they have enormous capacity for love, do not develop on the sex-plane until long after the average. Once the blossom flowers, it flowers magnificently. All the tenacity of the bull comes into play, and every hope may be entertained of settled happiness.

At all times, however, the magnetism of the sign is manifest, and people with this position often present baffling mysteries to their admirers. They give all the physical signs of great passion and are perfectly aware of how well they are fitted both to inspire and to reciprocate devotion; yet they will not yield themselves until the right person arrives. When that happens, the surrender is often instant and the fidelity eternal.

The same characteristics, transmuted to other planes, obtain there. There is often great amiability, though tact is rarely fine. Fortune in small matters is steady, but not sudden or capricious; and the artistic side of the native is likely to be solid, sensible, and free from erratic and hysterical manifestations. The word "domesticity," if it be extended to cover all the many qualities combined in Venus, gives a good idea of what is meant.

Taurus is preëminently the sign of material form and tends to bring everything to operation on the physical plane. The sex instinct, when Venus is in this sign, is consequently very simple and natural, as direct and intelligible as the marriage service in the Church of England prayer-book. Selection is determined primarily by physical fitness; other considerations hardly apply. The native is particularly fond of comfort, and strives actively and persistently to create this in his environment. While the sex instinct is direct and, as it were, plainly spoken, it in no way violates delicacy. The absence of shame is in itself a guarantee of modesty. Gentleness and kindliness go naturally with this position and contribute to the increase of its magnetism. Sense of sex, although somewhat animal, is perfectly clean and normal. There is no tendency to its perversion or degeneration, unless Venus should be afflicted by Saturn, or Uranus, or Neptune.

Apart from actual sex relations, this position means a great deal of geniality in the temperament, which very often stands for great popularity. Other people are naturally sympathetic to this type. Much of the success of such people as Joseph Pulitzer, W. J. Bryan, W. T. Stead, Levi P. Morton, Chauncey M. Depew, David Hummel Green and Marconi may be attributed to this position. In art, we see Daniel Chester French, whose sculptures show a massive, majestic and somewhat florid style. Sometimes the sympathy becomes more nearly universal yet, embracing all nature, as we see in such people as Walt Whitman and Luther Burbank. The extraordinary feeling of the unity of nature possessed by both these men caused them to be looked upon at first with disfavor by their contemporaries, and as if there were something eccentric in their outlook; but a better understanding has shown this to be the very quintessence of sanity. It is not just, therefore, to speak of such ideas as unconventional. However, that in them which was original is not to be attributed to the position of Venus. Whitman, for example, has Neptune and Uranus in conjunction, square to Saturn, an admirable configuration for epoch-making force. Unless there is something of this sort, one must not look to this position for originality, even of presentation.

One may cite the point of view of Thomas Hardy and Thomas Moore in literature, or even that of Alphonse Daudet. There is a certain conventionality in the outlook which prevents extravagances, even those of genius. The sanity and glow of Turner and Dürer may be ascribed to this position of Venus. Wagner illustrates it even better; and the steady correctness of Bachhaus as a pianist is very much in keeping. Wagner's Venus is, however, rendered singularly brilliant by the conjunction of Sol within one degree.

W. B. Yeats is rather a difficult case. His Venus qualities are decidedly nebulous and airy; the only explanation appears to be that she is attacked by Mars.

With ordinary people—not artists—the effect is clear enough. We have such sincere and sober folk as George V, Bismarck, Cromwell, Alexander II and Lord Wolseley. The domestic affairs of these people never gave cause for anxiety!

But what about Nero? Well, his Venus is in the twelfth house with Mars conjoined and Jupiter in opposition—and it appears likely that if we were to calculate the positions of Uranus and Neptune for that remote epoch, we should find further trouble.

The following are the names of well known persons who have Venus in the sign Taurus:

"Bud" Fisher
Norma Talmadge
Luther Burbank
Clarence S. Darrow
Alan Dale
William H. Crane
Norman Hapgood
Chauncey M. Depew
Daniel Chester French
Charlie Chaplin
Artemus Ward

For the benefit of those who are not in possession of Raphael's Ephemeris, or who are not able to interpret the symbols contained therein, the years when Venus is in the sign Taurus are as follows:

From	May	11th	through	June	3rd	1840
	March	4th	"	April	12th	1841
	May	4th	"	July	6th	1841
	April	11th	"	May	4th	1842
	May	26th	"	June	19th	1843
	March	13th	"	April	7th	1844
	April	26th	"	May	19th	1845
	June	5th	"	July	1st	1846
	March	27th	"	April	20th	1847
	May	10th	"	June	3rd	1848
	March	4th	"	April	18th	1849
	April	23rd	"	July	6th	1849
	April	11th	"	May	4th	1850
	May	25th	"	June	18th	1851
	March	12th	"	April	6th	1852
	April	25th	"	May	19th	1853
	June	5th	"	July	1st	1854
	March	27th	"	April	19th	1855
	May	10th	"	June	2nd	1856
	March	4th	"	July	6th	1857
	April	10th	"	May	3rd	1858
	May	25th	"	June	18th	1859
	March	12th	"	April	6th	1860
	April	25th	"	May	18th	1861
	June	5th	"	June	30th	1862
	March	26th	"	April	19th	1863
	May	9th	"	June	2nd	1864
	March	4th	"	July	6th	1865
	April	9th	"	May	3rd	1866
	May	24th	"	June	17th	1867
	March	12th	"	April	6th	1868
	April	24th	"	May	18th	1869
	June	4th	"	June	30th	1870
	March	26th	"	April	18th	1871

From	May	9th	through	June	1st	1872
	March	4th	"	July	7th	1873
	April	9th	"	May	2nd	1874
	May	24th	"	June	17th	1875
	March	11th	"	April	5th	1876
	April	24th	"	May	17th	1877
	June	4th	"	June	30th	1878
	March	25th	"	April	18th	1879
	May	8th	"	June	1st	1880
	March	4th	"	July	7th	1881
	April	8th	"	May	2nd	1882
	May	23rd	"	June	16th	1883
	March	11th	"	April	5th	1884
	April	23rd	"	May	16th	1885
	June	4th	"	June	29th	1886
	March	25th	"	April	17th	1887
	May	8th	"	May	31st	1888
	March	5th	"	July	7th	1889
	April	8th	"	May	1st	1890
	May	23rd	"	June	16th	1891
	March	10th	"	April	4th	1892
	April	23rd	"	May	16th	1893
	June	3rd	"	June	29th	1894
	March	24th	"	April	17th	1895
	May	7th	"	May	31st	1896
	March	5th	"	July	7th	1897
	April	7th	"	May	1st	1898
	May	22nd	"	June	15th	1899
	March	11th	"	April	5th	1900
	April	23rd	"	May	16th	1901
	June	4th	"	June	29th	1902
	March	24th	"	April	17th	1903
	May	8th	"	May	31st	1904
	March	6th	"	May	8th	1905
	May	28th	"	July	7th	1905
	April	8th	"	May	1st	1906
	May	23rd	"	June	16th	1907
	March	10th	"	April	5th	1908

From	April	22nd	through	May	16th	1909
	June	4th	"	June	29th	1910
	March	24th	"	April	17th	1911
	May	7th	"	May	31st	1912
	March	7th	"	May	1st	1913
	May	31st	"	July	7th	1913
	April	7th	"	May	1st	1914
	May	22nd	"	June	15th	1915
	March	10th	"	April	5th	1916
	April	22nd	"	May	15th	1917
	June	3rd	"	June	28th	1918
	March	23rd	"	April	16th	1919
	May	7th	"	May	30th	1920
	March	7th	"	April	25th	1921
	June	2nd	"	July	7th	1921
	April	7th	"	April	30th	1922
	May	22nd	"	June	14th	1923
	March	9th	"	April	4th	1924
	April	21st	"	May	15th	1925
	June	3rd	"	June	28th	1926
	March	23rd	"	April	16th	1927
	May	6th	"	May	29th	1928
	March	8th	"	April	19th	1929
	June	3rd	"	July	7th	1929

VENUS IN GEMINI

GEMINI has the precisely opposite effect to Taurus. In this sign Venus is easily aroused, but has little or nothing physical or positive about it. It is inconstant, and always mental or ideal. People having this position of Venus are constitutionally and ~~congenitally~~ incapable of understanding passion as ordinary men and women do. In the case of Shakespeare, for example, he is a master of Neptunian love (Venus and Neptune are conjoined in his horoscope), as shown in "As You Like it" and "Twelfth Night" and "Midsummer Night's Dream," rather than of the ordinary passion between man and wife.

In Petrarch we have a somewhat warmer Venus, but the love is still ideal and therefore incomprehensible to the average man. One must be a poet to read Petrarch with pleasure.

Where science is already elsewhere indicated as the pursuit in life, this position in Gemini comes naturally to strengthen that disposition, or at least to avoid weakening it by a counter-pull. Thus Kant, Huxley, and Herbert Spencer were undisturbed in their life's work by the claims of love or pleasure, and all their Venus-quality was manifested on the mental plane.

People with this position are never quite satisfied. "Ah but a man's reach should exceed his grasp; or what's a heaven for?" is a Browning quotation which they import into private life. They are often frivolous, fickle, and incapable of any but the most superficial affection. Nor is the object of affection ever single; such people are often terribly puzzled as to which of several admirers to prefer. In truth, they want none of them; they like the titillation, and would be seriously annoyed if one of their pigeons turned out a hawk—as sometimes happens!

The intellectuality of Gemini often enables the native to understand passion, even though he does not feel it. The examples of Shakespeare and Petrarch given above are to the point. The difficulty comes in the power of expression, for though, as Oscar Wilde observed, "genuine emotion is the root of all bad art," yet it is also the root of all good art, and its absence renders the portrayal of human character to some degree unsatisfying. In America we have an extremely satisfactory example of the attitude which we are discussing. It is that of Elbert Hubbard. He regarded the mind, or rather the mental plane, as the most real and the only important one of the planes, and his whole doctrine, being based on this assumption, finds both its strength and weakness therein. Some writer has asserted that all phenomena are but phantoms of the mind, and much of the teaching of Elbert Hubbard was very similar in this underlying assumption. This attitude is, of course, very distasteful to the average man, who regards it as evidence alike of lack of feeling and of instability of brain. The distinction between these points of view touches the emotions so closely that ill-feeling is bound to exist between people who happen to be on opposite sides of the fence. Without presuming to take sides in so embittered a controversy, or to give judgment in so delicate a dispute, one is bound to say that Gemini may be regarded as by no means sympathetic to Venus. Her presence in that sign is a limitation, for her nature is earth and water, while Gemini is pure air, and there is bitter hostility between air and earth. The effect of air upon Venus makes her dispersed and frivolous, which is a vice of Venus, whose excellence consists in form, in plasticity, in repose.

The following are the names of well known persons who have Venus in the sign Gemini:

William Randolph Hearst
William C. de Mille
Frank H. Damrosch
George M. Cohan
Charles Hayden
Margaret Lawrence
Maxfield Parrish
Edwin Markham
William Shakespeare
H. Rider Haggard
Elbert Hubbard
Lord Northcliffe
John W. Weeks

For the benefit of those who are not in possession of Raphael's Ephemeris, or who are not able to interpret the symbols contained therein, the years when Venus is in the sign Gemini are as follows:

From	June	4th	through	June	28th	1840
	April	13th	"	May	3rd	1841
	July	7th	"	August	7th	1841
	May	5th	"	May	29th	1842
	June	20th	"	July	14th	1843
	April	8th	"	May	4th	1844
	May	20th	"	June	13th	1845
	July	2nd	"	July	27th	1846
	April	21st	"	May	15th	1847
	June	4th	"	June	27th	1848
	April	19th	"	April	22nd	1849
	July	7th	"	August	7th	1849

From	May	5th	through	May	28th	1850
	June	19th	"	July	13th	1851
	April	7th	"	May	4th	1852
	May	20th	"	June	12th	1853
	July	2nd	"	July	27th	1854
	April	20th	"	May	14th	1855
	June	3rd	"	June	27th	1856
	July	7th	"	August	6th	1857
	May	4th	"	May	28th	1858
	June	19th	"	July	12th	1859
	April	7th	"	May	4th	1860
	May	19th	"	June	11th	1861
	July	1st	"	July	26th	1862
	April	20th	"	May	14th	1863
	June	3rd	"	June	26th	1864
	July	7th	"	August	6th	1865
	May	4th	"	May	27th	1866
	June	18th	"	July	12th	1867
	April	7th	"	May	4th	1868
	May	19th	"	June	11th	1869
	July	1st	"	July	26th	1870
	April	19th	"	May	14th	1871
	June	2nd	"	June	26th	1872
	July	8th	"	August	6th	1873
	May	3rd	"	May	27th	1874
	June	18th	"	July	11th	1875
	April	6th	"	May	4th	1876
	May	18th	"	June	10th	1877
	July	1st	"	July	25th	1878
	April	19th	"	May	13th	1879
	June	2nd	"	June	25th	1880
	July	8th	"	August	5th	1881
	May	3rd	"	May	26th	1882
	June	17th	"	July	11th	1883
	April	6th	"	May	4th	1884
	May	17th	"	June	10th	1885
	June	30th	"	July	25th	1886
	April	18th	"	May	13th	1887

From	June	1st	through	June	25th	1888
	July	8th	"	August	5th	1889
	May	2nd	"	May	26th	1890
	June	17th	"	July	10th	1891
	April	5th	"	May	4th	1892
	May	17th	"	June	9th	1893
	June	30th	"	July	24th	1894
	April	18th	"	May	12th	1895
	June	1st	"	June	24th	1896
	July	8th	"	August	5th	1897
	May	2nd	"	May	25th	1898
	June	16th	"	July	10th	1899
	April	6th	"	May	5th	1900
	May	17th	"	June	10th	1901
	June	30th	"	July	25th	1902
	April	18th	"	May	13th	1903
	June	1st	"	June	25th	1904
	July	8th	"	August	5th	1905
	May	2nd	"	May	26th	1906
	June	17th	"	July	10th	1907
	April	6th	"	May	5th	1908
	May	17th	"	June	9th	1909
	June	30th	"	July	24th	1910
	April	18th	"	May	12th	1911
	June	1st	"	June	24th	1912
	July	8th	"	August	5th	1913
	May	2nd	"	May	25th	1914
	June	16th	"	July	10th	1915
	April	6th	"	May	5th	1916
	May	16th	"	June	9th	1917
	June	29th	"	July	24th	1918
	April	17th	"	May	12th	1919
	May	31st	"	June	23rd	1920
	July	8th	"	August	5th	1921
	May	1st	"	May	25th	1922
	June	15th	"	July	9th	1923
	April	5th	"	May	5th	1924
	May	16th	"	June	8th	1925

From June	29th	through	July	23rd	1926
April	17th	"	May	11th	1927
May	30th	"	June	23rd	1928
July	8th	"	August	4th	1929

VENUS IN CANCER

One might generalize the effect of the elemental attribution of the signs upon Venus by calling fire passionate, earth affectionate, air ideal or romantic, and water voluptuous. The passivity of Cancer certainly makes Venus extremely emotional. It is hard for a person with this position to resist the advances of another; at the same time, the lunar force in Cancer makes the nature changeable. There is little disposition to seek companionship or love, but, when these are offered, they are gladly accepted. There is often deep sentimentality, and the native is apt to take his affairs too seriously; in reality, wounds heal quickly. It is very unfortunate for any native with this position to be deprived of free normal expression of his or her tendencies; in such cases the health may suffer.

This sign is in many ways the most suitable of all for Venus; she seems to dissolve into a swoon therein. However, the tendency is to sensuality in a very marked degree, though not so much so as we shall find when we come to Scorpio. It is desirable to find some aspect with a tendency to correct any exaggeration of this quality.

The desire for comfort in life and general good fortune in minor matters is to be expected in natives with Venus in Cancer. In art and music, and in literature also, the effect appears to be very intense; the feelings are very quiet and deep-seated, permeating the whole atmosphere. This quality will be recognized in the work of Dante, Balzac, and Schumann. The peculiar pathos and melancholy of the last-mentioned is, of course, due to the conjunction of the Lord of the Ascendant, Saturn, with Neptune. In all these determinations it must constantly be remembered that one practically never finds any single uncomplicated aspect; and crude, superficial research is consequently bound to be misleading.

A good example of the quiet sentimentality of the configuration is given by Abbas Effendi, who sought to build up a religion on generalities of purely pacific and amiable type.

Franz Josef II, Nicholas II, and Maximilian of Mexico all had this position; the effect is recognizable in the softness and ductility of their characters. In the last case, this became actual weakness and contributed largely to his ruin.

We have however three very remarkable cases of a quite opposite tendency. Sometimes Cancer appears to remember quite suddenly that it is a cardinal sign with Jupiter exalted, and to act accordingly! Even in the types of face given when it is rising, we see these two contrasted, the round, flat, pale moon-like face for one, and the aquiline, red, dominant, aggressive, hatchet-profile for the other.

Jay Gould certainly possessed none of the characteristics which we have cited, but his Venus is conjoined with Jupiter, and squared by the conjunction of Luna and Saturn. This is sufficient to determine the sign to activity.

Cecil Rhodes had very little of the true Cancer effect on Venus; but here again Saturn interferes.

Another example is Napoleon. Here Venus in Cancer, sextile to Uranus, Neptune, and Mars, accounts for his easy amours, and that indulgence in the pleasures of the table which led to his death. His general method, too, was quite in keeping with this position. It is his actions as a soldier and a statesman which make us think at first of him as an unlikely person to have this position. But such actions hardly come under Venus at all; they are only indirectly influenced by her in the same way as hip-disease might interfere with oratory by limiting the use of gestures; and we may therefore call the very particular attention of the student to this case as highly and aptly illustrative of the effect.

There are, however, many manifestations of Venus besides the obvious one. In Cancer, she frequently gives humorous good-nature—a gentle and ingratiating method—which endears the observer to the native without his quite knowing why it should be so. An excellent illustration of this quality is Oliver Wendell Holmes, and on the stage we see it in Harry Lauder. Julia Marlowe has this same indefinable charm; but, in her case, it is fortified with a more definite appeal, because Venus is in aspect to the Moon, Uranus and Neptune.

Cancer always makes for popularity, because it is ruled by the Moon, and the presence of Venus in the sign should cause the native to be generally beloved. Napoleon, of course, owed his elevation to the hold which he had upon the affections of the people, and it was no doubt the personal popularity of Franz Josef II, more than anything else, which enabled him to harmonize and build up the nations which he ruled, into one great empire. Their dissensions always stopped short of the person of the emperor, and many a time they were restrained from going to extremes, only by considerations of him. Cecil Rhodes, again, is a figure who struck the popular imagination. So, to turn once more to our own country, did Henry Ward Beecher. Here there is no question of the popularity, and it is also possible that certain other facts which made considerable stir at the time may partially, at least, be attributed to this position.

The following are the names of well known persons who have Venus in the sign Cancer:

Benito Mussolini
Robert J. Collier
Harrison Fisher
William Winter
Gifford Pinchot
James Stillman
Ex-President Coolidge
Percy Stickney Grant
John Jacob Astor
General Ballington Booth
Joseph Cannon
Honoré Balzac
Dante

For the benefit of those who are not in possession of Raphael's Ephemeris, or who are not able to interpret the symbols contained therein, the years when Venus is in the sign Cancer are as follows:

From	June	29th	through	July	22nd	1840
	August	8th	"	September	3rd	1841
	May	30th	"	June	23rd	1842
	July	15th	"	August	7th	1843
	May	5th	"	June	7th	1844
	July	25th	"	September	4th	1844
	June	14th	"	July	7th	1845
	July	28th	"	August	21st	1846
	May	16th	"	June	10th	1847
	June	28th	"	July	22nd	1848
	August	8th	"	September	3rd	1849
	May	29th	"	June	22nd	1850
	July	14th	"	August	7th	1851
	May	5th	"	June	8th	1852
	July	19th	"	September	5th	1852
	June	13th	"	July	6th	1853
	July	28th	"	August	21st	1854
	May	15th	"	June	9th	1855
	June	28th	"	July	21st	1856
	August	7th	"	September	2nd	1857
	May	29th	"	June	22nd	1858
	July	13th	"	August	6th	1859
	May	5th	"	June	10th	1860
	July	13th	"	September	5th	1860
	June	12th	"	July	6th	1861
	July	27th	"	August	20th	1862
	May	15th	"	June	9th	1863
	June	27th	"	July	21st	1864
	August	7th	"	September	2nd	1865
	May	28th	"	June	21st	1866
	July	13th	"	August	6th	1867
	May	5th	"	June	12th	1868
	July	7th	"	September	6th	1868
	June	12th	"	July	5th	1869
	July	27th	"	August	20th	1870
	May	15th	"	June	9th	1871
	June	27th	"	July	20th	1872
	August	7th	"	September	2nd	1873

From	May	28th	through	June	21st	1874
	July	12th	"	August	5th	1875
	May	5th	"	June	17th	1876
	June	28th	"	September	6th	1876
	June	11th	"	July	5th	1877
	July	26th	"	August	19th	1878
	May	14th	"	June	8th	1879
	June	26th	"	July	20th	1880
	August	6th	"	September	1st	1881
	May	27th	"	June	20th	1882
	July	12th	"	August	4th	1883
	May	5th	"	September	7th	1884
	June	11th	"	July	4th	1885
	July	26th	"	August	19th	1886
	May	14th	"	June	8th	1887
	June	26th	"	July	19th	1888
	August	6th	"	September	1st	1889
	May	27th	"	June	20th	1890
	July	11th	"	August	4th	1891
	May	5th	"	September	7th	1892
	June	10th	"	July	4th	1893
	July	25th	"	August	18th	1894
	May	13th	"	June	7th	1895
	June	25th	"	July	19th	1896
	August	6th	"	August	31st	1897
	May	26th	"	June	19th	1898
	July	11th	"	August	3rd	1899
	May	6th	"	September	8th	1900
	June	11th	"	July	4th	1901
	July	26th	"	August	19th	1902
	May	14th	"	June	8th	1903
	June	26th	"	July	19th	1904
	August	6th	"	September	1st	1905
	May	27th	"	June	20th	1906
	July	11th	"	August	4th	1907
	May	6th	"	September	8th	1908
	June	10th	"	July	4th	1909
	July	25th	"	August	18th	1910

From						
From	May	13th	through	June	8th	1911
	June	24th	"	July	18th	1912
	August	6th	"	August	31st	1913
	May	26th	"	June	19th	1914
	July	10th	"	August	3rd	1915
	May	6th	"	September	8th	1916
	June	10th	"	July	3rd	1917
	July	25th	"	August	18th	1918
	May	13th	"	June	7th	1919
	June	24th	"	July	18th	1920
	August	6th	"	August	31st	1921
	May	26th	"	June	19th	1922
	July	10th	"	August	3rd	1923
	May	6th	"	September	8th	1924
	June	9th	"	July	3rd	1925
	July	24th	"	August	17th	1926
	May	12th	"	June	7th	1927
	June	24th	"	July	17th	1928
	August	5th	"	August	30th	1929

VENUS IN LEO

Leo is by far the noblest of the signs and brings out the best qualities of Venus. Venus in Leo is not so passionate as in Aries, but she is loyal and warm-hearted. She becomes capable even of that highest virtue of self-sacrifice without which all is in vain. She becomes that Charity of which the apostle Paul waxed eloquent. This, however, depends as usual upon aspects; an attack of Saturn (for example) may undo all the good and transform it into evil; yet this is not so easily accomplished as when she is in a more passive and sensitive sign. However fallen, she always retains some memory of her ancient dignity.

Thus we find many of the greatest-hearted people born with this position. Alexander of Greece is a fine instance, and so is Cicero, if we remember him as the author of *De Senectute* and *De Amicitia*. In more recent times we have Colonel Olcott, one of the kindest-hearted men that ever lived, Tolstoi, George Sand, and Maurice

Maeterlinck. One will note the flavor of humanitarianism in its best sense in all these.

It is to be observed, with some care, that three of the most popular British statesmen of the generation just passed—Balfour, Chamberlain, and Asquith, all have this position. They were of very different types, yet all acquired popularity in a way that hardly any others have done. Their positive qualities are in each case ill-fitted to inspire affection; it is something deeper in their natures which has attracted the love of their fellow countrymen.

In the middle ages, who stands more for the ripe, kindly spirit of generous love than Cornelius Agrippa? It is not openly apparent in his writing, but it gilds the whole.

The same remark, with necessary modification, applies to Bernard Shaw. Venus in Leo is not self-assertive and blatant; it lurks hidden, its abiding glow warming the hands of life, but never scorching them.

There is no better position for Venus to attract warm feeling on the part of others; even where respect is not given to the native, he yet acquires sympathy and kindly consideration because he is such a good fellow. Barney Barnato was decidedly the most popular of the South African millionaires, because it was recognized that, for all his roughness and his questionable methods of business, he had a real human heart. The geniality of former President Taft was very characteristic. His bitterest political opponents never said a word against him personally. Another very good example is Irvin Cobb; Venus in Leo is very well characterized by his kindly, humanitarian humor and also by his personal characteristics. In a wider way, a more serious way, we see the same quality in Jane Addams; and the graciousness and good feeling of Dr. Felix Adler are almost equally well known.

To return to the by-paths of history, we may cite the great-hearted and magnanimous Garibaldi, as illustrative of this position, while its nobility and good-feeling were also very clearly manifest in the character of Cardinal Richelieu. Curiously enough, his successor, Mazzarin, has the same position, but in Mazzarin, these qualities were by no means strongly marked. A glance at his nativity explains why Mercury is in conjunction with Venus, masking her warmth by his rational and calculating acumen, and she is seriously afflicted by a square of Uranus on the one side, and of Saturn on the other. The position of Saturn, which dominates the horoscope from the Mid-heaven, emphasizes the selfishness of the native, and Uranus, being in bad aspect to Venus, hinders the emancipation and breadth which a friendly aspect might have restored to her. These aspects might not have been sufficient to destroy her influence, had not Saturn been so extremely powerful in the horoscope. Not only is he in the Mid-heaven, but Lord of the Ascendant. Saturn is, therefore, the key of the complex, and is sufficiently powerful to out-weigh the influence of Leo upon Venus.

Nature presents itself to people with Venus in Leo as primarily an emotional phenomenon. There is not the materialism which we found in Taurus or the intellectualism given by her presence in Gemini. The native may acquiesce in the dictum of Schopenhauer, that the world is a reflection of will and that both the material and mental aspects of it are subsidiary.

The following are the names of well known persons who have Venus in the sign Leo:

John Wanamaker
Gen. John Pershing
George H. Lorimer
Booth Tarkington
William Howard Taft
Dr. Felix Adler
James B. Gilder
Hamlin Garland
Harrison Grey Fiske
Charles Dana Gibson
Mary Baker Eddy
Gen. George W. Goethals
Archbishop John Ireland
James J. Hill
Chauncey Olcott
Cornelius Vanderbilt
Mrs. C. Pankhurst
Maurice Maeterlinck

For the benefit of those who are not in possession of Raphael's Ephemeris, or who are not able to interpret the symbols contained therein, the years when Venus is in the sign Leo are as follows:

From	July	23rd	through	August	16th	1840
	September	4th	"	September	29th	1841
	June	24th	"	July	18th	1842
	August	8th	"	August	31st	1843
	June	8th	"	July	24th	1844
	September	5th	"	October	8th	1844
	July	8th	"	August	1st	1845
	August	22nd	"	Septembmer	15th	1846
	June	11th	"	July	7th	1847
	July	23rd	"	August	15th	1848
	September	4th	"	September	29th	1849
	June	23rd	"	July	17th	1850
	August	8th	"	August	31st	1851
	June	9th	"	July	18th	1852
	September	6th	"	October	8th	1852
	July	7th	"	July	31st	1853
	August	22nd	"	September	15th	1854
	June	10th	"	July	7th	1855
	July	22nd	"	August	15th	1856
	September	3rd	"	September	28th	1857
	June	23rd	"	July	17th	1858
	August	7th	"	August	30th	1859
	June	11th	"	July	12th	1860
	September	6th	"	October	8th	1860
	July	7th	"	July	30th	1861
	August	21st	"	September	14th	1862
	June	10th	"	July	7th	1863
	July	22nd	"	August	14th	1864
	September	3rd	"	September	28th	1865
	June	22nd	"	July	16th	1866
	August	7th	"	August	30th	1867
	June	13th	"	July	6th	1868
	September	7th	"	October	8th	1868
	July	6th	"	July	30th	1869

From	August	21st	through	September	13th	1870
	June	10th	"	July	6th	1871
	July	21st	"	August	13th	1872
	September	3rd	"	September	27th	1873
	June	22nd	"	July	16th	1874
	August	6th	"	August	29th	1875
	June	18th	"	June	27th	1876
	September	7th	"	October	7th	1876
	July	6th	"	July	29th	1877
	August	20th	"	September	13th	1878
	June	9th	"	July	6th	1879
	July	21st	"	August	13th	1880
	September	2nd	"	September	27th	1881
	June	21st	"	July	15th	1882
	August	5th	"	August	29th	1883
	September	8th	"	October	7th	1884
	July	5th	"	July	29th	1885
	August	20th	"	September	12th	1886
	June	9th	"	July	6th	1887
	July	20th	"	August	12th	1888
	September	2nd	"	September	26th	1889
	June	21st	"	July	15th	1890
	August	5th	"	August	28th	1891
	September	8th	"	October	7th	1892
	July	5th	"	July	28th	1893
	August	19th	"	September	12th	1894
	June	8th	"	July	6th	1895
	July	20th	"	August	12th	1896
	September	1st	"	September	26th	1897
	June	20th	"	July	14th	1898
	August	4th	"	August	28th	1899
	September	9th	"	October	8th	1900
	July	5th	"	July	29th	1901
	August	20th	"	September	12th	1902
	June	9th	"	July	7th	1903
	July	20th	"	August	12th	1904
	September	2nd	"	September	26th	1905
	June	21st	"	July	15th	1906

From	August	5th	through	August	28th	1907
	September	9th	"	October	7th	1908
	July	5th	"	July	28th	1909
	August	19th	"	September	12th	1910
	June	9th	"	July	7th	1911
	July	19th	"	August	12th	1912
	September	1st	"	September	26th	1913
	June	20th	"	July	15th	1914
	August	4th	"	August	28th	1915
	September	9th	"	October	7th	1916
	July	4th	"	July	28th	1917
	August	19th	"	September	11th	1918
	June	8th	"	July	7th	1919
	July	19th	"	August	11th	1920
	September	1st	"	September	25th	1921
	June	20th	"	July	14th	1922
	August	4th	"	August	27th	1923
	September	9th	"	October	7th	1924
	July	4th	"	July	27th	1925
	August	18th	"	September	11th	1926
	June	8th	"	July	7th	1927
	July	18th	"	August	11th	1928
	August	31st	"	September	25th	1929

VENUS IN VIRGO

THE cold and earthy and mercurial nature of Virgo may be described as the very opposite to that of Venus. The planet, too, is in her fall and never develops properly. She may make a woman a careful housewife and a good hostess—for Virgo distributes the affections, forbids friendships but encourages acquaintanceships —but never a loving wife or a passionate mistress, unless there are some remarkably warm aspects to intensify her nature. Women of the town, many of whom are incapable of true feeling of any kind, often have this position. The native, too, is usually fastidious about people. Others are inclined to consider him cold, heartless and repellent. On the other hand, the *sang-froid* and aplomb which his indifference gives often make him a favorite on the lecture platform or the stage.

We find it, for example, in the horoscope of Marshall P. Wilder, the dwarf humorist. A very good example of its peculiar manifestation in art is the painter Millet. The perception is extraordinarily keen and accurate.

We find little development of the emotional nature in this position. Some of the most notoriously cold and even callous people in history have possessed it. However, it does not always turn to evil, and, in many cases, the position is a decided advantage in life. For example, one may attribute much of Anna Kingsford's high mentality to this cause. Her tenderer feelings were distributed through intellectual channels. We find a similar case in Thomas Mott Osborne, and these two examples may be considered the very flower of this position. The same development of emotion on humanitarian rather than on personal lines is clearly marked in Samuel Taylor Coleridge, but here it is noticeable how Virgo works upon Venus in courting the native to be, or at least to seem, cold, and to hold himself aloof, if not exactly from the society of his fellows, at least from any close intimacy with them. Similar qualities are observable in the horoscopes of President Hayes, President Carnot, President Kruger, Cardinal Gibbons, and Edward VI of England. In none of these can the position be described as having worked unfavorably. With Ludwig of Bavaria, however, the theatrical tendency is seen in an exaggerated form. He may be said rather to have acted his life than to have lived it. However, there are worse cases. In Caesar Borgia, this position produced downright callousness. This is, no doubt, emphasized by the shutting up of Venus in the twelfth house, her aspect to Saturn in the eleventh, and the fact that Virgo is actually the rising sign. It may seem at first sight surprising that Goethe, Dumas, and Guy de Maupassant should have this position, but further investigation clears up the difficulty. Goethe's Venus has the sextile of Neptune and the opposition of Jupiter and also the semi-sextile of Mercury, and Venus is powerfully placed in the tenth house. Dumas has the conjunction of Jupiter and Saturn, the semi-sextile of Sol and that of Uranus. De Maupassant has Mercury semi-sextile, Mars and Jupiter in conjunction. Such aspects from such great planets overpower the isolated influence of the sign, to a very large extent. It can still be traced, but only in minor matters.

The position of Venus does not exactly lack magnetism, but it is a different kind of magnetism from that which is usually understood by that word. James Coates, the mesmerist, had this position. The quality that enables a man to hypnotize successfully is very different from that which makes him a great lover. The position is admirable for a lawyer, giving him the power of insinuating his ideas into the minds of his hearers. Many very attractive speakers have this same position. People with Venus so situated have the power to express emotion without really feeling it. They can weep very convincingly for "Hecuba."

The position is also admirable for a nurse, where the greatest care and tenderness are required, yet where any trace of true pity or emotion would diminish the efficiency.

However, while not wishing to say anything derogatory to the natives who have this position, we must say that, so far as the development of Venus is concerned, it is not her highest development. It is a decided modification of her qualities and a limitation of her powers. It is, however, not to be regarded as so thoroughgoing an affliction as when she is in Aries.

The following are the names of well known persons who have Venus in the sign Virgo:

Henry Ford
Robert Treat Paine, Jr.
Edward W. Bok
John D. Rockefeller, Sr.
Leonard Wood
Sydney Rosenfeld
William Osborne Stoddard
William Gillette
Cardinal Gibbons
Melville E. Stone
Anna Kingsford
Alexander Dumas

Guy de Maupassant
Johann Wolfgang von Goethe

For the benefit of those who are not in possession of Raphael's Ephemeris, or who are not able to interpret the symbols contained therein, the years when Venus is in the sign Virgo are as follows:

From	August	17th	through	September	9th	1840
	September	30th	"	October	24th	1841
	July	19th	"	August	12th	1842
	September	1st	"	September	25th	1843
	October	9th	"	November	5th	1844
	August	2nd	"	August	25th	1845
	September	16th	"	October	9th	1846
	July	8th	"	August	7th	1847
	August	16th	"	September	8th	1848
	September	30th	"	October	23rd	1849
	July	18th	"	August	12th	1850
	September	1st	"	September	24th	1851
	October	9th	"	November	4th	1852
	August	1st	"	August	25th	1853
	September	16th	"	October	9th	1854
	July	8th	"	August	8th	1855
	October	17th	"	October	27th	1855
	August	16th	"	September	8th	1856
	September	29th	"	October	23rd	1857
	July	18th	"	August	12th	1858
	August	31st	"	September	24th	1859
	October	9th	"	November	4th	1860
	July	31st	"	August	24th	1861
	September	15th	"	October	8th	1862
	July	8th	"	August	8th	1863
	October	8th	"	November	1st	1863
	August	15th	"	September	7th	1864
	September	29th	"	October	22nd	1865
	July	17th	"	August	11th	1866
	August	31st	"	September	23rd	1867
	October	9th	"	November	4th	1868

From	July	31st	through	August	24th	1869
	September	14th	"	October	8th	1870
	July	7th	"	August	9th	1871
	October	1st	"	November	3rd	1871
	August	14th	"	September	7th	1872
	September	28th	"	October	22nd	1873
	July	17th	"	August	11th	1874
	August	30th	"	September	22nd	1875
	October	8th	"	November	3rd	1876
	July	30th	"	August	23rd	1877
	September	14th	"	October	7th	1878
	July	7th	"	August	10th	1879
	September	25th	"	November	4th	1879
	August	14th	"	September	6th	1880
	September	28th	"	October	21st	1881
	July	16th	"	August	10th	1882
	August	30th	"	September	22nd	1883
	October	8th	"	November	3rd	1884
	July	30th	"	August	23rd	1885
	September	13th	"	October	7th	1886
	July	7th	"	August	11th	1887
	September	19th	"	November	5th	1887
	August	13th	"	September	6th	1888
	September	27th	"	October	21st	1889
	July	16th	"	August	10th	1890
	August	29th	"	September	21st	1891
	October	8th	"	November	2nd	1892
	July	29th	"	August	22nd	1893
	September	13th	"	October	6th	1894
	July	7th	"	August	13th	1895
	September	13th	"	November	6th	1895
	August	13th	"	September	5th	1896
	September	27th	"	October	20th	1897
	July	15th	"	August	10th	1898
	August	29th	"	September	21st	1899
	October	9th	"	November	3rd	1900
	July	30th	"	August	23rd	1901
	September	13th	"	October	6th	1902

From July	8th	through	August	17th	1903
September	6th	"	November	8th	1903
August	13th	"	September	6th	1904
September	27th	"	October	21st	1905
July	16th	"	August	10th	1906
August	29th	"	September	21st	1907
October	8th	"	November	2nd	1908
July	29th	"	August	22nd	1909
September	13th	"	October	6th	1910
July	8th	"	November	8th	1911
August	13th	"	September	5th	1912
September	27th	"	October	20th	1913
July	16th	"	August	10th	1914
August	29th	"	September	21st	1915
October	8th	"	November	2nd	1916
July	29th	"	August	21st	1917
September	12th	"	October	5th	1918
July	8th	"	November	8th	1919
August	12th	"	September	4th	1920
September	26th	"	October	20th	1921
July	15th	"	August	9th	1922
August	28th	"	September	20th	1923
October	8th	"	November	2nd	1924
July	28th	"	August	21st	1925
September	12th	"	October	5th	1926
July	8th	"	November	9th	1927
August	12th	"	September	4th	1928
September	26th	"	October	19th	1929

VENUS IN LIBRA

VENUS in Libra is in her own house and, on the whole, stronger even than she is in Taurus. The only drawback to her excellence comes from the airy nature of the sign, which, conflicting with her earthy disposition, tends to diminish her domesticity. It is also important to note that Saturn is exalted in Libra, and in dealing with the aspects of Saturn and Venus it is shown how generally sinister is his effect upon her. In this sign, the Venus quality tends to be mysterious and bizarre, and suffers dark and inexplicable perversions. The ordinary bourgeois is usually very afraid of people having her in this position. She is too fine and subtle for the average man. The amatory side of Venus is not obvious; the feeling is refined into æstheticism. People with this position, however, often possess sincere affection, but it is important to express such affection more on the mental and spiritual planes than on others. The limitations of marriage are keenly felt. On the artistic side this is the best sign for Venus. She gives a magnificent sense of proportion, harmony and color, which can amount to genius. Vulgarity and blatancy are very distasteful, and uncongenial surroundings cause extreme unhappiness, and upset the nervous system. With all this there is a great love of simplicity in art. The Egyptian, Grecian and Chinese styles are preferred to the flamboyant and rococo.

Thus we see that, when Venus is in Libra, love is nearly always more and less than love, as understood by the average man. It is, to some extent, a religion, possessing its own ritual. Where disappointment occurs, the feeling is not that of a wounded heart, but rather as if a blasphemy had been uttered, or a crime against God committed. At times, the religious feeling in connection with this matter amounts almost to fetichism. This attitude often causes the native to dread the commonplace exceedingly, and, endeavoring to avoid that Scylla, he may be devoured by the Charybdis of the abnormal. Perversity of one sort or another is consequently common. This may not be actual vice—it results from refinement, delicacy and imagination.

Venus in this sign is released from earthy bondage. She takes wings and flies. She dwells in realms of air and the worst torture which she can suffer is her enchainment by bodily expression or material condition. Not only is *mariage de convenance* impossible to her, but even true love may be revolting as soon as it takes physical form. It is in some ways not altogether fortunate that so important a branch of life should be thus divorced from what Nature evidently intended as its limitation. Love was originally intended as a mere physical appetite. Its exaltation as amorism, romanticism, mysticism, æstheticism and the rest are superstructed, built upon that basis by the idealism of the Great Architect and His fellow-builders on the aspiring human plane.

The reader must not forget that Saturn is exalted in Libra, and, for this reason, there is much melancholy in the sign, which therefore transforms Venus from her simplicity, frankness and laughter into a subtle, secret, and somewhat austere Goddess, to be worshipped in secret shrines, rather than in the meadows. She is not content with offerings of flowers; she demands human sacrifice.

Of course, this is only a description of the action of this position on a single plane. The escape from flesh may be into many different fallacies. The effect of air, to which element Libra belongs, connects it with intellectuality; not only is it the ideal which is adored, even on the material plane, but the ideal frequently roots itself in devotion to causes of a religious, artistic or humanitarian character. In this connection we may mention the names of Madame Blavatsky, Frances Willard and Christabel Pankhurst.

The attitude of Savonarola towards love has Venus in Libra for its foundation, but, in his case, the planet is afflicted by the conjunction of Saturn within three degrees, while the Moon is square to her. Erasmus, with Jupiter trine, was rendered practically normal by this aid.

We have more characteristic examples still in Edward VII, and Queen Elizabeth. Here the influence of Libra as the judicial sign is very evident. These two monarchs were unquestionably the greatest diplomatists that ever occupied the throne of England. One sees a similar subtlety of judgment in Lord Brougham and Annie Besant. The position has a more obviously physical influence in the careers of Marie Bashkirtseff, Cleo de Mérode and Oscar Wilde. But the most powerful illustration of all is afforded by Martin Luther. Here it reached an extraordinarily powerful development, owing to the conjunction of Mars and Jupiter.

Venus is not sufficiently big to bear the whole weight of destiny. No amount of support can make her anything but yielding. Even in the most favorable cases, therefore, there is an element of possible disaster. Sooner or later, the clay pot bumps against the brass pot and is smashed. Louis XVI is a particularly striking instance. All his tact and sympathy failed to meet the situation which confronted him.

Those born with Venus in Libra are extremely careful about their surroundings. Harmony and beauty are as necesary to them as the air they breathe. They are much more particular about the manners of their friends than about their moral standards. They possess great personal dignity and a certain seriousness of attitude toward life which makes them almost pontifical. They possess charm, tact, a gravely sympathetic manner and much real kindness of heart. But they never allow this to degenerate into geniality. They dislike familiarity and do not allow anyone to take liberties with them.

There is a certain gaiety in the disposition, but it is kept below the surface. Frederick MacMonnies had Venus in Libra and his famous "Bacchante" might almost do for an astrological picture of this position at its brightest. There is always the feeling of the dance in Libra, but it is not the vulgar dance which is a mere expression of animal spirits. These exist, and exist strongly, but they are veiled by the religious instinct. The dance is, therefore, a religious dance, a subtle and esoteric ritual "inscrutable to the profane." In its highest expression, therefore, this position of Libra becomes almost divine. The perversities which have already been described may be considered as the trials of a pilgrim. At the end of the journey is the palace of that truth and beauty which are one.

The following are the names of well known persons who have Venus in the sign Libra:

Paul Von Hindenburg
Archduke Rudolph of Austria
Arnold Daly
Jonathan O. Armour
Ethel Barrymore
Henry Clay Barnaby
Walter H. Page
Theodore Dreiser
Frederick MacMonnies
Charles F. McKim
Kate Douglas Wiggin

For the benefit of those who are not in possession of Raphael's Ephemeris, or who are not able to interpret the symbols contained therein, the years when Venus is in the sign Libra are as follows:

From	September	10th	through	October	3rd	1840
	October	25th	"	November	17th	1841
	August	13th	"	September	8th	1842
	September	26th	"	October	19th	1843
	November	6th	"	November	30th	1844
	August	26th	"	September	19th	1845
	October	10th	"	November	2nd	1846
	August	8th	"	December	8th	1847
	September	9th	"	October	3rd	1848
	October	24th	"	November	17th	1849
	August	13th	"	September	7th	1850
	September	25th	"	October	18th	1851
	November	5th	"	November	30th	1852
	August	26th	"	September	18th	1853
	October	10th	"	November	2nd	1854
	August	9th	"	October	16th	1855
	October	28th	"	December	8th	1855
	September	9th	"	October	2nd	1856
	October	24th	"	November	16th	1857
	August	13th	"	September	7th	1858
	September	25th	"	October	18th	1859
	November	5th	"	November	29th	1860
	August	25th	"	September	18th	1861
	October	9th	"	November	1st	1862
	August	9th	"	October	7th	1863
	November	2nd	"	December	8th	1863
	September	8th	"	October	2nd	1864
	October	23rd	"	November	16th	1865
	August	12th	"	September	7th	1866
	September	24th	"	October	17th	1867
	November	5th	"	November	29th	1868
	August	25th	"	September	17th	1869
	October	9th	"	November	1st	1870
	August	10th	"	September	30th	1871
	November	4th	"	December	8th	1871
	September	8th	"	October	1st	1872
	October	23rd	"	November	15th	1873
	August	12th	"	September	7th	1874

From	September	23rd	through	October	16th	1875
	November	4th	"	November	28th	1876
	August	24th	"	September	17th	1877
	October	8th	"	October	31st	1878
	August	11th	"	September	24th	1879
	November	5th	"	December	8th	1879
	September	7th	"	September	30th	1880
	October	22nd	"	November	14th	1881
	August	11th	"	September	6th	1882
	September	23rd	"	October	16th	1883
	November	4th	"	November	28th	1884
	August	24th	"	September	16th	1885
	October	8th	"	October	31st	1886
	August	12th	"	September	18th	1887
	November	6th	"	December	8th	1887
	September	7th	"	September	30th	1888
	October	22nd	"	November	14th	1889
	August	11th	"	September	6th	1890
	September	22nd	"	October	15th	1891
	November	3rd	"	November	27th	1892
	August	23rd	"	September	16th	1893
	October	7th	"	October	30th	1894
	August	14th	"	September	12th	1895
	November	7th	"	December	8th	1895
	September	6th	"	September	29th	1896
	October	21st	"	November	13th	1897
	August	11th	"	September	6th	1898
	September	22nd	"	October	15th	1899
	November	4th	"	November	28th	1900
	August	24th	"	September	16th	1901
	October	7th	"	October	30th	1902
	August	18th	"	September	5th	1903
	November	9th	"	December	9th	1903
	September	7th	"	September	30th	1904
	October	22nd	"	November	14th	1905
	August	11th	"	September	7th	1906
	September	22nd	"	October	15th	1907
	November	3rd	"	November	27th	1908

From August	23rd	through	September	16th	1909
October	7th	"	October	30th	1910
November	9th	"	December	8th	1911
September	6th	"	September	29th	1912
October	21st	"	November	13th	1913
August	11th	"	September	6th	1914
September	22nd	"	October	15th	1915
November	3rd	"	November	27th	1916
August	22nd	"	September	16th	1917
October	6th	"	October	29th	1918
November	9th	"	December	8th	1919
September	5th	"	September	29th	1920
October	21st	"	November	13th	1921
August	10th	"	September	6th	1922
September	21st	"	October	14th	1923
November	3rd	"	November	26th	1924
August	22nd	"	September	15th	1925
October	6th	"	October	29th	1926
November	10th	"	December	8th	1927
September	5th	"	September	28th	1928
October	20th	"	November	12th	1929

VENUS IN SCORPIO

It is very unfortunate for Venus to find herself in a sign which is both martial and watery. It completely destroys any altruistic tendencies, and it may turn her amiability not only into sensuality but into something grosser still. Her influence is often extremely violent; passion is intense and physical; unless gratified it is likely to turn into hatred; and, even when it is reciprocated, its career is likely to be stormy, in particular afflictions it may end in treacheries and tragedies. People with this position run the greatest danger of getting themselves into social trouble. It is particularly important to guard against misalliance either with or without the assent of the law. The extreme violence of the feelings may also react ultimately upon the health; since, great as the capacity is, the desires are still stronger and may easily lead to dangerous excess.

A disappointment also frequently arises from too great straightforwardness. Such people are likely to frighten the birds which they wish to ensnare. They are sometimes unscrupulous in the pursuit of their plans. No consideration seems to weigh with them. This naturally results in what may pass with the world for success, and unquestionably the physical magnetism is as great of its kind as in any other sign. In fact Libra alone rivals it. But the magnetism of Libra is subtle and perverse, whereas that of Scorpio is coarse and gross.

In dealing with the nativities of people who have lacked the refining influences of education, this position stands for quite animal dissipation and is nearly always associated with drunkenness. People of a higher type naturally escape such extremes. But frequently the cynical temperament develops as a result of satiety. This is marked in the cases of Sainte Beuve, Benjamin Disraeli, and Marie Antoinette. In the last case one may regard this position of Venus in her horoscope as one of the principal causes of the French Revolution. One has only to examine the innumerable pamphlets which were written against her to see how this came about.

Venus in Scorpio does not appear compatible with any striking tendencies towards artistic development, and she is also here very weak in tact and amiability. It must be remembered that in this sign she is in her detriment. Of course, the usual modifications caused by aspects are always to be considered, but the position is so sensual that it takes a great deal to overcome its natural tendencies.

People with this position are extremely self-possessive in the matter of affection. Jealousy with them is a passion far more consuming than the love which has given birth to it. A trifling disappointment will turn love into hate, relentless and unscrupulous. The character of the passion is as physical as when Venus is in Taurus, but in the earthy sign, she connects with all the natural, genial, domestic, human qualities. Venus in Scorpio may be called almost demoniac; weary, but unsatisfied, is her motto. She never rests. Scorpio in many of its aspects is symbolized by the sea in storm, and the qualities of that element accurately symbolize this temperament.

The magnetism is extraordinarily strong, but may be called primitive. There is a kind of fascination which the innocent frequently fail to recognize, and which consequently makes them fall an easy prey. This type is curiously open to flattery. A compliment is always taken as surrender, as a tribute to the superiority of the native.

Venus in Scorpio is extremely passionate and irresistible. It will not be content with anything but exact fulfillment of its desires. It is consequently necessary for the loved one to comply absolutely, or at least to seem to comply with sufficient skill to pretend; and this is, evidently, by no means a dignified or worthy position for anyone to maintain.

It is noticeable that few people with this position have attained great fame, and the reason is clear. However brilliant may be the other qualities in the nativity, this one influence leads us so frequently to plain dissipation that it is not possible to pursue the career with that single-mindedness and greatness of heart which are necessary to consummate success.

It must be borne in mind that, when Venus is in Scorpio, the Sun and Mercury may, at the same time, be in either Libra or Sagittarius; in such case, much that has been said would be largely modified, or the education and circumstances of the native would be such that the qualities imparted by the pure Venus in Scorpio would be latent and never be brought to the surface. They might be expressed through a feeling of great dissatisfaction and suppression.

The following are the names of well known persons who have Venus in the sign of Scorpio:

A. J. Drexel-Biddle
Henry George
Frederick Remington
George W. Vanderbilt
John Philip Sousa
Duke of York
Mahatma Gandhi
Edith Cavell
Ralph Waldo Trine
Col. William Mitchell

For the benefit of those who are not in possession of Raphael's Ephemeris, or who are not able to interpret the symbols contained therein, the years when Venus is in the sign Scorpio are as follows:

From	January	1st		through	January	6th	1840
	October	4th		"	October	27th	1840
	November	18th		"	December	11th	1841
	September	9th		"	October	6th	1842
	October	20th		"	November	12th	1843
	December	1st		"	December	25th	1844
	September	20th		"	October	14th	1845
	November	3rd		"	November	26th	1846
	December	9th	1847	"	January	6th	1848
	October	4th		"	October	27th	1848
	November	18th		"	December	11th	1849
	September	8th		"	October	6th	1850
	October	19th		"	November	11th	1851
	December	1st		"	December	24th	1852
	September	19th		"	October	13th	1853
	November	3rd		"	November	26th	1854
	December	9th	1855	"	January	5th	1856
	October	3rd		"	October	26th	1856
	November	17th		"	December	10th	1857
	September	8th		"	October	6th	1858
	October	19th		"	November	11th	1859
	November	30th		"	December	24th	1860
	September	19th		"	October	13th	1861
	November	2nd		"	November	25th	1862
	December	9th	1863	"	January	5th	1864
	October	3rd		"	October	26th	1864
	November	17th		"	December	10th	1865
	September	8th		"	October	6th	1866
	October	18th		"	November	10th	1867
	November	30th		"	December	23d	1868
	September	18th		"	October	13th	1869
	November	2nd		"	November	25th	1870
	December	9th	1871	"	January	5th	1872
	October	2nd		"	October	25th	1872

From	November	16th		through	December	9th	1873
	September	8th		"	October	6th	1874
	October	17th		"	November	9th	1875
	November	29th		"	December	23rd	1876
	September	18th		"	October	12th	1877
	November	1st		"	November	24th	1878
	December	9th	1879	"	January	4th	1880
	October	1st		"	October	25th	1880
	November	15th		"	December	8th	1881
	September	7th		"	October	6th	1882
	October	17th		"	November	9th	1883
	November	29th		"	December	22nd	1884
	September	17th		"	October	12th	1885
	November	1st		"	November	23rd	1886
	December	9th	1887	"	January	4th	1888
	October	1st		"	October	24th	1888
	November	15th		"	December	8th	1889
	September	7th		"	October	7th	1890
	October	16th		"	November	8th	1891
	November	28th		"	December	22nd	1892
	September	17th		"	October	11th	1893
	October	31st		"	November	23rd	1894
	December	9th	1895	"	January	3rd	1896
	September	30th		"	October	24th	1896
	November	14th		"	December	7th	1897
	September	7th		"	October	7th	1898
	October	16th		"	November	8th	1899
	November	29th		"	December	22nd	1900
	September	17th		"	October	12th	1901
	October	31st		"	November	23rd	1902
	December	10th	1903	"	January	4th	1904
	October	1st		"	October	24th	1904
	November	15th		"	December	8th	1905
	September	8th		"	October	8th	1906
	December	16th		"	December	25th	1906
	October	16th		"	November	8th	1907
	November	28th		"	December	22nd	1908
	September	17th		"	October	11th	1909

From October	31st		through	November	23rd 1910
December	9th	1911	"	January	4th 1912
September	30th		"	October	24th 1912
November	14th		"	December	7th 1913
September	7th		"	October	9th 1914
December	6th		"	December	30th 1914
October	16th		"	November	8th 1915
November	28th		"	December	21st 1916
September	17th		"	October	11th 1917
October	30th		"	November	22nd 1918
December	9th	1919	"	January	3rd 1920
September	30th		"	October	23rd 1920
November	14th		"	December	7th 1921
September	7th		"	October	10th 1922
November	29th	1922	"	January	1st 1923
October	15th		"	November	7th 1923
November	27th		"	December	21st 1924
September	16th		"	October	11th 1925
October	30th		"	November	22nd 1926
December	9th	1927	"	January	3rd 1928
September	29th		"	October	23rd 1928
November	13th		"	December	6th 1929

VENUS IN SAGITTARIUS

Venus is in some ways at her best in this sign. She has not the passion which we have noticed in the other two fiery signs. She is more impulsive and less constant. The slightest rebuff kills the interest. And in no case is affection likely to be long-lived. These remarks apply to love rather than to friendship, for, in the latter, the fact that Jupiter rules Sagittarius comes into play.

For this reason we call Venus at her best; she has an aspiring and spiritual quality which tends to remove from her any taint of earthy grossness. This very quality, however, may in some eyes appear as a defect. Those who imagine that the only kind of love is that which is expressed in accordance with social conventions may be unmeasured in the hatred of such tendencies as this sign confers, particularly upon women.

It is very common to find fantastic passions such as have been celebrated by Baudelaire, Verlaine and Swinburne, as well as by the one supreme poetess that ever lived, Sappho. Those things which are gross and unrefined do not appeal. It is necessary to satisfy mental and spiritual cravings and also to content the imagination. The lack of earthiness, the absence of physical bonds, causes rapid changes which may be mistaken for caprice, but which are really not so; on the contrary, they are symptoms of fidelity to the ideal. People with this position are proud and high-spirited, and they demand the same qualities in those whom they love. Indelicacy shocks. Further it may be said that any attempt to bind down the affections is intensely resented. To fish for such people one must employ the finest lines and the smallest flies; though the more brightly they are colored, the more successful is likely to be the sport.

Examples of the peculiar delicacy or spirit conferred by this position are afforded by George Eliot, Robert Louis Stevenson, Chatterton, and Lewis Carroll. Perhaps, too, the unfortunate relations of Charles I with his ministers may be attributed to this position. He never seemed able to trust constantly to them. He would trust too much, become disappointed for quite insufficient reasons, and then betray them. One might also look at the political careers of Gladstone, Bright, John Burns, Winston Churchill and Theodore Roosevelt. The extraordinary rashness in speech of the last named is very typical of this position.

With most ordinary people, these qualities manifest as something not much better than heartlessness and fickleness. Love sparkles and glitters, but is without warmth. Venus does not expand sufficiently to glow or to ennoble the life with true affection. There is never any excess energy to waste. The native has just so much of the Venusian qualities as suits his own purpose. He has none to give to others. As the swift spark is very attractive to those who really seek love, people with Venus in this sign often cause the greatest disappointment—they attract the passion of really warm-hearted people and then fail to satisfy it. Often they cannot understand how they are failing. Similarly, they may cause much anxiety to those who love them because they do not reciprocate the affections of the other party, who may consequently believe that he is failing in kindness, when, in reality, it is merely that he is trying to rekindle a shooting star. Very often true passion is altogether lacking or, if it exists, it is as transient and ephemeral as we learn that certain brightly colored insects are.

It often happens that the natural instincts are replaced by fantasies, forms of love which are expressed by symbol rather than by sense. Hence, the natural purpose of Venus, which is, after all, vitally important to the race, is frequently thwarted. Venus in Sagittarius often induces the native to act in such ways as to avoid what is, after all, the one great glorious human attribute, willing sacrifice. Thus, a woman with Venus in Sagittarius might prefer to adopt a child rather than to go through the pains of bearing one.

In art, we find a very interesting expression of this position in Mark Twain. Here we see an art, extraordinarily jeweled, with brief scintillations, but we rarely find in his writings the large, sustained humor, elaborated and rendered complex by the interplay of one idea with another, such as we find in the greatest masters.

One may also recommend to the reader without comment, the study of three people very different in this position who are yet united by the presence of Venus in this sign: Hetty Green, Maude Adams and Evelyn Thaw.

The following are the names of well known persons who have Venus in the sign of Sagittarius:

Ramsay MacDonald
George Eliot
Will Carlton
Harriet Stanton Blatch
Henry E. Dixey
Maude Adams
Rev. George Clark Houghton
Andrew Carnegie
Nicholas Longsworth
Augustus Thomas
Henry Clay Frick
William E. Gladstone
Havelock Ellis
Rudyard Kipling
Robert Louis Stevenson

Forbes-Robertson
Fritz Kreisler
Theodore Roosevelt

For the benefit of those who are not in possession of Raphael's Ephemeris, or who are not able to interpret the symbols contained therein, the years when Venus was in the sign Sagittarius are as follows:

From	January	7th		through	February	1st	1840
	October	28th		"	November	21st	1840
	December	12th	1841	"	January	4th	1842
	October	7th		"	November	12th	1842
	December	14th	1842	"	February	2nd	1843
	November	13th		"	December	6th	1843
	December	26th	1844	"	January	18th	1845
	October	15th		"	November	8th	1845
	November	27th		"	December	20th	1846
	January	7th		"	January	31st	1848
	October	28th		"	November	20th	1848
	December	12th	1849	"	January	4th	1850
	October	7th		"	November	15th	1850
	December	6th	1850	"	February	3rd	1851
	November	12th		"	December	5th	1851
	December	25th	1852	"	January	18th	1853
	October	14th		"	November	8th	1853
	November	27th		"	December	19th	1854
	January	6th		"	January	31st	1856
	October	27th		"	November	20th	1856
	December	11th	1857	"	January	3rd	1858
	October	7th	1858	"	February	3rd	1859
	November	12th		"	December	4th	1859
	December	25th	1860	"	January	17th	1861
	October	14th		"	November	7th	1861
	November	26th		"	December	19th	1862
	January	6th		"	January	31st	1864
	October	27th		"	November	19th	1864
	December	11th	1865	"	January	2nd	1866

From	October	7th	1866	through	February	4th	1867
	November	11th		"	December	4th	1867
	December	24th	1868	"	January	17th	1869
	October	14th		"	November	7th	1869
	November	26th		"	December	18th	1870
	January	6th		"	January	30th	1872
	October	26th		"	November	19th	1872
	December	10th	1873	"	January	2nd	1874
	October	7th	1874	"	February	4th	1875
	November	10th		"	December	3rd	1875
	December	24th	1876	"	January	16th	1877
	October	13th		"	November	7th	1877
	November	25th		"	December	18th	1878
	January	5th		"	January	30th	1880
	October	26th		"	November	18th	1880
	December	9th	1881	"	January	1st	1882
	October	7th	1882	"	February	4th	1883
	November	10th		"	December	3rd	1883
	December	23rd	1884	"	January	16th	1885
	October	13th		"	November	6th	1885
	November	24th		"	December	17th	1886
	January	5th		"	January	29th	1888
	October	25th		"	November	18th	1888
	December	9th	1889	"	January	1st	1890
	October	8th	1890	"	February	5th	1891
	November	9th		"	December	2nd	1891
	December	23rd	1892	"	January	15th	1893
	October	12th		"	November	6th	1893
	November	24th		"	December	17th	1894
	January	4th		"	January	29th	1896
	October	25th		"	November	17th	1896
	December	8th		"	December	31st	1897
	October	8th	1898	"	February	5th	1899
	November	9th		"	December	2nd	1899
	December	23rd	1900	"	January	15th	1901
	October	13th		"	November	7th	1901
	November	24th		"	December	17th	1902
	January	5th		"	January	29th	1904

From October 25th		through	November 18th 1904
December 9th 1905		"	January 1st 1906
October 9th		"	December 15th 1906
December 26th 1906		"	February 6th 1907
November 9th		"	December 2nd 1907
December 23rd 1908		"	January 15th 1909
October 12th		"	November 6th 1909
November 24th		"	December 17th 1910
January 5th		"	January 29th 1912
October 25th		"	November 17th 1912
December 8th		"	December 31st 1913
October 10th		"	December 5th 1914
December 31st 1914		"	February 6th 1915
November 9th		"	December 2nd 1915
December 22nd 1916		"	January 14th 1917
October 12th		"	November 6th 1917
November 23rd		"	December 16th 1918
January 4th		"	January 28th 1920
October 24th		"	November 17th 1920
December 8th		"	December 31st 1921
October 11th		"	November 28th 1922
January 2nd		"	February 6th 1923
November 8th		"	December 1st 1923
December 22nd 1924		"	January 14th 1925
October 12th		"	November 6th 1925
November 23rd		"	December 16th 1926
January 4th		"	January 28th 1928
October 24th		"	November 16th 1928
December 7th		"	December 30th 1929

VENUS IN CAPRICORNUS

'HIS sign brings out the colder and more earthy side of Venus, and xercises a restricting influence, in many cases, upon the tempera- ient. While it gives strong and permanent attachments, yet the ature may be called capricious. The native loves the comic or Panic de of intrigue; he is likely to be somewhat gross and even lustful in the expression of attachment; he will waste time, health and money in the search for pleasure; yet at the same time he will be extremely petty about it. There is little amiability. Indifference is the real interior attitude. And this is only modified by gusts of storm. The native is usually jealous and exacting. He expects too much of other people; but that not through optimism or idealism, but, on the contrary, from self-interest.

People with Venus thus situated are usually very slow in developing the sexual instinct, and the later they marry the better their chances to make a success of it. Sometimes this tardiness is such that it never develops at all during the life time. This is often the case when other instincts happen to be tremendously powerful. We find many instances of people whose human side has failed to develop through the occupation of the mind with loftier ideals. We may notice the cases of William Blake, Swami Vivekenanda, Joseph Smith and Jeanne d'Arc, all of whom were occupied primarily with mystic conceptions. In the case of the Indian sage Venus took her revenge, as she nearly always does when slighted, and that which might have been after all quite as holy as any amount of meditation expressed itself in ways which nearly led to open scandal.

We have examples of a somewhat different kind of enthusiasm in John Ruskin, Dr. Zamenhof and Sir Edward Durning-Lawrence. In Ruskin's case, as is well known, there was actual physical disability. Science furnishes us with the names of Pasteur, Davy and Alfred Wallace, while an example of pure coldness of nature, with no enthusiasm to replace it, is given by William III.

It may be a little surprising at first sight to find that Alfred de Musset had this position of Venus. But the explanation is simple, for in his nativity Venus is on the cusp of the twelfth house, squared by Mars, and she is just turning retrograde. The mental attitude displayed in *Gamiani*, in which he was at least an accomplice, and many other of his writings, and the extraordinary developments of his personal character are fully explained by these facts.

Venus in Capricornus is a little inclined to be suspicious. The native demands that advances shall be made to him unmistakably, before he commits himself. He dreads rebuff. It is, therefore, necessary in dealing with such a person to give encouragement if it is really desired to accept him.

There is no danger of perversion in the sign in the ordinary sense of the word, but the native is very likely omnivorous. This applies to all the appetites equally. The native cannot bear to be bothered with refinement of any of the appetites. He wishes possession and demands the response, even more emphasized than his demand. He desires open demonstration of affection and if he imagines that he is being neglected, or if his pride be hurt, he is likely to change from great warmth of affection to the most icy indifference, but once being on intimate terms with a native of this sign, he may be trusted to behave admirably, so long as those conditions persist. He is constant, and a lover of home, preferring the fireside and domestic joys to social functions and the like.

There is no great aptitude for art connected with this sign and no great feeling for beauty in itself. The native is attracted by strength of character and other peculiarities which do not appeal to the ordinary man. Sometimes the character of the native is undeveloped on ordinary Venusian lines. Moral beauty appeals to him more than any other kind. We may mention in this connection the name of the Preacher Moody and of Arthur Brisbane, but much more characteristic of the usual development of character given by this position is the late Stanford White.

The following are the names of well known persons who have Venus in Capricorn:

George Harvey
Otto H. Kahn
Peter A. B. Widener
Frank O. Lowden
Hudson Maxim
Robert E. Peary
Pres. A. L. Lowell of Harvard
E. H. Sothern
Martin W. Littleton
Adelina Patti
Joseph Smith
Alfred de Musset
Cicero
John Ruskin

Sir Humphrey Davy
Richard Le Gallienne
Alexander Agassiz
Samuel Gompers
George Jay Gould
John Drew
Gatti-Cassazza

For the benefit of those who are not in possession of Raphael's Ephemeris, or who are not able to interpret the symbols contained therein, the years when Venus is in the sign Capricorn are as follows:

From	February 2nd	through	February 26th 1840
	November 22nd	"	December 15th 1840
	January 5th	"	January 28th 1842
	November 13th	"	December 13th 1842
	February 3rd	"	March 7th 1843
	December 7th	"	December 30th 1843
	January 19th	"	February 11th 1845
	November 9th	"	December 5th 1845
	December 21st 1846	"	January 13th 1847
	February 1st	"	February 25th 1848
	November 21st	"	December 15th 1848
	January 5th	"	January 27th 1850
	November 16th	"	December 5th 1850
	February 4th	"	March 7th 1851
	December 6th	"	December 29th 1851
	January 19th	"	February 11th 1853
	November 9th	"	December 4th 1853
	December 20th 1854	"	January 12th 1855
	February 1st	"	February 25th 1856
	November 21st	"	December 14th 1856
	January 4th	"	January 27th 1858
	February 4th	"	March 6th 1859
	December 5th	"	December 28th 1859
	January 18th	"	February 10th 1861
	November 8th	"	December 4th 1861
	December 20th 1862	"	January 12th 1863

From	February	1st		through	February	25th	1864
	November	20th		"	December	14th	1864
	January	3rd		"	January	26th	1866
	February	5th		"	March	6th	1867
	December	5th		"	December	28th	1867
	January	18th		"	February	10th	1869
	November	8th		"	December	4th	1869
	December	19th	1870	"	January	11th	1871
	January	31st		"	February	24th	1872
	November	20th		"	December	13th	1872
	January	3rd		"	January	26th	1874
	February	5th		"	March	6th	1875
	December	4th		"	December	27th	1875
	January	17th		"	February	9th	1877
	November	8th		"	December	4th	1877
	December	19th	1878	"	January	11th	1879
	January	31st		"	February	24th	1880
	November	19th		"	December	13th	1880
	January	2nd		"	January	25th	1882
	February	5th		"	March	6th	1883
	December	4th		"	December	27th	1883
	January	17th		"	February	9th	1885
	November	7th		"	December	4th	1885
	December	18th	1886	"	January	10th	1887
	January	30th		"	February	23rd	1888
	November	19th		"	December	12th	1888
	January	2nd		"	January	25th	1890
	February	6th		"	March	5th	1891
	December	3rd		"	December	26th	1891
	January	16th		"	February	8th	1893
	November	7th		"	December	4th	1893
	December	18th	1894	"	January	10th	1895
	January	30th		"	February	23rd	1896
	November	18th		"	December	12th	1896
	January	1st		"	January	24th	1898
	February	6th		"	March	5th	1899
	December	3rd		"	December	26th	1899
	January	16th		"	February	9th	1901

From November 8th		through	December	5th	1901
December 18th	1902	"	January	10th	1903
January 30th		"	February	23rd	1904
November 19th		"	December	12th	1904
January 2nd		"	January	25th	1906
February 7th		"	March	6th	1907
December 3rd		"	December	26th	1907
January 16th		"	February	8th	1909
November 7th		"	December	5th	1909
December 18th	1910	"	January	10th	1911
January 30th		"	February	23rd	1912
November 18th		"	December	12th	1912
January 1st		"	January	24th	1914
February 7th		"	March	6th	1915
December 3rd		"	December	26th	1915
January 15th		"	February	7th	1917
November 7th		"	December	5th	1917
December 17th	1918	"	January	9th	1919
January 29th		"	February	22nd	1920
November 18th		"	December	11th	1920
January 1st		"	January	24th	1922
February 7th		"	March	5th	1923
December 2nd		"	December	25th	1923
January 15th		"	February	7th	1925
November 7th		"	December	5th	1925
December 17th	1926	"	January	8th	1927
January 29th		"	February	22nd	1928
November 17th		"	December	11th	1928
December 31st	1929	"	January	23rd	1930

VENUS IN AQUARIUS

The general characteristic which we have noticed with the other two airy signs still applies to Aquarius. There is, however, a very strong tendency to a development of the affections on humanitarian lines. It is rare to find domesticity; nor is there any great tendency to intensity of passion. The plane of the affections is mostly spiritual and mental. Such love as exists has always the wings of the eagle and the head of the man. With this position of Venus, the religious and humanitarian instincts often take the place of those natural to the great mass of humanity. The founder of the Christian religion had Venus placed in this sign, and so had Brigham Young and Dr. Steiner. The humanitarian impulse is still visible, though in a perverted form, in the anarchist Vaillant; and the perversity is readily explained, since his Venus is squared by a rising Mars.

In science we have the great names of Copernicus, Newton, and Nostradamus. It is very clear in these cases that the interest of the heart was cosmic, and could not be fettered by deep personal attachments.

In the domain of the arts we find the names of Lord Byron and of Chopin. Both these men acquired considerable notoriety in the matter of their love affairs; but this fact must not mislead the reader. In both cases the intention was idealistic. And if, in their search for the rarest thing on earth, they fell from time to time into the hands of vampires, it is to be taken as confirming, not as refuting, our judgment of their quality. Their misfortune, indeed, is common. Unless Venus is extraordinarily well dignified, so as to remove her operations altogether from the personal plane, the native is likely to be called unmoral. He or she may try innumerable experiments, all equally disastrous; but no blame should be attached to such good people. The intention is invariably ideal. One may go further and say that they are deserving of every sympathy, for Aquarius makes them very clear sighted. And, even when most under the dominion of some temporary illusion, the native is all the while aware that he has not gotten what he wants.

It might be surprising, at first glance, to find Pope Alexander VI in this class, but, on reference to the horoscope, one sees immediately that Mars is in exact conjunction. It is only one further illustration of the fatal action of this combination.

People with Venus in this sign often arouse quite unreasonable jealousy in the marriage partner. Attracted intellectually to a stranger on a first meeting, a person under this influence may treat him or her as an intimate friend. The husband or wife frequently fails to realize that this means nothing. It is because love with such people is so entirely divorced from physical considerations that this occurs. They are extraordinarily constant, unselfish and sincere in love; their motto is to render unto Cæsar the things which are Cæsar's and to God the things which are God's. Having given themselves unreservedly on the physical plane to one person, they regard the matter as closed, but naturally see no reason why that should interfere with a warm intellectual friendship. It is just because they know there is no danger that they act in such a way as to make people think that there is.

Venus in Aquarius gives extraordinary power to divine character. In the case of a portrait artist, for example, he may be able to paint the spiritual rather than the physical image of the sitter, showing in the portrait qualities which perhaps are yet undeveloped. Similarly, especially when Mercury is in the same sign, one finds an excellent diagnostician who, with practically no symptoms to guide him, can yet discover in his patients the root of some deep-seated malady. Aquarius is so very spiritual a sign that its action is almost always likely to cause the native to perceive the transcendental reality beneath the mask of form. We have already insisted that the position of Venus exhibits the primary shape in which the non-ego presents itself to the ego, and, when Venus is in Aquarius, one may say that the native sees things, not so much as they are but as they will be.

While the native is not domestic, in the same way as when Venus is in Taurus, the same qualities are manifest, but in a much more intelligent form. A mother with Venus in Taurus is likely to spoil her children; if Venus is in Aquarius she is equally devoted but never foolish. She will pick out the best nurse, not merely the nicest one. She will criticize the child in a most impersonal way and thus develop its real talents, instead of being deluded by imaginary or desired talents into encouraging the wrong one. One may say that the ties of blood are not very important to people with this position of Venus; yet they act as admirably as if they were important, for they base their actions upon the real necessity of the situation, instead of upon mere traditional sentimentality.

The same characteristics apply in such matters as patriotism. President Wilson is a first-grade example of the action of this position. He did not allow himself to be swayed by the cries of the mob. He considered everything with what many people regard as undue deliberation, and took no action until he was absolutely satisfied as to the wisdom of the course proposed. He never allowed prejudice or passion to sway him. This is remarkably indicative of the power exercised by this sign, since Mars is in conjunction with Venus. His personal prejudices were extraordinarily strong, and his character dictatorial and overbearing, yet he did not allow this, as a rule, to hurry him into inconsiderate actions. As an example of the seriousness and general excellence of this position, we have such people as the sculptor Gutzon Borglum, the astrologer Ebenezer Sibley, Ellen Terry, Dr. Weir Mitchell, and George Ade. We have also Admiral Dewey, Bramwell Booth and Elihu P. Root, in whom these qualities may be studied to advantage.

We may pay a little more detailed attention to the case of Robert Burns. Here again, Mars is in conjunction with Venus; but, Venus being the lady of ascendant, the effect upon the personality is as great as in the case of President Wilson, just considered; but the Sun is also in conjunction and lends additional violence to the combination. Hence we find the Scottish poet really very passionate and very fickle, and the influence of the sign is shown mostly by the idealism which gave birth to that fickleness. We also find the humanitarian impulse extremely strong, expressing itself in the broad-mindedness and tolerance which was rather rare for his generation.

The following are the names of well known persons who have Venus in Aquarius:

Frank B. Kellogg
Jack London
Gloria Swanson
David Lloyd George
Gelett Burgess
David S. Bispham
John D. Rockefeller, Jr.
George Ade
Arthur Foote
William Dean Howells
Admiral George Dewey
John La Farge
Frederick François Chopin

Sir Isaac Newton
Lord Byron
Ellen Terry
Josef Hoffman
Franklin D. Roosevelt

For the benefit of those who are not in possession of Raphael's Ephemeris or who are not able to interpret the symbols contained therein, the years when Venus is in the sign Aquarius are as follows:

From	February	27th		through	March	22nd	1840
	December	16th	1840	"	January	9th	1841
	January	29th		"	February	21st	1842
	March	8th		"	April	3rd	1843
	December	31st	1843	"	January	23rd	1844
	February	12th		"	March	7th	1845
	December	6th	1845	"	January	3rd	1846
	January	14th		"	February	6th	1847
	February	26th		"	March	21st	1848
	December	16th	1848	"	January	8th	1849
	January	28th		"	February	20th	1850
	March	8th		"	April	3rd	1851
	December	30th	1851	"	January	22nd	1852
	February	12th		"	March	7th	1853
	December	5th	1853	"	January	3rd	1854
	January	13th		"	February	5th	1855
	February	26th		"	March	21st	1856
	December	15th	1856	"	January	8th	1857
	January	28th		"	February	20th	1858
	March	7th		"	April	2nd	1859
	December	29th	1859	"	January	22nd	1860
	February	11th		"	March	6th	1861
	December	5th	1861	"	January	4th	1862
	March	13th		"	March	24th	1862
	January	13th		"	February	5th	1863
	February	26th		"	March	20th	1864
	December	15th	1864	"	January	8th	1865

From	January	27th		through	February	19th	1866
	March	7th		"	April	2nd	1867
	December	29th	1867	"	January	21st	1868
	February	11th		"	March	6th	1869
	December	5th	1869	"	January	4th	1870
	March	4th	1870	"	March	28th	1870
	January	12th		"	February	4th	1871
	February	25th		"	March	20th	1872
	December	14th	1872	"	January	7th	1873
	January	27th		"	February	19th	1874
	March	7th		"	April	2nd	1875
	December	28th	1875	"	January	21st	1876
	February	10th		"	March	5th	1877
	December	5th	1877	"	January	5th	1878
	February	25th		"	March	30th	1878
	January	12th		"	February	4th	1879
	February	25th		"	March	19th	1880
	December	14th	1880	"	January	7th	1881
	January	26th		"	February	18th	1882
	March	7th		"	April	1st	1883
	December	28th	1883	"	January	20th	1884
	February	10th	1885	"	March	5th	1885
	December	5th	1885	"	January	6th	1886
	February	19th		"	April	1st	1886
	January	11th		"	February	3rd	1887
	February	24th		"	March	19th	1888
	December	13th	1888	"	January	6th	1889
	January	26th		"	February	18th	1890
	March	6th		"	April	1st	1891
	December	27th	1891	"	January	20th	1892
	February	9th		"	March	4th	1893
	December	5th	1893	"	January	8th	1894
	February	13th		"	April	2nd	1894
	January	11th		"	February	3rd	1895
	February	24th		"	March	18th	1896
	December	13th	1896	"	January	6th	1897
	January	25th		"	February	17th	1898
	March	6th		"	March	31st	1899

From	December	27th	1899	through	January	19th	1900
	February	10th		"	March	5th	1901
	December	6th	1901	"	January	11th	1902
	February	7th		"	April	4th	1902
	January	11th		"	February	3rd	1903
	February	24th		"	March	19th	1904
	December	13th	1904	"	January	7th	1905
	January	26th		"	February	18th	1906
	March	7th		"	April	1st	1907
	December	27th	1907	"	January	20th	1908
	February	9th		"	March	4th	1909
	December	6th	1909	"	January	15th	1910
	January	29th		"	April	4th	1910
	January	11th		"	February	2nd	1911
	February	24th		"	March	18th	1912
	December	13th	1912	"	January	6th	1913
	January	25th		"	February	17th	1914
	March	7th		"	April	1st	1915
	December	27th	1915	"	January	19th	1916
	February	8th		"	March	4th	1917
	December	6th	1917	"	April	5th	1918
	January	10th		"	February	2nd	1919
	February	23rd		"	March	18th	1920
	December	12th	1920	"	January	6th	1921
	January	25th		"	February	16th	1922
	March	6th		"	March	31st	1923
	December	26th	1923	"	January	19th	1924
	February	8th		"	March	3rd	1925
	December	6th	1925	"	April	5th	1926
	January	9th		"	February	1st	1927
	February	23rd		"	March	17th	1928
	December	12th	1928	"	January	5th	1929

VENUS IN PISCES

In this sign Venus is in her exaltation. The watery nature of the sign does not make her so voluptuous as we saw to be the case with

Cancer and Scorpio. Pisces is too psychic for that to happen. Softness and tenderness are brought out strongly, but are expressed as an unequalled capacity for devotion and self-sacrifice. A very striking example of this is given in the relations of Sir Richard Burton with his wife. In all other respects his nature was fiery, arrogant and domineering; but he treated her with a chivalry which did not even succeed in getting itself understood or appreciated. The same spirit, with a slightly wider field of expression, is found in "Chinese" Gordon.

As a general rule, indeed, the affections are likely to be widely distributed. When art is concerned, this position seems to give the faculty of handling large groups of people with ease. This is evident in the cases of Michael Angelo, Zola, Dickens, Victor Hugo and, with slightly less lustre, Rosa Bonheur. The affections, generally speaking, are simple and natural. There is a calm kindliness of feeling towards humanity in general, and there is very little tendency to snobbery, none at all to arrogance.

Possibly as a consequence of this, the native does not easily make enemies. On the other hand, he is likely in some measure to spoil his friends. This position does not excite in others that depth of emotion which leads to grand passions and great sacrifices. Relations with others seem to be taken too easily, and their devotion is not likely to develop, as it does often enough in the case of people far less calculated at the first sight to inspire the noblest sentiments. People with this position are usually devoted to their families. They not only love others, but care for and cherish them. Self-sacrifice is natural to the native, whenever his tender feelings are in question.

There is a great deal of romance mingled with these feelings. The native dissolves himself into the beloved, making a true union, and the greatest sorrow that can be experienced by a person with this position is when the beloved fails to appreciate his devotion to the full. Venus in this sign is not particularly fastidious; she is too ready for the pleasure the yielding gives to others. In some respects this is the highest possible development of Venus. The reader will remember Browning's poem in which one of the competing lovers says that she does not care what may be the qualities of the beloved, let him be an absolute scoundrel, with no good qualities at all; such a man gives the greatest opportunity for the exhibition of the noblest qualities of love, and the abbé called in to decide the case ends his judgment:

"The love which to one, and one only has reference, seems terribly like what perhaps gains God's preference."

Venus in Pisces is not in the least intellectual; she is intuitive, and this intuition is the outcome of her extraordinary nobility. Her willingness to pay the price, however great, gives her the privilege of a knowledge almost divine in its immediateness.

One of the most beautiful examples of this position is Edgar Allan Poe. In him, as critics have often pointed out, the instinct of love is almost abnormally pure. There is not a word in his writings which can be called coarse, gross or even free, yet his conception of passion is more romantic, more poetic than that of almost any other writer. In his very rhythm one feels the nature of his love. "Annabel Lee" and "Lenore" illustrate magnificently the vision which the poet has of women.

Of course, it is not always to be expected that we shall find this influence in such purity. George Washington took a much more practical view of sex.

Sometimes, we discover a romanticism and idealism not necessarily connected with sex. We may put down the passion for exploration which characterized H. M. Stanley and the Duke of the Abruzzi to this position, at least in part. It is the romantic view of things which is indicated. As we have seen in other signs, Venus represents the exterior of things. These explorers translated into the actions of manhood, boyhood's dream of the romance of geography. Flammarion is in very much the same position with regard to astrology, and the attitude of C. W. Leadbetter towards the astral plane may also be ascribed to this position.

It is a very good position for actors, who, when they possess it, incline to prefer to undertake the representation of romantic and heroic parts. Henry Irving and William Terris illustrate this point. There is also the example of Mary Garden; the comprehensive character of her art and its extraordinary romance and glow recall the very similar qualities otherwise expressed in Michael Angelo.

The following are the names of well known persons who have Venus in Pisces:

George Washington
Geraldine Farrar
Howard Chandler Christy
Will Levington Comfort
Thomas A. Edison
Dr. William S. Bainbridge
"Buffalo Bill" (Wm. S. Cody)
Rev. Leighton S. Parks
Richard Watson Gilder
Walter J. Damrosch
Charles E. Hughes
Charles M. Schwab
William Faversham
Robert Mantell
Algernon Blackwood
Charles A. Lindbergh
Antonio Scotti
Rosa Bonheur
Victor Hugo
Cammille Flammarion
Sir Henry Irving
William Terris
Charles Dickens
Emile Zola

For the benefit of those who are not in possession of Raphael's Ephemeris, or who are not able to interpret the symbols contained therein, the years when Venus is in the sign Pisces are as follows:

From	March	23rd	through	April	15th	1840
	January	10th	"	February	4th	1841
	February	22nd	"	March	17th	1842
	April	4th	"	April	29th	1843
	January	24th	"	February	16th	1844
	March	8th	"	April	1st	1845
	January	4th	"	May	6th	1846
	February	7th	"	March	2nd	1847

From	March	22nd	through	April	15th	1848
	January	9th	"	February	3rd	1849
	February	21st	"	March	16th	1850
	April	4th	"	April	29th	1851
	January	23rd	"	February	16th	1852
	March	8th	"	March	31st	1853
	January	4th	"	May	6th	1854
	February	6th	"	March	1st	1855
	March	22nd	"	April	14th	1856
	January	9th	"	February	3rd	1857
	February	21st	"	March	16th	1858
	April	3rd	"	April	28th	1859
	January	23rd	"	February	15th	1860
	March	7th	"	March	30th	1861
	January	5th	"	March	12th	1862
	March	25th	"	May	6th	1862
	February	6th	"	March	1st	1863
	March	21st	"	April	14th	1864
	January	9th	"	February	3rd	1865
	February	20th	"	March	15th	1866
	April	3rd	"	April	28th	1867
	January	22nd	"	February	15th	1868
	March	7th	"	March	30th	1869
	January	5th	"	March	3rd	1870
	March	29th	"	May	6th	1870
	February	5th	"	February	28th	1871
	March	21st	"	April	13th	1872
	January	8th	"	February	2nd	1873
	February	20th	"	March	15th	1874
	April	3rd	"	April	27th	1875
	January	22nd	"	February	14th	1876
	March	6th	"	March	29th	1877
	January	6th	"	February	24th	1878
	March	31st	"	May	6th	1878
	February	5th	"	February	28th	1879
	March	20th	"	April	13th	1880
	January	8th	"	February	2nd	1881
	February	19th	"	March	14th	1882

From April	2nd	through	April	27th	1883
January	21st	"	February	14th	1884
March	6th	"	March	29th	1885
January	7th	"	February	18th	1886
April	2nd	"	May	6th	1886
February	4th	"	February	27th	1887
March	20th	"	April	12th	1888
January	7th	"	February	2nd	1889
February	19th	"	March	14th	1890
April	2nd	"	April	26th	1891
January	21st	"	February	13th	1892
March	5th	"	March	28th	1893
January	9th	"	February	12th	1894
April	3rd	"	May	5th	1894
February	4th	"	February	27th	1895
March	19th	"	April	12th	1896
January	7th	"	February	1st	1897
February	18th	"	March	13th	1898
April	1st	"	April	26th	1899
January	20th	"	February	13th	1900
March	6th	"	March	29th	1901
January	12th	"	February	6th	1902
April	5th	"	May	6th	1902
February	4th	"	February	27th	1903
March	20th	"	April	12th	1904
January	8th	"	February	2nd	1905
February	19th	"	March	14th	1906
April	2nd	"	April	27th	1907
January	21st	"	February	13th	1908
March	5th	"	March	28th	1909
January	16th	"	January	28th	1910
April	5th	"	May	6th	1910
February	3rd	"	February	27th	1911
March	19th	"	April	12th	1912
January	7th	"	February	2nd	1913
February	18th	"	March	13th	1914
April	2nd	"	April	26th	1915
January	20th	"	February	13th	1916

From	March	5th	through	March	28th	1917
	April	6th	"	May	6th	1918
	February	3rd	"	February	26th	1919
	March	19th	"	April	11th	1920
	January	7th	"	February	2nd	1921
	February	17th	"	March	12th	1922
	April	1st	"	April	26th	1923
	January	20th	"	February	12th	1924
	March	4th	"	March	27th	1925
	April	6th	"	May	6th	1926
	February	2nd	"	February	26th	1927
	March	18th	"	April	11th	1928
	January	6th	"	February	2nd	1929

MARS SYMBOLICALLY CONSIDERED

MARS is the God of War. Pestilence and famine are his captains; before him goes terror, and after him gallops the phantom of Death.

Mars is a vigorous and fiery god; he is the soldier "seeking the bubble reputation even in the cannon's mouth." He is force, but not fruition. He is still in the heat of the struggle. He has not acquired that authority, dignity, repose which come with success.

Mars is a male and strenuous power; but he is the prey of Venus. He is Samson in the arms of Delilah; for all men must resist Kundry, or Lilith, or Venus, in whatever form she may appear, in order to attain mastery of life. Mars was caught by Vulcan in the embraces of Venus; the angry god, arising from Etna, threw his net over the pair, and exposed them to the inextinguishable laughter of the Gods. Vulcan is volcanic fire; he forges the thunderbolts of Jove, and therefore Venus is his lawful spouse.

Only with reverence, and by law, sustained by high and holy purpose, dares one enter the most sacred relationship of life. To go with lightness is to expose oneself to scandal, and to ridicule; more, it is to lose virtue, the armor of man's soul. Man should not lay aside his sword and shield. He should remember a hundred other warriors of history and of legend, betrayed to shame and death by their own weaknesses. In "Parsifal," Wagner tells once more the story. Beware lest the sacred lance that should subdue the heathen be snatched from you in a moment of dalliance, and thrust into your own side.

The doctrine of the prophets and saints has been more misunderstood than any other. It is not the surrender of the body that destroys; but the abdication of the soul. It is the divorce of Passion from Religion that works mischief. Creation is the special function of Deity; and when we create either by art or by love, we are like God. Therefore, to prostitute art or love to commerce or even to pleasure is the unpardonable sin.

Life is a sacrament, and the energy of Mars is the red flame of the fire upon the altar. Mars is manhood; he is the knight vowed to serve his lady; and that lady must be to him the ideal, adored and not to be attained. Only at the end of his knight-errantry may he look for his reward. He is a warrior; his duty is first to his liege lord.

So, then, let Mars rear his fiery crest upon the heavens. He is the chosen guardian of the fortress of the soul. All depends upon his courage and his valor and his vigilance. He must have knocks. He must expose his breast to the violence of the foe, and he must not allow himself to be surprised and slain.

Jupiter needs Mars to girdle him with steel, or the kingdom may be lost forever. Most in the stress of life, in the violence of circumstance, do we need character and energy. We must be stern and tireless. We must spare no drop of blood in the defense of our soul's welfare. Since life is a contest for the great prize of godhead, falter, and the sword is at the throat. Avert your glance for the fraction of a second from the eyes of your antagonist, (whether it be courage or attention that fails, it matters not) and his rapier slips past your guard. Let your wrist weaken, whether from insufficient training or from exhaustion through a breach of will, and the glittering point is in your heart.

This is the interpretation that a wise man puts on Mars, and this is the spirit in which he seeks to use the vital and dangerous energy with which he is endowed from on high.

Without Energy, Being itself could not manifest; Motion is necessary to Matter if a Universe is to exist. But this Energy and Motion must be directed and controlled. It must not be allowed to dissipate, or to escape in ways unwilled. The fire of the Sun is the first weapon of mankind; but fire let loose is a destroying energy.

All force is necessary, but the forces of Nature are the natural foes of man; it is only when he confines them and tames them that they serve him. Let us see to it that we ride as kings upon the stallion of our own desires. Thus shall we course upon the heavens; thus shall we enter in triumph the gates of the City of God.

MARS IN THE SIGNS

It is important at the outset to make a distinction, subtle on the surface, but fundamentally cardinal, between the esoteric qualities of Mars and Uranus. The latter is happily phrased as "the magical will," while Mars is understood to mean "will-power." Yet there should be no confusion here. Uranus is a will, deep-seated, spiritual, transcendental, and may exist without the activity, energy and potency to make itself operative. One can conceive of a most powerful character physically paralyzed; and, on the other hand, of a person of enormous flaming energy scattering it abroad to no purpose. The first of these would be indicated by a strong Uranus and an afflicted Mars; the last by a weak Uranus and a powerful Mars.

Mars represents the muscular system; it is often found that a weak brain goes with great development of physical strength, and vice versa. It might even occur that the whole of the higher faculties might be harmonious and strong, yet fail to make good, owing to the lack of practical energy, boldness, and capacity for rather brutal work. The material plane continually presents obstacles to the higher nature; Mars is the force which pushes such obstacles aside, or demolishes them. We shall find similarly that Venus gives the power of dealing with them tactfully and adroitly, and that Mercury bestows discrimination with regard to them. Hence we have as it were, a higher and a lower triad dependent upon the soul Neptune.

Uranus = the magical will
Saturn = the ego and its divine wisdom
Jupiter = the altruistic qualities; the spiritual love
Mars = the human will

Mercury = the human reason
Venus = the affections and physical love.

The Sun and Moon complete the triad of Neptune; the Sun being the essence of life itself, the Moon the psychic envelope, the aura, or animal soul, and Neptune, the spiritual soul.

It is thus at last that we are able to obtain in some detail the full idea of Astrology, to understand how each horoscope presents a complete picture of the native, and thereby enables us to describe him in every detail.

To return to Mars, his external influence upon the man as distinguished from his internal influence within the character, is that of excitement, inflammation, violence, and accident. Thus a square of Mars to the Sun might give a rugged constitution and dauntless energy, and at the same time subject the native to fevers and accidents from fire or steel.

The power of Mars will, of course, as before, be modified by his position in the Zodiac, and, owing to his material and therefore easily-moulded nature, the variations will be, on the whole, more extreme than we have found to be the case with planets of greater spirituality.

Yet so great is his importance, that a badly afflicted Mars practically inhibits the native from making wise use of his enormous energy. It is a curious and somewhat paradoxical situation, and the student cannot pay too much attention to its study.

MARS IN ARIES

In Aries, Mars is in his own house, tremendously strong. The fiery and precipitate nature of Aries blends admirably with his, and the essential passion of the character, as indicated by Uranus, leaps forward unchecked, to its fullest development. We have, therefore, a long list of famous persons with this position; it will be apparent that even those with inherent weakness of disposition accomplish their ends; the petty, crazy, or ignoble purpose is executed as surely as the lofty configuration and the wise desire.

We have a very characteristic and salient illustration of the action of Mars in the nativity of Jesus of Nazareth, where he is conjoined with Neptune, opposed to Jupiter, square to the Sun and Mercury, and sextile to Saturn. In this extraordinary complex, Mars on the cusp of the seventh house is very strong to deal with public affairs, and Saturn adds wisdom to that force. But the opposition of Jupiter interferes with material power, and the square of Mars and the Sun acting externally predicts the danger of violent death.

We find the Mars of Emmanuel Swedenborg in the third house, giving great excitability to the mind, but the opposition of Saturn is not very favorable, as this should tend to deny the higher wisdom to that mind. It is interesting to observe Mars thus usurping the position of the mental ruler, Mercury, who is rising. The subjective mind is, therefore, much stronger than the objective or rational mind; so that the intuitions of the native were more nearly correct than his arguments.

Swami Vivekananda, with Mars in opposition to Jupiter, exactly squared by a rising Venus, and Jupiter in square to the Sun, was hindered as a practical propagandist. The gentleness of his nature was too great to enable him to use a battering-ram against the inertia of other minds. Mars, however, is again in the third house, and we see in him the same forceful intellect, the same iron will to solve the problems of existence. Per se, Mars was adequate; it was only in connection with the non-ego that the weakness appeared.

To turn to political types, one of the most successful in the world's history was Queen Victoria. Astute to the point of hiding her political aims from even many of the wise, she aggrandized her throne and held back the republican movement in England with matchless skill. The sextile of Jupiter to her Mars must have been of unqualified assistance in this matter, and accounts for the good fortune which attended her indomitable purpose.

Franz Josef, again, who achieved an even more difficult task in Austria-Hungary, has a Mars sextile to Uranus, square to Jupiter, and placed on the cusp of the seventh house. Jupiter being in the fourth house, the affliction by Mars accounts to some extent for his domestic tragedies. But the Aries power of Mars himself is to be thanked for the courage and energy displayed in his policy.

Nicholas II, on the other hand, has no strength of Mars beyond this position in Aries; and, as he is in the twenty-eighth degree, some of this influence is more Taurian than Arian, and Mars is, therefore, not a strong or favorable planet. Venus on the cusp of the eleventh in conjunction with Uranus seems to imply that the Tsar trusted to alliances, and was deceived therein. Saturn in the fourth indicates his tragic end.

Contrast this weak character with the fiery Cromwell. Here Mars, Lord of the Ascendant, is just above the eastern horizon, with the Sun, Venus, and Mercury rising just below him. Saturn opposed, denies far-sighted political wisdom; perhaps this made it impossible for him to found the dynasty he so dearly hoped for; but the primary position of the planet of battles rendered it impossible for him to fail in courage or energy, as soldier or as ruler.

In George III Mars appears as obstinacy. The Moon and Uranus square him, making the king deluded and stupid; hence his loss of the American colonies through sheer mismanagement. But Mars is on the cusp of the tenth house, very powerful; so that the ultimate issue of England's war with Napoleon, who had Saturn in the midheaven, could never have been in doubt to any enlightened astrologer.

Gambetta, who "stamped his foot amid the ashes of the glory of France, and sparks of manhood sprang armed to life at his summons," has the Sun and Mercury very near conjunction to Mars, with Venus and Uranus semi-sextile, and Neptune sextile.

In literary men, artists, and musicians, this position of Mars seems to imply great mastery of technique, great power of execution. It further seems to mean much brilliancy and energy; even originality is enhanced where Uranus is well placed and favorably aspected.

Among novelists, for example, Zola and Dickens may be fairly classed together. Their pugnacity and propagandism is all decidedly characteristic of Mars in Aries. Zola's Mars is exceedingly strong, with Mercury conjoined, the Sun and Moon not far off, Uranus semi-sextile, Neptune sextile, and Saturn trine. Dickens had not nearly so powerful a Mars as this, and it is in the fifth house, confining his pugnacity to his art. It would never have occurred to Dickens to placard London with a violent political squib, as Zola did in Paris. He had to work indirectly through his novels.

Compare now the virile, forceful Baudelaire with the dreamy and gentle Maeterlinck. The latter only has Uranus sextile to Mars which is in the fifth house; it is good enough to win out, but the force is hardly strong enough to be called revolutionary. Baudelaire has Mars in a tremendous complex. Neptune and Uranus conjoined, are square to him—hence, his eventual paralytic insanity; the Moon stands apart; but all the other five planets are in conjunction with him. Here is overwhelming force indeed; and we understand how his passion for the Infinite yet burns in those words of his that seem to corrode the soul like acid!

Albrecht Dürer has Mars culminating in the ninth house. There is no particular support, so the effect is limited to craftmanship, especially in working upon metals or with them. Mars, incidentally, is a very angry, passionate, impatient planet when excited to the full; the student will do well to contrast carefully the extremes as presented by Dürer and Baudelaire.

In music we have two more great originators of superb technique; Chopin and Richard Strauss. The former has Neptune trine and the Sun semi-sextile; Saturn, too, is close to Neptune; and all this tends in a way to modify the fire of Mars, and lead him into subtle channels. Yet in his "Polonaises" the essential force of the spirit is well represented, as well as the general firmness and conciseness of his technique.

Strauss has Venus sextile, Saturn in opposition, Neptune in conjunction; this is a somewhat great excitation of Mars, who, moreover, is in the tenth house, dominating the horoscope. Hence, we may judge, come the wrath and fury of his "Electra" and his "Salome," and the violent perfections of his technique; the conjunction of Neptune obviously accounts for their eccentricity.

Havelock Ellis, to conclude, another militant person, has this same position of Mars. Venus is square, Saturn trine, Uranus sextile on one side and the Moon on the other. It is a strong but not a violent complex, and fairly descriptive of his method.

For the benefit of those who are not in possession of Raphael's Ephemeris, or who are not able to interpret the symbols contained therein, the years when Mars is in the sign Aries are as follows:

From March	7th	through	April	14th	1840
February	14th	"	March	26th	1842
January	23rd	"	March	3rd	1844
December	22nd 1845	"	February	6th	1846
June	17th	"	August	4th	1847
May	18th	"	June	27th	1849
April	26th	"	June	3rd	1851
April	4th	"	May	13th	1853
March	15th	"	April	23rd	1855
February	22nd	"	April	2nd	1857
February	1st	"	March	13th	1859
January	5th	"	February	17th	1861
July	6th 1862	"	January	14th	1863
May	28th	"	July	8th	1864
May	4th	"	June	12th	1866
April	12th	"	May	20th	1868
March	23rd	"	April	30th	1870
March	2nd	"	April	10th	1872
February	9th	"	March	21st	1874
January	17th	"	February	27th	1876
December	10th 1877	"	January	30th	1878
June	9th	"	July	23rd	1879
May	13th	"	June	21st	1881
April	21st	"	May	29th	1883
March	31st	"	May	8th	1885
March	11th	"	April	18th	1887
February	17th	"	March	28th	1889
January	26th	"	March	7th	1891
December	28th 1892	"	February	10th	1893
June	23rd	"	August	18th	1894
October	13th	"	December	30th	1894
May	22nd	"	July	1st	1896
April	29th	"	June	6th	1898
April	8th	"	May	16th	1900
March	19th	"	April	26th	1902
February	27th	"	April	6th	1904
February	5th	"	March	16th	1906
January	11th	"	February	22nd	1908

From	July	21st	through	September	26th 1909
	November	21st 1909	"	January	22nd 1910
	June	3rd	"	July	15th 1911
	May	8th	"	June	16th 1913
	April	17th	"	May	25th 1915
	March	27th	"	May	4th 1917
	March	7th	"	April	14th 1919
	February	13th	"	March	24th 1921
	January	21st	"	March	3rd 1923
	December	19th 1924	"	February	4th 1925
	June	15th	"	July	31st 1926
	May	17th	"	June	25th 1928

MARS IN TAURUS

In Taurus, Mars is in his detriment, and his fiery energy is largely transformed into obstinacy. The heaviness of Taurus weighs him down, and, though he fights with desperate courage, there is not that élan which we found him to possess in Aries. Nor is the Venusian character of the sign favorable to his full development; since, Taurus being earthy, it sometimes occurs that he is degraded to be cruel and callous. Yet, at his best, he is steady and earnest; not so original, brilliant, nor lucky as when in Aries, nor so confident of the issue; but dogged, and as the saying goes: "Dogged does it."

We have examples of this in two of the most patient and persevering of those noble men who have given their lives to extend the empire of knowledge; Sir Isaac Newton and Huxley. The latter, with the Sun in conjunction and Mercury very close, an exact trine of Uranus and a near one of Neptune, has an almost ideal Mars. He is in the eleventh house, showing the influence of the native working through friends and colleagues. Newton's Mars has sextiles of Jupiter and the Moon and a trine of the Sun within seven degrees; and Uranus is very near the opposition. He was by no means a great fighter, like Huxley, as Mars is not so important in his nativity. Here we see only the patience and labor involved in his work, and the indomitable courage with which he attacked problems.

The Mars of Annie Besant is formidable enough, with Jupiter and the Moon sextile and Uranus semi-sextile. Mars is rising just below Uranus, and Aries is on the Ascendant. This makes the whole personality militant and ambitious, but, in the absence of help from the Sun or Saturn—or even Venus—one cannot but regard the complex as unfortunate. Colonel Olcott, on the contrary, has the Sun and Venus square on one side, Uranus square on the other, and Saturn trine. Mars is not the center of activity, but Venus, as Lady of the Ascendant; it is excellent, on the whole, making him an admirable and trustworthy subordinate.

The horoscope of Houdini gives an excellent example of the extreme power of Mars on the material plane, even enabling him to overcome the strongest oppositions of such material objects as fetters, etc. Saturn and Uranus in opposition to each other are both squaring Mars, a most unusual development of occult powers.

In the world of literature and art, we find a group deserving careful contrast with those who have Mars in Aries. Compare Reynolds with Dürer, the easy voluptuous style of the one with the austere sincerity of the other. Set Tchaikovsky against Strauss and Chopin; George Sand and Alphonse Daudet against Zola. It at once appears how the brilliancy of the Aries-Mars is weighed down and subdued in Taurus. Against Dickens we may put Dumas, and, though it would be possible to maintain that Dumas is a much more brilliant writer than Dickens, this is a matter of the higher planets; the technique of Dickens sparkles and fumes with brilliancies often ill-harmonized; that of Dumas is infinitely smoother and more voluptuous.

Among soldiers, compare Cromwell with Charles George Gordon. The latter, daring and courageous as he was, was yet "a Christian gentleman." His Mars is toned down by Taurus; and, indeed, one may attribute his failure in the Soudan to a lack of grip in dealing with the fierce Mohammedan spirits that surrounded him.

Worthy of our most careful consideration are two very strong examples of Mars corrupted, the one to the earth of Taurus, the other to its Venus; Jay Gould and Nero.

The financier has Saturn in direct opposition, and Uranus sextile. The former aspect is here abominably bad. Mars is in the house of friends and we can well understand how he sold out his colleagues. Nero has Jupiter in opposition, a presage of weakness, and Venus in conjunction makes Mars excitable and passionate without giving him strength. There is a trine of Saturn, which renders him effective, however; in this case with most unfortunate results.

For the benefit of those who are not in possession of Raphael's Ephemeris, or who are not able to interpret the symbols contained therein, the years when Mars is in the sign Taurus are as follows:

From	April	15th		through	May	26th	1840
	March	27th		"	May	6th	1842
	March	4th		"	April	15th	1844
	February	7th		"	March	25th	1846
	August	5th	1847	"	February	24th	1848
	June	28th		"	August	10th	1849
	June	4th		"	July	15th	1851
	May	14th		"	June	23rd	1853
	April	24th		"	June	3rd	1855
	April	3rd		"	May	14th	1857
	March	14th		"	April	24th	1859
	February	18th		"	April	2nd	1861
	January	15th		"	March	8th	1863
	July	9th		"	August	25th	1864
	June	13th		"	July	24th	1866
	May	21st		"	June	30th	1868
	May	1st		"	June	10th	1870
	April	11th		"	May	21st	1872
	March	22nd		"	May	2nd	1874
	February	28th		"	April	10th	1876
	January	31st		"	March	19th	1878
	July	24th	1879	"	February	13th	1880
	June	22nd		"	August	3rd	1881
	May	30th		"	July	10th	1883
	May	9th		"	June	18th	1885
	April	19th		"	May	29th	1887
	March	29th		"	May	9th	1889
	March	8th		"	April	19th	1891
	February	11th		"	March	28th	1893
	August	19th		"	October	12th	1894
	December	31st	1894	"	March	1st	1895
	July	2nd		"	August	15th	1896

From						
From June	7th		through	July	18th	1898
May	17th		"	June	26th	1900
April	27th		"	June	6th	1902
April	7th		"	May	17th	1904
March	17th		"	April	28th	1906
February	23rd		"	April	6th	1908
January	23rd		"	March	13th	1910
July	16th		"	September	5th	1911
November	30th	1911	"	January	30th	1912
June	17th		"	July	28th	1913
May	26th		"	July	5th	1915
May	5th		"	June	14th	1917
April	15th		"	May	25th	1919
March	25th		"	May	5th	1921
March	4th		"	April	15th	1923
February	5th		"	March	23rd	1925
August	1st	1926	"	February	21st	1927
June	26th		"	August	8th	1928

MARS IN GEMINI

THE sign Gemini exercises upon Mars its usual influence; it transforms its potency to the mental plane, but it tends to disperse the force and to make it excitable and irritable rather than powerful.

Compare Thomas Hardy, whose Mars is in this position, with Dickens on the one hand and Daudet on the other, with Mars respectively in Aries and Taurus. Hardy's technique lacks alike brilliancy and softness; it is not simple or direct, and yet it is far more intellectually developed than in either of the others. Mercury and the Sun in conjunction naturally tend to emphasize this point, and they are certainly of great assistance; without them the style would have been abrupt and obscure.

In the world of music, Schumann offers us just the illustration we need, of a very refined and intellectual, but rather thin, technique. Here, again, the conjunction of the Sun saves the situation. Mars is, however, not the important factor in this nativity and it must be remembered that, in speaking of style in these sections, we do not mean the matter or even the manner of an artist, but the actual technical method by which he executes his ideas.

Sir David Wilkie is another case in point; he may be contrasted with Reynolds. His method may be called almost perky in comparison with the smooth voluptuousness of the other. The sextile of Jupiter prevents this from too great effect; without it, he would perhaps have been as agitated, violent, and distracted as a futurist.

The trine of the Sun to Mars doubtless helped to make Lord Roberts a successful soldier, but even here the Gemini influence is apparent. His efforts were bound to be intermittent, and his influence on the army, while it uplifted, did not bind. Devoted to him as his soldiers were, he never succeeded in forming a phalanx like Cromwell's.

The same failure in method is seen in Joseph Chamberlain and Cecil Rhodes. Mars in Gemini represents a fault which is best expressed in the language of sport, where it is the very commonest of all errors. In golf and billiards it is called "failing to follow through," in rowing "being short with the finish." You cannot get full results from a stroke unless you give it power enough to carry to the end. So Chamberlain, with Neptune trining his Mars, and Uranus squaring it, giving it idealism, but lack of continuity, seemed unable to persist in any policy.

Rhodes had a little more assistance than this from the Sun, Moon, Mercury, Saturn, and Uranus. The conjunction of Saturn in particular gave more power of persistency. It is an exceptionally strong, if not very well-balanced complex; but the influence of Jupiter, lord of the Ascendant, in opposition to Mars, is really the key to the nativity.

Queen Elizabeth showed extraordinary caprice in method, none at all in main lines of policy; Uranus was very strong; Mars has Jupiter in opposition, and a trine of Mercury lends her cleverness.

For the benefit of those who are not in possession of Raphael's Ephemeris, or who are not able to interpret the symbols contained therein, the years when Mars is in the sign Gemini are as follows:

From	May	27th	through	July	8th	1840
	May	7th	"	June	19th	1842
	April	16th	"	May	30th	1844

From March	26th		through	May	10th	1846
February	25th		"	April	17th	1848
August	11th		"	October	7th	1849
December	9th	1849	"	March	14th	1850
July	16th		"	August	29th	1851
June	24th		"	August	5th	1853
June	4th		"	July	16th	1855
May	15th		"	June	26th	1857
April	25th		"	June	7th	1859
April	3rd		"	May	18th	1861
March	9th		"	April	27th	1863
August	26th	1864	"	March	30th	1865
July	25th		"	September	9th	1866
July	1st		"	August	13th	1868
June	11th		"	July	24th	1870
May	22nd		"	July	3rd	1872
May	3rd		"	June	15th	1874
April	11th		"	May	25th	1876
March	20th		"	May	5th	1878
February	14th		"	April	11th	1880
August	4th		"	September	23rd	1881
January	12th		"	February	25th	1882
July	11th		"	August	23rd	1883
June	19th		"	July	31st	1885
May	30th		"	July	11th	1887
May	10th		"	June	22nd	1889
April	20th		"	June	3rd	1891
March	29th		"	May	13th	1893
March	2nd		"	April	21st	1895
August	16th	1896	"	March	21st	1897
July	19th		"	September	2nd	1898
June	27th		"	August	9th	1900
June	7th		"	July	20th	1902
May	18th		"	June	30th	1904
April	29th		"	June	11th	1906
April	7th		"	May	22nd	1908
March	14th		"	May	1st	1910
September	6th		"	November	29th	1911

From January	31st	through	April	4th 1912
July	29th	"	September	15th 1913
July	6th	"	August	18th 1915
June	15th	"	July	27th 1917
May	26th	"	July	8th 1919
May	6th	"	June	18th 1921
April	16th	"	May	30th 1923
March	24th	"	May	9th 1925
February	22nd	"	April	16th 1927
August	9th	"	October	2nd 1928
December	20th 1928	"	March	10th 1929

MARS IN CANCER

In Cancer, Mars is in his fall; but Cancer is so receptive a sign that its influence is not antagonistic. In fact, it makes the martial energy subtle and profound, dissolving it, as it were, and thus making it more active, just as a solution of phenol is more corrosive than the crystals themselves.

Some of the very greatest artists that have ever lived have this position of Mars; it seems as if the specialized energy which he represents were somehow made universal. There is not that same concentration upon a single line that is shown, for example, by Mars in Aries; there have been found very few instances of politicians or conquerors or even great generals with this position. Every one of our illustrations has worked for the general good, not the particular good of any person or even any country, unless we consider Alexander II as having done so. But even his action with regard to the serfs should be regarded as the limited expression of a wide humanitarian intention. And in this case Mars has the opposition of Jupiter, though it is directed wisely by Saturn's trine, and made gentle by the sextile of Venus.

There is, of course, one very unfortunate career to consider; that of Marie Antoinette. Here Mars is very strong, rising trine to Uranus, with no affliction but a square of the Moon. The Moon ruling the female life, and in this case being Lady of the Ascendant, we must regard her rather than Mars as the key to the complex. We must say then that her Moon is afflicted by the presence in the Ascendant of Mars in his fall. All the good she gets from the complex is a towering practical ambition, which was indeed successful, so far as it went, Uranus trined by Mars being in her tenth house. But Saturn, lord of the seventh, being in his own house in the eighth, afflicting and afflicted by the square of the Moon, even the marriage which gratified her ambition resulted in her death.

To return to artists, we have the most amazing galaxy; Shakespeare, Petrarch, Michael Angelo, Byron, Balzac, Dante, and, in their wake, Coleridge. It is to be noted how, in each case, the universality of sympathy is evident. Each has an enormous field of expression. There is not the intensity of Baudelaire or the single-minded passion of Blake; it is, rather, breadth and objectivity of outlook, and completeness of comprehension of humanity that stand revealed. And to this heavenly court of artists we may add a philosopher, one of the greatest, in every way, that ever lived: Immanuel Kant; while, should they need an astronomer to observe more accurately their heaven, they may include in their ranks the shining name of Copernicus.

For the benefit of those who are not in possession of Raphael's Ephemeris, or who are not able to interpret the symbols contained therein, the years when Mars is in the sign Cancer are as follows:

From	July	9th	through	August	23rd	1840
	June	20th	"	August	4th	1842
	May	31st	"	July	15th	1844
	May	11th	"	June	27th	1846
	April	18th	"	June	6th	1848
	October	8th	"	December	8th	1849
	March	15th	"	May	14th	1850
	August	30th	"	October	23rd	1851
	February	4th	"	April	5th	1852
	August	6th	"	September	22nd	1853
	July	17th	"	August	31st	1855
	June	27th	"	August	11th	1857
	June	8th	"	July	23rd	1859
	May	19th	"	July	4th	1861
	April	28th	"	June	15th	1863
	March	31st	"	May	23rd	1865

From September	10th		through	November	25th	1866
December	8th	1866	"	April	25th	1867
August	14th		"	October	1st	1868
July	25th		"	September	8th	1870
July	4th		"	August	18th	1872
June	16th		"	July	30th	1874
May	26th		"	July	11th	1876
May	6th		"	June	22nd	1878
April	12th		"	June	1st	1880
September	24th	1881	"	January	11th	1882
February	26th		"	May	7th	1882
August	24th		"	October	14th	1883
August	1st		"	September	16th	1885
July	12th		"	August	26th	1887
June	23rd		"	August	6th	1889
June	4th		"	July	19th	1891
May	14th		"	June	29th	1893
April	22nd		"	June	10th	1895
March	22nd		"	May	17th	1897
September	3rd		"	October	30th	1898
January	16th		"	April	14th	1899
August	10th		"	September	26th	1900
July	21st		"	September	4th	1902
July	1st		"	August	14th	1904
June	12th		"	July	27th	1906
May	23rd		"	July	7th	1908
May	2nd		"	June	18th	1910
April	5th		"	May	27th	1912
September	16th	1913	"	May	1st	1914
August	19th		"	October	7th	1915
July	28th		"	September	11th	1917
July	9th		"	August	22nd	1919
June	19th		"	August	2nd	1921
May	31st		"	July	15th	1923
May	10th		"	June	25th	1925
April	17th		"	June	5th	1927
October	3rd		"	December	19th	1928
March	11th		"	May	12th	1929

MARS IN LEO

Where the fire of Mars burns brightly, he obliterates minor distinctions. The Sun is, himself, fire; in fact, Mars is but the fiery part of the Sun, so that Leo is as favorable to the development of Mars as even Aries; indeed, more so. For the solar influence tends to balance, breadth, and fullest development in the fiery impulses; Aries is, as it were, too martial to be the highest good for Mars.

We shall find as a rule, therefore, people with less passionate intensity of action, but with wider sympathies, than we found in Aries. Of course, in some cases Saturn's influence may override this; one cannot expect a person intensely narrow and selfish to act in accordance with sentiments better illustrated by Jupiter. Yet, all things considered, his method will be broader than had Mars been in Aries.

In the horoscope of General Boulanger, Mars is very strong; but the square of Saturn in Scorpio produces a certain restraint which proved fatal. This square should not have worked so badly had Mars been in Aries and Saturn in Capricornus.

George Eliot has a most noble and beautiful Mars, trine to the Sun and Venus; it lent force and fire to a rather cramped and disappointed ego. (Her Saturn is sextile to the Moon and square to Uranus and Neptune, implying melancholy.) Hence the brilliance and color of her work is objective; the expression is more genial than that which it expresses.

Lily Langtry has Mars in the tenth house very powerful, but squared by Uranus. It is not the important complex. A certain amount of scandal is implied; but the dominant position and generous Zodiacal situation of Mars tend to make this innocuous. The scandal is so big that it becomes a negligible factor.

Lord Brougham, again, a man of a most acrid and vitriolic spirit, had Mars in Leo to thank for his breadth of action. He could not (luckily for him) express himself in mean ways.

William Blake is an example of the other side of the picture. Here we find the most tremendous development of the higher faculties, but no adequate and equal disposition of Mars, which, besides being in this exuberant and generous sign, is squared by Mercury. Hence his failure to realize practically his immense conceptions.

Herbert Spencer, on the other hand, has a grand Mars with Saturn trine and the Sun square. Here is great wisdom combined with great activity, steadily forcing the idea upon a reluctant world, by open and honest methods, and indomitable courage, pluck, and perseverance. The square of the Sun implies opposition, and gives some threat to the health.

Another great-hearted and successful man was General Grant, whose generous action at Appomattox is altogether characteristic of this Mars in Leo position. Lord Lytton is a similar case of great success won by geniality of action.

The warmth and persuasiveness of the eloquence of Cicero may also be put down to the Leonine position of Mars which is approaching conjunction with Mercury. The square of Jupiter and Saturn accounts for the polemical character of much of his writings and speeches; but this has nothing to do with the method, which remains as a model of grace and vigor.

Cæsar Borgia, by contrast, has Mars in conjunction with Saturn, in opposition to Jupiter, and square to Uranus, with no help but the sextile of the Sun and the semi-sextile of Venus. This tends to mask the Leo influence; however, we still see it to some extent in the range of his action; in the pride and splendour with which he worked.

Edward VI of England, on the other hand, has Mars approaching an opposition to the Moon, square to Jupiter, and in conjunction with Uranus, with only the trine of Neptune to counter balance these misfortunes; and yet we see the Leo influence on Mars still peeping through in the shape of those qualities which make kings lovable. And as he was the best-loved king, save Cœur-de-Lion and Henry the Fifth, that ever ruled England, so was James II the most hated. Here Mars was rising, alone in the horoscope without any important aspects. There is no complex of importance in the whole heaven; Mars was therefore free to rule the life; and here we must argue that Leo only brought obstinacy and haughtiness into the method. The Sun, lord of Leo, is in Scorpio, badly aspected by a conjunction of Neptune and a square of the Moon; and, as Leo is rising, the influence is all the more evil.

The vivid warmth and generosity of Turner's method of painting is also very characteristic, though, happily, of this position. Here Mars is square to the conjunction of Jupiter and Venus, and this appears to have given the force and directness which is the wonder of his technique.

Benjamin Disraeli is a great example of this Leo effect on Mars. His eccentricities were all of a gorgeous order; and he made them part of his career, of his method of influencing his contemporaries. Mars being also lord of the Ascendant, of course made this tendency inevitable.

Lord Wolseley is a case of the exuberance of this position of Mars. He was too good-natured and too popular to become a Napoleon. Neptune, too, is in opposition, which would tend to thwart the material benefits of Mars.

The strength of the Mars of Madame Steinheil is enormous. It is not only semi-sextile to Uranus and sextile to the Moon, but also trine to the Sun, Neptune, Mercury and Venus on the one hand, and to Saturn on the other. Here is a tremendous complex of eight planets, which stamps her with the very hall-mark of success. But the Leo influence still shines in her method; whatever she might do, she would give a sunny smile, and "get away with it."

One is at first heartily surprised to find Robespierre in this long list. But a little investigation soon clears away the difficutly. Mars is in the sixth house, conjoined with Neptune, and square to the Sun. The trine of Jupiter seems here merely to make him effective. Now, Saturn rising and lord of the Ascendant is, with his aspects, the key to the horoscope, and there is no relation between him and Mars. So we see that, after all, the method of the man was totally distinct from his purpose. And what was that method? Leo all over! Big, frank, open talk, generous sentiments, noble aspirations, the phraseology of a Mazzini or a Lincoln! It is an admirable illustration of the "mask" in astrology. Had Saturn and Uranus aspected Mars, all these sentiments would have been genuine.

Rosa Bonheur is excellent for our purpose. Mars rising, trine with Saturn, is a great influence upon her for masculinity and force. But see how Leo operates to make this generous and frank and noble. In Aries, we should have had a person of far more push and with no qualities so lovable. For one does not class her as a "mannish woman," but as a great-hearted, loyal comrade and friend.

Much geniality is evident in the method of the late J. Pierpont Morgan. He was indeed the Napoleon of finance; there was nothing underhanded, sly or treacherous about his ways; and he was interested in many things beyond his business. The conjunction of Jupiter accentuates this tendency.

Similarly genial, but not so effective, is the Mars of W. B. Yeats. Here Neptune is trine, and Venus square, neither of great help to the practical side of Mars. It is an admirable picture of the easy openness of his method, both in art and in life. With Saturn trine, instead of Neptune, he might have been as austere as Blake, and as successful as Maeterlinck.

The glow and riot of Swinburne's early verse is also to be attributed to this position of Mars. Once again we must insist that we refer to the actual technique, not to the matter or the manner. With Jupiter conjoined, Mercury and Venus trine, and Neptune in opposition, we can well explain the rhythms with which he enriched the English language.

For the benefit of those who are not in possession of Raphael's Ephemeris, or who are not able to interpret the symbols contained therein, the years when Mars is in the sign Leo are as follows:

From	August	24th		through	October	10th	1840
	August	5th		"	September	20th	1842
	July	16th		"	August	31st	1844
	June	28th		"	August	13th	1846
	June	7th		"	July	25th	1848
	May	15th		"	July	5th	1850
	October	24th	1851	"	February	3rd	1852
	April	6th		"	June	11th	1852
	September	23rd		"	November	16th	1853
	March	23rd		"	April	27th	1854
	September	1st		"	October	19th	1855
	August	12th		"	September	27th	1857
	July	24th		"	September	8th	1859
	July	5th		"	August	20th	1861
	June	16th		"	August	2nd	1863
	May	24th		"	July	13th	1865
	November	26th		"	December	7th	1866

From April	26th		through	June	21st	1867
October	2nd		"	December	5th	1868
February	1st		"	May	22nd	1869
September	9th		"	October	28th	1870
August	19th		"	October	5th	1872
July	31st		"	September	15th	1874
July	12th		"	August	27th	1876
June	23rd		"	August	9th	1878
June	2nd		"	July	20th	1880
May	8th		"	June	30th	1882
October	15th	1883	"	June	4th	1884
September	17th		"	November	8th	1885
August	27th		"	October	13th	1887
August	7th		"	September	22nd	1889
July	20th		"	September	4th	1891
June	30th		"	August	15th	1893
June	11th		"	July	28th	1895
May	18th		"	July	8th	1897
October	31st	1898	"	January	15th	1899
April	15th		"	June	15th	1899
September	27th		"	November	22nd	1900
March	2nd		"	May	10th	1901
September	5th		"	October	23rd	1902
August	15th		"	October	1st	1904
July	28th		"	September	12th	1906
July	8th		"	August	23rd	1908
June	19th		"	August	5th	1910
May	28th		"	July	16th	1912
May	2nd		"	June	25th	1914
October	8th	1915	"	May	28th	1916
September	12th		"	November	1st	1917
August	23rd		"	October	9th	1919
August	3rd		"	September	18th	1921
July	16th		"	August	31st	1923
June	26th		"	August	12th	1925
June	6th		"	July	24th	1927
May	13th		"	July	3rd	1929

MARS IN VIRGO

Mars and Mercury are not altogether unfriendly, and certainly Virgo has no such detrimental effect on Mars as we found exerted by Gemini, but the combination is a little cold-blooded. There is a certain passionate chastity about it; real warmth of heart in the conventional sense appears to be denied. It will be seen that, of all upon our list, though many are great men and women, not one can be called a great lover. This remark applies as much to method as in the preceding sections; it refers to a certain coldness and detachment of action, as if the enthusiasms were not awakened. Yet the will may be extremely strong. The women on our list are almost ostentatiously passionless, and the men hardly less so. In the devotion to a cause, we find two of the greatest women enthusiasts that ever lived, Jeanne d'Arc and Madame Blavatsky.

Before adding the name of Anna Kingsford to these, we must anticipate the objection that she boasted of an intensely sensual disposition, but here Virgo is warmed by the Sun, Venus, and Mercury, the first of these being in very close conjunction with Mars. However, there is no trace of eroticism in her work, and it is the actual method of expressing the personality which is denoted by Mars, not the nature of that personality itself.

Among men we have Balfour, whose cold intellectualism is at once his charm and his weakness; Kruger, notably the most dexterous and cool politician of his period; Dreyfus, whose detachment made him so unpopular with his men, and thus led to his being accused by his brother officers; Archbishop Laud, whose lack of warmth lost him his friends; William III, most unpopular as a king, owing to his "Dutch coldness"; and Louis XVI, whose lack of sympathy with the needs of his people caused his downfall.

Finally, we have two of the greatest conquerors that the world has known: Alexander the Great, and Napoleon Bonaparte. Both of these owed their greatness very largely to this power of detachment in their method; both, however keenly interested in a matter, were able to view it and treat it as if it hardly concerned them; and this is the chief virtue of Mars in Virgo.

For the benefit of those who are not in possession of Raphael's

Ephemeris, or who are not able to interpret the symbols contained therein, the years when Mars is in the sign Virgo are as follows:

From	October	11th		through	December	1st	1840
	September	21st		"	November	7th	1842
	September	1st		"	October	18th	1844
	August	14th		"	September	29th	1846
	July	26th		"	September	10th	1848
	July	6th		"	August	22nd	1850
	June	12th		"	August	1st	1852
	November	17th	1853	"	March	22nd	1854
	April	28th		"	July	8th	1854
	October	20th		"	December	13th	1855
	September	28th		"	November	15th	1857
	September	9th		"	October	26th	1859
	August	21st		"	October	6th	1861
	August	3rd		"	September	18th	1863
	July	14th		"	August	29th	1865
	June	22nd		"	August	10th	1867
	December	6th	1868	"	January	31st	1869
	May	23rd		"	July	18th	1869
	October	29th		"	December	30th	1870
	March	18th		"	June	15th	1871
	October	6th		"	November	24th	1872
	September	16th		"	November	2nd	1874
	August	28th		"	October	13th	1876
	August	10th		"	September	25th	1878
	July	21st		"	September	5th	1880
	July	1st		"	August	18th	1882
	June	5th		"	July	27th	1884
	November	9th	1885	"	July	1st	1886
	October	14th		"	December	5th	1887
	September	23rd		"	November	10th	1889
	September	5th		"	October	21st	1891
	August	16th		"	October	1st	1893
	July	29th		"	September	13th	1895
	July	9th		"	August	25th	1897
	June	16th		"	August	5th	1899

From November	23rd	1900	through	March	1st	1901
May	11th		"	July	13th	1901
October	24th		"	December	19th	1902
April	20th		"	May	30th	1903
October	2nd		"	November	19th	1904
September	13th		"	October	29th	1906
August	24th		"	October	9th	1908
August	6th		"	September	21st	1910
July	17th		"	September	2nd	1912
June	26th		"	August	14th	1914
May	29th		"	July	22nd	1916
November	2nd	1917	"	January	10th	1918
February	26th		"	June	23rd	1918
October	10th		"	November	29th	1919
September	19th		"	November	6th	1921
September	1st		"	October	17th	1923
August	13th		"	September	28th	1925
July	25th		"	September	10th	1927
July	4th		"	August	21st	1929

MARS IN LIBRA

In Libra, Mars is in his detriment; but he is not so weak as might appear from this first consideration. Libra rather tempers his activity with judgment; and, if he be well dignified, he may be as strong here as anywhere. He becomes more effective through being more controlled. But, in every case we examine, we shall find an excellent quality of direction given to him; just as the explosive force of gunpowder gains in effectiveness by virtue of the very limitation of the barrel of the rifle.

Sadi Carnot, for instance, was by no means so ambitious as Cromwell, who had Mars in Aries; but he did not need to use the same violence. His method was admirably adjusted to circumstances, and he attained his ends without recourse to undue force. He measured his actions carefully, and there was no lack of power, but at the same time no excess. Felix Faure, with the same position of Mars, gives exactly similar evidence of its action.

Shelley had the same quality; it appears in his work continually.

It is indeed admirable, this harmony of motion which one perceives in his rhythm. If it be contrasted with that of Swinburne, the difference between Leo and Libra will appear quite obvious.

Another admirable illustration of the judicial temperament is the method of Sir William Hamilton, dignified, well-considered, convincing. One can hardly say the same of Luther, but in this case Venus and Jupiter are both in conjunction with Mars, tending to over-excitement. Still, Libra's influence is visible even here; impassioned and intense as Luther was, he never went beyond the bounds of prudence.

There are two well-known British statesmen with this position for Mars, Mr. Asquith and Winston Churchill. The same tempered and adroit energy is characteristic of both.

Sir Humphrey Davy, too, has this admirably moderated fire. Without violence or controversy, he managed to have his way, owing to the proper control of his energy by his judgment. In the case of Alfred de Musset, one may say, this is not so obvious. There was a good deal of overproduction of energy in his machine, which made for vehemence of expression. But his Mars is powerfully excited by the square of Venus, the semi-sextile of Uranus; and the sextiles of a conjunction of Sol, Mercury and Saturn make up a formidable complex, to which, however, Mars is not the key, but Saturn. It is a very powerful combination, and the calming influence of Libra is to be thanked for the restraint of his method. This should be contrasted with that of Baudelaire, whose complex key is equally powerful, but who has Mars in Aries.

Occasionally it may occur that Libra is too powerful. Much of Bernard Shaw's apparent inconsistency is due to the fact that he has unrivaled capacity for seeing both sides of every argument with equal clarity, and often sets both together on the same page, or even in the same sentence. And here Mars is very weak, having no particularly close or strong aspects. Libra, therefore modifies his action much more than in the other cases which we have had occasion to consider.

For the benefit of those who are not in possession of Raphael's Ephemeris, or who are not able to interpret the symbols contained therein, the years when Mars is in the sign Libra are as follows:

From			through			
December	2nd	1840	through	February	4th	1841
April	12th		"	July	14th	1841
November	8th		"	December	27th	1842
October	19th		"	December	4th	1844
September	30th		"	November	14th	1846
September	11th		"	October	25th	1848
August	23rd		"	October	7th	1850
August	2nd		"	September	17th	1852
July	9th		"	August	27th	1854
December	14th	1855	"	July	30th	1856
November	16th	1857	"	January	7th	1858
October	27th		"	December	13th	1859
October	7th		"	November	21st	1861
September	19th		"	November	2nd	1863
August	30th		"	October	14th	1865
August	11th		"	September	25th	1867
July	19th		"	September	4th	1869
December	31st	1870	"	March	17th	1871
June	16th		"	August	12th	1871
November	25th	1872	"	January	22nd	1873
May	20th		"	June	24th	1873
November	3rd		"	December	21st	1874
October	14th		"	November	29th	1876
September	26th		"	November	9th	1878
September	6th		"	October	21st	1880
August	19th		"	October	2nd	1882
July	28th		"	September	12th	1884
July	2nd		"	August	21st	1886
December	6th	1887	"	February	26th	1888
March	10th		"	July	21st	1888
November	11th		"	December	31st	1889
October	22nd		"	December	7th	1891
October	2nd		"	November	16th	1893
September	14th		"	October	29th	1895
August	26th		"	October	9th	1897
August	6th		"	September	20th	1899
July	14th		"	August	31st	1901
December	20th	1902	"	April	19th	1903

From May	31st	through	August	6th 1903
November	20th 1904	"	January	13th 1905
October	30th	"	December	16th 1906
October	10th	"	November	25th 1908
September	22nd	"	November	6th 1910
September	3rd	"	October	17th 1912
August	15th	"	September	28th 1914
July	23rd	"	September	8th 1916
January	11th	"	February	25th 1918
June	24th	"	August	16th 1918
November	30th 1919	"	January	31st 1920
April	24th	"	July	10th 1920
November	7th	"	December	25th 1921
October	18th	"	December	3rd 1923
September	29th	"	November	13th 1925
September	11th	"	October	25th 1927
August	22nd	"	October	5th 1929

MARS IN SCORPIO

Although Mars is in his own house, he cannot be called strong for good. We have noticed that Aries did not bring out the highest qualities of Mars; Scorpio brings out his worst. Mars is the most unbalanced of the planets; the one most in need of restriction or direction. Almost any influence but his own touches his fire to rationality, generosity, or grace. But Scorpio, while in some ways the most powerful of the signs, may be described as snake-tempered; and in it he easily becomes bloodthirsty. It is even amusing to note how one of the gentlest spirits that ever dwelt within the human form, Robert Louis Stevenson, is often in method outrageous almost beyond the "penny dreadful." In "Treasure Island," cold-blooded murderers tumble over each other's heels, in circumstances of unparalleled atrocity. Who, without the help of Mars in Scorpio, could have invented Long John Silver, hopping after his comrade and braining him with his crutch, or the attempt, in "The Ebb-Tide," of Hurst to throw vitriol over Atwater, and the breaking of the bottle in his hand by the ready rifle of the pearler?

There is a complete lack of adaptability in this position of Mars; it is sometimes replaced by treacherous cunning; but, as a general rule, the method of the native tends to be blind and brutal. The anarchist Vaillant may be cited as an illustration. Such extreme cases are fortunately rare and imply bad aspects. In this particular instance, Mars has the sextiles of Jupiter and Saturn, which make him effective, but his quality is deteriorated by the square of Venus. The violence of Mrs. Pankhurst, again, is undoubtedly due to this position, for Mars is not otherwise afflicted. On the contrary, he is helped by a sextile of the Moon and trines of Neptune and the Sun. Her undoubted nobility of character and the altruism of her violent action indicate the vision conferred by the trines of Neptune and the Sun which the sextile of the Moon directs toward the masses of women. Miss Frances E. Willard may be advantageously compared with Mrs. Pankhurst. Mercury is sextile to Mars, Jupiter semi-sextile; and the complex is important, Sagittarius being the rising sign and Mars only six degrees above the Eastern Horizon. Hers is a far more rational and effective method than that of the later suffragist. Mme. Patti has Mars trined by Uranus, and squared by the Sun and Neptune in conjunction, which appears an extremely advantageous disposition. Sir Richard Quain has the Sun, Lord of the Ascendant, in conjunction with Mars, and Venus and are semi-sextile. These aspects go far to minimize the effect of Scorpio.

Henry VI of England is another example of the unfortunate influence which this sign exerts on Mars. He has the softening trine of Neptune exact, and only the slight help of a semi-sextile of the Sun.

For the benefit of those who are not in possession of Raphael's Ephemeris, or who are not able to interpret the symbols contained therein, the years when Mars is in the sign Scorpio are as follows:

From	February	5th		through	April	11th	1841
	July	15th		"	September	6th	1841
	December	28th	1842	"	February	21st	1843
	December	5th	1844	"	January	19th	1845
	November	15th		"	December	28th	1846
	October	26th		"	December	8th	1848
	October	8th		"	November	19th	1850
	September	18th		"	October	30th	1852

From	August	28th		through	October	10th	1854
	July	31st		"	September	16th	1856
	January	8th		"	March	21st	1858
	April	29th		"	August	12th	1858
	December	14th	1859	"	January	30th	1860
	November	22nd	1861	"	January	5th	1862
	November	3rd		"	December	16th	1863
	October	15th		"	November	26th	1865
	September	26th		"	November	7th	1867
	September	5th		"	October	17th	1869
	August	13th		"	September	26th	1871
	January	23rd		"	May	19th	1873
	June	25th		"	August	29th	1873
	December	22nd	1874	"	February	11th	1875
	November	30th	1876	"	January	14th	1877
	November	10th		"	December	23rd	1878
	October	22nd		"	December	3rd	1880
	October	3rd		"	November	14th	1882
	September	13th		"	October	25th	1884
	August	22nd		"	October	5th	1886
	February	27th		"	March	9th	1888
	July	22nd		"	September	10th	1888
	January	1st		"	February	28th	1890
	June	17th		"	July	21st	1890
	December	8th	1891	"	January	24th	1892
	November	17th		"	December	31st	1893
	October	30th		"	December	11th	1895
	October	10th		"	November	21st	1897
	September	21st		"	November	2nd	1899
	September	1st		"	October	14th	1901
	August	7th		"	September	22nd	1903
	January	14th		"	August	21st	1905
	December	17th	1906	"	February	4th	1907
	November	26th	1908	"	January	9th	1909
	November	7th		"	December	19th	1910
	October	18th		"	November	29th	1912
	September	29th		"	November	10th	1914
	September	9th		"	October	21st	1916

From	August	17th		through	September	30th	1918
	February	1st		"	April	23rd	1920
	July	11th		"	September	4th	1920
	December	26th	1921	"	February	18th	1922
	December	4th	1923	"	January	19th	1924
	November	14th		"	December	27th	1925
	October	26th		"	December	7th	1927
	October	6th		"	November	18th	1929

MARS IN SAGITTARIUS

We have already had occasion to note the transitory nature of the sudden action of Sagittarius. The symbol of the arrow was chosen to express that curious quality. In the case of a heavy and slow-moving planet, the action will be, perhaps, to quicken it to some extent; but with Mars, which is already fast and fiery, there is no such compensating influence. Mars tends to become meteoric when in this sign. Unless the energy be carried on for a reasonably long period, it does not begin to have a fair chance to work. What can be done in a moment may be done exceedingly well; but works involving the element of time are likely to be failures. Our examples, therefore, will give us people scintillating rather than solid, dashing rather than enduring.

The swift brilliance of Oscar Wilde is to the point. He was incapable of large construction; his ideas were like shooting stars. Lewis Carroll has an identical limitation, and so had Rudyard Kipling, whose forte is short stories of extreme brilliance and who has written but two novels of any length, both of which are little more than a series of brilliant episodes.

Exceedingly curious and highly illustrative is the case of "Datas." His marvelous memory never forgets a date, but he remembers only disconnected items. It is not at all the same memory as that of Gladstone, who knew Homer by heart. Extremely typical this of the syncopating action of Sagittarius.

Charles I showed the same in his kingship. He would start a strong man's policy one evening, and weaken on it before lunch next day, only to conceive something else equally violent at supper time.

This was an effect in method of action, not at all in the will to govern, which was perfectly consistent.

Louis XIV is a surprising conclusion to the list, especially as Mars is squared by Mercury, and has nothing better than a sextile of Uranus and a semi-sextile of Neptune to offset this affliction. Mars, however, is very strong by position, rising; and he is the lord of the Ascendant.

It is not wonderful that so few persons of note are born with this position of Mars; for, however great they may be within themselves, this fatal defect of discontinuity usually prevents them from translating themselves to the external and objective world.

For the benefit of those who are not in possession of Raphael's Ephemeris or who are not able to interpret the symbols contained therein, the years when Mars is in the sign Sagittarius are as follows:

From	September	7th		through	October	19th	1841
	February	22nd		"	September	16th	1843
	January	20th		"	March	8th	1845
	December	29th	1846	"	February	10th	1847
	December	9th	1848	"	January	18th	1849
	November	20th		"	December	30th	1850
	October	31st		"	December	9th	1852
	October	11th		"	November	19th	1854
	September	17th		"	October	28th	1856
	March	22nd		"	April	28th	1858
	August	13th		"	October	1st	1858
	January	31st		"	March	22nd	1860
	January	6th		"	February	19th	1862
	December	17th	1863	"	January	27th	1864
	November	27th	1865	"	January	6th	1866
	November	8th		"	December	18th	1867
	October	18th		"	November	27th	1869
	September	27th		"	November	6th	1871
	August	30th		"	October	13th	1873
	February	12th		"	April	19th	1875
	June	16th		"	August	31st	1875
	January	15th		"	March	1st	1877

From December	24th	1878	through	February	4th	1879
December	4th	1880	"	January	13th	1881
November	15th		"	December	25th	1882
October	26th		"	December	5th	1884
October	6th		"	November	14th	1886
September	11th		"	October	22nd	1888
March	1st		"	June	16th	1890
July	22nd		"	September	23rd	1890
January	25th		"	March	13th	1892
January	1st		"	February	13th	1894
December	12th	1895	"	January	22nd	1896
November	22nd	1897	"	January	1st	1898
November	3rd		"	December	13th	1899
October	15th		"	November	23rd	1901
September	23rd		"	November	2nd	1903
August	22nd		"	October	7th	1905
February	5th		"	April	1st	1907
January	10th		"	February	23rd	1909
December	20th	1910	"	January	31st	1911
November	30th	1912	"	January	10th	1913
November	11th		"	December	21st	1914
October	22nd		"	December	1st	1916
October	1st		"	November	10th	1918
September	5th		"	October	18th	1920
February	19th		"	September	13th	1922
January	20th		"	March	6th	1924
December	28th	1925	"	February	8th	1926
December	8th	1927	"	January	18th	1928
November	19th		"	December	28th	1929

MARS IN CAPRICORN

Mars in Capricorn is in his exaltation. His fierce energy is tempered to obstinacy by the earthy and Saturnian nature of the sign, but, on the other hand, the leaping Goat lends additional power and élan to his activity. He becomes tremendously magnetic and commanding, but also dour and tenacious. A striking instance of his quality expressed in the world of action is Theodore Roosevelt. One has only to contemplate his method to understand the full effect of Mars in Capricorn.

In the world of science, we have two men of incomparable vigor and persistence, Pasteur and Edison; while, to return once again to political life, we find Edward VII with this position of Mars. This is a very astonishing case; there is little of high ability to be found in this monarch, but Mars, rising in this sign, gave him the executive force to carry through the Triple Entente, one of the greatest diplomatic achievements in the world's history.

Goethe also has this position; in this connection we notice the brusquerie of much of his verse, its leaping, forceful, direct quality. That any man could win such signal triumph is amazing; the art of poetry seems to demand smoothness rather than this abrupt sledge-hammer method. Rossetti, for example, with the same position, scores only partial success. The rough scansion of much of his verse must be called a flaw, whereas with Goethe it was a virtue. But Rossetti's Mars is in conjunction with Neptune and in opposition to Saturn, with no buttress to such aspects but a distant trine of the Sun, while Goethe's Mars is trine to Mercury and the Sun.

Ruskin and Tolstoi have also this position, but Ruskin's Mars is the storm-centre of a great complex, which considerably modifies the effect, while Tolstoi's is in conjunction with Neptune, increasing its eccentricity and violence by harnessing materialism with mysticism. A better illustration of the effect of this position is Savonarola. Here we see clearly the sudden fierce resolution and the tenacity of purpose. Afflictions by Saturn and the Moon tended to increase the asperity of the method, and doubtless they contributed to its failure; but the method is indicated clearly enough by the position.

Among women we have Cleo de Mérode with the Moon trine and the Sun and Venus in square to Mars. From this comes her incomparable power to have her own way in everything. Incidentally, the planet is on the cusp of her eleventh house, and its main effect is therefore to enable her to influence friends. The trine of the Moon includes the public among such friends, and modifies the fierceness of her method by masking it with a show of yielding grace. In reality, she was just as full of will and determination as Cromwell.

For the benefit of those who are not in possession of Raphael's

Ephemeris, or who are not able to interpret the symbols contained therein, the years when Mars is in the sign Capricorn are as follows:

From	October	20th		through	November	28th	1841
	September	17th		"	November	1st	1843
	March	9th		"	April	27th	1845
	February	11th		"	March	24th	1847
	January	19th		"	February	27th	1849
	December	31st	1850	"	February	7th	1851
	December	10th	1852	"	January	17th	1853
	November	20th		"	December	28th	1854
	October	29th		"	December	6th	1856
	October	2nd		"	November	12th	1858
	March	23rd		"	June	9th	1860
	June	23rd		"	September	29th	1860
	February	20th		"	April	3rd	1862
	January	28th		"	March	8th	1864
	January	7th		"	February	15th	1866
	December	19th	1867	"	January	26th	1868
	November	28th	1869	"	January	5th	1870
	November	7th		"	December	15th	1871
	October	14th		"	November	22nd	1873
	April	20th		"	June	15th	1875
	September	1st		"	October	23rd	1875
	March	2nd		"	April	16th	1877
	February	5th		"	March	18th	1879
	January	14th		"	February	22nd	1881
	December	26th	1882	"	February	2nd	1883
	December	6th	1884	"	January	12th	1885
	November	15th		"	December	23rd	1886
	October	23rd		"	December	1st	1888
	September	24th		"	November	5th	1890
	March	14th		"	May	6th	1892
	February	14th		"	March	27th	1894
	January	23rd		"	March	2nd	1896
	January	2nd		"	February	10th	1898
	December	14th	1899	"	January	21st	1900

From	November 24th	1901	through	January	1st	1902
	November 3rd		"	December	11th	1903
	October 8th		"	November	17th	1905
	April 2nd		"	October	13th	1907
	February 24th		"	April	9th	1909
	February 1st		"	March	13th	1911
	January 11th		"	February	18th	1913
	December 22nd	1914	"	January	29th	1915
	December 2nd	1916	"	January	9th	1917
	November 11th		"	December	19th	1918
	October 19th		"	November	27th	1920
	September 14th		"	October	30th	1922
	March 7th		"	April	24th	1924
	February 9th		"	March	22nd	1926
	January 19th		"	February	27th	1928
	December 29th		"	December	31st	1929

MARS IN AQUARIUS

THE Uranian and airy influence of Aquarius tends to cause Mars to spend his energy more in the direction of intellectual force—and we may add, moral force. The method will be expansive, free, open, and yet full of wisdom. There are, of course, unfortunate exceptions. If over-excited by some dangerous aspect, the airy formula may be as distracting as that given by Gemini.

Mary, Queen of Scots, suffered from this airy temperament in her mode of action, for, though the Sun was sextile, Saturn was square, and Uranus in opposition.

Another instance is Marie Bashkirtseff. No doubt, as in the previous case, Mars is active enough. That is not the point; the point is that Mars is too active. Here Jupiter is in opposition and Neptune semi-sextile, and the Sun is square, a most unfortunate combination. Her peculiar temper and her method of attempting to achieve her ends, as described in her diary, are admirably pictured by these planets.

Aquarius, on the whole, gives far more freedom of action to Mars than does Capricorn; hence occasionally we find looseness in its mėthod, and, in all cases, the native is more a man of thought than of action. Even such tremendous driving forces, practical as ever lived, as Gladstone, Bismarck, Alexander VI, and John Bright, all shared in this expansive—one may almost dare to say imaginative—type of action. With all but the very greatest, there is likely to be some hindrance implied. Alfred Russell Wallace was not the fighting force that his intellectual capacity would have stood for. The Earl of Strafford, in particular, was afflicted sorely in this matter. In his situation he needed an extraordinarily close-knit, terrible Mars. The opposition of Neptune on one side and the squares of the Sun and Mercury on the other were certainly detrimental, and the Aquarius tendency asserted itself unchecked.

A last example of weakness is Ludwig II of Bavaria, whose Mars is made fatally eccentric in its action by the conjunction of Neptune with no counter-balance. Here the royal power itself was actually frittered away in whimsical intellectualities.

Richard Wagner has the same position of Mars, but the aspects are so different that Aquarius brings out the best instead of the worst. Jupiter is in square to Mercury and opposition to Mars, it is true; but Venus and the Sun in conjunction are trine, and Mars is culminating in the tenth house. It is, therefore, a great and important complex, and it is never to be forgotten that, in such circumstances, it is less important whether planets have "good" or "bad" aspects; the fact of their existence in the complex is itself an element of strength; half a loaf is better than no bread!

Another figure of amazing stature with this position is Victor Hugo. Mars has only a trine of Uranus and approaching a sextile of Mercury; there is therefore something lacking in his method. Gigantic as his soul was—quite equal to that of Wagner—he yet failed to influence Europe to the same extent. The fact is explicable by the inferior disposition of his Mars, and in no other manner.

For the benefit of those who are not in possession of Raphael's Ephemeris or who are not able to interpret the symbols contained therein, the years when Mars is in the sign Aquarius are as follows:

From January	1st	through	January	28th	1840
November	29th 1841	"	January	5th	1842
November	2nd	"	December	12th	1843

From	April	28th		through	July	10th	1845
	July	28th		"	October	27th	1845
	March	25th		"	May	4th	1847
	February	28th		"	April	8th	1849
	February	8th		"	March	17th	1851
	January	18th		"	February	24th	1853
	December	29th	1854	"	February	4th	1855
	December	7th	1856	"	January	14th	1857
	November	13th		"	December	22nd	1858
	June	10th		"	June	22nd	1860
	September	30th		"	November	20th	1860
	April	4th		"	May	17th	1862
	March	9th		"	April	17th	1864
	February	16th		"	March	25th	1866
	January	27th		"	March	4th	1868
	January	6th		"	February	12th	1870
	December	16th	1871	"	January	23rd	1872
	November	23rd		"	December	31st	1873
	October	24th		"	December	5th	1875
	April	17th		"	June	6th	1877
	March	19th		"	April	28th	1879
	February	23rd		"	April	2nd	1881
	February	3rd		"	March	12th	1883
	January	13th		"	February	19th	1885
	December	24th	1886	"	January	30th	1887
	December	2nd	1888	"	January	9th	1889
	November	6th		"	December	16th	1890
	May	7th		"	November	8th	1892
	March	28th		"	May	9th	1894
	March	3rd		"	April	11th	1896
	February	11th		"	March	20th	1898
	January	22nd		"	February	28th	1900
	January	2nd		"	February	8th	1902
	December	12th	1903	"	January	19th	1904
	November	18th		"	December	27th	1905
	October	14th		"	November	28th	1907
	April	10th		"	May	25th	1909
	March	14th		"	April	22nd	1911

From			through		
From	February	19th	through	March	29th 1913
	January	30th	"	March	9th 1915
	January	10th	"	February	16th 1917
	December	20th 1918	"	January	26th 1919
	November	28th 1920	"	January	4th 1921
	October	31st	"	December	11th 1922
	April	25th	"	June	24th 1924
	August	25th	"	October	19th 1924
	March	23rd	"	May	3rd 1926
	February	28th	"	April	7th 1928

MARS IN PISCES

In Pisces Mars reaches the very depths of misfortune. The sign is watery, receptive, sensitive, psychic, the very antithesis of the fiery, dominant, brutal, material planet. Very few people with this detrimental position, unless strongly aspected, reach any remarkable goal; even the greatest men are so hampered in their external expression that their greatness passes unremarked in a world that can only be conquered by battle-axes and sledge-hammers. A great tragedy of the Victorian period stands witness to this fact.

We have already called attention to the horoscope of Sir Richard Burton. Uranus is conjoined with Neptune, and four other planets fortify the complex. Mars himself in conjunction with Venus and semi-sextile to Saturn, is lord of the Ascendant, while, without much straining, these two complexes may be unified through the Moon and Mercury. Here, then, are the nine planets all more or less related, as in the case of Shakespeare; and truly the mind of Burton was no less than his. Yet the effect of Pisces on Mars is so deadly that the whole of his externalization was nullified. He should have been Viceroy of India and Governor-General of Egypt; but, as he himself said, he "possessed every talent but that of making use of the others!"

Erasmus was another individual of rare distinction—the greatest scholar of the Middle Ages. But here again there was no capacity for externalizing his powers; even poor old Cornelius Agrippa had a far greater influence in Europe; while Paracelsus outshone both.

Nell Gwyn has this position, too, but Mars is a very curious planet in the case of women. It is difficult to assert anything positively with so little evidence as is forthcoming, but one may suspect that Mars and Venus are counterchanged for feminine horoscopes rather as are the Sun and the Moon, though not so effectively. In any case, Mars has the trine of Jupiter on one side and that of the Moon on the other, which would amply redeem any radical weakness of the planet, especially as he is rising.

Mars in Pisces, the house of Neptune, is badly placed; in fact the worst position of the twelve.

For the benefit of those who are not in possession of Raphael's Ephemeris or who are not able to interpret the symbols contained therein, the years when Mars is in the sign Pisces are as follows:

From	January	29th		through	March	6th	1840
	January	6th		"	February	13th	1842
	December	13th	1843	"	January	22nd	1844
	July	11th		"	July	27th	1845
	October	28th		"	December	21st	1845
	May	5th		"	June	16th	1847
	April	9th		"	May	17th	1849
	March	18th		"	April	25th	1851
	February	25th		"	April	3rd	1853
	February	5th		"	March	14th	1855
	January	15th		"	February	21st	1857
	December	23rd	1858	"	January	31st	1859
	November	21st	1860	"	January	4th	1861
	May	18th		"	July	5th	1862
	April	18th		"	May	27th	1864
	March	26th		"	May	3rd	1866
	March	5th		"	April	11th	1868
	February	13th		"	March	22nd	1870
	January	24th		"	March	1st	1872
	January	1st		"	February	8th	1874
	December	6th	1875	"	January	16th	1876
	June	7th		"	December	9th	1877
	April	29th		"	June	8th	1879
	April	3rd		"	May	12th	1881

From March	13th		through	April	20th	1883
February	20th		"	March	30th	1885
January	31st		"	March	10th	1887
January	10th		"	February	16th	1889
December	17th	1890	"	January	25th	1891
November	9th		"	December	27th	1892
May	10th		"	June	22nd	1894
April	12th		"	May	21st	1896
March	21st		"	April	28th	1898
March	1st		"	April	7th	1900
February	9th		"	March	18th	1902
January	20th		"	February	26th	1904
December	28th	1905	"	February	4th	1906
November	29th	1907	"	January	10th	1908
May	26th		"	July	20th	1909
September	27th		"	November	20th	1909
April	23rd		"	June	2nd	1911
March	30th		"	May	7th	1913
March	10th		"	April	16th	1915
February	17th		"	March	26th	1917
January	27th		"	March	6th	1919
January	5th		"	February	12th	1921
December	12th	1922	"	January	20th	1923
June	25th		"	August	24th	1924
October	20th		"	December	18th	1924
May	4th		"	June	14th	1926
April	8th		"	May	16th	1928

JUPITER SYMBOLICALLY CONSIDERED

Zeus, or Jupiter, is more than lord of air. He is the heir of Saturn, and the Father of the Gods. In him is to be found the principle of human generation and of the joy of life. The nine moons which surround Jupiter are the nine months of gestation. The vast body and glory of this planet are the marvel of the sky. Neptune, Uranus and Saturn are somewhat sinister, solitary and austere. Their remoteness has something inhuman. But great Jupiter swings grandly and joyously in his orbit, divine indeed, but warm toward man in his normal life, protector of the hearth and also of the shrine.

There is no strife or turmoil in Jupiter; only victory, success and the rewards of success. But he is a Protean God; to attain his end he cast veils over the eyes of those whom he would bless. To one he appears as a bull, to another as a swan; again is he perceived only as a dove, or as a shower of gold. These fables contain the truth enshrined in that wonderful hymn "God moves in a mysterious way His wonders to perform."

Now, then, let us fix Jupiter in our minds as man in authority. He is the father blessing his children, but also he chastises them. He is the judge to acquit, but also to condemn. He is the Bishop at mass, but he has bell, book and candle at his need. Yet all these functions, properly considered, are benefic. The father desires to train, the judge to reform, the bishop to save. If we are afflicted by Jupiter, it is for our own good.

Great is Jupiter, firm, four-square, unshakeable in his mighty course. Behold him lord it over the sky at night, a blaze of gold and azure. Venus never moves far from the Sun; here is a twilight star. But Jupiter leaps upon the saddle of midnight, like a warrior king on his black mare.

To one who loves Jupiter his grace is urgent, returning tenfold all adoration. Blessings flock about his feet as dogs greet their master at his homecoming. Success rides laughing at his right hand, and on his left is Love. Before him Fame stalks forth with silver trumpet, and the invisible hosts of power follow his footsteps.

And here is danger—the danger of plethora. Even Jupiter may sit too long at the banquet; the friend of Jupiter may occupy himself with things too earthy to be permanent. It is important for each of us to emphasize the noble and the religious aspects of Jupiter. He is in a dangerous position, between the leaden Saturn and the iron Mars. His true relations are Venus and the Sun and Mercury, and they are far off. He represents the utmost height of achievement merely human, and thus may fall by success into desuetude, or by failure into heaviness of wrath.

Remember that, though Jupiter is supreme, there are three spheres beyond. This is the summit of life, but in life is more than life, for beyond life is death, and beyond death new life,—strange, mystical, and glorious. When you have touched success, aspire to that which is above; and, as to the blessings of this earthly life, let it be your pleasure to shower them on those that have need of them.

So shall you fulfill the divine economy; so shall you attain the holy mountains whose snow-pearls glitter beyond the peaceful river of the fullness of life.

JUPITER IN THE SIGNS

Jupiter, in a general classification, may be said to be the precise contrary of Saturn. The latter constricts and conserves; the former expands and spends. The one is egoism; the other altruism. In religious symbolism Saturn is Jehovah—"I am that I am"—which is only a theocratic way of saying "everything for myself." Jupiter is the divine Son, Jesus—the benevolently spendthrift heir—who gives his very life for others. Jupiter is the instinct of creation, of generosity and hospitality, and of the religious emotions generally; and, of course, in so far as the man is passive to Jupiter, he represents these qualities in the cosmos bestowed upon the man, and hence "Good fortune." Naturally, his action depends, with regard to its scope, upon Neptune and Uranus. Unless these planets, signifying respectively the soul and the divine will, indicate bigness in the career, a good Jupiter will be no more than a luck-bringer in business or profession, and make the character noble, generous, and easy-going; and a weak Jupiter will only defeat advancement in life, and tend to enfeeble the character by making it spendthrift, luxurious, and unable to resist the influence of others.

The power of Jupiter, therefore, will not always be easy to recognize in many of the horoscopes with which we have hitherto been able to illustrate our propositions; for only when the private lives of the natives are fairly well known, or where "luck" has played a great part in their careers, shall we be able to trace his action to our satisfaction. There will, however, be no great difficulty in detecting the modifying influence of the signs, for Jupiter is far more impressionable than Saturn, for the reason that he is so expansive and warm-hearted.

We have intimated above through what channels Jupiter comes

to express his creative and generous tendencies in material prosperity; but another point which should be emphasized in this regard is that Jupiter represents to a very great extent the ambition of the native. The force, quality, and degree of success of this ambition will be indicated by the strength and position of the planet, and the direction or channel through which this ambition may work out its best prosperity will be shown by the sign which Jupiter occupies, modified of course by other contributory conditions.

JUPITER IN ARIES

Aries increases the energy of Jupiter, and makes him decidedly militant. If Jupiter is not afflicted seriously, the combination promises a generous, ardent, and high-minded disposition, with a strong inclination to the study of science, literature, or religion. The more purely benevolent qualities of Jupiter, however, are somewhat repressed, and, at times this position may even mean the complete transmogrification of the religious instinct into something very like ambition. It will, in any case, make the native, to a considerable extent, a pioneer or an innovator, with a very positive and material outlook on those subjects which are accepted by the majority of men with passive reverence; and, while actual atheism is not necessarily implied, there is very likely to be a tendency to that unspoken skepticism which is characteristic of those who regard religious organizations as a branch of politics.

The most typical example of this is, perhaps, Pope Alexander VI whose Jupiter, conjoined with the Moon, is in the third house squared by a rising Saturn. Jupiter is weakened by the latter aspect, and here the power of Saturn quite overwhelms him; such religious instinct as may remain is due to the conjunction of the Moon with Jupiter. But the complete obliteration of any noble or generous quality in the character is clearly marked. Sir Richard Burton, on the contrary, has a very strong Jupiter, both Mercury and Saturn being in conjunction with him. The conjunction of Uranus and Neptune gives deep mysticism, but the Aries position keeps him in the middle path. Hence his strong leaning toward the religion of Mohammed, and the sentiments so splendidly expressed in his "Kasidah," one of the greatest religious and philosophical poems ever written. Very different is Alfred Tennyson, whose Jupiter is softened by the sextile of Venus (but what amazing good fortune it brought him!) and is somewhat irritated by the square of Mercury. Both weaken and conventionalize Jupiter; hence we find the religion of Tennyson quite orthodox and ritualistic, picturing rather its sentimental spirit. Contrast this with Baudelaire, where the Sun, Venus, Mars, and Saturn are all in conjunction with Jupiter. The man is all religion, his whole life one strenuous protest against the limitations of earthly life. That he failed to find a solution of his problems is due to the fact that, like Burton, he had Uranus and Neptune square to this immense combination. Bernard Shaw is a good type of the sceptic. Saturn squares Jupiter, as with Alexander VI, but fortunately Venus is trine and the Moon sextile. Here, then, we get a soft hearted and kindly man, but with his religious instincts quite inhibited from ordinary channels by the fact that the inspired vision is denied to him. Even the trine of the Sun does not make up for this defect; it acts here more on the material plane, and gives him great success, but does not illuminate. Had Jupiter been in a more religious sign, belief would have been easier for Shaw.

Consider, in this connection, Chopin. Here Jupiter has Venus sextile, the same softening influence as with Tennyson; but Mercury is in conjunction with Venus, and his religious feeling is of a deeper intelligence than that of England's laureate. In the case of Madame Steinheil, we see much greater strength of Jupiter, who is in conjunction with the Sun and Venus and not far from conjunction with Mercury and Neptune. But Jupiter is not by any means the strongest of these planets, and so does not control the complex; Saturn in the tenth house, trining all these planets, dominates the horoscope, so that all these varied impulses of her nature tended to subserve her selfishness. Had Jupiter and Saturn been in each other's places, we should have had in her horoscope the figure of a great religious leader.

These cases should be sufficient to indicate not only the nature of the limitations which Aries imposes upon Jupiter but also the favorable indications of natural success and prosperity which the combination furnishes when Jupiter is not badly aspected. It gives ability in managing large enterprises or organizations, self-confidence, and a desire to be at the head of the undertakings.

The following well known persons were also born with Jupiter in the sign Aries:

Alan Leo
Elihu P. Root
Melville E. Stone
Spencer Trask
Warren Leland
Christabel Pankhurst
William H. Woodin
Charles H. Sabin
Woodrow Wilson
Mary Baker Eddy
Clarence Darrow
Emile Coué
George C. Lorimer

For the benefit of those who are not in possession of Raphael's Ephemeris, or who are not able to interpret the symbols contained therein, the years when Jupiter is in the sign Aries are as follows:

From	June	3rd		through	September	13th	1844
	January	20th		"	June	1st	1845
	May	9th		"	November	3rd	1856
	December	15th	1856	"	May	14th	1857
	April	20th	1868	"	April	28th	1869
	April	3rd	1880	"	April	11th	1881
	March	17th	1892	"	March	24th	1893
	March	1st		"	August	8th	1904
	September	1st	1904	"	March	7th	1905
	February	12th		"	June	25th	1916
	October	27th	1916	"	February	12th	1917
	June	6th		"	September	10th	1927
	January	23rd		"	June	3rd	1928

JUPITER IN TAURUS

THERE is much harmony between Jupiter and Taurus, for their power and constructiveness are alike. The native is fixed in his religious beliefs, and in his opinions generally, is of devout and warm-hearted nature and clothed with much pride. But, unless the planet is well posited and dignified, there is danger of crassness and of extravagance. For example, Ludwig II of Bavaria, whose Jupiter is squared by Saturn, lacked wisdom; his extravagant enthusiasms cost him his throne and his life. One sees, too, in his religious ideas, the obstinacy of the earthy Taurus; the decorum of religion was all in all to him. Contrast his nativity with that of Dante, the central religious figure of the most religious age of mankind—we speak here of the outward forms of religion, for ancient Egypt and even pagan Greece were really far more deeply spiritual. In Dante's horoscope, Jupiter is powerfully placed just above the eastern horizon, with the Sun and Mercury in conjunction; semi-sextile to Saturn and Venus, and sextile to Mars.

The figure of Alfred de Musset may well be contrasted with that of Baudelaire whose Jupiter was in Aries. Here Jupiter in Taurus and in the third house has a semi-sextile of the Moon, no other planet affecting these influences. This indicates a mind incapable of real religious thought, Jupiter here meaning only preoccupation with self-indulgence, a situation leading naturally to boredom and despair. A stronger Jupiter in a more spiritual sign could have saved him from this sad end. The Jupiter of Louis Pasteur is in the eighth house, the natural position of Scorpio, whose influence thus blends with the Taurus qualities to give an instinct for laborious inquiry into scientific matters, and additional energy is given by the trine of Mars to Jupiter. The religion of such a man must be material and practical; expressed in no emotional or sentimental manner, but none the less deep and sincere. He may also be assured of good fortune with such a disposition of Mars, that fortune depending on his own energy and will.

Turner is another fine example of a good Jupiter in Taurus. Here Neptune is trine, Venus in conjunction, and Mars square. There is a mystical element in his work from the first planet, softness and richness and beauty of form from the second, and intense realistic power from the third. Jupiter on the cusp of the fourth house, the natural place of Cancer, may explain his great success in painting the sea, and indeed for his choice of canvas as the medium through which to express his religious emotion.

Schumann, for example, has Mars semi-sextile to Jupiter in conjunction with the Sun. This is not nearly so strong a combination as Turner's, though Jupiter is again in the fourth house, indicating the reflective method of expression. But the expansive part of his nature is not strong, and the conjunction of Saturn and Neptune in the Orient turns the strain into a minor key.

Rosa Bonheur is a far more jovial figure. Mercury and Venus are sextile, the Sun semi-sextile; and Uranus trine to her Jupiter, who is on the cusp of the house of her profession, and her predilection for painting bulls or stallions is indicated by Taurus. The whole figure is massive, strong, expansive, and genial.

We might have contrasted with Pasteur another man of science, Alfred Russell Wallace. Here the Sun, Venus, and Mercury are fairly near the trine of Jupiter, though not very close; the religious side of the nature is stimulated thereby, indeed, but the combination is not nearly so strong a motive as is the trine of Saturn to Uranus and Neptune. Hence the intellect ruled for a time, but, when old age came, the religious nature was more prominent, and this proved rather conventional—a surprise to his friends and colleagues and disciples, for there was little harmony between the former and latter views. General Grant has a robust Jupiter, rising in Taurus, with the Sun and Saturn in conjunction, and with Neptune and Uranus close to the trine. The effect of Saturn in conjunction with the Sun appears to be contrary to any deep spirituality; this seems to bring all forces to work on the plane of normal life; and, though Grant had a hearty sort of faith, one is more impressed by the extreme good fortune which attended him, no doubt largely due to the position of Jupiter. Edward VI of England has a fine Jupiter, trined by Saturn. This may explain why, despite his early death, the causes of which are explained elsewhere in this volume, he remains famous as a monument of early piety, learning, and good disposition.

The native with Jupiter in Taurus is fond of home and unlikely to travel much unless under the compulsion of business, or because of other planetary combinations. The position, unless Jupiter is badly afflicted, is fortunate for gain through agriculture, building and mining.

Though generous, he may, in some cases, be over-fond of money for its own sake.

The following well known persons were also born with Jupiter in the sign Taurus:

Bessie Leo (Mrs. Alan)
Chauncey M. Depew
Jules Sardou
William H. Taft
Ray Long
Horace Greeley
Hugo Stinnes
Adolph Ochs
P. T. Barnum
Oscar Hammerstein
Nat Goodwin
Geraldine Farrar
Booth Tarkington

For the benefit of those who are not in possession of Raphael's Ephemeris, or who are not able to interpret the symbols contained therein, the years when Jupiter is in the sign Taurus are as follows:

From	June	2nd	1845	through	June	10th	1846
	May	15th	1857	"	May	25th	1858
	April	29th	1869	"	May	9th	1870
	April	12th	1881	"	April	21st	1882
	March	25th		"	August	20th	1893
	October	20th	1893	"	April	1st	1894
	August	9th		"	August	31st	1904
	March	8th		"	July	20th	1905
	December	5th	1905	"	March	9th	1906
	June	26th		"	October	26th	1916
	February	13th		"	June	29th	1917
	June	4th	1928	"	June	11th	1929

JUPITER IN GEMINI

ALTHOUGH Mercury, the Lord of Gemini, is the herald of Jupiter, Jupiter himself is in detriment in this sign, because the dispersive effect of Gemini upon the mentality cools the generous and magnanimous influences of the altruistic planet. Fiery and watery signs, especially the latter, are far more suitable for the development of these sides of Jupiter's nature. In Gemini, while Jupiter's position is favorable for culture and the intellectual side of religion, the native is mentally restless or changeable, and there is often a tendency to mysticism or to the eclectic in religious expression. As, however, there is no antagonism between Jupiter and the Lord of the sign, much, as usual, will depend upon the elevation and aspects.

One of the greatest religious geniuses of modern times—very Jupiterian both in devotionalism and humanitarianism—was Anna Kingsford. Here Jupiter, though in Gemini, has the sextile of Uranus, which prevents any conventionality in the religious nature; and the square of Mars and the Sun makes it necessary for her to realize her convictions rather than blindly to believe. Jupiter being in the tenth house is easily the most important planet in the figure, so that he moulds the native's whole life to his liking.

It must always be remembered that the most important point in judging a figure is to diagnose from the start the key to the horoscope. In every fortunate nativity, there is one planet, and one only, cardinal to it; the others group themselves naturally around this significator. Where, as in the case of Dr. Wallace, recently mentioned, we find two independent and contradictory groups, there is usually a clash sooner or later, with disastrous results. Another religious genius, now somewhat obscured in the mists of antiquity, was Proclus. Here Saturn is in close conjunction with Jupiter in the second house, but with no planet ascending above them. It is a very strong combination; but, with no help from Uranus, revolutionary tendencies could hardly be expected. Saturn kept Proclus to a scholarly and wise type of orthodoxy; Gemini emphasizes the intellectual side of the religious impulse.

A very great scholar was Erasmus, with a trine of Mercury and a square of Mars to Jupiter. Jupiter is in the ninth house, giving much force to the aspiration toward religion and science; but, once again, Uranus has no part in the complex, and the religious impulse is bounded by the limitations of the period in which he lived, and the schools in which he studied. He clarified and organized; he could not overturn.

Compare with this figure Archbishop Laud's Jupiter, also in the ninth house. Here there is a close square of the Moon and another of Mars from the other side. There is a semi-sextile of Neptune, but this appears as additional weakness, and, perhaps, gives a strain of hypocrisy. Neptune is close to the cusp of the Midheaven, which may account for the extraordinary fame of Laud; there are not half a dozen archbishops in English history whose names are as well known. But Jupiter being decidedly weak, the religious qualities are shallow, perhaps merely assumed as a cloak for the ambition. The Sun rising, and Saturn on the cusp of the third house, are far more significant factors in this nativity.

Dickens has a much stronger Jupiter, hence his strong sense of humanitarianism. There are no aspects, however, to influence his quality one way or the other except the trine of the Sun, and accordingly there is some diffuseness—some, perhaps, may say even shallowness—in the expression of the religious instinct in his art. His is a very good example of a strong Jupiter in Gemini without the admixture of other influences. Two other and greater stars of literature have this position of Jupiter, Balzac and Byron.

With Balzac, Jupiter is in the tenth house. Mars and Venus are semi-sextile; so, on the other side, is Mercury; and the Sun is only seven degrees from exact conjunction. The humanitarian aspect is stronger than in Dickens, and the whole configuration is more compact and better directed. Mars and Mercury, friendly, add truth; Venus, tenderness and beauty of form; while the Sun adds to the fire and art. The vast superiority of the close-knit intensity of *La Comédie Humaine* to the more diffuse novels of the English author is in exact accordance with the prediction of their horoscopes.

Byron's Jupiter is helped by the semi-sextile of Mars and a trine of Neptune, but the Neptunian influence makes the action of Jupiter rather sporadic and intermittent, and he is further constricted by being in the twelfth house. A rising Mars with Uranus just below him seem more important significators in the nativity; and the Moon, as Lady of the Ascendant in close conjunction with Uranus, is easily discernible as the key of the complex. Hence we do not find any great humanitarianism, but that strong love of freedom which is given to the Moon by Uranus.

Of the truly religious type, Cardinal Gibbons furnishes a fine example. Jupiter being in the house of friends, preferment was sure; but a trine of Saturn makes the religious nature strong and sincere; a square of Venus is in this respect favorable, since her affliction makes asceticism the rule of his life.

In Edison, the square of Venus to Jupiter indicates the life of self-denial; Saturn, however, also square, forbids any religious bias; while Uranus being sextile to Jupiter turns the development all to the side of science.

A study of the Jupiter of Wilhelm II is of unusual interest, since its analysis should indicate whether he is the ambitious, self-seeking tyrant and despot his enemies contend, or whether he really did his best to keep the peace in Europe. Astrology gives no uncertain answer. Jupiter has the sextile of Saturn, and the trine of the Sun and, though Jupiter is near the cusp of the twelfth house, and Saturn is rising in the second, the opposition of the Sun to the latter seems to make it unreasonable to call Saturn stronger than Jupiter. The matter is, however, complicated by the conjunction of Mars and Neptune in the tenth house, which dominates the horoscope. On the whole, it appears that the European catastrophe was a fatality beyond the power of any man to cause or avert, or even to hasten or retard to any great extent. In any case the Kaiser's Jupiter in Gemini is a very evident cause of the airy way in which he ventilates his religious convictions, and his "I and my God" goes one better than Cardinal Wolsey's "I and my King."

The occupations and material affairs, over which Jupiter rules, will develop prominently in the native's life, with a natural tendency to professional or diplomatic pursuits; but, if Jupiter is afflicted, this position often tends to produce differences with, or separations from, the near relatives. There is much sympathy, benevolence, and charity in the disposition, and the diplomacy of the native usually amounts to a positive gift, enabling him to get his own way without arousing opposition.

The following well known persons were born with Jupiter in the sign Gemini:

C. W. Leadbetter
Harry Thaw
Joseph Pulitzer
Thomas W. Lamont
Col. George Goethals
Cardinal Gibbons
Roy Howard
George Westinghouse
Theodore Roosevelt
Augustus Thomas
Julia Marlowe
Charles Hayden

For the benefit of those who are not in possession of Raphael's Ephemeris, or who are not able to interpret the symbols contained therein, the years when Jupiter is in the sign Gemini are as follows:

From	June	11th	1846	through	June	25th	1847
	May	26th	1858	"	June	9th	1859
	May	10th	1870	"	May	23rd	1871
	April	22nd		"	September	19th	1882
	November	18th	1882	"	May	4th	1883
	August	21st		"	October	19th	1893
	April	2nd		"	August	18th	1894
	January	2nd		"	April	10th	1895
	July	21st		"	December	4th	1905
	March	10th		"	July	30th	1906
	June	30th	1917	"	July	12th	1918
	June	12th		"	December	31st	1929

JUPITER IN CANCER

In Cancer, Jupiter is in the house of his exaltation; and that sign being above all a symbol of pleasure, we may naturally expect that it will bring out the truly "jovial" qualities of the planet. This is undoubtedly the case; the native is good-humored, benevolent, and humane; the emotional nature and the imagination are strong; but the pleasantest qualities are more evident in the nativities of private persons than in those of the great.

In these there will nearly always be a counterbalance, or life would be dissipated into mere pleasure. These tendencies are well illustrated in William Shakespeare, whose Jupiter in the eleventh house is decidedly stronger than the Saturn with whom he is conjoined. There is a fairly close square, too, of the Sun and the Moon; and the result is the regrettable weakness of character which we still deplore. It is really Venus and Neptune in the tenth house that dominate the horoscope, and these have a semi-sextile aspect of Mars, and a sextile aspect of Jupiter and Saturn, and the Sun and the Moon semi-sextile on the other side from Mars. Uranus is in opposition to Neptune. Here, then, is a marvellous complex; even Mercury is near enough to the trine of Uranus to allow us to say that in this nativity, all nine planets are in aspect. To dissociate Jupiter and isolate his influence, is therefore no easy task. One sees the poet yielding to jollity and boon companionship; he has no strong religious feeling in the ordinary sense of the word, and little humanitarianism. But with Uranus square to Neptune culminating, all personal characteristics fall into the background. The problem of Shakespeare is the problem of genius.

Let us look at the Jupiter of three strong, self-centered men, Cromwell, Jay Gould, and Joseph Chamberlain, and of one weak, selfish man, James II. Cromwell has the Sun and Mercury sextile to Jupiter, the one bringing out the material qualities, the other assisting these by strengthening the intelligence. The Moon, too, is sextile to Jupiter on the other side, and Saturn is square. The last of these aspects removes the last trace of religious or philanthropic development from Jupiter; moreover, Uranus rising and trined by Neptune, is the most powerful planet of the horoscope, especially as Mars is above him. Jay Gould has Jupiter in conjunction with Venus, which turns the self-indulgence shown by Cancer into love of money, and of course implies great luck in getting hold of it. There are no good aspects. Chamberlain has Saturn square, with the usual effects, as noted above with Cromwell. James II has Uranus square to Jupiter, and the Moon semi-sextile. This is weakness. Jupiter is lord of the ninth house; so we find, as we should expect, religious bigotry, the affliction by Uranus denying illumination. Still more unhappy was Dreyfus. Here Jupiter is strong with Neptune and the Moon trine, and Saturn semi-sextile, while Mars is close to a sextile on the other side. But the Sun, Venus, and Mercury are square; the material aspects threaten. It is a cramped position.

Dr. Zamenhof, with his benevolent idea, should have a strong Jupiter; and, indeed, the planet has a semi-sextile of the Moon and Saturn and a trine of Neptune. But these are not strong enough to carry the idea to a successful accomplishment; for this, Uranus and Mercury should have coöperated; had they done so, we might indeed have had a "universal language" that would have commended itself to the world. John Bright, one of the really fine religious and humanitarian types of the Victorian era, has Jupiter just above the Ascendant; and, as he is the only planet in the east, this gives a singular importance.

In everyday life, the native who has Jupiter in Cancer is imaginative and intuitional, sometimes with inclinations for psychism or other mysteries. The position gives excellent aptitude for money-making and the ability to hold money after it has been acquired. He is likely to travel much by water, but is fond of home and is apt to find himself very closely bound by affection to his mother.

The following well known persons were also born with Jupiter in the sign Cancer:

"Bud" Fisher
William J. Bryan
Samuel Insull
Joseph B. Cannon
Dr. John Duncan Quackenbos
Harry Payne Whitney
Harold McCormick

Rudolph Spreckels
Nathan Strauss
David Belasco
Agassiz
Rudolph Valentino
Andrew Carnegie
Mussolini

For the benefit of those who are not in possession of Raphael's Ephemeris, or who are not able to interpret the symbols contained therein, the years when Jupiter is in the sign Cancer are as follows:

From	June	26th	1847	through	July	15th	1848
	June	10th	1859	"	June	29th	1860
	May	24th	1871	"	June	11th	1872
	September	20th	1882	"	November	17th	1882
	May	5th	1883	"	September	26th	1883
	January	17th	1884	"	May	21st	1884
	August	19th	1894	"	January	1st	1895
	April	11th	1895	"	September	4th	1895
	March	1st	1896	"	April	17th	1896
	July	31st	1906	"	August	18th	1907
	July	13th	1918	"	August	1st	1919

JUPITER IN LEO

Leo brings out to the full the frank, expansive, exuberant nature of Jupiter, but the materializing influence of the Sun, as Lord of Leo, is felt markedly, and therefore the religious qualities of Jupiter are not very strong. In the case of Rudolph Steiner, the only definitely religious type on our list, Jupiter is very strong, being in the ninth house near the cusp of the Mid-heaven. The Leonine materiality of Jupiter's religious nature is shown very clearly in Brigham Young, who was more of a theocratic state-builder than a truly spiritual descendant of Joseph Smith. His Jupiter has the Sun, Venus, and Mercury sextile, all accentuating this influence of Leo; Uranus, too, is sextile on the other side, giving that touch of originality which has made Mormonism a living force.

The floridity of Jupiter in Leo is well illustrated by Wagner and Swinburne. The Jupiter of Wagner has Mars in opposition, Venus and the Sun in sextile and Mercury square; an ideal combination for the production of theatrical effect. Swinburne's Jupiter has Mars in conjunction, lending an extreme passion to the higher emotions, and a trine of Venus and Mercury rendering their expression harmonious, sensuous, and lucid. There is also, however, a direct opposition of Neptune to Jupiter which gives a strain of instability and lack of balance. It must not be forgotten that the great poet was also a bitter pamphleteer and a polemical critic.

Similar considerations apply to the Jupiter of Huxley. We are to look here not for the science of the man, but for his religious feeling and his general outlook on life; we are to consider the man by his fireside and not in his laboratory. Saturn and Venus are sextile, giving a sort of conscientious bonhomie, and the Moon is trine; he must have been a singularly indulgent father, and tender to human weakness. A similar case is found in Arthur Balfour. As a statesman, he was callous and caustic; but he was universally beloved in private life, even by his bitterest opponents. The Sun and Venus in conjunction with Jupiter, and the Moon sextile, fully account for this radiant warmth of his private feelings; but Jupiter's position on the cusp of the house of friends makes the effect even stronger.

As a contrast, consider Marie Bashkirtseff, with Jupiter on the cusp of the tenth house, but with no help beyond a sextile of the Moon. Fame she has had, and to spare; but her hopes were all thwarted, and her nature repressed and blighted. She was constantly trying to expand, and was invariably balked. The opposition of Mars to Jupiter was sufficient to account for the thwarting of her impulses. So, too, with Louis XVI, whose humanitarianism was so ill-suited to his period—Jupiter is conjoined with the Sun and Mercury, and their forces tend to overwhelm him. Some distant support, such as a trine, (or even the counter action of a square) seems always desirable to moderate the vehemence of a major conjunction. Henry VI was the Louis XVI of England. He, too, was tender hearted at the wrong time and place. His Jupiter has a rather distant trine of the Sun; but this may have developed his religious instincts and his gentleness. Some sterner element is valuable in the emotional apparatus of a king. The late J. Pierpont Morgan had Jupiter with Mars conjoined, Neptune in opposition, and Saturn nearly square on the other side. This restricts any great outpouring of the higher emotion; Jupiter is tied down very firmly to the material plane, but on that plane he is made very strong. He is externalized, as it were, to signify good fortune within the limits of the ambition.

The native with Jupiter in Leo is sincere, generous and magnanimous, ambitious, fond of power, often with much of the dramatic in his make-up, and usually well-fitted for success in public life. The position increases the intuition and strengthens the vitality, and it is most favorable for the development of such genius as may be indicated by the horoscope.

The following well known persons were born with Jupiter in the sign Leo:

Ex-President Coolidge
Marshall P. Wilder
Jane Addams
George Bernard Shaw
John Wanamaker
General Pershing
Charles A. Peabody
Harrison Grey Otis
Luther Burbank
Bliss Carman
John Burroughs
The late J. P. Morgan

For the benefit of those who are not in possession of Raphael's Ephemeris, or who are not able to interpret the symbols contained therein, the years when Jupiter is in the sign Leo are as follows:

From	July	16th	1848	through	August	11th	1849
	June	30th	1860	"	July	25th	1861
	June	12th		"	November	15th	1872
	January	17th		"	July	7th	1873
	September	27th	1883	"	January	16th	1884
	May	22nd		"	October	17th	1884
	February	26th		"	June	14th	1885
	September	5th	1895	"	February	29th	1896
	April	18th		"	September	27th	1896
	August	19th	1907	"	September	11th	1908
	August	2nd	1919	"	August	26th	1920

JUPITER IN VIRGO

In Virgo, Jupiter is again in detriment, as this sign tends to bring out his duller and more earthly qualities. We, therefore, shall not expect to find here much expansion or altruism or even strong religious feeling. Petrarch and Victor Hugo may immediately strike the casual observer as apparent exceptions to this rule, but the former has Jupiter wonderfully developed by sextiles of Neptune and Venus, and a semi-sextile of the Sun and Mercury on one side and Saturn on the other. The latter has Jupiter in the tenth house conjoined with Saturn, semi-sextile to Uranus, and in opposition to the Sun and Venus. In general, the native is very practical in his religious views, which are intellectual, even materialistic, rather than devotional or spiritual. A more typical example, therefore, is Paul Kruger whose Jupiter has Mars in conjunction, Neptune in trine, and Uranus not far off it, Venus only five degrees from exact conjunction, and Mercury semi-sextile. In this powerful complex, however, Mars, lord of the Ascendant, is the key, and Jupiter merely adds good fortune to Mars. Thus, while the religious and humanitarian nature was extremely strong, it remained strictly subservient to more important material forces.

The anarchist Vaillant had Saturn in conjunction with Jupiter, chilling him, and Neptune in opposition, rendering his movements eccentic; Mars is sextile, denoting activity; hence the strong-headedness and strong-handedness of his essentially humanitarian impulses. Lord Brougham, cold-blooded lawyer, also has Jupiter in

Virgo. The square of Uranus weakens the benignancy of Jupiter, while the sextile of Saturn constricts it into prudence; there is nothing to expand or fortify its benevolent impulses. The Jupiter of Bulwer-Lytton, on the other hand, has a sextile of Neptune, lending a mystical tendency, though not a very powerful or precise one, to the religious element, which is also made rather superficial by a square of Mercury. But Jupiter is strengthened by Saturn applying to a conjunction within twelve degrees; and, as Saturn is in the third house, his influences tinge the whole mind.

Albrecht Dürer, saturnine though the austerity of his mind declares him, has yet a deep reverence. Venus is trine to Jupiter, and Uranus semi-sextile, giving what might be called a good average development. The Virgo influence, however, leaves some coldness. Sir Humphrey Davy, with Neptune exactly in conjunction with Jupiter, Venus trine and Saturn sextile, is genuinely religious. Having taken laughing gas as an experiment, he came back from unconsciousness exclaiming "The universe consists of nothing but ideas." The greatest saint in his highest trance could hardly have known much more. It is a striking example of a truly religious subconsciousness, in one whose conscious mind was preoccupied with the affairs of exact science.

Alexander Dumas has Jupiter conjoined with Venus and Saturn, the Sun semi-sextile on one side, and Uranus on the other. From these influences comes the jovial raciness of his famous stories. In Guy de Maupassant, Jupiter rising, in conjunction with Venus and Mars and with no help from without, is completely obsessed by this pair of passionate planets; and so we regretfully observe this brilliant author the slave of passions which ultimately slew him.

The materialistic qualities of Jupiter in Virgo tend to permeate the higher side of the mind in all directions, and the native is practical, analytical, and skeptical to the point of requiring proofs. Naturally, this position gives marked ability for scientific research, and generally for teaching and for service to others. It also, as in Taurus, gives great constructive power which may manifest itself in success in manufacturing, building, agriculture, or even in literature, according to the bent of the mentality.

The following well known persons were also born with Jupiter in the sign Virgo:

Sir Henry Irving
Whitelaw Reid
J. J. Hill
Nicholas Murray Butler
Charles Evans Hughes
Daniel Chester French
John R. Delafield
Charles M. Schwab
George W. Perkins
Admiral George Dewey
Clarence Mackay
Houdini

For the benefit of those who are not in possession of Raphael's Ephemeris, or who are not able to interpret the symbols contained therein, the years when Jupiter is in the sign Virgo are as follows:

From	August	12th	1849	through	September	10th	1850
	July	26th	1861	"	August	24th	1862
	November	16th	1872	"	January	16th	1873
	July	8th		"	December	12th	1873
	February	19th		"	August	6th	1874
	October	18th	1884	"	February	25th	1885
	June	15th		"	November	15th	1885
	March	30th		"	July	15th	1886
	September	28th	1896	"	October	27th	1897
	September	12th	1908	"	October	11th	1909
	August	27th	1920	"	September	25th	1921

JUPITER IN LIBRA

In Libra, Jupiter encounters two apparently contradictory strains of influence, since Venus, Lady of the sign, softens or sentimentalizes the religious impulses, while Saturn, exalted in Libra, is able to give at least a tinge of asceticism. These influences blend, however, in developing sincerity in the religious instincts, which are expressed with an imaginative mysticism. The influence of Libra in itself contributes a sense of justice and impartiality. Therefore, the student of religions will not be surprised to learn that this sign held Jupiter at the nativities of Jesus of Nazareth, of Percy Bysshe Shelley, of Robert Louis Stevenson, of Swami Vivekananda, and of Maurice Maeterlinck. All these have the deepest religious instinct, combined with a sort of shrinking from the superficial facts of life, seeing humanity, as it were, through rose-colored glasses. It is the gentle spirit in these people which made them great. "Blessed are the pure in heart, for they shall see God." Jupiter in every case above cited is prominent in the nativity, but, at the same time, the tendencies of the sign account for what must at least be reckoned partial material failure.

In the nativity of Jesus, Jupiter, rising, is trined by Saturn; he suffers from the opposition of Mars, and the square of the Sun and Mercury. Without the fiery energy of Paul, the gentle teaching of Jesus would hardly have spread widely, and Christianity might have remained largely a matter of pious local sentiment. The humanitarianism of Shelley was very strong. Mars is in conjunction with Jupiter, making the poet active in protest; but Neptune, also in conjunction, seriously weakens the effect by making his revolt fantastic and intermittent. Stevenson's Jupiter has not even so much strength. Saturn is in opposition, and there is nothing to help but a semi-sextile of Mercury. The gentle spirit is there, but it shows in a glow of kindliness, very lovable, but not to be feared by the unkindly-minded. The Jupiter of Swami Vivekananda is in all respects the best of the group. It is finely balanced by reason, and brought into action by will. A square of Venus prevents the mere sentimentality which her conjunction with the Sun might have allowed. Unfortunately, Mars is in opposition, or he might have made as successful a religious leader as Mohammed. Maeterlinck's Jupiter has the opposition of Neptune, which gives his religious nature its wonderful mysticism.

Consider, now, a very ungentle spirit, but a great religious genius, Luther. Here Jupiter has Mars and Venus conjoined, with the Moon and Uranus sextile with powerful aspects of other planets. There is a lever to move the world; there could be no question of resistance to a bolt of this calibre! Another great builder, genial enough in private life, but adamant in affairs of state, was

Bismarck. Here Jupiter is opposed to the Sun and square to the Moon; Uranus, however, is sextile, and Mars and Saturn are in trine to Jupiter. The chief influence of Libra here is, doubtless, the sense of Justice and the balance which we have already noted as characteristic. Contrast with this the horoscope of Winston Churchill. Here Mars is in conjunction, making Jupiter powerful and energetic; but Neptune's opposition in this complex gives eccentricity. Jupiter acts vigorously, but by fits and starts; set-backs are certain to injure the career from time to time.

There is one religious genius whom we omitted in our first consideration, because her religion was orthodox, though mystical, and was expressed not in propaganda, but in patriotism. We refer to Jeanne d'Arc. Her Jupiter has Venus square, the Moon in conjunction, Mars semi-sextile, and Uranus trine. It is a magnificent combination for the peculiar gift indicated. Uranus gives the illumination, and Mars the practical power. Libra, too, assures good judgment; she was as simple and sensible as she was inspired. This is not a common quality of alleged inspiration!

Jupiter in Libra favors comradeship and association in domestic affairs, especially where dispassionate judgment is a factor, and promises popularity. It gives especially good judgment in handling the money of others and in impartiality in decision; hence, judges and bankers are numerous among the natives of this position. It also promises success in occupations involving efficiency in the higher mathematics.

The following well known persons were also born with Jupiter in the sign Libra:

Henry Ford
Franz Hartmann
Francis Bret Harte
John D. Rockefeller, Jr.
Harrison Fisher
George Washington
John D. Rockefeller, Sr.
Dr. Felix Adler
Frederick MacMonnies

For the benefit of those who are not in possession of Raphael's Ephemeris, or who are not able to interpret the symbols contained therein, the years when Jupiter is in the sign Libra are as follows:

From	September	11th	1850	through	October	11th	1851
	August	25th	1862	"	September	24th	1863
	December	13th	1873	"	February	18th	1874
	August	7th	1874	"	January	12th	1875
	March	21st		"	September	6th	1875
	November	16th	1885	"	March	29th	1886
	July	16th		"	December	16th	1886
	April	29th		"	August	15th	1887
	October	28th	1897	"	November	26th	1898
	October	12th	1909	"	November	11th	1910
	September	26th	1921	"	October	26th	1922

JUPITER IN SCORPIO

So powerful and so aggressive is Scorpio, that its influence in modifying any planet which comes into its "war zone" can hardly be estimated too highly. Mars and Jupiter make the most forceful combination of any two planets, and the Martial energy which Jupiter receives from the Lord of Scorpio is even more effective than that in Aries. For Jupiter is the Father of the Gods and has a strong creative instinct, while Scorpio is the sign of Sex. Hence, people with Jupiter in this sign have the religious idea developed to an overwhelming extent and indissolubly linked with that of generation. Whatever views may be generally held today as to religion, there is no doubt that the deepest reverence for the natural forces of creation makes for enormous strength, and especially for sincerity of religious conviction; since, in such a case, to deny one's own physical power is to fail in faith.

If Jupiter is strong in this sign, we find people with a positively fanatical faith in themselves. God is omnipotent, and He abides within them; how, then, can they ever falter on the path? The effect of ill-dignity—say an evil aspect to Jupiter from Saturn or Mercury—would be to upset the mental balance in this respect and to give evidence of deep-seated perversion.

To take such weak and perverse configurations before the others, we have two remarkable cases of what evidently amounts to sex-mania of a religious type. The case of Edith Allonby, who committed suicide in order to call attention to a book she had written, shows Saturn and Uranus square to Jupiter, one on either side, and Mercury is near a conjunction. On the grand scale, this type of religious hysteria is exhibited by Tolstoi. Venus and Saturn are square to Jupiter, but the sextile of Neptune adds a touch of mysticism intensified by the conjunction of Mars and Neptune. Here is a case of a bad affliction transformed into exaltation and issuing in comparatively harmless channels; but it explains the spirit of the "Kreutzer Sonata."

We find two instances in women of normal sex instincts raised to a high power and made useful in securing material advancement. The Jupiter of Nell Gwyn is trined by Mars, giving exceptional potency; while the Moon, also trine on the other side, adds a softness, which, in view of the strength given by Mars, is decidedly an advantage, especially as the square of Venus tends to prevent too great sentimentality. Cleo de Mérode has the Sun and Venus semi-sextile to Jupiter and Neptune square; the Moon is sextile on one side, and Mars on the other. Each of these combinations is very strong and subtle.

Among writers with Jupiter in Scorpio, we see great preoccupation with, and insistence upon the importance of, the sex-nature. One need only quote Rossetti, Zola, Thomas Hardy, Alphonse Daudet, and Sainte Beuve; and one might also include Cicero on the strength of the hidden implications of "Scipio's Dream." Rossetti's Jupiter, softened by the trine of Venus, and afflicted by the square of Mercury, becomes decidedly sensuous, while the will power is weakened by a square of Uranus. The sex-feeling is strong, but very feminine in quality; and the religious instinct is somewhat unsettled by this combination.

Very different is the case of Zola, whose Jupiter, although trined by Venus, is redeemed by the trine of Uranus which is in conjunction with Venus; and, though the square of Neptune contributes mysticism, yet Jupiter remains extremely strong on the plane indicated; and creation, virility and constructiveness mark his feeling and his work. Venus, especially through her conjunction with

Uranus, accounts for much of the animalism which has been criticized in his writing, but the Uranus-Jupiter trine elevates all this in the grand result. Indeed this case should be very instructive to the student, illustrating how each planet and aspect has its particular effect, persisting in spite of contrary aspects, and becoming reconciled in a higher complex. This principle is immensely important; it explains the infinite variety of mankind, and shows the folly of attempting the solution of astrological problems by mere consideration of the superficial elements of a horoscope.

Thomas Hardy's sex-religion complex very closely resembles Zola's. Here however, the Moon, instead of Venus, is trine to Jupiter; and, though Uranus is also trine, it is from the other side and not in a conjunction. It is a magnificent figure; but, unfortunately, as the Moon is in the mid-heaven in Cancer, the centre of gravity tends toward her rather than to the greater planets, thus diminishing the intensity of both Jupiter and Uranus. Had Jupiter been in the ascendant, Hardy would have been much greater than Zola. The Jupiter of Alphonse Daudet has also the trine of Uranus; it is evidently a most important aspect for constructiveness. Mars, Venus, and the Sun all come near to squaring Jupiter, but hardly succeed. There is, therefore, not the same vivid direction to the force which we have seen in the previous cases. The Scorpio influence, however, is evident as dominating the Jupiter motive, while a semi-sextile of Saturn may be responsible for the touch of melancholy which one perceives in his mood. In the case of Nero, who has Jupiter in this position, the Scorpio influence upon Jupiter took a decidedly troublesome form; the insane perversity of his action toward Sporus is conclusive on this point. The conjunction of Mars and Venus in opposition to Jupiter doubtless determined this sex-madness.

In a much more heroic shape was moulded the grand nativity of Napoleon. Jupiter is just within the second house, but rising; he has Uranus in opposition, but Mars is sextile. It is not to be wondered at, that he had faith in his star. And here a word of explanation may be in place. This sublime self-confidence appearing to be a kind of insane egoism, it may be asked, "Why not rather judge this quality from the point of Napoleon's Saturn?" But it really is not fundamentally egotistic at all. Napoleon's belief was a true religious feeling; in him self-aggrandizement was a secondary matter; he quite seriously believed himself to be the divine instrument to right Europe, and that such a belief should take an apparently egoistic form involves no real change in its Jupiterian character.

Benjamin Disraeli is another instance of a man who rose through an extreme belief in himself. Indeed, in his earlier days, he was much of a coxcomb. Here Neptune and Venus are both in conjunction with Jupiter, which gives just the fantastic affectation which distinguished him. The semi-sextile of Uranus prevented him from going too far on this line, especially as the Sun is also semi-sextile on the other side. The Moon, too, is square, and the result of this was a skeptical feeling in religion. Asked what his religion was, "The religion of every sensible man." "And what is that?" "No sensible man ever tells." Such an attitude is very characteristic of this aspect.

From Scorpio's tendency to scientific investigation, Jupiter in this sign may sometimes have a very technical application to eminence in medicine and surgery, as in the case of Richard Quain. Jupiter is in the fourth house, trine to the Moon and semi-sextile to Neptune, not very notable dignities. Saturn, too, is square. The Sun, excited by the conjunction of Mars and the trine of the Moon, is Lord of the Ascendant, and is applying to Jupiter within eleven degrees. It is only in this indirect way that Jupiter becomes at all important, and such secondary and obscure indications rarely lead to the highest pinnacles. Exact aspects, with elaborate complexes, and simplicity and directness in the references, are characteristic of the greatest sons of the earth.

As an exception to the general implication of the sex-element in the religious idea, we have Sir William Hamilton. But this is through no fault of Scorpio; it is the conjunction of Neptune that turns the religious instinct to metaphysics, and the square of Venus that neutralizes the sensual quality of the sign. The skeptical side remains, and is indeed accentuated by a near square of Mercury, who is Lord of the Ascendant. This is a very interesting and instructive complex.

In music, we have two composers of the first rank in whom the sex-idea may be considered paramount, Strauss and Tchaikovsky. The latter has Neptune square to Jupiter, and Mars and the Sun in opposition, indicating the inversion of sex-impulse; but Uranus is trine, giving constructive ability, which the bad aspects also tend to transpose into a minor key. Strauss has a Jupiter of much greater power; he is not interfered with by any other planet, and is culminating. It is a grand example of "splendid isolation."

From all the cases cited, it will appear that Jupiter in Scorpio indicates an active, self-confident mind, well centered upon its object, with much perseverance and generous enthusiasm. The position is favorable for success in engineering and chemistry and also for matters of transportation, especially marine. Many surgeons, dentists, machinists and railroad officials are found among those born under this combination.

While the imagination and the emotional nature are strengthened, the native will be extremely fond of pleasure and have not a little of showiness in his personality.

The following well known persons were born with Jupiter in the sign Scorpio:

Barney Barnato
John Jacob Astor
Palmer Cox
The late Thomas E. Mitten
Thomas F. Ryan
Thomas Coleman DuPont
Perry Belmont
Lee Shubert
Napoleon
Edward W. Bok
George F. Baker
Edward Markham
Col. George Harvey
Robert J. Collier
William McAdoo

For the benefit of those who are not in possession of Raphael's Ephemeris, or who are not able to interpret the symbols contained therein, the years when Jupiter is in the sign Scorpio are as follows:

From January	1st		through	November	23rd	1840
October	12th	1851	"	November	7th	1852
September	25th	1863	"	October	22nd	1864
January	13th		"	March	20th	1875
September	7th	1875	"	February	9th	1876
April	24th		"	October	3rd	1876
December	17th	1886	"	April	28th	1887
August	16th	1887	"	January	14th	1888
June	3rd		"	September	10th	1888
November	27th	1898	"	December	25th	1899
November	12th	1910	"	December	9th	1911
October	27th	1922	"	November	24th	1923

JUPITER IN SAGITTARIUS

As Jupiter is Lord of Sagittarius, he cannot but be strong therein; yet the abruptness of the fiery sign gives some acerbity to his easy disposition, and there is a certain sharpness of temper associated with this position unless the planet be very well dignified. Even so, we need not expect to find a very genial Jupiter, for Sagittarius is dry as well as swift.

The most expansive persons illustrative of this position are Edward VII and President Faure of France. The former has Jupiter very well placed, only seven degrees above the eastern horizon, and with a sextile of Venus. The square of Uranus accounts for the fact that a good deal of his joviality led to scandal. Felix Faure has this same square of Uranus; in this case, the affliction led directly to his death. There is no help but a sextile of the Sun, and Jupiter, being in the third house, is not so powerful as in the case of the founder of the Triple Entente.

Lily Langtry's Jupiter is also in the third house, but it has no bad aspects except a rather distant square of Neptune. The Sun is sextile, exactly; and, as he is Lord of the eleventh house, one can see how much the friendship of exalted persons must have meant in her career. The Jupiter of Queen Elizabeth is very strong by position, being just above the Orient. But he is afflicted by a square of Neptune and another of the Sun, while Mars is in opposition.

Mercury is sextile, but this only signified the exploitation of Jupiter by shrewdness. From a moral point of view, the afflictions are about as bad as it is possible to imagine.

In the giant figure of Cecil Rhodes, the square of Neptune may perhaps have aided Jupiter by making him spiritual and *large-ideaed*, while the trine of Mercury made those ideas not only broad and benevolent, but *widely* conceived and well calculated. Sagittarius without doubt lent a fierce impetuosity to their development. A similarly ambitious, though selfish, example is Robespierre. The great ability is shown plainly by the trine of Mars to Jupiter. Neptune is close to Mars, and contributes wildness. Uranus, again, is nearly square. We cannot call this Jupiter exactly weak; indeed, he is rather finely placed in the eleventh house, and doubtless the "sea-green incorruptible" was extremly adroit in making use of his friends, but there is nothing to bring out the naturally noble qualities of Jupiter.

Since Sagittarius is a peculiarly mysterious influence, the mystical side of the religious instinct may sometimes be strongly developed. From a psychic standpoint, its influence is even better—and far less liable to corruption—than that of Pisces. Joseph Smith was without doubt a truly religious man, however little one may feel inclinded to subscribe to, or even to examine seriously, his strange belief. Here Saturn and Uranus are conjoined sextile to Jupiter on the one side, and Venus is sextile to the other. There is a semi-sextile of Mercury, and another of Neptune. Here then is a most powerful development of the religious impulse; it is clear that the most sincere conviction went with his belief, and that this intense and honest passion was the real lever that moved so many of his contemporaries to endure the most sinister persecutions for their faith.

W. B. Yeats is a visionary of lesser calibre, though of more intellectual power. Saturn is sextile to his Jupiter, but Uranus and the Sun are in opposition. The complex is not so important, since the rising Moon conjoined with Neptune dominates his nativity.

Melanchthon, who, from the purely religious side, was a greater element in the development of Protestantism than Luther himself, has his Jupiter strengthened by the conjunction of Mars. The Sun is square, Uranus sextile and Neptune semi-sextile. It is a big and genuine complex; and, as in the case of Joseph Smith, the moral earnestness of the man was a tremendous asset. Few would have trusted the volcanic Luther alone, but nobody could have doubted Melanchthon. Such men, in themselves often without initiative, are the backbone, or perhaps the heart, of every great religious movement. Woe to the man of brains who cannot find a man of heart to back him!

And such again was William Blake, one of the truest and noblest seers that England had produced up to that time. The conjunction of the Sun and Mercury with Jupiter assures the intensity and fervor of true faith, though the square of Mars inhibits a practical propaganda. Neptune rising is, however, the dominant force in the element of vision; the Jupiter complex affects the definitely religious connection with the vision. Saturn being in opposition to Neptune gives greater importance still to Jupiter, because the selfish instinct is repressed and spiritualized, thus leaving the expansive qualities to develop at will.

It is doubtful if any of the signs promise more favorably for Jupiter's influence upon financial prosperity than does Sagittarius. Its natives seldom hold subordinate positions, being natural financiers; they are fortunate as directors or managers of large enterprises. It gives a generous disposition and brings honor and esteem not only from friends but even from enemies.

The following well known persons were also born with Jupiter in the sign Sagittarius:

Arthur Brisbane
Stanford White
James Montgomery Flagg
John D. Spreckels
Gifford Pinchot
Senator Borah
August Belmont
Senator Aldrich
E. H. Fallows
John Drew
Charles G. Dawes

Hudson Maxim
Charles E. Mitchell

For the benefit of those who are not in possession of Raphael's Ephemeris, or who are not able to interpret the symbols contained therein, the years when Jupiter is in the sign Sagittarius are as follows:

From	November	24th	1840	through	December	17th	1841
	November	8th	1852	"	December	1st	1853
	October	23rd	1865	"	November	14th	1865
	February	10th		"	April	23rd	1876
	October	4th	1876	"	February	28th	1877
	June	10th		"	October	25th	1877
	January	15th		"	June	2nd	1888
	September	11th	1888	"	February	5th	1889
	July	24th		"	September	25th	1889
	December	26th	1899	"	January	18th	1901
	December	10th	1911	"	January	2nd	1913
	November	25th	1923	"	December	17th	1924

JUPITER IN CAPRICORN

JUPITER being in his fall in Capricorn, the earthy qualities of the sign detract from the buoyancy and good humor of the planet and tend to "freeze the genial currents of the soul." The mind is more serious and less hopeful than is usual with Jupiter; and, while the position may incline the nature to philosophy and contemp-plative learning, the religious instincts, though serious, are not always orthodox. Jupiter badly aspected may become the demon of debauch. This is evidently the case with Michael Angelo and Oscar Wilde, in both of which cases the legend of Ganymede may be remembered.

Wilde's Jupiter is squared by the Sun, which is apt to make its influence loose and gross, and the trine of Uranus and sextile of Neptune can give no counterbalance to such impulses, for these rather tend to accentuate so-called perversions. Jupiter, too, is in the house of pleasures, allowing the full development of the sensual side of his nature; and we have seen that Venus in Libra tends to strange refinements of the sex life. It is, taking it altogether, a most unfortunate position. Michael Angelo, though "immoral" in just the same way as Wilde, has Mercury and Venus sextile to Jupiter on one side and the Moon and Uranus on the other. But the opposition of Saturn steadies this combination and Jupiter is in the eleventh house which does not allow such loose rein to these impulses as the fifth house.

We have one great visionary, Swedenborg, with this position of Jupiter, and the material character of his visions is no doubt due to this. No man ever went so far in bringing angels to earth; his heaven is as objective as that of the orthodox Christian; indeed, more so, because it is more detailed. No man was ever less mystic in the true sense of the word, or held together more firmly the bonds of spirit and matter. Uranus, in conjunction with the Moon, is trine to Jupiter; and here the Moon stands for materiality, while Uranus gives the illumination and the originality. A touch of the fleshly may be conferred by Venus rising twelve degrees above Jupiter, who, as the Lord of the Ascendant, is certainly the key of the complex.

It is extremely interesting to observe through such cases, how, in every complex, the key dominates the entire configuration on the large scale, and yet how every single aspect insists upon achieving its own special signification. The position gives a curiously paradoxical combination of economy and extravagance; the native being apt to be parsimonious in small matters and to spend liberally in large amounts. Many successful merchants and manufacturers are found with this position; and, of course Capricorn endows Jupiter with fortunate influences in any occupation connected with the earth.

The following well known persons were also born with Jupiter in the sign of Capricorn:

Andrew Mellon
Ramsay MacDonald
Charlie Chaplin
Camille M. Flammarion

Prof. J. H. Hyslop
DeLancey Nicoll
Francis Wilson
Rudyard Kipling
Bolton Hall
Will Levington Comfort
Edith Cavell
Gelett Burgess

For the benefit of those who are not in possession of Raphael's Ephemeris, or who are not able to interpret the symbols contained therein, the years when Jupiter is in the sign Capricorn are as follows:

From	December	18th	1841	through	January	4th,	1843
	December	2nd	1853	"	December	18th	1854
	November	15th	1865	"	April	11th	1866
	June	29th	1866	"	November	29th	1866
	March	1st		"	June	9th	1877
	October	26th	1877	"	March	14th	1878
	August	12th		"	November	3rd	1878
	February	6th		"	July	23rd	1889
	September	26th	1889	"	February	22nd	1890
	January	19th	1901	"	February	6th	1902
	January	3rd	1913	"	January	21st	1914
	December	18th	1924	"	January	5th	1926

JUPITER IN AQUARIUS

The Uranian qualities of Aquarius are rather helpful in steadying Jupiter against the tendency to laxity, which we have seen is his chief danger. His religious side is, however, not strongly developed, though there may be a tendency to uncommon religious beliefs of a mystical or occult nature. In general, however, political astuteness is far more to the front in Jupiter's activity, as is witnessed by Queen Victoria and Cæsar Borgia, whose careers, despite the difference of their eras, are not altogether unlike. The sextile of Mars from Aries assures the efficiency of Victoria's Jupiter; he culminates in the tenth house, and there is no trace of any aspect from a planet to disturb his political bent. The real character of Cæsar Borgia is not altogether unlovable. The Sun is trine to Jupiter, making him open and scornful of meanness, but Mars and Saturn in conjunction oppose Jupiter, and these aspects doubtless brought his ultimate ruin.

Another interesting comparison is in George Eliot and John Ruskin. The same coldness is apparent in both. In the former, a sextile of Venus to Jupiter tends to loosen the conventional ties, and the opposition of Mars must have been a great handicap. But in this complex, Mars, as Lord of the Ascendant, is the important factor, especially as he is near the cusp of the Mid-heaven, and Jupiter is in a subordinate position. John Ruskin's Jupiter is seriously afflicted by a conjunction of Mars and by the opposition of the Moon to both these planets; and, the Moon being in the sixth house, an actual physical defect was apparently the cause of his physical incapacity. But had Jupiter not been in zero of Aquarius, taking on some of the coldness of Capricorn, the calamity of the aspects might not have been so serious.

Coleridge's Jupiter was squared by Uranus and opposed by the Moon; fortunately, however, the Sun is nearly trine. Observe how each of these has its own peculiar effect. Jupiter, Lord of the Ascendant, is the key to the complex; and, as he is rising (though rather low in the second house), the personality is altogether suffused with expansive, generous, and noble religious instincts. But Uranus makes his character rather original (to our profit, indeed, though to the poet's own material detriment) and turns it into unusual channels. The weird horror of the one great poem and the two fragments by which he lives in literature are admirably suggested by this aspect plus the Lunar opposition. The trine of the Sun is yet deeper and more personal; it is the undertow of his thought to love all. Hence all the fantastic and gruesome imagery of the Ancient Mariner only decorates the simple truth:

"He prayeth best, who loveth best,
All things both great and small."

It is a noble, unfortunate complex, highly instructive to the student, and it operates on every plane. Jupiter afflicted by Uranus in the house of pleasure squared by the Moon could only mean, on the physical side, addiction to drugs.

Immanuel Kant, on the contrary, has a powerful Jupiter in the tenth house; the Sun and Mercury are square, and Saturn is semi-sextile. This is all very well balanced. The trine of the Sun and Mercury to Saturn is, however, more important in itself than any Jupiter aspect, and it is only the strong position of the latter planet that gives him enough influence to make the religious side of the nature of real importance.

Jupiter in Aquarius gives to the native sincere friends who bring both benefit and pleasures. It strengthens the intuition, inclines to originality in ideas, and favors the acquirement and development of almost any of the higher mental qualities. It gives little love for money as such, and great sensitiveness to the material needs of others. Its natives develop as physicians, lecturers, teachers and promoters of large schemes, especially when they are of a philanthropic kind.

The following well-known persons were also born with Jupiter in the sign Aquarius:

Eugene V. Debs
Dr. Richard Hodgson
Joseph W. Harriman
Otto Kahn
Joseph E. Otis
Dean Cornwell
Gutzon Borglum
George Eliot
Jackie Coogan

For the benefit of those who are not in possession of Raphael's Ephemeris, or who are not able to interpret the symbols contained therein, the years when Jupiter is in the sign Aquarius are as follows:

From	January	5th 1843	through	January	16th 1844
	December	19th 1854	"	May	11th 1855
	August	3rd	"	December	27th 1855

From						
From April	12th		through	June	28th	1866
November	30th	1866	"	April	14th	1867
September	16th		"	November	30th	1867
March	15th		"	August	11th	1878
November	4th	1878	"	March	25th	1879
February	23rd	1890	"	March	7th	1891
February	7th	1902	"	February	19th	1903
January	22nd	1914	"	February	3rd	1915
January	6th	1926	"	January	17th	1927

JUPITER IN PISCES

In Pisces, Jupiter is strong, and the passive, receptive, somewhat psychic character of the sign enables the religious element in Jupiter to develop to its fullest extent, though in a quite unconventional and mystical manner. For example, in the case of Colonel Olcott, a sextile of Neptune is Jupiter's only important aspect; this, perhaps, led him to Theosophy rather than to Presbyterianism. Savonarola, with the trine of Uranus to Jupiter, is very dominant and constructive. Neptune is in opposition within four degrees, giving intense mysticism to the religious spirit. This is, however, far from the strongest complex of his figure.

Tom Mann, the socialist agitator, has this position of Jupiter. Apart from near conjunctions of Venus and Neptune, there is no aid, and Saturn is square. It is a bad and selfish as well as a weak and untrustworthy complex.

We have, however, three really great men with this position. Each has the true religious feeling; yet, in each case, it is somewhat masked by the scientific spirit. Herbert Spencer, for example, has no aspects to Jupiter but the sextile of the Sun, the semi-sextile of Mercury and square of Venus. It is by far the weakest of his three great complexes. Goethe has Neptune trine to Jupiter; hence the mystical tinge in his religious thought, and Venus is in opposition. Saturn rising is within ten degrees of making a triple trine with the two former planets, and adds a much-to-be desired severity to the mind. The Venus aspect here only insists on beauty of form, and no doubt determined him as primarily a poet. Sir Isaac Newton has Saturn conjoined to Jupiter, lending wisdom and austerity to his religious conceptions, while the Sun is sextile, illuminating the vision and balancing by his warmth the coldness of Saturn. Uranus, moreover, is trine, giving originality and freedom to the idea. It is an altogether admirable combination, one of the finest that we have had to consider.

Jupiter in Pisces indicates travel, principally by water, and brings good fortune through occupations ruled by Neptune. It inclines the disposition to be kind, quiet and unassuming. It develops the social instincts, but is apt to leave the native rather easy going and unambitious, unless the planet is well-dignified.

The following well-known persons were also born with Jupiter in the sign Pisces:

Stanley Baldwin
J. P. Morgan
H. Rider Haggard
Bishop Greer
Elbert Hubbard
Ellen Terry
Robert Goelet
Abraham Lincoln
Ethel Barrymore
Stanley Baldwin
William Faversham
President Lowell of Harvard.

For the benefit of those who are not in possession of Raphael's Ephemeris, or who are not able to interpret the symbols contained therein, the years when Jupiter is in the sign Pisces are as follows:

From	January	17th		through	June	2nd	1844
	September	14th	1844	"	January	19th	1845
	May	12th		"	August	2nd	1855
	December	28th	1855	"	May	8th	1856
	November	4th		"	December	14th	1856
	April	15th		"	September	15th	1867
	December	1st	1867	"	April	19th	1868

From	March	26th 1879	through	April	2nd 1880
	March	8th 1891	"	March	16th 1892
	February	20th 1903	"	February	29th 1904
	February	4th 1915	"	February	11th 1916
	January	18th	"	June	5th 1927
	September	11th 1927	"	January	22nd 1928

THE EFFECTS OF JUPITER ON VOCATION

In the days when a man was either a lord or a serf, a knight or an innkeeper, it was comparatively easy to determine with exactness a man's vocation. In modern days, however, there are thousands of different and characteristic types of employment. While Jupiter is the key to the type of work which may bring a man money or profit, it does not necessarily follow that it is the kind of vocation for which he has the greatest inclination. Too often, indeed, his inclination is not that for which he is best adapted, or it is incompatible with his environment and education. On the other hand, an accurate observer may often see a person with distinct abilities for a certain type of work, and yet he recognizes that, for some other reason, he had an inability to make a success of that work.

For example, those born with Jupiter in Aries are seldom contented and happy unless they can be in a type of work where leadership, personal self-assertiveness, and pioneering are necessary to success. Those with Jupiter in Aries are never contented with a routine job, or one in which their personalities are constantly subjected to others.

These people have ability in managing large enterprises or organizations, and have a desire to be at the head of any undertaking in which they may be engaged. They find it necessary, however, to guard against giving the impression that they are over-confident and that their ideas are not practical. Men active in politics, club or organization work, and those who meet with success in military life, or in any business connected with fire, railroads, or machinery, are born with Jupiter in Aries. Even if not personally interested in these undertakings, investments in them should yield good returns. People born between March 21st and April 21st, July 21st and August 21st, and November 21st and December 21st prove fortunate to those having Jupiter in this sign in a business way, and undertakings which lead up to them at these times in any year will stand a good chance of succeeding, or may prove to be connecting links to more important things later on.

Those born with Jupiter in Taurus require a kind of work where constructiveness, systematic building, and a certain amount of routine bring success. Even though the mind may be radical in interest and advanced in thought, the method of procedure will be one of careful and conservative action.

These people are natural builders; but it largely depends upon circumstances whether they use their constructive force in erecting a skyscraper, in running a ranch, in opening a new mine, in building a factory, or establishing a rundown business on a paying basis. As Taurus rules the throat, Jupiter in this sign often gives one a sympathetic speaking or singing voice. It is interesting to note that Jupiter was in this sign in the horoscopes of Sarah Bernhardt and Geraldine Farrar. Women having Jupiter in Taurus make natural home builders, devoted mothers, and are successful as interior decorators or in activities with or for children.

People born between December 21st and January 21st, April 21st and May 21st, and August 21st and September 21st, prove fortunate in a business way to those having Jupiter in this sign; and undertakings, which lead up to them at these times in any year, will stand a good chance of succeeding or prove to be connecting links to greater things later on. Landed property will prove to be one of their safest forms of investment.

Those born with Jupiter in Gemini will have a natural desire to make money through some professional, diplomatic or mental pursuit. Seldom will any form of manual labor be agreeable. Brilliance takes the place of routine, and any routine task will be obnoxious. Patience and persistence are not characteristic virtues of this type.

Many bankers, brokers, promoters, lawyers, diplomats, public speakers, actors, artistic and professional men have been born with Jupiter in Gemini. These people should guard against allowing their interests to be too much divided, although their Jupiter being in Gemini often makes them successful in two different enterprises at the same time. They should guard against going into new ventures before looking into them most carefully, as they naturally attract schemers. These people have an ability to get their own way, without arousing opposition, which amounts almost to a gift.

The cut-and-dried business man, unless he is very polished, does not appeal to the average woman having Jupiter in this sign.

People born between January 21st and February 21st, May 21st and June 21st, and September 21st and October 21st will prove fortunate in a business way to those having Jupiter in this sign; and undertakings which lead up to them at these times in any year will stand a good chance of succeeding or will prove to be connecting links to more important things later on.

People born with Jupiter in Cancer have a splendid sense of the practical and natural values of life. The disposition allows for a wider range of vocation, but not for any wider attitude toward the work at hand. Some of our most successful politicians, manufacturers, wholesale merchants, chemists or men interested in shipping or other enterprises connected with liquids, have Jupiter placed in Cancer. It often causes them to deal with something that is used in the home or on the person, and gives excellent aptitude for making money, as well as the ability to accumulate it, although they are often too conservative in business, frequently missing opportunities through too great caution. It makes one a gracious host and a liberal provider for the home.

Women having Jupiter in this sign frequently marry men in public life. They make excellent nurses, meet with success in domestic science or in the care of children and the home, also in work connected with food.

People born between February 21st and March 21st, June 21st and July 21st, and October 21st and November 21st, will prove fortunate in a business way to those having Jupiter in this sign, and undertakings which lead up to them at these times in any year will stand a good chance of succeeding or will prove to be connecting links to more important things later on.

Those born with Jupiter in Leo find any phase of work which requires subjection irksome and difficult. Such a nature could not possibly be happy in being a personal servant or a clerk behind the counter. He would be in perpetual revolt, and only those phases of work where some opportunity for command is possible, interest these personalities. Many officers of banks, directors and superintendents of important enterprises, captains of industry, and heads of departments are born with Jupiter in Leo. If circumstances over which these people have no control force them to fill inferior positions, they will not only find it almost impossible to adapt themselves to conditions, but they will be in danger of stirring the jealousy or enmity of their superiors. Furthermore, if they are in a subordinate position they may never know their latent possibilities; for until there is something great at stake, they will not be stirred to do their best and the powers lying dormant will not come to the surface.

People with Jupiter in Leo should look into any opportunities which lead up to them between March 21st and April 21st, July 21st and August 21st, and November 21st and December 21st of any year; even though they may not seem important, they may prove to be, directly or indirectly, stepping stones to greater things later on. These would also be propitious times to inaugurate new ventures, or for extending their business activities. People born at these periods in any year may be in a position to benefit them, or, because of their disposition or temperament, may bring to the surface their most desirable side.

Those born with Jupiter in this sign have many generous impulses and inspire confidence in people of wealth or power; they naturally attract and enjoy much good fortune, provided they make use of their opportunities. They must, however, guard against going to extremes in the expenditure of money, particularly on friends or those they love.

Those born with Jupiter in Virgo are exceedingly systematic; and, when they have this position, can carry on, with great force and precision, any phase of routine task which requires detail and persistence. They have pronounced technical command. They have two fields of activity open to them. Some of our most successful literary men, accountants, secretaries and teachers, as well as successful manufacturers, builders, miners, foresters, biologists and agriculturists were born with Jupiter in this sign.

Women having Jupiter in Virgo are successful in business life, or as librarians, private secretaries, teachers or in any position where practical, analytical, critical or constructive faculties are required. The natural tendency to be constructive makes both men and women judicious in the expenditure of money, regardless of the income, and gives them a dislike for undue extravagance or waste. They make wise buyers.

People with Jupiter in Virgo should look into any opportunities which may lead up to them between December 20th and January 20th, April 20th and May 20th, August 20th and September 20th; for, even though these opportunities may not appear vital at the time, they may prove connecting links to greater things later on. People born at these times will usually prove fortunate to them in a worldly way. They would do well to consider, as investments, real estate, mining property, manufacturing enterprises, or mortgages.

Those born with Jupiter in Libra show a type of vocational interest where breadth of concept or even balance of judgment is of supreme worth. It is a position of such sensitiveness that rough, manual tasks or the stress of war would be most irksome. There is that type of personal balance and discrimination which might make the native a jeweler, a painter or a judge, but he could not be a butcher or a general. It gives a keen sense of justice and the ability to come to fair and just conclusions, even though adverse to their own personal interests. In fact, these people often show better judgment in the management of money belonging to others than in the management of their own, particularly if connected with speculation. For this reason, unless circumstances seem very favorable, it would be well for them to be a part of a large organization or have a partner who has qualities which complement their own, rather than to be in business for themselves. Some of our most successful lawyers, judges, bankers, brokers, engineers, architects, electricians, as well as artists, are born with Jupiter in Libra. Therefore, any of the above professions or lines of business would prove more agreeable as a calling than anything purely commercial. If forced into the commercial world, they will feel dissatisfied, even though they meet with financial success. If they choose a hobby or an avocation, this will help to make their life seem more nearly complete.

It would be well for those having Jupiter in Libra to look into opportunities which lead up to them from January 20th to February 20th, May 20th to June 20th, and September 20th to

October 20th; for, although they may not appear to be of vital importance at the time, they may prove to be connecting links to more important things later on. These would also be propitious times for making greater effort to advance their interests, to increase their business, or for adjusting misunderstandings. Even though adverse aspects are operating in any particular year, these periods will usually bring some favorable conditions or assist them in taking an attitude which will help to mitigate whatever may be threatened. People born during the above mentioned dates may, in some way, contribute toward their financial interests.

Those born with Jupiter in Scorpio would be well qualified for a general or for anyone like, let us say, a detective; they are interested in all subtle, secret and exact forms of activity. They would not delight in an open, jolly, offhand type of work, such as travelling salesmanship. These people are very tenacious in the attainment of their desires and ambitions, whether they be for power in the financial, artistic, or social world. They have a great sense of self-protection, but must guard against being too self-absorbed. Scorpio is the sign of great extremes, and can either make one very spiritual and unselfish or very material. It is, therefore, necessary that those who have Jupiter so placed live up to their best, as well as to the letter of the law. Many successful critics, musicians, chemists, and those engaged in mechanical pursuits, as well as officials in large organizations, have Jupiter in Scorpio.

Women with Jupiter in this sign often make magnetic healers, nurses, masseuses and dentists, or attendants in physicians' offices.

It would be well for these people to look into opportunities which lead up to them, from February 20th to March 20th, June 20th to July 20th, and October 20th to November 20th; people born between these times are likely to benefit them in a business way.

Those born with Jupiter in Sagittarius would find sympathetic any sphere of work where clear, penetrating, intellectual precision would produce essential success. A mere social task or emotional occupation, or a material routine kind of work would prove distasteful. These people are natural financiers, and if in a subordinate position, or if forced to deal in small figures, will never get the full benefit of their "luck." It is so much a part of their destiny to have money and to do everything in a princely way, that, if they force themselves to economize and to save the pennies, they will so change their nature that they will cut themselves off from what would otherwise come to them. Jupiter in this position frequently brings money, through inheritance, and because people of influence, wealth and power have confidence in the judgment of those who have it so placed. These people just naturally attract much good fortune, and, unless they neglect opportunities, they will meet with unusual success and be a power in their world.

They should look into any opportunities which lead up to them between March 21st and April 21st, July 21st and August 21st, November 21st and December 21st; even though they may not seem important, they may prove to be, directly or indirectly, stepping stones to greater things later on. These would also be propitious times for adjusting any difficulties, or for asking favors. People born at these periods will be in a position to benefit them, or, because of their disposition or temperament, may bring to the surface their most desirable side and have a cheering influence over them.

Women with Jupiter in this sign are rarely forced to be self-supporting, but, if desirous of earning money, they can be successful in some enterprise of their own, or as advisors, directors, and financial managers.

Those born with Jupiter in Capricorn have an enormous capacity for detail and routine and are conscientious plodders. They make successful manufacturers, wholesale clothiers, builders, real estate dealers, miners, agriculturists and foresters.

They should look into any opportunities which lead up to them between April 20th and May 20th, from August 20th to September 20th, and from December 20th to January 20th. These would be propitious times to adjust any business difficulties or for asking favors. People born at these periods of any year are likely to be in a position to benefit them; or, because of their disposition or temperament, they may coöperate sympathetically and have an altogether cheering influence over them.

Those born with Jupiter in Aquarius enjoy all phases of work relating to human beings. It is a splendid position for diplomats, labor leaders, psychologists, sociologists, and for those types of business men or women who handle many employees. In a business way, these people often prove more fortunate to others than to themselves, and for this reason they should hesitate before assuming the responsibility of conducting a business of their own; they would do better by being the part of a large organization or in an advisory capacity. If they are following a profession, they would do well to have a competent secretary who will look after the financial end in a businesslike manner; otherwise, because of their leniency, they are likely to suffer from delinquent accounts or from attracting too many clients who take advantage of their humanitarianism. Many competent physicians, architects, inventors, bankers, brokers, ambassadors, statesmen, lecturers and teachers, as well as promoters of big schemes, particularly of a philanthropic kind, or where the object is to improve the general condition of the masses, have Jupiter thus placed. They are often bored by ordinary commercial business; and, if forced into this channel, they should also have a hobby or other interest, in order that their life may be complete.

They should look into any opportunities which lead up to them between January 20th and February 20th, May 20th and June 20th, and September 20th and October 20th of any year. These would also be propitious times to adjust any difficulties or for asking favors. People born at these periods may be in a position to benefit them, or because of their encouraging disposition, may bring to the surface their most desirable side and have a very beneficial influence over them.

Those born with Jupiter in Pisces would be bored if obliged to confine their efforts to any mere intellectual type of work; emotion, human association, drama and responsiveness must enter into the vocational interests. Because of their ability to coöperate with their associates, they succeed when connected with large manufacturing concerns; they are also successful in a business connected with steamship companies, waterways or those concerned with liquids. Those engaged in research work for the benefit of humanity, secretarial workers, teachers, orators, dramatists, actors and dancers are frequently born with Jupiter in this sign.

They should look into any opportunities which lead up to them between February 20th and March 20th, June 20th and July 20th, and October 20th and November 20th. These would also be favorable periods for them to adjust any business difficulties or for approaching those who can advance their interests. People born at these times should play a constructive part in their lives in a business way.

It must be borne in mind, naturally, that there are many modifying factors which should be taken into consideration when determining the type of vocation which is most favorable to the native. But the position of Jupiter is to be looked for as the prime influence in the native's capacity for making money.

As an example, the Sun favors positions of authority, responsibility and dignity, and those born strongly under Leo, which is ruled by the Sun, or where the Sun is the dominating influence in the horoscope, would naturally be enabled to hold such positions.

The Moon, which governs the masses and the public and brings about journeys and much travelling, is fortunate for politicians, the heads of clubs, travelling salesmen, sailors, fishermen, dealers in liquids, nurses, employment in connection with children, dressmakers and general tradesmen. Those born strongly under the sign Cancer, which is ruled by the Moon, or where the Moon is the dominating influence in the horoscope, could fill any of the above positions admirably.

Mercury is fortunate for journalists, orators, lawyers, accountants, school teachers, secretaries, messengers, letter carriers, book dealers. Those born strongly under either Gemini or Virgo, or where Mercury is the dominating influence in the horoscope, could be successful in any of the above employments.

Venus is favorable for musicians, painters, singers, dancers, poets, actors, toymakers, florists, beauty specialists, stylists and apparel designers, and domestic servants. Those born strongly under the signs Taurus and Libra, or who have Venus as the dominating influence in the horoscope, could show aptitude for any of the above mentioned vocations.

Mars favors military men, surgeons, dentists, chemists, workers with metals, especially iron and steel, engineers, railroad men, trades which use sharp tools, including barbers; people born strongly under Aries and Scorpio, or who have Mars as the dominating influence in the horoscope, could fill any of the above professions or employments successfully.

Jupiter is propitious for senators, judges, ministers, deaconesses, bankers, philanthropists, financiers, and the financial heads of any business. Those born strongly under Sagittarius, or who have

Jupiter as the dominating influence in the horoscope, could be successful in any of the above.

Saturn favors earthy occupations, builders, real estate dealers, farmers, landscape gardeners, geologists, miners, foresters; it is also propitious for jailors, undertakers and night watchmen. Those born strongly under Capricorn, or who have Saturn as the dominating influence in the horoscope, could easily attain success in any of the above mentioned employments.

Uranus is favorable for government officials, astrologers, psychoanalysts, psychologists, mesmerists, metaphysicians, scientists, inventors, lecturers, explorers, aviators, radio operators, and electricians. People born strongly under Aquarius, or where Uranus is the dominating planet in the horoscope, would be attracted by, or could be successful in, any of the above vocations.

Neptune favors philosophers, occultists, magicians, inspirationalists, artistic and literary geniuses, and occupations in connection with water and ether. Those born strongly under Pisces, or where Neptune is the dominating influence in the horoscope, would be attracted by, or could attain success in, any of the above mentioned callings.

SATURN SYMBOLICALLY CONSIDERED

Chronos, or Saturn, is called the eldest of the gods, that is, of those who are known upon earth. When Saturn ruled the earth, it was the age of gold. In Parsifal, Saturn is Titurel, the holy primæval king, in whose day all went well. But age has withered him. Jupiter, the only child of his that he did not devour, has tricked him of his throne. Now, this golden age is the age of agriculture unfettered, the patriarchal age of Abraham. There was no pressure from without or from within. Mankind lived freely and easily. Love had no after taste of bitterness, and death itself was, indeed, the twin brother of sleep.

But Time, devouring his children, has also eaten into his own bones. Jupiter being crowned, Saturn becomes a "back number." He is no longer thought of as the clement king, but as the old man, envious of his juniors. It is chiefly this aspect which we see in the planet called after him. Saturn represents agriculture, indeed, but from the point of view of the townsman; the work seems coarse, heavy, laborious, and dull. And he has all the vices of age, as well as its disabilities.

Man may be master of life and of death—if he will. To the worker in the fields of the intelligence, the farmer of mind, the harvest grows continually. Saturn is once again the golden god. The brain of the brain worker improves constantly until the age of sixty, and even then retains its vigor until the end. Such old men we often see. Instead of the vices and infirmities of age, they have consolidated virtues, conserved strength. Dignity and austerity crown and cloak them. They are simple, strenuous and lofty-minded. Even if they are of solitary habit, they are kind. The purpose of their lives has crystallized; and, because they have desired only the infinite, satiety does not touch them. Life is to them a religion of which they are the priests, an eternal sacrament of which perhaps the ecstasy is dulled, but which they consume with ever-increasing reverence. Joy and sorrow have been balanced, and the tale thereof is holy calm. They know that peace of God which passeth all understanding.

The commoner aspect of Saturn, however, is this: the malicious oldster, envious of youth, hating life because he has failed to live it according to the law of righteousness. His will-power is merely obstinacy, opposition to reform, failure to accomodate himself to changed conditions, the conservatism of the hardened brain. He feels his waning powers and tries to receive—to receive, when all his sensibility is gone! Feeling himself impotent, he vents his toothless rage upon the young. Unhappy himself, he seeks to make others wretched. Sordid and heartless, he sneers at enthusiasm and generosity. Weary of life, he thinks life holds no joy.

And so, unless Saturn be dignified nobly—the best of all his dignities is illumination by the Sun—he represents malefic force. Cold, hostile, merciless, bitterly calculating life in terms of his own disaster, he blights all that he gazes on. He is the curse of disappointment, not of anger. He freezes the water-springs; he is the dry-rot and the death of the ungodly. He looks upon the Sun, despairs; in cynic bitterness his draught is brewed, and he drinks it, wishing it were poison. His breath withers up love; his word is malediction.

Happy are we, if we escape his fatal influence! But in each one of us this principle exists; it is the most unescapable of all our fates. On us, on our wisdom and our vitality, the burden lies, how we will live so that our old age may be beautiful. There is no token of the triumph of life like a noble close to it; no proof of our salvation like the love borne us by the young when we have hailed the bark of Charon from afar. Let us see to it that our age

> "Is as lusty winter,
> Frosty but kindly."

> "Be humble, if thou wouldst obtain wisdom
> Be humbler still, when wisdom thou hast gained."

SATURN IN ARIES

Here we find the planet in his fall; it is in many ways the most unfavorable position for him. It is not that the martial disposition of the sign is so unfavorable; but Aries is the sign par excellence of initiative, and to find delay in that which is essentially of prompt decision is fatal. The Sun, too, being exalted in Aries, can hardly rejoice to find his brilliance usurped by the dull planet, his joy replaced by that leaden melancholy. However, Saturn is obstinate enough, and when in this sign, he appears to mean that the will is working under great disadvantages; it represents persistent struggle against overwhelming obstacles. It means usually patience; but if success comes to the native, it can only be at the end of the journey, and that with pain and sorrow. There seems no right adaptation possible of the means available to his end—the native is indeed a round peg in a square hole. He must take courage that all experience is for the good of the soul, and so miss no spiritual profit. Circumstances prove usually too much for the sturdiness of the personality. Even those who achieve greatness are likely to miss full measure, because Fate seems to say "thus far and no further."

An example of such restriction to effort is Philip Bourke Marston's blindness. His Moon, one of the "lights," is in Scorpio, in opposition to Uranus, which is only 9 degrees from Saturn. The

Rising Sun is in trine to Saturn, and Marston seems to have made splendid use of the Sun's reinforcement and found strength to make headway against his misfortune. His case seems especially one caused by the soul's election of special discipline—for the unfavorable aspect of Luna indicates calamity beyond prevention.

The world will not soon forget Robert Louis Stevenson's heroic cheer and industry under the lash and inescapable grind of physical suffering. What might his pen have wrought unhampered! Yet the discipline and "trying out" of his fine soul counts on the side of eternal profit and, though the physical man could not surmount the affliction of ill-health, and an early death cut short his effort, yet his courage and cheer were never dimmed, and "pity" must hesitate to judge. Saturn rising, afflicted by the opposition of Jupiter, and the Sun in conjunction with Mars, and Neptune rising in conjunction with Luna indicate his test. Who shall compute or deny his eternal profit?

The limiting power of Saturn in Aries worked out similarly through the ill health that handicapped Herbert Spencer. Here, however, is a formidable personality and a will capable of overcoming anything and everything; although a persistent invalid, he not only accomplished his gigantic task, but lived to great age. Uranus and Neptune are rising in conjunction; the Moon and Sun in opposition and squared by Mars is unfortunate, but Saturn, semi-sextile to Sol and trine to Mars, influences baleful but strengthening balance. The Will of the man tips the scales, and the Will of Spencer pulled with Neptune and Uranus, and set patience, courage and concentrated industry in the balance. Materially, he "beat" fate with success. But who shall compute his greater riches, won under the discipline of his Saturn in Aries?

Sir Richard Burton's obstacle is external. His ill-health was caught in the jungles. His Moon is directly opposed by his Saturn in Aries, which is conjoined with Mercury, lord of the house of his friends. Jupiter too is with Saturn. Burton displays indomitable courage, yet cannot counteract the limitation of his Moon. His walls of success fall as fast as he lays the stones.

The Saturn of Erasmus spoke limitation from Aries, though enlightened by Uranus, opposite in fair Libra. We find Erasmus foremost scholar of his time, and his limitation represented by that time. Patient, persevering, indomitable, he seems to have laid hold upon the steadfastness of Saturn and accomplished the utmost possible—but the bar could not be lifted.

Inescapable limitation is manifested curiously in the career of Rosa Bonheur, whose sex shackles her. Sturdily she laid hold of all that Saturn trined by Mars could give. She never faltered in purpose and we know the splendid measure of her success.

Guy de Maupassant succumbs to the forces of his own emotional nature. His Venus is rising in conjunction with Mars and Jupiter. This is the test that seems dictated by Saturn in Aries—and de Maupassant seemed unable to lay hold on any reinforcement to his will. Lamentable indeed was the climax of that most brilliant and most unfortunate life!

We end the series with Charles Baudelaire. Saturn is in conjunction with the Sun; Mercury, Venus, Mars and Jupiter are all approaching them. Obstacle and limitation and powers of opposition! And also an array of strengthening influences to equip him in the fight to which the soul is called. All these planets, however, are in the eighth house—the house of death. His preoccupation was ever with death and the appurtenances and ornaments of death. His Uranus and Neptune are conjoined exactly in the fourth house, inviting an inner solemnity to the soul.

The poet walks in his garden of cypress, and tends his monkshood, his nightshade, and his vervain—darkness and sorrow his limitation! Not for him the blossoms of the May, nor the rose-bowers of happier though not holier bards! The edict of Saturn in Aries is fulfilled.

From all the cases cited it appears that Saturn in Aries tends to bring the native prominently forward in his own sphere of activity; he has ambition, is diplomatic, though somewhat distrustful, and has self-confidence, though he may be austere and a lover of retirement. With many acquaintances, he has few intimates, and there may be traces of selfishness and sometimes great irritability. One of the greatest limitations imposed by Saturn in Aries is upon the physical health. Such material success as may be obtained is likely to be through the relations with the public.

The following well known persons were born with Saturn in the sign Aries:

Queen Wilhelmina of Holland
Lord Kitchener
General Joffre
Guy de Maupassant
George Washington
Mary Baker Eddy
King Ludwig II of Bavaria
Ethel Barrymore
Perry Belmont
George M. Cohan
Cecil de Mille

For the benefit of those who are not in possession of Raphael's Ephemeris, or who are not able to interpret the symbols contained therein, the years when Saturn is in the sign Aries are as follows:

From	April	4th	1849	through	June	3rd	1851
	November	5th	1851	"	February	22nd	1852
	May	15th	1878	"	September	15th	1878
	February	6th	1879	"	April	5th	1881
	March	19th	1908	"	May	16th	1910
	December	15th	1910	"	January	19th	1911
	May			"	October		1937
	February		1938	"	June		1939
	October		1939	"	March		1940

SATURN IN TAURUS

In Taurus the heaviness of Saturn is accentuated by that of the sign, and so his obstinacy, pertinacity and dullness are accentuated. But as all this makes for steadiness, the moral character is firm and capable of overcoming obstacles by sheer determination; while, on the other hand, those obstacles themselves are not apt to be particularly violent. So we shall expect to find natives with the capacity to push steadfastly forward, and to conquer.

One of the weakest examples of this position is given by Shelley, whose Saturn, being in only two degrees of Taurus, retains perhaps some portion of the Aries qualities. It is just at the Nadir, and has no support of any kind from any other planet, and is indeed in opposition to Neptune. Hence we see in Shelley a moral instability, which is contrary to the general nature of Saturn in Taurus; fine aspirations given by the Sun, Venus and Uranus in conjunction without the power to fully coördinate them or cause them to cohere; impatience and frivolity indicated by Mars and Neptune in conjunction with Jupiter from the effects of which an iron and indomitable resistance would have saved him.

The nativities of three great conquerors present an utterly different picture. It was the military genius of Grant that turned the fortunes of the Civil War, and Grant had Saturn rising on the cusp of Taurus in conjunction with the Sun and Jupiter and trined by a conjunction of Neptune and Uranus. An astrologer looking at this horoscope might easily have predicted the famous words, "I propose to fight it out on this line, if it takes all summer."

Similar doggedness is shown by Cecil Rhodes whose Saturn has the sextile of Venus and is only ten degrees from the conjunction of Mars. The figure is not so strong as Grant's, and one cannot be surprised that he died saying "So much to do; so little done." But the patience and moral force of the man are not in doubt; it was the inertia of the Sun and Moon in Cancer that hindered him from more complete success.

The third example is Alexander the Great. Here Saturn is sextile to the Sun and trine to the Moon and Mars, an ideal disposition for a great conqueror. Only the most concentrated patience and steadiness of push could have carried him through into India; an expedition, by the way, which would appear hopeless for a modern army of any size, with all the advantages of railways. His name is still known and honored throughout Persia and North India; his is an example of Saturn in Taurus at his best.

Nor must we forget the extraordinary case of Jeanne d'Arc, with her Saturn trined by Venus and Mars. Here we see a simple, ignorant peasant girl, in days when even a born queen was seldom more than a puppet, with the moral strength to shoulder the burdens of a great kingdom in the very hour of its collapse, and drive out the invader. And in her trial, how patiently and courteously she withstood the infamous Bishop of Meaux, battling long months with no armor but her virtue against every engine that the law of those tyrannous times could set in motion. This is a finer Saturn than even that of Alexander.

Two of the most patient observers that science can claim are Alfred Russell Wallace and Louis Pasteur. The Saturn of the former is trined by Uranus and Neptune; but squared by Mars; without that detriment he might have been as great as Huxley or Darwin. Pasteur has no such trouble; with the Sun, Uranus, Neptune, Mercury and Venus, all in conjunction, trine to Saturn, it is no wonder that he became the foremost of the men of science of France. There could be no doubt or wavering in a Saturn so brilliantly aspected.

In mundane affairs Saturn in Taurus is not very good for financial matters; unless extremely well aspected, money comes slowly or wastes away. The native, however, may somewhat counteract this danger, since the same influence that begrudges his financial success makes him careful and saving, sometimes indeed quite frugal. In all cases there is apt to be some selfishness.

The following well known persons were born with Saturn in the sign Taurus:

General French
Shelley
U. S. Grant
Edwin Markham
Dr. Felix Adler
August Belmont
Ray Long
Roy Howard
Frederick Collins

For the benefit of those who are not in possession of Raphael's Ephemeris, or who are not able to interpret the symbols contained therein, the years when Saturn is in the sign Taurus are as follows:

From	June	4th		through	November	4th	1851
	February	23rd	1852	"	July	29th	1853
	October	30th	1853	"	April	14th	1854

From						
From April	6th	1881	through	May	23rd	1883
May	17th	1910	"	December	14th	1910
January	20th	1911	"	July	6th	1912
December	1st	1912	"	March	25th	1913
July		1939	"	September		1939
April		1940	"	May		1942

SATURN IN GEMINI

The sign Gemini is altogether too airy to harmonize entirely with Saturn; the only quality in common is the intellectuality. But the intellectuality of Gemini is inspirational, rather like a child's; while that of Saturn is the wisdom of age and experience. When both sign and planet are dignified, the combination is superb. In any case, however, the native is out of the region of patient effort and struggle; with Saturn in Gemini the character of the action is removed to the mental plane. A great example is that of Jesus of Nazareth, who had Saturn in the ninth house, that of religion, with a trine from Jupiter rising. Saturn, thus culminating, is by far the most powerful planet in the figure, and accordingly rules the horoscope, especially as Venus, Lady of the Ascendant, makes very nearly a trine to both Saturn and Jupiter. This triple trine describes very accurately the teachings recorded as having been actually given out by Jesus Himself.

With this chart may be compared that of Dante, with only a trine of the Moon to assist Saturn, which is in the Ascendant. No aspect from Jupiter or Venus mitigates the temperament of the mind, with its trend toward melancholy; he found solace only in dreams. However, this trine is sufficient to strengthen the character and make it patient in its afflictions; the scholarship and labor involved in his "Divine Comedy," begun and completed while he ate the bitter bread of exile, are hardly to be conceived, still less appreciated, in an age like the present.

Another very great man with this position, equally sombre, is Albrecht Dürer, whose "Melancholia" inspired James Thomson to one of the greatest masterpieces of literature, "The City of Dreadful Night." Dürer is one of the most austere and pure draughtsmen that ever took pencil in hand; but the Sun and Mercury being in conjunction with Saturn in the tenth house, the point of view is broader and there is in him less pure melancholy than in Dante.

Sometimes Saturn may quite overpower Gemini, and give merely a stubborn mind. Such is the case with "Oom Paul" Kruger, whose Saturn, being squared by the Moon, has no trace of idealism. The trine of the Sun adds great moral strength and pertinacity, and it may be that the 150 degrees of Uranus helps to confer great shrewdness. In any case there is no great strength in Mercury, tied up in the twelfth, so that Gemini is only evidenced by the childlike innocence with which he was wont to mask his astuteness, and by the fact that the action of his Saturn took effect in the fields of diplomacy.

Stubborn, too, was George III, and lost America by his mulishness. Here Venus and Neptune are both conjoined with the leaden planet, a very unfortunate combination, making his temperament eccentric and unaccountable, and turning persistence into obstinacy, and moral force into pig-headedness. Mercury, too, is conjoined, or the result should have been even more disastrous; he might have lost his throne; as it was, he lost his reason.

The case of Oscar Wilde is very unfortunate. Here Saturn in the Mid-heaven is squared by Neptune; the moral character is ruined by eccentricity. With all his splendid qualities given by the trine of the Sun, he was doomed to catastrophe.

Nell Gwyn and Lily Langtry had very similar careers in that each enjoyed the friendship and confidence of a king. In both cases Saturn is strong; Nell Gwyn has the trine of the Sun and the opposition of Uranus and Neptune, and Lily Langtry's Saturn is elevated, opposed by Venus in Scorpio and squared by Neptune and the Moon from the fifth house. The cases are interesting as showing purpose and resolute ambition working with Neptunian cleverness to attain their ambition.

Saturn in Gemini in many cases indicates trouble or hardships in the early life, such being often connected with the education or literary work. It naturally follows from the nature of the planet and sign that such success as is gained should come through intellectual matters. Unless well aspected the intellect is likely to be rather hard, with some bitterness or cynicism, and at times a lack of candor.

The following well known persons were born with Saturn in the sign Gemini:

Oscar Wilde
Lily Langtry
Harriet Stanton Blatch
Bolton Hall
Eugene Debs
"Bud" Fisher

For the benefit of those who are not in possession of Raphael's Ephemeris, or who are not able to interpret the symbols contained therein, the years when Saturn is in the sign Gemini are as follows:

From	July	30th		through	October	29th	1853
	April	15th	1854	"	October	4th	1855
	October	21st	1855	"	May	27th	1856
	May	24th	1883	"	July	5th	1885
	July	7th		"	November	30th	1912
	March	26th	1913	"	August	24th	1914
	December	7th	1914	"	May	11th	1915
	June		1942	"	June		1944

SATURN IN CANCER

Cancer is the sign particularly significant of domesticity and of repose. It is indolent to a degree, and saps the morality of Saturn. His persistence degenerates into laziness, and his austere concentration into mere inertia. Notwithstanding the galaxy of great names whose nativities show Saturn in this sign, which might lead the careless student to assume the position a fortunate one, the exceptions to this rule will be found few, and a careful study of the cases cited will prove that the successes were not because of, but in spite of Saturn's detriment in Cancer.

We have as examples of this position a trio of amazing geniuses in literature and art—Shakespeare, Balzac, and, in a lesser degree, Rossetti. But Saturn's influence, so far from contributing anything to the greatness of these men, was not by all their good aspects prevented from achieving on each an effect that may not unfairly be described as debauching. Their conscience was manifest only in the sphere of their work; the famous epigram of Catullus may be reversed for them. In their lives they were extravagant and idle; pleasure made them slaves. No sooner was the work of the moment over than they plunged into dissipation.

The Saturn of Shakespeare was in conjunction with Jupiter, squared by the conjunction of the Sun and Moon. Neptune, too, is within six degrees of the sextile of the former pair, and he is in conjunction with Venus and in opposition to Uranus. The astrologer will be in little doubt as to the significance of the much-debated sonnets, or disposed to whitewash the carousals at the "Mermaid." He will not be surprised at the accurate drawing of the Falstaff scenes, or be bewildered by the exquisite ambiguity of Rosalind and Viola.

The Saturn of Balzac afflicted by the conjunction of Venus and Mars, has no assistance but the sextile of Mercury. While free of perversions, it is evident how these positions led him into excess and careless extravagances.

Rossetti's Saturn has the opposition of Mars and Neptune conjoined. From this we see how, in spite of his great genius, anger and whimsy interfered with his proper concentration, how idleness and folly ate up his soul, demoralizing the good of a trine of the Sun to both Mars and Neptune, and found their culmination in madness.

For yet another example we may take Queen Elizabeth, whose policy was much marred by her pursuit of pleasure. Here Saturn, in conjunction with Uranus, is squared by Mercury, making her temper eccentric and unreliable, in spite of a sextile from the Sun, which could only save her from going to too great extremes. It was not strong enough to counteract the danger of sensuality of Saturn in Cancer, and the title of "England's Virgin Queen" requires quotation marks.

In the case of Napoleon, Saturn is far stronger, not only because he is culminating, but also because Libra, the Ascendant, is the sign of his exaltation. The opposition of the Moon is not therefore so powerfully unfavorable. His moral character was developed well enough for self-restraint against his propensities, although of course he was in some ways as sensual as those already considered. But he never allowed pleasure to interfere with his ambition. Note well, however, that Saturn took his revenge upon the body, since his loss of the battles of Leipzig and of Waterloo came largely through his illness, by reason of indigestion, and he died from a cancer of the stomach, an organ that is ruled by this sign.

The case of William III is interesting. Saturn has no help but the sextile of Mars. His wisdom was practical but not deep. Saturn, being in the twelfth house, is peculiarly inert in his map. The causes of his good fortune are elsewhere indicated.

In the case of Nostradamus, we have Saturn dominating the nativity in the fullest sense. He is in the third house in conjunction with Jupiter and trined by the Moon, which dignities easily overcome all the lax tendencies of the Cancer position. We have here a fine picture of the famous astrologer, sinister, severe, pious, noble, commanding austerity dominant in his manner, and vision in his eyes. Neptune elevated in the tenth house, opposing Saturn and Jupiter, completes the sketch, adding a certain aloofness to the character, and causing incredible stories to gather around his name like demons about the circle of an enchanter. Of very similar character was the great Copernicus. Saturn is trined by Uranus and by the Sun and hence comes the illumination of his wisdom. There is an opposition of Jupiter and the Moon, and a square of Mercury. The latter prevents any tinge of unreality from contaminating the intelligence, while the oppositions prevent that indulgence in pleasure which Saturn in Cancer, alone, might have predicted.

The following well known persons were born with Saturn in the sign Cancer:

Balzac
H. Rider Haggard
Shakespeare
William H. Taft
Woodrow Wilson
Michael Angelo
David Bispham

Charlie Chaplin
Jackie Coogan
Emile Coué
Clarence Darrow
Napoleon

For the benefit of those who are not in possession of Raphael's Ephemeris, or who are not able to interpret the symbols contained therein, the years when Saturn is in the sign Cancer are as follows:

From	October	5th		through	October	20th	1855
	May	28th	1856	"	July	9th	1858
	July	6th	1885	"	August	18th	1887
	March	10th		"	April	20th	1888
	August	25th		"	December	6th	1914
	May	12th	1915	"	October	16th	1916
	December	8th	1916	"	June	23rd	1917

SATURN IN LEO

Leo cannot be considered a favorable position for Saturn for there can be no real sympathy between the slow, restricting, heavy, dull rays of the planet and the frank, free, swift, generous glory of the sign. The effect of this antipathy will vary according to the dignity as usual. It may mean sorrow to the heart of the native, where he is passive to its influence, or a constriction in his own emotion. When under adverse aspects, he receives it actively. The currents of the blood are then frozen; there is apt to be a critical and cold outlook on life, and the sentiment it gives is tinged with diplomacy. The native is skeptical of compliments or attentions bestowed on him by others.

The greatest name we find in this position is that of Tolstoi, whose Saturn on the cusp of the sign still holds some trace of Cancer, and is also excited by the conjunction of Venus. The opposition of Uranus gives mystic sight, but the emotional nature is warped and distorted and turned to morbidity by the Saturn influence further corrupted by Venus; hence his "Kreutzer Sonata," as well as his attitude toward his wife and family.

An example of Saturn in Leo at his worst is given by Franz Josef of Austria, where the planet is afflicting a conjunction of the Sun and the Moon. The Emperor's nature was doubtless itself somewhat callous, but the Saturnian influence is most seen in the repeated mattock-blows of fate that struck him. King Lear is a very petty figure of tragedy beside Franz Josef. In this nativity Saturn's conjunction with the Sun and the Moon is in the eleventh, the house of hopes and of friends. That the two luminaries become the slayers seems to indicate that the conjunction of Saturn is peculiarly fatal to the New Moon, and a further deadliness may be conferred by the influence of the fixed star Regulus, martial and strident, close to whom the conjunction occurs. Saturn's only aid is a semi-sextile of Venus, quite powerless against such afflictions. We are the more inclined to attribute the catastrophes of the Emperor's life to the Regulus influence, when we remember that the outbreak of the great war occurred when Mars was rising at the solstice in conjunction with Regulus, and the eclipse following had the Sun and Moon exactly on that spot.

Wilhelm II, with a Saturn in opposition to the Sun and sextile to Jupiter, who therefore also trines the Sun, has enjoyed far better fortune, in spite of the loss of his kingdom and the downfall of all his hopes.

A great example of the influence of Saturn in Leo, making its native cold and calculating in matters of the heart is found in Brigham Young, who grafted polygamy on to Mormonism for economic and political reasons and not at all from the lustful motive usually credited to him. In his case an opposition of the Moon increases the coldness of the outlook.

Cæsar Borgia is a case of a violent yet cold disposition, at once cynical and of ungovernable passion. Here Saturn opposed by Jupiter, is in conjunction with Mars, which is warmed by a semi-sextile of Venus and a sextile of the Sun. This is a most extraordinary complex, and well worth tracing out in every detail, for it shows a marvelous medley of passions. Restricting ourselves to the immediate subject, we must observe that while Saturn is strengthened by these aspects and the character is thus made more dominant, this fact only accentuates the callousness of Saturn in Leo; it in no wise mitigates it.

The case of Havelock Ellis, the calm dissector of the sex problems of his fellow-creatures, next occupies our attention. Saturn, opposed by the Sun and Moon, is trine to Mars and sextile to Jupiter. It is a fortunate combination for character so far as its effective control is concerned; he is indeed one of the few men that have been able to immerse themselves in the study of such subjects without the least suspicion of taint therefrom; but it is not suggestive of any great degree of warmth from the more human points of view.

The following well known persons were born with Saturn in the sign Leo.

Kaiser Wilhelm II
Emperor Franz Josef
Raymond Poincaré
Theodore Roosevelt
General Carranza
Tolstoi
David Belasco
General Ballington Booth
John Brown
William Jennings Bryan
Augustus Thomas
Frank Damrosch
Henry E. Dixey

For the benefit of those who are not in possession of Raphael's Ephemeris, or who are not able to interpret the symbols contained therein, the years when Saturn is in the sign Leo are as follows:

From July	10th	1858	through	August	25th	1860
August	19th	1887	"	March	9th	1888
April	21st	1888	"	October	6th	1889
February	25th		"	June	27th	1890
October	17th		"	December	7th	1916
June	24th	1917	"	August	11th	1919

SATURN IN VIRGO

There is no doubt that Saturn and Mercury are great friends—just as in life one often sees attraction between an old philosopher and a clever child. So Virgo is found even more sympathetic to Saturn than Gemini. The heights may not be so high as the best dignities in Gemini, but there is never danger of any real trouble. Virgo being an earthy sign is more of the nature of Saturn, and the agricultural implication is also present to link them. This kinship tends greatly to stability of moral character, and to the confirmation of practical wisdom. It gives an orderly, critical and analytical mind, usually of a serious cast if Saturn is well dignified. The intellect should be capable and original.

The affliction of the Lord of Virgo would, of course, detract from these elements, and perhaps wring reason dry. So, too, would any serious damage wrought on Saturn himself. In fact, we shall find not only some of the wisest but some of the most foolish of mankind with this position; and it will be our duty to make it clear why it should act rather as Caliban supposed Setebos to act. One may add, before proceeding to examples, that, Virgo being the Hermit in the Tarot, the solitariness of Saturn is brought out and emphasized by this sign. Every one of our examples will be found a person of solitary habit and disposition. This must be taken as modifying and illustrating everything that may be said of them in other ways. Three great theosophists, H. P. Blavatsky, Rudolf Steiner and Colonel Olcott have all this position of Saturn, H. P. Blavatsky is enormously strong, being in exact conjunction with Mars, and very close conjunction with Mercury. These indicate the extraordinary strength of will and persistence which she possessed, so far as the mental plane was concerned.

Mr. Steiner's Saturn is not so unique or so dominant. He has the opposition of Sol, but luckily the square of Uranus lends illumination, and the trine of Mars practical power. However, the main point is abundantly confirmed. The forces which concentrate and resist disintegration are supreme; the opposition of Sol only indicates that this is accomplished somewhat at the expense of the vitality.

Colonel Olcott's Saturn received no assistance from any quarter beyond a trine of Mars and semi-sextile of the Sun and Venus. Here, then, is a case of a moral character strong enough, but not more than enough. He made consequently an admirable Chief of Staff, but lacked great originality. He was a modern St. Paul to theosophy.

Rather like him in character are three British Generals, best known of any in their day; Roberts, Wolseley and Gordon. The first of these has Jupiter rising, in exact opposition, and Mercury in exact conjunction, and trine to Neptune. The latter gave him the insight to foresee the Great War. The former shows that his warning would fall upon deaf ears. The whole configuration caused him to become a prominent figure in that war.

Gordon, on the other hand, a much less fortunate soldier, was of tremendous moral force, influencing the whole trend of English thought, even from the distance of China. His Saturn, too, is opposed by Jupiter, but the trine of Mars, Mercury and Neptune more than atones for this.

Lord Wolseley, least of the three, has a very flabby Saturn. Venus is trine, and Neptune and Mercury nearly trine, and this is all the help that he gets. We have, therefore, an able soldier, whose moral force is weak, and in the end he was shelved, as might be expected with the Sun squared by Saturn.

Another soldier is seen in Garfield, and again there is only the aid of a trine of the Moon, a sextile of Mars and a semi-sextile of Venus. There is, however, no affliction and we may take it that Saturn in a sympathetic sign like this is strong enough for all the ordinary purposes of life. It is only in serious crises that additional help is required; and doubtless Saturn's position in the twelfth (the house of treachery) was responsible for his assassination.

Maximilian of Mexico was also unfortunate. Here Saturn has only the sextile of Mercury, the Sun and Venus. He stands at the Nadir, isolated and unprotected.

A king of a very different sort was Nero, although his early promise was so bright. But though Saturn was sextile to Jupiter, it was square to the Sun, and the effect seems to have been to loosen the moral sinews. This is further accentuated by Mars being in Taurus, in opposition to Jupiter and conjunction with Venus, which explains the terrible part he played as dictator of Rome.

We may now consider the case of the anarchist Vaillant, who has the conjunction of Jupiter and the opposition of Neptune, as well as the square of Uranus and Mercury. Jupiter counteracts the firmness of Saturn and Neptune attacks the weakened planet with the full force of his eccentricity. The result we know. Note, however, in particular how the disturbance takes place in the mind on its practical side: Saturn in Taurus (for instance) with similar aspects, would have furnished a totally different picture.

Another example is Marie Bashkirtseff. Here Saturn, in the Midheaven, is square to Uranus and Mercury. Her Venus in Libra, trine to Uranus, was incapable of diverting her abnormal mentality into normal channels.

It will be instructive to contrast the dreamy melancholy mind and temper of Coleridge with the bright, positive, firm yet whimsical mind and temper of Lewis Carroll. The poet has Saturn in conjunction with Venus and Neptune. The will to resist is altogether eaten up, and opium naturally had no trouble in enslaving him.

The author of "Alice in Wonderland" on the contrary had the trine of Mercury, and Saturn rides gaily in the ninth house, like that of Coleridge, but uninterfered with by any weakening forces. Yet the brighter planets helped Coleridge far more; in all that really counts he was the greater man. It is only on the plane of life, in the bonds of time and space, that he failed. "His giant wings interfered with his walking."

Half way between these two stands Bulwer-Lytton. Saturn is in the third house, and neither very strong nor very weak. But there is nothing to interfere with his free action, and so the native was able to manage his affairs remarkably well, and with prudence and cunning. He never obtruded his moral strength, but it never relaxed; and this is one of the principal keys to a successful career.

In the case of George Sand there is a trine of Mars, and a sextile of Neptune, making the character vivacious, kaleidoscopic, and full of genius. There is no hindrance, but great help to the self-control and in addition there is the inestimable quality of variety.

The character of Maurice Maeterlinck now claims our attention. Here Saturn has the square of Herschel, good for mystic insight but rather tending to disturb the concentration. But Mercury is not far from conjunction, so we see the self-interested qualities reinforced by shrewdness and cleverness. Saturn, incidentally, is in the tenth house; from this it appears that the ego occupies itself intensely with the fruits of fame.

Victor Hugo has the conjunction of Jupiter, the semi-sextile of Herschel, and the opposition of Sol and Venus. This complex is difficult to disentangle; one need, however, only remark that the absence of help from Mars diminished the possibilities of his becoming the hammer; he had to take the part of the anvil. Saturn, however, is strong enough, and on the mental plane he was able to do great work, culminating from his exile with very great effect against the tyrant who had put him there.

The following well known persons were born with Saturn in the sign Virgo:

Lord Roberts
Bulwer-Lytton
Emerson
Victor Hugo
James A. Garfield
Charles E. Hughes
Jane Addams
Bliss Carman
Coleridge
Alan Dale
Walter Damrosch
Josephus Daniels
Reginald de Koven
Alexander Dumas
Dean Cornwell

For the benefit of those who are not in possession of Raphael's Ephemeris, or who are not able to interpret the symbols contained therein, the years when Saturn is in the sign Virgo are as follows:

From	August	26th 1860	through	October	22nd	1862
	April	23rd	"	July	9th	1863
	October	7th 1889	"	February	24th	1890

From	June	28th 1890	through	December	26th 1891
	January	23rd	"	August	29th 1892
	August	12th 1919	"	October	7th 1921

SATURN IN LIBRA

In Libra Saturn is in his exaltation, and is therefore very strong and beneficent. The Venusian character of the house tempers his asperity, even though there is always some sinister implication in the association of Venus with Saturn, and the judicial function of Libra assures good balance to the conservative and concentrative force of the dark planet. We shall therefore expect to find that the natives are well able to take care of themselves, and exercise both tact and judgment in the management of their personal affairs. The exceptions will, as before, be due to some unusual affliction either of the planet or the ruler of the house.

Both the philosophical and religious temperament are well developed in this position. In orthodoxy we have Cardinal Gibbons with Saturn trined by Jupiter on one side and by Neptune on the other. There is no impediment to the ego, and, with all else favorable, his ambition was certain of gratification. Savonarola, though a reformer, was only so in his denunciation of corruptions in Church and State. Mars and the Moon square his Saturn, so that dreams of violence haunt his dark spirit, and place obstacles continually in his path. His is a good example of a strong Saturn thwarted.

Two great heresiarchs now attract our notice: Swedenborg and Joseph Smith. The former has Mars in opposition to Saturn but the Sun is trine, and this latter aspect always means great stability of moral character. The affliction of Mars prevents the Saturnian wisdom from operating on the material plane; therefore with vision probably superior to that of Mohammed, he accomplished no more than the foundation of a new sect.

Joseph Smith's Saturn has Uranus in conjunction, and the Moon square, while Neptune stands semi-sextile. To him, therefore, we might look for the doctrinal founding of a sect; but it was the energy and practical genius of Brigham Young that made Mormonism a living force.

Another religious genius and one of high order was Swami Vivekananda. Here Saturn has a conjunction of the Moon, an opposition of Neptune, and Venus is nearly trine. Although the position of Saturn in Libra gave him the philosophical religious bent, the afflictions give clear explanation of the sources of his collapse, to which the softening aspect from Venus materially contributed.

Disraeli and Lord Northcliffe form a pair suitable for comparison, both showing immense ambition. The Saturn of Disraeli is in the Mid-heaven, conjoined with Uranus and squared by Mercury; thus both enlightenment and a sense of reality modify the ambition and there is also a sextile of Mars, adding efficiency.

Lord Northcliffe also has Saturn in the tenth house, but the Moon is in opposition, and the Sun square. The offhand prediction would be an inevitable failure, but the student must not forget that the evil effects of an opposition may be greatly mitigated by the interposition of another planet in trine to one and sextile to the other of the opposing forces. And here Jupiter, in his own sign, Sagittarius, is sextile to Saturn and therefore trine to the Moon, which also accounts for Northcliffe's great wealth. The square of the Sun and opposition of the Moon, operating generally as a threat against the constitution, indicate his comparatively early death.

A great artist will illustrate the good tendencies of a well-aspected Saturn in Libra. Petrarch's Saturn has the sextile of the Sun and Mercury and semi-sextiles of Neptune and of Jupiter. Here we see a very harmonious, beautiful attitude towards self, a mellowness in strength which made him so lovable a character.

The Saturn of Turner has the trine of the Moon, Uranus and Venus, which similarly soften the asperity of the ego-feeling and ripen it to artist-altruism. The opposition of Mercury, however, gave a practical tinge to Saturn's natural selfishness which showed in the frugality of the artist's life, even though it afterward appeared that his stinginess was really inspired by altruism, in order that he might bequeath to the nation the greater part of his imperishable work.

In a material way the position of Saturn in Libra is favorable for partnerships, especially with persons older or of better position than the native. It diminishes somewhat the austerity and selfishness of Saturn, moves the sympathies, and slightly favors the mystical side in religion.

The following well known persons were also born with Saturn in the sign Libra:

Prince of Wales
Don Carlos of Portugal
Billy Sunday
King George V
Duke of Clarence
John Jacob Astor
Edward Bok
Senator Borah
Arthur Brisbane
Charles G. Dawes
Chauncey M. Depew

For the benefit of those who are not in possession of Raphael's Ephemeris, or who are not able to interpret the symbols contained therein, the years when Saturn is in the sign Libra are as follows:

From	October	23rd	1862	through	April	22nd	1863
	July	10th	1863	"	January	20th	1865
	February	28th		"	September	29th	1865
	December	27th	1891	"	January	22nd	1892
	August	30th	1892	"	November	6th	1894
	October	8th	1921	"	December	19th	1923
	April	6th		"	September	13th	1924

SATURN IN SCORPIO

The quality of secretiveness in Scorpio, and its order in the Zodiac as the natural sign for the house of death, make it a sympathetic menstruum for Saturn's rays. There is naturally, however, something deep, obscure and sinister in this position of the planet, and where it has a fair chance it will give such a tone to the Akankara, the name given by the philosophers of India to the "ego-making faculty," or the Saturn force in the human character. While this position of Saturn tends to produce a character both masterful and subtle, the evidence of this peculiar effect is not easy to find on account of its very habit of concealing itself. In the case of Tennyson it was so covered by external graces, (in particular, the influence of Venus) that it is only from private sources that we know that traces of this Scorpio selfishness ever existed.

Similar remarks apply to Lord Brougham. Here Saturn in Scorpio gives a harsh, unscrupulous purpose, which is developed in material affairs by the sextile of Jupiter; but Mercury and Venus just above the Ascendant conceal Saturn effectively, though he is the real director of the inner thought. The self-seeking of the great lawyer wore a mask of tact, wit and amiability, beneath which the corrosive acid of his purpose ate away his enemies.

Compare with this the nativity of Archbishop Laud. Here Saturn has the conjunction of Venus, a square of the Moon and an opposition of Jupiter, who in the ninth house signifies religion, with no help beyond a semi-sextile of the Sun. Here is the typical selfish and intriguing prelate; Saturn on the cusp of the third house constantly occupying the mind with ambition and the lust of power. But Saturn's strength is not aided by fortune; the afflictions were bound to bring the native's ultimate downfall.

Cicero is a great example of this position; Saturn is in conjunction with Jupiter and squared by Mars, Venus and Mercury. The operation of the sign is intensified by these dispositions. He pursued cruelly and relentlessly his secret schemes of self-aggrandizement. But there is also to be considered and ranked in the same category, though on the surface so different, his more lasting achievement, the "Somnium Scipionis" almost the only mystical treatise which the Latins have left to us.

That unfortunate monarch, Charles I of England, had this position. Here Saturn, in opposition to Uranus, is close to the cusp of the fourth house, for an ill end to the matter, and he receives no notable help. But we can gauge the desperate quality of the native's struggle to hold his inheritance, the secret and mendacious and fatal paths trodden by him in that attempt.

An example of over-development of the self is seen in Thomas Moore. Mars and the Moon are in conjunction with Saturn to give recklessness and dissipation; Mercury in opposition to make it blind; only the sextile of Jupiter adds a touch of geniality, which made him welcome only as the companion of an hour in a tavern or a parlor.

Compare particularly in this matter the case of the late J. Pierpont Morgan. Saturn is squaring Mars, Jupiter and Neptune, sextile to the Moon, while trine to Uranus. While there is plenty of self-preservation, the Moon and Uranus both bring vision. The dispositions are consequently not altogether bad, but the great wisdom was undoubtedly used for material ends.

Sir Humphrey Davy has Saturn in Scorpio, but Jupiter and Neptune are conjoined in sextile, Venus is sextile, and the Sun and Mars semi-sextile. Here is much favorable modification of Saturn, who is rising. Thus the self-force, rendered bright and tender by such aspects, is in complete harmony with the personality. Here strength is wedded with gentleness, and we can understand readily how he was able to give his life to its purpose without upsetting his contemporaries by bitterness of controversy.

We may now turn to the grand yet sinister figure of Martin Luther. Here the conjunction of the Sun with Saturn gives violent pride to the sense of self, though Mercury, four degrees off, makes this sense intelligent. That his mind, his life force and his self-pride are all brought together in Scorpio by this conjunction, may explain this secret, though perhaps unconscious, real source of his break with Rome; though of course the conjunction of Mars with Venus is a further stimulus to this inherent dissatisfaction with clerical celibacy.

In Goethe we find less violence, and more adroitness in the emphasis of his ego. Saturn just above the horizon is trined by the Moon, and has the illuminating square of Uranus, all of which harmonizes the personality with the instinct of self-preservation. This instinct is strong but clever, and we comprehend, if we do not altogether applaud, his sword and his diamond buckles.

In many ways, as has been seen, Saturn in Scorpio has critical tendencies; it imperils the reputation, may bring scandal or unpopularity and, badly aspected, may cause reverses or downfall. Its influence upon the health is rather perilous in early life, though, that period safely passed, it promises a long life. It is, however, a position very favorable for association with mystical or secret societies.

The following well known persons were born with Saturn in the sign Scorpio:

General Boulanger
Lord Tennyson
Goethe
Mark Twain
Grover Cleveland
Sir Henry Irving
John Wanamaker
Edith Cavell
Rudolph Valentino
Agassiz
Ralph Waldo Trine
Stanley Baldwin
Gutzon Borglum
Andrew Carnegie
Gelett Burgess
John Burroughs
Norma Talmadge
Joseph Cannon
John O'Hara Cosgrave
Sir Humphrey Davy

For the benefit of those who are not in possession of Raphael's Ephemeris, or who are not able to interpret the symbols contained therein, the years when Saturn is in the sign Scorpio are as follows:

From January	21st		through	February	27th	1865
September	30th	1865	"	December	16th	1867
June	29th		"	September	5th	1868
November	7th	1894	"	February	6th	1897
April	10th		"	October	26th	1897
December	20th	1923	"	April	5th	1924
September	14th	1924	"	December	2d,	1926

SATURN IN SAGITTARIUS

THERE is in nature perhaps little harmony between Saturn and Sagittarius. Saturn is slow and heavy, Sagittarius swift and transient; the sign is one of many-colored light; the planet as dull as lead. But Jupiter is Lord of Sagittarius, and, just as in the Roman mythology the heir of the elder god overthrew his father, the impulses of the active and spendthrift planet accelerate the slowness and loosen the selfishness of the greater orb when he enters his house, so that Saturn's normal quality in this position is a thrifty disposition not at all incompatible with real altruism.

An excellent example of a strongly spiritualized Saturn is given by Abraham Lincoln. Although in the twelfth house, he has only passed one degree above the Ascendant, in which Neptune is rising in conjunction with him; Venus is trine and Mercury square to both. It is easy to see the effect of these aspects upon the wisdom of the martyr-president. Sagittarius prepares Saturn to open more responsively to the illumination of Neptune and the warmth of Venus. The altruism is therefore very spontaneous and yet well restrained by great practicality. Mercury shows excellently the influences of both Saturn and Neptune, in the restricting delays and obstacles to early education and the sensitiveness of the mind, touched upon under another chapter, which explains her influences toward unfaltering devotion to an ideal. Altogether the figure is one of great faith fortified by far-seeing wisdom.

In the case of Emile Zola, Saturn is trined by Mars and Mercury and squared by Uranus. The deep insight into human nature, which wrought itself into a philosophy of life expressed in the forty or more volumes of novels, short stories and essays, is amply accounted for by the Saturnian aspects of these three planets. That Saturn occupied the fifth, the house of pleasure, is significant in view of the fiction form chosen to convey his philosophy. That altruism of the most courageous and uncompromising kind was an essential part of his character was proved by his action in the Dreyfus case; that it manifested itself to the world at so late a period in his life may have been due to the fact that his Saturn was retrograding.

An example of great and shining activity of the preservation-energy of Saturn is shown in the horoscope of Gladstone. Neptune and Venus excite the former by conjunction, and Jupiter supports the combination by a trine. Here, then, we have a complete harmony of Jupiter and Saturn, which also steadies and strengthens against the weakening indicated by the conjunction, the softness of which merely adds grace and originality to the character.

Thomas Hardy's insight into human nature, which is not dissimilar to that of Zola, apparently comes from the same aspect of Saturn squared by Uranus. But Saturn is in opposition to the Sun and has no help beyond a sextile of Neptune, which is rather a disadvantage in this regard. The nature is retiring and modest; the ambition is not aggressive; a novelist with a tenth of his talent, and more push, might have gained a far greater popular reputation.

James II has Saturn in the fourth house, trined by the Moon, squared by Venus; his character, as is well known, was cold and selfish to a degree, and also weak and irresponsible. Saturn is developed, but not enough to save the native from his downfall.

Tchaikovsky has an excellent Saturn. Uranus is square, Mercury and Venus trine, and Neptune sextile. The wonderful comprehension with which he has expressed the mingled fire and melancholy of the Slavonic race is described by these aspects, especially the square of Uranus and the sextile of Neptune. The relief from the domestic difficulties of his early life and the subsequent freedom which enabled him to devote himself to his work come through the strength of his Saturn; and his success, creating masterpieces in every branch of Music, is due to the same cause. The versatility is of course indicated by the aspect with Mercury in Aries.

Madame Steinheil furnished perhaps the most convincing example of all these characters. Her Saturn in the Mid-heaven, opposing the Moon, is trined by Mercury, Neptune, Venus, the Sun and Jupiter, and Mars is in exact trine on the other side. Here then is a case where the whole cohort of heaven (one may say) concentrate upon Saturn to make him swift, subtle, active, even vehement. It is a marvelous example for successful self-seeking. Even the opposition of the Moon, which pulled her down from high eminence and placed her life in jeopardy, could not compass her entire defeat against such fortified power.

In its more material significance, Sagittarius being the natural sign to ocupy the ninth house, Saturn's influence in that sign tends to give prominence and power through activity in the religious or legal world; under good aspects this activity should bring prosperity. Philosophy, science, voyaging or shipping may afford scope for the influence, according to the native's station in life, with corresponding results depending upon the nature of Saturn's aspects.

The following well known persons were born with Saturn in the sign Sagittarius:

Abraham Lincoln
Senator Aldrich
Dr. William S. Bainbridge
George F. Baker
P. T. Barnum
Booth Tarkington
William Faversham
Horace Greeley

For the benefit of those who are not in possession of Raphael's Ephemeris, or who are not able to interpret the symbols contained therein, the years when Saturn is in the sign Sagittarius are as follows:

From	December	17th	1867	through	June	28th	1868
	September	6th	1868	"	December	14th	1870
	February	7th		"	April	9th	1897
	October	27th	1897	"	January	20th	1900
	July	19th		"	October	16th	1900
	December	3rd	1926	"	March	14th	1929
	May	5th	1929	"	November	29th	1929

SATURN IN CAPRICORN

Saturn being in his own sign in Capricorn, he is naturally strong, even without help from outside sources. His quality here, however, is rather rough and crude, and this does not tend to produce the best results, in so far as the effect upon the external world is concerned. There will be no altruistic thought to soften the egotism, and opposition will be likely to infuriate. In a word, Saturn in this sign makes the native harsh and overbearing, unless there be some very strong counteracting influence to soften its asperity.

The most dense form of the arrogant selfishness which Saturn in Capricorn may give is well illustrated by Louis XVI and Marie Antoinette. In both charts, Saturn is badly afflicted and is situated in the fourth and eighth houses respectively. Not only was this evil Saturn the moral cause of their downfall, but his house position also predicted their tragic end.

Edward VII had Saturn rising in Capricorn, but with little affliction; even the semi-sextile of Mercury could save him from the stupidity of allowing such tendencies to manifest themselves, while his other planets gave him many lovable qualities which ensured his popularity. The Saturn of Sir Isaac Pitman has a conjunction of the Sun, a semi-sextile of Neptune and Venus, and a sextile of Mars. We get in this a very good astrological map of the kind of force required for proper development of the ego, a steady and vigorous push, but executed on proper lines with tact and with intelligence.

In the nativity of Richard Wagner, we find no specially strong support to Saturn. In fact it is a good illustration of what the planet can do by himself. There is a great deal of brusquerie and instability, which was a serious limitation to the greatness of the man. He wasted incalculable energy in sterile and fruitless controversy, antagonizing some whose support might have been most valuable.

Immanuel Kant has a much more harmonious Saturn. The Sun and Mercury are trine and Jupiter is semi-sextile; the Moon, too, is trine on the other side. There is nothing aggressive in this configuration; it is splendidly smooth and harmonious, and at the same time perfectly strong. Consequently, without the need of strenuous effort or self-assertion, it carried him onward and upward in calm self-confidence.

The general influence of Saturn in Capricorn is to give ambition, independence, power, authority or rulership to the native, according to his station in life. This may be accompanied by great selfishness and loneliness, or isolation may be characteristic of the life. It is frequently the case that this position of Saturn gives an unusual degree of melancholy to the mind.

The following well known persons were born with Saturn in the sign Capricorn:

Carmen Sylva
Sir Isaac Pitman
Stephen A. Douglas
Edward VII
Maude Adams
Marie Antoinette
Victor David Brenner
Richard Carle
Howard Chandler Christy
Calvin Coolidge
Joseph P. Day

For the benefit of those who are not in possession of Raphael's Ephemeris, or who are not able to interpret the symbols contained therein, the years when Saturn is in the sign Capricorn are as follows:

From	February	8th		through	June	17th	1841
	November	7th	1841	"	February	2nd	1844
	December	15th	1870	"	March	13th	1873
	July	14th		"	December	10th	1873
	January	21st		"	July	18th	1900
	October	17th	1900	"	January	19th	1903
	March	15th		"	May	4th	1929
	November	30th	1929	"	February		1932
	September			"	November		1932

SATURN IN AQUARIUS

Aquarius is by far the best house which Saturn can occupy. The airiness of the sign lightens the heaviness of the planet, and therefore there is no such harshness as is given by the sign of the Goat. Aquarius, too, is par excellence the sign of Science; and it gives free scope to the wisdom-quality of Saturn in a way that no other sign can do, while the humanitarian impulses of the sign tend to lessen the selfishness of the planet. Even when unoccupied by Saturn, his influence tends to make its natives comprehend the true significance of the ego, tempering the crude consciousness of the self with some understanding of its cosmic importance. Of course, evil aspects are able to upset even so favorable a position. We have, for example, Ludwig II of Bavaria, whose Saturn, in conjunction with Mars and Neptune, is squared by Jupiter; this entirely unbalances the ego, loosening all the natural restraints and slackening even the cords of reason. Saturn being on the cusp of the ninth house, the attack was peculiarly severe, and we cannot be surprised that madness should have terminated the concourse of these forces.

Consider however, such scholars as Sir Richard Quain, the medical lexicographer, and Picus de Mirandola. The former has Jupiter square to Saturn as in the case of the Bavarian King, but Neptune and Uranus are sextile, and Saturn is in the sixth house, where there is no menace to the mind. Moreover, the Jupiter aspect is from Scorpio, and Scorpio and Aquarius make a good, scientific combination, especially for a doctor. The Saturn of Picus de Mirandola, is in conjunction with Mercury, trine to Neptune, and square to the Moon. Such a combination gives deep penetrating insight to the mind, and an isolation which, coupled with the normal persistency of Saturn, promises a great philosophic scholar.

In the starry career of Cleo de Mérode, we have Saturn just above the Ascendant, trined by Mercury and opposed by Uranus; the ego is therefore selfish enough, but clear-sighted and clever; hence a resourceful and shrewd pushfulness, adroit and subtle, landed her quite early in life at the top of the ladder of success in her ancient profession.

Let us now turn to Louis XIV, one of the cleverest and most resourceful rulers that ever lived; a man as sucessful in aggrandizing his ego as was Queen Victoria. Here Saturn has a square of Jupiter from Scorpio, and an opposition of the Moon and Venus. It is a purely selfish combination, but extremely strong; for Venus and the Moon are so overpowered by Saturn that all the gracious and feminine qualities of the man are constrained to serve his selfishness as its handmaidens.

A very successful type, too, was Byron, whose Saturn is trine to

Jupiter and also to Neptune. Venus is in conjunction—this is always a corruption to Venus, but where Saturn is so radically strong, she cannot hinder his success, although her influence is shown in the arrogance and vanity of the poet.

Sir David Wilkie in a quieter manner gained a good deal of reputation. The sextile of Jupiter exercises its beneficent influence on Saturn and the trine of Mars adds driving force, while Mercury is also sextile and gives intelligence to the assertion of the self. Small wonder, then, that of so little talent he made so considerable a fame.

Bismarck, for contrast, has Saturn conjoined with Mars, sextile to the Sun and Uranus, and trine to Jupiter. The square of Venus confirms, rather than detracts from, this general broad, deep and persistent vigor of the ego, which was marred by no petty personal selfishness.

There are two great mystics, Anna Kingsford and William Blake, whose Saturn is in Aquarius. The former, who was by far the more practical of the two, wrote two definitely propagandist books, and did really make, in the desert of Victorianism, a small oasis of a spiritual movement. Here Saturn is in conjunction with Neptune and Jupiter is approaching a trine. The Neptune aspect gives illumination to her wisdom, although it probably lessens her material success, by depriving her to some extent of the plain common sense which is necessary to genius, if that genius is to bear fruit in its own time.

Blake's Saturn is in opposition to Neptune, and this not only contributed to his illumination, but probably inhibited him from caring to achieve the material success that his Sun in conjunction with Jupiter should have made easy for him. Wisdom without strength crieth in the streets, and no man regardeth her; but with a proper appreciation of the value of publicity even folly can obtain a hearing!

In the material affairs, Saturn in Aquarius, if free from serious affliction, gives power and good fortune, especially in connection with associations or with public affairs. Its influence is much more democratic than that in Capricorn, though the native may still be conservative and autocratic. There is an instinct for mysticism and occultism, and the native is usually widely known in his own station in life.

The following well known persons were born with Saturn in the sign Aquarius:

King Albert of Belgium
Queen Alexandra
A. J. Drexel Biddle
Bjerregaard
Lord Byron
Spencer Trask
Henry Carmichael
William H. Crane
"Buffalo Bill" (William Cody)
Frank Howard Dodd

For the benefit of those who are not in possession of Raphael's Ephemeris, or who are not able to interpret the symbols contained therein, the years when Saturn is in the sign Aquarius are as follows:

From	February	3rd	1844	through	May	9th	1846
	July	14th	1846	"	January	24th	1847
	March	14th		"	July	13th	1873
	December	11th	1873	"	February	29th	1876
	January	20th	1903	"	April	12th	1905
	August	17th	1905	"	January	7th	1906
	March			"	August		1932
	December		1932	"	February		1935

SATURN IN PISCES

Saturn and Jupiter represent opposite magical formulas, the intending and the extending, or the centripetal and centrifugal forces, but we have already seen from Saturn's action in Sagittarius that the blending of the qualities of these two planets produces good results. Indeed, although the centripetal and centrifugal forces are exactly opposite, it is their balance that holds the universe together.

Pisces is a mutable and receptive sign, and in these respects it is, in the element of water, very similar to what Saturn is in that of the earth. The expectation therefore is that Saturn will be somewhat softened of his asperity by the pleasing solvent in the waters of Pisces, even as we saw to be the case with regard to his position in Cancer. But there is no detriment to the force of Saturn here, as there is in Cancer, and its peculiarly psychic nature gives a modification of the worldly wisdom of Saturn by some touch of faerie and other-world gnosis. It adds imagination, if well dignified, especially by Neptune or Uranus, and we have only to mention such names as those of Newton, Ruskin and Edison to perceive the practical application.

The first of these has Jupiter in conjunction with Saturn, harmonizing planet and sign; Uranus is trine, giving philosophical comprehension, and Mercury square, emphasizing the scientific spirit, while the sextile of the Sun assures success. The trine of Saturn and Uranus gives the essential harmony between the magical will and the personal force of bringing it into action; here then are all the elements of extraordinary greatness.

The Saturn of Edison has Venus in conjunction with Jupiter square, and Mars and the Moon in sextile. In itself this is not really a very favorable combination for exceptional greatness; there is plenty of energetic application and success, but, were it not for Mercury's conjunction with Neptune and sextile to Uranus, we would see but little of the quality of the scientific philosopher. And after all the imagination turns not so much to fundamental problems as to the adaptation to practical ends of truths already known.

Ruskin's Saturn has the square of Uranus, conjoined with Neptune, and the semi-sextile of the Sun. The constructive ability of Saturn, helped only by this very weak Sun, is not highly developed. Hence he failed as a painter; failed to a great extent even as a critic by the eccentricity and acerbity of some of his judgments, although the illumination and insight of his wisdom enabled him to write that fascinating prose which has been so highly esteemed by many of his contemporaries.

A good illustration of the softening of the ego under this position is afforded by Czar Alexander II. There is a sextile of Jupiter to Saturn, a square of Uranus, and a trine of Mars. From these aspects we can analyze the emancipation of the serfs. Jupiter gave the benevolent thought, Uranus the imagination required to perceive a method of effecting it, and Mars the executive force needed to carry out the will, against the opposition of all the bureaucracy and aristocracy that surrounded him.

Contrast with this horoscope that of Robespierre! Here we find Saturn with only the hardening square of Mercury, rising just under the horizon, and thus enormously strong by position. We see utter selfishness unredeemed by any other quality; the Mercury aspect itself, ordinarily good, here means nothing more than the cold perspicacity which, harnessed to the plough of his egotism, and stimulated by a conjunction of Mars and Neptune square to the Sun, drove ruthlessly through the furrows of France, where, sowing only murder, he reaped terror and desolation.

Two British politicians may close our study of this position of Saturn. Balfour has Saturn in trine to Mercury, approaching a trine of Venus, Jupiter and the Sun, and we get an instant picture of the amazing cleverness and success of the man, as well as the depth of his philsopohic wisdom. The semi-sextile of Uranus is enough to aid his ego by a glimpse of vision in statesmanship, but only by a glimpse.

Rosebery's Saturn has no strong aspects, except a sextile of the Sun, though Mars and Neptune are in conjunction ten degrees away from Saturn. The latter is a source of trouble, making his career episodical and confused, yet the sextile of the Sun always kept his head above water. Without that, any single one of his moods might have ruined him.

Notwithstanding the softening influence of Pisces in the psychic development of the ego and its wisdom, the position is not generally a fortunate one for the material affairs. Unless Saturn is very well aspected, it is unfavorable to the occupation, public position, reputation and popularity of the native. If he occupies a high position in life, he may suffer severely from attacks of his inferiors and be subjected to much criticism from friends and enemies alike. In an inferior position he is apt to find hostility on the part of his superiors. But here it may once again be emphasized that the material trials of the world are the distillment of the wisdom of the soul, and it is particularly to that wisdom that all the benefits of Pisces for Saturn apply.

The following well known persons were born with Saturn in the sign Pisces:

Alexander II of Russia
John Ruskin
George Eliot
Robert Burns
Queen Victoria
Prince Albert (Consort of Queen Victoria)
Alexander Graham Bell
Luther Burbank
Louis Tiffany
Robert J. Collier
Will Levington Comfort

For the benefit of those who are not in possession of Raphael's Ephemeris, or who are not able to interpret the symbols contained therein, the years when Saturn is in the sign Pisces are as follows:

From	May	10th		through	July	13th	1846
	January	25th	1847	"	April	3rd	1849
	March	1st	1876	"	May	14th	1878
	September	16th	1878	"	February	5th	1879
	April	13th		"	August	16th	1905
	January	8th	1906	"	March	18th	1908
	March		1935	"	April		1937
	November		1937	"	January		1938

URANUS SYMBOLICALLY CONSIDERED

Ouranos, Uranus, or heaven, is said to have been the father of Saturn, who, jealous lest another son should appear, mutilated him with his scythe. This legend is but an apologue of the nature of this planet, often called Herschel after the man who rediscovered it.

This planet swims lonely in the vast abyss that separates Saturn from Neptune. If we have compared Neptune to the outpost, we may continue by saying that Uranus is the moat of the fortress, and its secret passages. And if we have called Neptune the soul of the sea, then Uranus is the essence of volcanic fire. There is no planet so strange, so revolutionary, so occult and mysterious, or so contradictory.

For this is in the shocking story of Uranus, the principle of heaven bereft of fatherhood by the jealousy of time.

This planet is the planet of genius, the planet of the secret magical power in man that lies (according to the Indian mythology) coiled at the base of the spine like a snake, ready to strike up and illuminate the whole, or downward to damnation. Genius may break; it will not bend.

Gil de Rais, de Sade, Borgia, were men of genius, just as truly as Michael Angelo and Isaac Newton. All genius desires the infinite, and the infinite is one, not many. Only the mediate steps are diverse. Darwin regretted his limitations as bitterly as did Alexander; and the love of Christ equally with the malice of Satan would destroy the world were each not thwarted by that world's inertia.

The essence of genius is this occult but overmastering lust of achievement in practical and material shape. If Neptune makes the saint or hermit, Uranus makes the magician, the man who calls forth from the Unseen not only its peace but its power. The dream of the Uranian is universal dominion by and for his Idea. This Idea may obsess him, blind him to all else, ruin him by narrowness. He rarely understands that Being must take Form before it can be perceived, and he often misses his opportunities. He does not know how many veils must be thrown over the splendour of his Virgin before men can bear to gaze upon her without going mad.

All genius is equally "good," but unless it be accompanied with utmost breadth of sanity, with moral strength as of a god, and above all with humor, it thickens, it ferments, it turns to deadly poison.

It is characteristic of the infatuation with an idea that all sense of proportion is lost. Even so, a diplomatist plunges his country into war at the cost of millions, both of men and money, in order to gain an advantage of negligible worth. So also Uranus is the particular planet of all secret vices that tend to usurp the whole nature of a man. From religious fanaticism to indulgence in dangerous drugs the gamut runs; and, because of the obsession of the one idea, the defiance or neglect of circumstance attending it, we find what we call fame or infamy as our own bias determines. There is no good or evil absolute; to one man Cæsar is a hero, to another a fiend; the Puritans destroyed cathedrals; others, even today, hate pictures and statues. One critic thought Shelley a devil specially incarnated to plague mankind; another calls him a beautiful but ineffectual angel. So, let us clear our minds; let us realize that de Bruierlliers might have been Madame Curie, and Dean Swift, John Cleland!

Any genius, thwarted in the beneficent purpose of his life, turns either to self-indulgence or to revenge. The anarchist throws his bomb, in the spirit of philanthrophy! Unless all the "good" and "bad" of Uranus is fully understood, it is useless to try to judge mankind. For every man has this Uranus in him, strong or weak, subtle or gross, fortunate or unfortunate, and this is the Royal Snake of Egypt, the giver of Life and Death. If you will not allow him to create, he will devour.

The most important thing in the life of any man is to discover the secret purpose of his incarnation, and to follow it with wariness as well as passion; with wisdom, if possible. Astrology has no more useful function than this, to discover the inmost nature of a man, and to bring it out into his consciousness, that he may fulfill it according to the law of light.

The Uranus in us is the Sacred Dance of the legend; in the hands of the Holy King it built the Temple of the Grail; in those of Klingsor, the Garden of Evil Enchantments. Genius may be fertile or sterile, radiant or self-consuming; the one is White Magic, and the other Black. But the force is the same; and, being thus double, it is of the utmost importance to direct it aright. The purity of a strong and noble Jupiter is the greatest safeguard to this force; and the Sign of the Cross, in its fullest, holiest, most Pagan and most Christian sense, is its warrant. For not only is it the Redeemer, but must be itself redeemed.

URANUS IN THE SIGNS

As the race evolves, it seems that man must learn to adapt himself more and more to the vibrations of Uranus and its powerful influx, which appear to be growing more and more potent in the unfolding of genius, or the transcending of intellect. Through the harmonious vibrations of Uranus, it is found that people become prophetic, keen, perceptive, executive, inventive, original, given to roaming, untrammelled by tradition, impatient of creeds, opinionated, argumentative, stubborn, and eccentric. They speak to the point; asserting, with startling confidence, opinions far in advance of their fellows. They come into possession of wealth in unexpected and strange ways, yet often appear to pass under the yoke of discipline as though cast down for a purpose from opulence to poverty, only to rise again by the unfolding of unexpected resources. Always ahead of their time, the natives of Uranus are often dreamers in philanthropy; poetic, though their writings need interpretation and are often unintelligible even to the imaginative, because of their mystical origin and transcendental coloring.

In the few years during which Uranus has been under observation, it has been found that, if afflicted, it is the source of incurable organic diseases, collapse of fortune, and individual as well as national destruction. It is demonstrable that, in inharmonious nativities, evil Uranian influences, both through transits and directions, have brought about headlong destruction from bad habits, misdirected affection, illicit connections before or after legal marriage; according to the signification of the place of radical affliction in the horoscope.

Every psychic thus far studied by the writer has been found, by careful consideration of the authentic birth data, to be under powerful Uranian influence; and to this vibration may be attributed clairvoyance, warning dreams, second-sight, clairaudience and similar phenomena.

The occupations or avocations which seem in sympathy with this strange planet are progressive, inventive, exploring, and of a humanitarian nature. The influence of Uranus is the least personal, and the most universal in the Zodiac; consequently, any endeavor for the betterment of humanity is favored by those who are strongly responsive to its vibration.

"Uranus produces lecturers, public figures, travellers, inventors, aviators, radio operators, astrologers, electricians, scientists, physiologists, mesmerists, metaphysicians.

"Uranus makes one impulsive and extremely eccentric; the native does not know his own mind, but is continually moved by providential agencies; he often becomes a fatalist, feeling that his destiny is beyond his own control.

"Uranus emphasizes the will, causing the native to move spontaneously from an inner urge; the native is active, original, inventive, and is notable for his love of liberty and an idealistic sense of justice. The planet bestows leadership and causes the native to become a pioneer and to establish new orders of things.

"Uranus makes the mind independent, original, and not amenable to control. The native is unconventional, altruistic and subject to sudden changes of attitude. There is an uncanny ability to sense motives.

"Circumstances induced by Uranus are sudden changes, estrangements, exiles, blind impulses, catastrophes, suicides, romantic tragedies, inexplicable changes of fortune, accidents, secret enemies, and plottings, sudden elevations."

From what we have said in regard to the character of Uranus, it will be seen that his force is peculiarly sympathetic to Taurus, Leo, Scorpio, and Aquarius. We shall see, in the course of this chapter how his action is modified in each of these signs, the Aquarian menstruum bringing out his emancipating and scientific qualities; the Taurian exhibiting him as the fearful personification of earthquake and upheaval, since Taurus is the bull; the Leonine emphasizing his revolutionary and fighting quality; and, finally, the solvent of Scorpio, manifesting him as the Death-star, or as the treacherous and subtle power of poison, or as the Eagle, which, although it cries "The House of Death," makes whole the spirit. For Scorpio, always best and worst of the signs, brings out the quintessence of Uranus more strongly than even Leo or Aquarius, being indeed, in a way, the flux of these.

Every living soul is presumed to have a purpose, and that purpose single. Not one in a million, perhaps, is conscious of that purpose; we seem for the most part to be a mass of vacillations. Even the main objective career of an individual cannot be considered as necessarily an expression of the interior will.

But Uranus indicates divine will; and the reason why he is so explosive and violent and upsetting to human affairs is that he represents the real intention, which, lying deeper than the conscious purpose, often contradicts it. The outer and the inner are then in conflict; and whenever battle is joined, the inner must win. To the outer consciousness, this naturally appears as disaster; for the native does not recognize the force as part of himself, or, if so, he regards it as a disturbing entity, and resents its dominion. Uranus is, in Egyptian symbolism, the Royal Uræus Serpent; slow, yet sudden, Lord of life and death. It takes a great deal to move him; but, when once in motion, he is irresistible. This is why, to the normal mind, he appears so terrible.

As has been seen, the deep-lying interior purpose of any being is nearly always obscure and undecipherable to the mortal eye; but there is an indication or hieroglyph of it which is usually very significant. One can hardly call it more than the artistic expression of the purpose, and this appears a very good way to describe it. We call it the Temperament. It does not define the Will itself, but it sets limits to the sphere wherein the Will may work.

We have already found that the personality is imaged in the sign on the Ascendant; and from this we now turn to a consideration of the sign in which Uranus may be situated. Where these two factors are harmonious, we get a character with unity of moral purpose; where otherwise, a self-tortured waverer. It might be cited as an objection that those who have Uranus in the Ascendant are usually eccentric characters; but the argument is on the other side. Such eccentricity is temperament in its highest development; it shows the entire over-ruling of the superficial qualities by this deep-seated, turbulent, magical will. It is only to others that the person with Uranus rising appears so eccentric.

URANUS IN ARIES

Uranus in Aries gives a character intrepid, dauntless, fiery and indomitable, whether for good or evil.

Flaming, headstrong, hot-tempered, impetuous, self-willed, and obstinate is the type; but sometimes the native will make a sudden and complete turn-about-face, and pursue a new and contradictory course with the same energy as he did the former. Nor, as a rule, will he be capable of seeing that he has changed in any respect. There is nothing particularly constructive in this type of energy. A strong example of this temperament is found in Mrs. Annie Besant, Aries being the rising sign. In Pope Alexander VI, the same qualities are apparent; but here Capricorn is rising; and, although Mars is exalted in Capricorn, and so not inharmonious with the Aries temperament, yet a Saturnian element is super-added with the most unfortunate results.

People with Uranus in Aries are always so firmly convinced they are right that opposition to their wishes appears to them as something positively unjustifiable, and they are therefore entirely unscrupulous in crushing such opposition. Sometimes this masterful quality is confined to legitimate lines, as in the case of Edison. Scorpio is rising, and its Lord, Mars, is softened by the conjunction of the Moon in the third house; thus the powerful will implied works mostly on the mental plane, where the enemy is only stubborn Nature; and, in bending her to his will by the force of his genius, he has earned the thanks of humanity.

Contrast with Edison's Uranus the case of the Earl of Strafford, and Cromwell, who both had Uranus in Aries. It will also be instructive to compare them with each other. Each had an iron will, an unscrupulous determination to have his own way at any cost; but Strafford has Virgo rising. He prepared a plan for dealing with Ireland called "thorough," which was effectively to legalize massacre; but there is no passion in Virgo to coöperate with such violence, and Strafford was not strong enough to carry the plan out; he hung fire. Cromwell, with Aries rising, went through Ireland like a new Attila.

Lord Rosebery, on the other hand, has Aries rising, (the Ascendant being the twenty-eighth degree of Pisces); Uranus therefore occupies the Ascendant, and so we find a fair uniformity of disposition. But his career was interrupted by his sudden laying-down of things, and his equally sudden reassumption of them.

Anna Kingsford has Uranus in Aries, but it occupies the eighth house. Here, as in the case of Strafford, Virgo is rising, but its lord, Mercury, is in his own house and in conjunction with Venus, and the Ascendant is further dignified by the presence of the Sun and Mars in conjunction. Here we find, then, a great example of the driving force of these configurations; for Anna Kingsford, despite all disqualifications, disposed of an initiating force sufficient to arouse the thought of half the world. It is her work which made the growth of Theosophy and its analagous cults at all possible. She was, doubtless, the head of the battering-ram that broke in the gates of the materialistic philosophy of the Victorian Age.

Robert Louis Stevenson has the last degrees of Aquarius rising, but Pisces is intercepted in the Ascendant, and Uranus in the first degrees of Aries is just within it. There is no great natural harmony between Aries and Aquarius, but their presence together in the first house creates harmony. So we find Stevenson, despite the most distressing ill-health, producing masterpieces. Astrologic students of literature may attribute to Aquarius his curiously gentle, profound, psychology, and to Uranus in Aries the passion for bloodthirsty incident, which may also be credited to the position of his Mars in Scorpio. Saturn is also in the Ascendant, just above Uranus, and this adds the tinge of melancholy which so increases his incomparable charm.

Another example is Ludwig II of Bavaria. Here Uranus is in the tenth house. Cancer is rising, weak, feminine, and receptive, and assorting illy with the violence of Uranus in Aries. So we see a dreamy, easy, pleasure-loving temperament, which bursts out at times into maniacal enthusiasms and extravagances. The lack of harmony between these two configurations is the essential blot in the personality which ultimately manifested itself as madness.

A final example is Abbas Effendi. Aquarius is rising, and Uranus in Aries is just within the second house. Here is the same gentle profundity as Stevenson's. But Neptune is rising opposed to the Moon; and, instead of the tremendous will which enabled Stevenson to rank with the greatest masters, there is but a soft and somewhat undefined personality, its Will remaining interior, not externalized, since the forces that oppress it are too strong to overcome, and also since Neptune, opposing the Moon, exercises an inhibitory influence on all continuous activity.

The following well known persons were born with Uranus in the sign Aries:

Daniel Chester French
Charles N. Flagg
Bishop Greer
Samuel Gompers
Von Hindenburg
Rev. George C. Houghton
Oscar Hammerstein
Stanley Hall
Lord Kitchener
Thomas Edison

For the benefit of those who are not in possession of Raphael's Ephemeris, or who are not able to interpret the symbols contained therein, the years when Uranus is in the sign Aries are as follows:

From	April	19th		through	October	1st	1843
	February	10th	1844	"	July	5th	1850
	September	5th	1850	"	April	14th	1851
	March	31st		"	November	4th	1927
	January	13th	1928	"	May		1934
	November		1934	"	March		1935

URANUS IN TAURUS

This position is highly favorable for Uranus, for his great energy is set to honest constructive work. One can immediately instance such empire-builders as Napoleon, Cecil Rhodes, and Wilhelm II; and, on the higher planes, we find two persons who actually invented new theogonies, which philosophy declares to be the highest creative work possible to the human intelligence. We refer to Dante and Swedenborg, whose conceptions of Hell still hold sway over the minds of great masses of men. Such empires endure long after earthly thrones have crumbled.

Swedenborg has Sagittarius rising, and his Uranus is on the cusp of the fourth house; Dante has Gemini rising, and Uranus well above the horizon in the twelfth. Both these signs are far from material—Sagittarius more mystical, Gemini more intellectual.

These differentiations are, of course, at once apparent in the work which each accomplished. Wilhelm II has Cancer rising, and accordingly he has been criticized, by his own subjects, for that obstinate devotion to peace which delayed (and thus made more uncontrollable, ultimately), the outbreak of the Great War. Rhodes had Sagittarius rising, with Jupiter, its lord, just above the horizon. Swedenborg's Jupiter was exactly trine to Uranus, emphasizing the religious bent; that of Rhodes is squared by Neptune, which would tend to remove such bias from Jupiter, leaving his force to manifest itself on those more terrestrial lines which Sagittarius implies for Jupiter. Napoleon had Libra rising, and his Uranus is in the seventh house; but Libra and Taurus are sympathetic, through the fact that Venus rules both; and Venus is sextile to Uranus, and culminating. There lies the explanation of his extraordinary sense of justice; the Code Napoleon ranks with the achievements of the greatest law givers and is the basis of the laws of several European nations.

Tom Mann has this planet in the Ascendant, but Aries is on the cusp. The two signs are contrary in nature, so there is a lack of harmony. His Will-force is occupied entirely with Taurus in its lowest form, that of labor; the sextile of Neptune to Uranus lends eccentricity to the ideas involved, and Aries rising makes the temperament violent and abrupt. Uranus thus assumes its most explosive form, and the result is an extreme agitator. A superficially most dissimilar case is that of Charles I. Here Leo is rising, and Uranus is on the cusp of the tenth house, always a dangerous position for a malefic. Leo gives the good-heartedness characteristic of that unfortunate monarch, but Neptune rising made his temperament unstable; this, combined with the obstinacy of will shown by Uranus in Taurus, gave a disposition which could bring only disaster. There is a very cognate example in Mr. Asquith, whose obstinate patience kept him long at the head of a most unruly majority in the House of Commons. Here Cancer is rising, making him tactful and pliable on the surface; Uranus in Taurus, in the house of friends enables him to conceal beneath that apparent amiability a determination of steel.

A case of very similar persistence in a woman is furnished by Lily Langtry. In a woman's horoscope, one naturally expects to find the Venus influence of Taurus brought out fully, especially as Libra is rising; so the career is marked as singularly successful. The constructive force is able to develop itself without too great hindrance, especially as the Sun is rising, sextile to Jupiter. No doubt, this aspect determines the character of the object of her will; for example, had Saturn and the Moon been in the Ascendant, she might have become an indefatigable worker among the poor.

Finally, we have a large group of writers. We may pair, for convenience, Bernard Shaw and Havelock Ellis. The Uranus of the latter being in the third house caused his mind to occupy itself with very unusual subjects; Aquarius rising gave a scientific turn to the personality; and the result is his monumental study of the Psychology of Sex.

Shaw, with Gemini rising, has Uranus just above the eastern horizon; the unusual character of the man is thus emphasized; but the Moon, on the very cusp of the Ascendant, makes him vacillating and even self-contradictory. Gemini rising adds to the airy lightness of the personality, and conceals the tremendous driving force of Uranus. For, beneath the mask of easy wit and paradox, Shaw has undoubtedly done more to upset conventional ideas than any other man in England since Swinburne.

Among novelists, is Guy de Maupassant. It is hardly too much to say that he created the short story in France. Here is Virgo rising, with Venus on the horizon in conjunction with Mars. This violence of passion, with Uranus in the eighth house, presaged his melancholy and appalling death; but, before this effect could take place on the physical plane, it must first produce that miraculous labor whose fruit is still so sweet in our mouths.

With this we may compare the horoscope of Oscar Wilde. Here Uranus is again too near the tenth to make for permanence. Virgo rising has its lord, Mercury, near the opposition of Uranus; a careful consideration of the difference in these dispositions will make most significant the variation of his career from that of the great French writer. But we must once more point out that Uranus in Taurus has great constructive power; Wilde's work produced a tremendous effect upon the younger generation, and its permanence in literature seems now assured.

Then there is Mabel Collins, who also did much to make the success of the Theosophical movement by her interesting writings. As in the case of Lily Langtry, Libra is rising; but, Saturn being in exact conjunction with Uranus, Venus trine to them, and Neptune sextile, with Jupiter in the Ascendant, the career is less material; the direction of the will is more to power of a subtler and more permanent sort.

Lastly, we have two similar poets, Coleridge and Philip Bourke Marston. The former has Sagittarius rising, which adds its element of shy suddenness to the personality; it is refined and beautiful, like a deer. Uranus in the fifth house gives that mystic tinge which is the essence of the beauty of his poetry; but, alas! when it worked down to the material plane, it made him the slave of his pleasures. The pre-Raphaelite poet, on the other hand, has Leo rising, and was generous, frank and free. Uranus in the ninth house gave him another kind of mysticism. Both men were, however, strongly determined by Uranus in Taurus. Their work is patient, steady, and constructive. Coleridge's Uranus is hampered by the exact square of Jupiter, and Marston's blindness no doubt prevented his will from coming to full flower; but the determination, in both cases, is most evidently there.

The following well known persons were born with Uranus in the sign Taurus:

Andrew Mellon
Emile Coué
Samuel T. Coleridge
Clarence Darrow
John Drew
William Gillette
Elbert Hubbard
John Hays Hammond

For the benefit of those who are not in possession of Raphael's Ephemeris, or who are not able to interpret the symbols contained therein, the years when Uranus is in the sign of Taurus are as follows:

From						
From July	6th		through	September	4th	1850
April	15th	1851	"	May	31st	1858
January	4th		"	March	11th	1859
June			"	October		1934
April		1935	"	July		1941
November		1941	"	May		1942

URANUS IN GEMINI

The sign Gemini is by nature singularly unsympathetic with Uranus; for its force is dispersive and gentle, easily moved, but not persistent in motion, and the influence is accordingly weak. We shall find in this position few persons preëminent for driving force of will. Their power will be mainly that of idea; and, unless the rising sign be thoroughly harmonious, and both its lord and Uranus himself well-dignified, we may expect examples rather of failure than of success. We have, however, three great religious teachers, all distinguished for the gentleness of their doctrines and the suavity of their methods. These are Jesus of Nazareth, Swami Vivekananda, and Dr. Rudolph Steiner.

In the case of Jesus, Libra is rising, a sign peculiarly harmonious with Gemini. Jupiter is ascending, squared by the Sun (which is in exact conjunction with Mercury) and in direct opposition to Mars and Neptune. Uranus himself is on the cusp of the tenth house. This makes Uranus by far the strongest planet in the figure, so much so that we may regard his influence as paramount and unchecked, thus summing the career, in so far as the will is concerned, in the one word—emancipation.

The Hindu adept has Capricorn rising, with the Sun and Venus in the Ascendant, and these are square to Mars. Uranus is in the fifth house; this made him efficient as a teacher of occult philosophy. But there is no great harmony between Gemini and Capricorn, so that the complete temperament is not nearly so efficient as in the case just considered.

The German mystic, with Scorpio rising and Jupiter in the ninth, adds great scientific accomplishment to the Uranian force. Mars, too, its lord, is exactly semi-sextile to Uranus; but the latter is squared by the Sun, gravely diminishing the mundane potency of the planet, which is, moreover, in the seventh house, by no means a powerful position in such a case.

Another type is Maurice Maeterlinck; but here Scorpio is rising with its lord, Mars, in sextile to Uranus. Consequently, the driving force of the one compensates the weakness of the other.

An even better example is Lord Brougham, with Libra rising, and Venus in her own house just above the horizon. The influence is still mental; Gemini can never act on the material plane directly; but Uranus is in the eighth house, and so the great lawyer became what he was through dealing with the minds of the dead by his study of precedent. Libra, again, in material matters implies the judicial faculty, and Mercury, the mental ruler, is just below Venus.

An even more strenuous politician is John Burns. Once more the forceful Scorpio is rising, implying iron determination. Uranus in Gemini here gives the limit and the means. His strength is in his eloquence, and Uranus, being trined by Mars, makes him a great fighting orator. Both he and Brougham display the same dogged will, but the difference between them is most clearly characterized by the difference between Libra and Scorpio; the one "hacking through"; the other, adroit, subtle, weighing every word.

Not dissimilar to either, indeed a sort of mean proportional between them, is Theodore Roosevelt. Here Sagittarius is rising, and Uranus is in the fifth house. There is a sort of boyish pleasure in the will, a spontaneity in the eloquence, which appealed strongly to even his enemies. The breeziness, the spirit of the vast deserts wrung from the bison and the Indian, was in his words. Mars rising in Capricorn makes the temperament somewhat rash and tactless; if unable to sweep people off their feet by the first gust, he has no reserve of tact to influence their second thought. Here, then, we read the whole secret of his success and of his failure.

Not so far removed, either, from this category is Billy Sunday. Scorpio is rising, with Mars and Jupiter in close conjunction just above the cusp of the Ascendant, and once again we see the brutal thrust of the personality, breaking through all obstacles to attain its ends. And here again the effect is upon the minds of men. But there is nothing subtly persuasive; the only weapon is the bludgeon.

He literally tries to bully men into belief—or what, for the moment, passes for belief.

Another vigorous personality was Mrs. Pankhurst, with Aquarius rising. Aquarius and Gemini are friendly enough, and thus we observe that, within the narrow limitations, (Mercury is afflicted by the conjunction of Saturn in the sixth, a most unfortunate house for the mental ruler), her will has produced very remarkable results.

Richard Strauss has Cancer rising, and Uranus not far above the Orient. The Moon, lady of Cancer, is in the third house, in Virgo; thus the mind and the temperament are in tune; and Cancer is a sign most delicate and pleasing, receptive of harmonious impulses from without. The Sun, too, lord of Music, is with Uranus, and Venus stands the morning star above them. How beautiful a picture of the temperament of the composer of "Electra" and "Salome"!

J. M. W. Turner is another excellent example of this position. One may ask where lies the peculiar force of Gemini; but a further investigation of the horoscope will justify wisdom of her children. Capricorn is rising with Saturn in close trine to Uranus, thus harmonizing the personality, while Uranus himself is modified by the conjunction of Venus, the planet of gracious form and brilliant color. A certain ruggedness and power is added to these by the square of Mars.

Far less amicable dispositions are found in the nativity of Thomas Moore. Scorpio is rising, and there is the successful man, no doubt, especially as Mars is in his own house, just above the eastern skyline. But he is sorely weakened by the conjunction of the Moon and Saturn, while Uranus is squared by Jupiter. Hence, the extremely narrow limit of his art, and the monotony of his melody. Uranus, too, is in the seventh house, and it is never well for the will to conflict with the personality. Moore's ambition was never equalled by his achievement; and his best-known work is not vital or elemental.

One of the greatest chemists that ever lived was Sir Humphrey Davy. He, too, had Scorpio rising, but its lord Mars in Libra is in exact trine to Uranus, giving him that noble devotion to justice, in Nature, which made him so perfect an observer. Here, then, is a temperament of ideal balance, and the will worked freely at its gigantic and most honorable ambition. It may be objected that

Mars is in his detriment, but the trine of Uranus fully compensates for this weakness. Scorpio gives the inquiring mind, and the position of Uranus in the Zodiac could not but operate freely with such assistance. With Neptune and Jupiter in exact conjunction in the House of Fame, the native was assured not only of success, but of recognition.

The following well known persons were born with Uranus in the sign Gemini:

Bliss Carman
Alan Dale
Frank Damrosch
Reginald de Koven
Henry Ford
Harrison Grey Fiske
Lloyd George
Percy Stickney Grant
George Harvey
William Randolph Hearst

For the benefit of those who are not in possession of Raphael's Ephemeris, or who are not able to interpret the symbols contained therein, the years when Uranus is in the sign Gemini are as follows:

From	June	1st	1858	through	January	3rd	1859
	March	12th	1859	"	June	25th	1865
	February	22nd		"	March	22nd	1866
	August			"	October		1941

URANUS IN CANCER

So passive, so placid, so receptive, so conservative a sign as Cancer cannot be expected to accentuate the active, violent, creative, determined, revolutionary rays of Uranus. It will tend to soften his violence but may, under favorable conditions, be found to modify and expand the force, just as some pungent perfume needs to be spread out more thinly before the olfactory nerves can perceive it. We shall, then, expect to find the power of Uranus neutralized by

Cancer; and, whether this leaves a residuum potent and yet pleasant will depend far more than in other signs upon the Ascendant, and upon the dignities and aspects of the lord thereof, and upon those of Uranus himself.

We shall certainly not expect to discover many people who have revolutionized their age, who have dominated their contemporaries in any radical manner. We shall not find any great strength of will, any true masterfulness of temperament, unless the Sun is in a fixed sign. Nevertheless, Cancer is ruled by the Moon and therefore the position implies an unusual degree of psychic power, and renders the native capable of becoming truly submissive to the deep, subconscious will.

The facts bear out this prognosis. Savonarola, to take our best available example first, has Uranus in twenty-nine degrees, and its influence extends, therefore, to the cusp of Leo. In his case, moreover, Aries is rising, with Mars exalted in Capricorn; and his Uranus is trined by Jupiter. Mars is weakened by the conjunction of the Moon, but the square of Saturn adds determination, and somewhat embitters the configuration, while Mars being in the tenth house, dominates the figure. There is, therefore, much force in the personality; the temperament is directed to religion and confined within those limits, by the aforesaid trine of Jupiter.

In twenty-eight degrees of Cancer is the Uranus of Byron, and here, too, Leo has doubtless some influence. But Cancer is rising, and its lady, the Moon, is in close conjunction with Uranus. The temperament is therefore harmonious within itself, but easy-going, pleasure-loving, artistic, sensuous, eccentric, and mutable. The power of the character comes rather from Mars (in his fall) on the cusp of the Ascendant. This configuration seems admirably to describe the best and the worst of the poet. Strong-willed and self-willed he was, yet unable to persist in will; he was at once weak and violent, stormy and querulous; with all his advantages and his talents, his rank and his reputation, he died a disappointed man, having sought in vice that victory which comes only from virtue.

Another hot-tempered individual was Queen Elizabeth, whose Uranus is in conjunction with Saturn, in the house of marriage and of public enemies, the seventh; thus being practically in opposition to her Ascendant. Here is a fatal opposition of personality and temperament. The whole substance of her will was bound up in the seventh house, and, arrogant and masterful as her personality was, she could never secure her dynasty. In spite of all the glories of her reign, its tragedy was her failure to save her house.

There are two other persons of importance who have this position of Uranus—Alfred Harmsworth and Rudyard Kipling, both journalists—one in the wholesale and the other in the retail business! Kipling has Uranus on the very cusp of his Ascendant, and unquestionably there was never a more self-supporting personality. He strikes a very definite note, and rises at times to extraordinary heights. He is perhaps the only author who has really succeeded in understanding and portraying the ruling class of England. The conjunction of the Sun and Jupiter, and that of Mercury, Mars, and Venus, contribute greatly to his success. But this is a digression; the point here to be emphasized is the unique personal note struck by Uranus on the Ascendant, and its resolution in artistic form by the fact of that Ascendant being Cancer. With Harmsworth the case is different. Jupiter is rising in Sagittarius, and the Uranus in Cancer becomes of secondary importance. It merely ties him down to a method, that of working upon the people, by publicity. The suddenness and boldness of his schemes are determined by the rising sign.

Sir David Wilkie is a good example of this position. Gemini is rising, and its lord, Mercury, is weakened by the opposition of Mars, so that the influence of Uranus in Cancer comes out strongly. Uranus is trine to the Sun, confirming the artistic predisposition conferred by Cancer. Therefore, he was a successful painter with a keen sense of beauty, but with nothing in him to set the world on fire.

Our last example is Madame Steinheil. In this nativity Aquarius is rising, but there are no less than five planets in Aries, all just under the Ascendant, and Saturn, the lord of the Ascendant, is trine from the tenth house, to all of them in general, and to Neptune in particular. Here, then, is the insatiable ambition, limitless and indomitable, which devoured her. Uranus in Cancer is not important, except that, being in the fifth house, it gave her the temperament of pleasure, and laid down the lines along which she worked to aggrandize her vaulting personality. Saturn in the tenth house laid his scythe to the root of her tree in the very season of its blossoming.

The following well known persons were born with Uranus in the sign Cancer:

Edith Cavell
Richard Carle
Charles G. Dawes
William Faversham
Richard le Gallienne
Charles Hayden
Rudyard Kipling
Ramsay MacDonald

For the benefit of those who are not in possession of Raphael's Ephemeris, or who are not able to interpret the symbols contained therein, the years when Uranus is in the sign Cancer are as follows:

From	June	26th 1865	through	February	21st	1866
	March	23rd 1866	"	September	12th	1871
	January	2nd	"	June	27th	1872

URANUS IN LEO

There is a peculiar sympathy between Uranus and Leo, because it is in a solar sign, and Uranus is the secret generative force by which we call the Sun, "Father." Fierceness and subtlety alternate in his mode of action; he is weighty in his onset, but dangerously sudden; and he is the giver of life and death.

There is, however, one serious drawback to this position of Uranus, a danger that its very sympathy with the secret part of the Solar force creates. Apollo is called "creator and destroyer"; the Lingam is addressed by the Greeks as "all-begetter, all devourer," and this force is now seen to be concentrated in Uranus. Unless the Sun in a man's horoscope is reasonably well-dignified, there is danger to the life of the native. The presence of Uranus in the house of the Sun is itself an affliction of the Sun on the material plane;

and so the Sun must be well-dignified in other ways, or the native is likely to die before the occult power of the planet has time to manifest itself.

There is, accordingly, a notable paucity of examples of the proposition which we have put forward as to its natural action when isolated; since, from the nature of the case, such isolation is rather rare. Shelley is our one great example; and his case is, fortunately, very perfect. We see the revolutionary influence at work in Great-heart; the rebel against the fetters that bind humanity, overflowing with solar force and love which blazes on high, melting the cold passions of age and experience with his flaming jets of white-hot vapor of gold. Such works as "Prometheus Unbound" and "The World's Tragedy" are pure Uranus in Leo. Shelley was saved from premature death through illness by the conjunction of the Sun and Venus, six degrees from Uranus; Sagittarius is rising, and its lord, Jupiter, is in conjunction with Mars and Neptune. But, Uranus being in the eighth house, an accidental death was indicated. Early as this came, he had done his work; he had sown a new seed in the fields of humanity, one of the most fruitful ever planted.

Another case of the most promising talent cut short is King Edward VI, admittedly the most accomplished scholar of his period. At an age when most boys are still struggling with the elements of Latin, he spoke fluently not only that comparatively easy language, but also Greek and Hebrew. Here again, however, the Sun is only seven degrees from the square of Uranus, and is himself squared within one degree by the Moon. Mercury, lord of the Ascendant, Virgo, is squared by Mars, again within one degree; with such aspects it was impossible for the promise of youth to be fulfilled in the achievement of age.

Another striking example of the seductive, fascinating temperament given by Uranus in Leo is Mary Queen of Scots. She stands out from all other queens, for beauty and tragedy, not because these elements were so much greater than in the others, but on account of the temperament itself, which has the faculty of inspiring the most amazing extremes of attraction and repulsion. There is never anything half-hearted about the feeling with which such people are regarded. With Shelley, half the world made him Apollo incarnate; the rest thought, and even wrote, that he was, in sober truth, not a man at all, but a devil sent specially from hell to plague humanity. So with Mary Queen of Scots. She had Taurus rising, and Venus in semi-sextile to the Moon. The Sun is trine to Uranus; but, being in the eighth house, a violent death was presaged as soon as the directions permitted; which duly came to pass. Rather similar is the personality of Cleo de Mérode, whose fascination may be held to match that of the unhappy Stuart queen, having the same serpentine quality. Here Pisces is rising; the life is made secure by the trine of Mars to the Moon; and there are no afflictions to injure the native.

Another example of fascination is Winston Churchill, perhaps the most attractive personality in English politics. At an age when most men, even if they started with his advantages of birth and wealth, are just taking their seats for the first time in Parliament, he was a Cabinet Minister, holding the most responsible portfolios. Scorpio is rising, a most harmonious circumstance, and the Sun is in the Ascendant, sextile to Saturn, so that the life is well-protected. However, Uranus is rather near the cusp of the tenth house, and a sudden fall from power, such as took place in 1915, was naturally to be expected.

Sometimes the temperament of Uranus in Leo confers unique powers in some obscure direction. One may instance "Datas," with Cancer rising, and the Moon in opposition to Uranus, limiting the mental powers to his peculiar faculty of remembering dates. Somewhat like him, is Houdini, with unequalled dexterity in one trivial, but most unusual accomplishment, that of being able to extricate himself from bars or fetters. The squares of Mars and Saturn to Uranus indicate the special line in which the temperament is displayed.

The following well known persons were born with Uranus in the sign Leo:

Alfred W. Smith
Will Levington Comfort
Robert J. Collier
George M. Cohan
Howard Chandler Christy
Winston Churchill
Harrison Fisher

Charles E. Mitchell
Jack London

For the benefit of those who are not in possession of Raphael's Ephemeris, or who are not able to interpret the symbols contained therein, the years when Uranus is in the sign Leo are as follows:

From	September	13th 1871	through	January	1st 1872
	June	28th 1872	"	August	24th 1878

URANUS IN VIRGO

So earthy, mercurial, passive a sign as Virgo can have little in common with the fire and activity of Uranus. Sometimes, the influence, as in the case of Cancer, becomes harmonized and fixed; but this will only be in special cases. For the most part, one is likely to find eccentricity and mental instability, and it is not often that any great driving force is developed.

Nevertheless, we are at once confronted with the case of Balzac, presumably one of the greatest novelists that ever lived. But here Leo is rising, and Uranus, though just within the second house, has no planet between him and the horizon. The Sun, lord of the Ascendant, is in conjunction with Jupiter in the tenth house. There is no lack of harmony between the personality and the temperament, except for the mercurial touch given by Virgo, which made the master personally very eccentric in manner, and somewhat unintelligible in his actions, at least to the majority of his contemporaries.

Brigham Young has Uranus rising in Virgo, just within the second house, in exact sextile to Mars which is within four degrees of the conjunction of Jupiter. Mercury, the lord of Virgo, is in close conjunction with the Sun. This combination gives that tremendous energy and ability which he had, and which the mere position of Uranus would have denied him.

The following well known persons were born with Uranus in the sign Virgo:

Mussolini
Geraldine Farrar
"Bud" Fisher
Roy Howard
Ray Long
Balzac
Ethel Barrymore

For the benefit of those who are not in possession of Raphael's Ephemeris, or who are not able to interpret the symbols contained therein, the years when Uranus is in the sign Virgo are as follows:

From August	25th 1878	through	October	13th 1884
April	12th	"	July	28th 1885

URANUS IN LIBRA

Owing to the exaltation of Saturn in the house of Venus, there is a subtle suggestion of danger in the sign of Libra. Its own nature, too, is the balance; and when that balance is upset by casting such a flaming sword as Uranus into the scale, we may expect very astonishing results. Where Venus is afflicted, and Saturn strong, we shall find that the influence is often exceedingly dangerous; but good dispositions and dignities of Venus, and a harmonious rising sign and happy aspects to Uranus, himself, may bring about the development of the most useful forces. The freedom of Libra, an airy sign, will give play to the impulses of Uranus; in fact, one might almost say that he is never more himself than when he is in this sign.

Taking first some rather unfortunate examples, let us consider the nativity of Joseph Smith. Note, however, that it only appears unfortunate to us in so far as we may happen not to be Mormons; we must be tolerant with those expressions of genius with which we are not in sympathy. It is, however, quite permissible for the astrologer to give planetary reasons for thinking this prophet a mistaken one. At his birth Cancer was rising, a very suitable sign for the reception of inspired knowledge; unhappily, the Moon, close to Mercury, is in exact opposition to the cusp of the Ascendant; moreover, she is in her detriment, and square to Uranus, which is conjoined with Saturn. Libra itself is not very harmonious with Cancer, and though there is much power developed, such power is bound to work in a disordered manner.

There is much tragedy in the horoscope of James II of England. Here Uranus is in the third house, with a sextile of the Moon, and a semi-sextile of the Sun, but squared by Jupiter. The Sun is lord of the Ascendant, Leo, but he is in Scorpio; and Mars is rising in his own decanate of Leo, the third, which represents unsuccessful struggle. Uranus, too, is in the third house, so that the mentality is eccentric. The whole outlook is gloomy in the extreme, leading one to expect an increasing tension, due to tactlessness and ill-temper, qualities which indeed cost him his throne. Contrast these positions with those of Louis XIV, "le grand monarque." Here Scorpio is rising, its lord, Mars, sextile to Uranus. Instantly we see a harmony of temperament of the ambitious type; not very amiable, perhaps, but singularly strong and without inhibitions.

The severe quality of the vision of Dürer is determined by the conjunction made by Saturn with his Sun, lord of Leo, the Ascendant. Uranus is in the third house, making possible such pictures as the "Astrologer" and the "Four Witches." But there is a strong friendship between Leo and Libra, and the temperament is a symphony of these signs and planets.

A more Venusian type of artist is Sir Joshua Reynolds. Here Virgo is rising, but in twenty-nine degrees, so that Libra occupies almost the whole of the Ascendant. Uranus is just within the second house, but there is nothing rising above him. It is, therefore, evident that his influence is quite free from admixture. A sextile of Jupiter and Saturn to Uranus lends him exceptional force, and it is to be noted that the Sun, Venus, Mercury, and the Moon are all in the tenth house, and thus rule the entire figure. It may be remarked here that when there is any dispute, so to say, among the other planets, the tenth house assumes primary importance.

In literature we have, in Bulwer-Lytton, a figure analogous to that of Reynolds in painting. Here Cancer is rising, causing him to prefer antiquity to modern times, to write historical novels rather than modern, and, even when he wrote of modern times, as in "A

Strange Story," to introduce the ideas of the past and make them more prominent than those of the present. The Moon is on the cusp of the Ascendent, or he might have gone even farther than he did in this direction; as it was, his personality was diffuse; his tendency was to play first at magic, next at politics, then at literature. Were Cancer more appropriate to Libra, the result would have been happier; but the truth is that nothing goes well without a dash of fire somewhere in its composition. In any case this dispersion of interests is quite characteristic of Libra.

The influence of Uranus in this sign, at its best, emphasizing its most judicial quality, is seen in Sir William Hamilton, one of the greatest metaphysicians that Britain has produced. Here Gemini is rising, and Mercury is in his own house, Virgo, in conjunction with Venus. This gives the mental development full play; otherwise, Uranus in the fifth house might have caused trouble. The perfect harmony of the two airy signs, and the good dignity of Mercury, allow full play to the better side of Uranus. Hence we find the metaphysician probing deeply into the most recondite mysteries of existence, and displaying the most even judgment as well as the subtlest power of analysis.

In the case of Petrarch we find the emphasis is to be laid upon the fact that Venus rules Libra. Leo is rising, giving him a large and warm heart; especially as the Sun, its ruler, is close under the cusp of the Ascendant, while Mercury, exactly on it, adds keen intellect to the personality. Venus is trine to Uranus, and lends tenderness and beauty to his fierce and passionate rays. Is further explanation needed of the circumstances that he challenges even Dante as the Poet of Love? In the horoscope of Erasmus, Uranus is in nine degrees of Libra, just above the cusp of the Ascendant, while Venus is rising just below it. But Uranus is opposed by Saturn, making the temperament cold. Mercury, too, is ascending, and the Sun is in conjunction with the Moon and Neptune in Scorpio, which diminish his glow. Here, then, is the great scholar as opposed to the great lover.

A very incarnation of passion is to be found in George Sand, with 27 degrees of Aquarius rising, and Saturn sextile to Neptune. The temperament is harmonious enough, and the intellectual side of the woman is clearly indicated by the points given above, but Uranus in the seventh house, squared by the Sun from the fifth house, describes her varied affairs with men.

George Borrow has Uranus exactly on the Ascendant, squared by the Sun and Mercury, while Venus, the lady of the Ascendant, is squared by Saturn. This fully accounts for his queer, sardonic, temperament, its flashes of genius, and its strange outbursts of passion. In the nativity of Victor Hugo, Scorpio was rising with Mars in Aquarius not specially strong, high, or well-aspected. Aquarius is friendly to Libra, however, and, as Mars is within five degrees of the trine of Uranus, the personality and temperament go well enough together. One may easily understand that this combination gave the extraordinary power for work which the great poet and novelist possessed.

That cynical voluptuary, Sainte Beuve, had Pisces rising and Jupiter in conjunction with Venus and Neptune, a very apt description of the personality. Uranus has the conjunction of Saturn, squared by Mercury; and here is the temperament and the tone of his life's work—criticism. Dumas has Leo rising, with the Sun just above the horizon, sextile to Uranus. Here again is a splendid harmony, and its dominant note is the rich youthful glow always conferred by Leo, unless the Sun is most sorely afflicted, or Saturn present in the sign.

The following well known persons were born with Uranus in the sign Libra:

Charlie Chaplin
Victor Hugo
Bulwer-Lytton
Sir Joshua Reynolds
Sir William Hamilton
Petrarch
Albrecht Dürer

For the benefit of those who are not in possession of Raphael's Ephemeris, or who are not able to interpret the symbols contained therein, the years when Uranus is in the sign Libra are as follows:

From October	14th 1884	through	April	11th 1885
July	29th 1885	"	December	9th 1890
April	5th	"	September	25th 1891

URANUS IN SCORPIO

THE nature of Scorpio in its more spiritual aspects is so singularly like that of Uranus at his best, we may anticipate that his presence in this sign will be so strong as to dominate the personality, even where that is of an opposite character. The excellence of this position will depend upon the aspects to Uranus in a greater degree than is the case in other signs.

There is naturally a strong affinity between Uranus and Scorpio. With some respects, the spirit of scientific investigation, which is an important element of Scorpio, will be brought out very strongly; with others, the treacherous, subtle-witted quality of that mysterious sign; and, in a third group, we may find its sensuality and passion most deeply marked.

To begin with men of science and philosophy, we have three emancipating intelligences of the highest order; Copernicus, Newton, and Immanuel Kant. The first of these great men has Virgo rising, with Mercury in the eighth house trined by the Moon, and only eight degrees from the trine of Mars. Uranus is in the third house near the conjunction of Neptune, and is trined by Saturn. It is impossible to imagine a more perfectly harmonious disposition of the planets for intellectual and scientific eminence.

Sir Isaac Newton had Libra rising, giving the balanced judgment so requisite in scientific investigation. Uranus himself is within the Ascendant, and is trined by Jupiter, who is only six degrees from conjunction with Saturn. Here the differences from the previous example well describe the larger aspects taken by Newton's investigation. In the horoscope of Immanuel Kant we find Taurus rising, but in 29 degrees, so that most of the Ascendant is occupied by Gemini, whose lord, Mercury, is in exact conjunction with the Sun in Taurus; and these planets are trined by the Moon in Virgo and by Saturn in his own sign Capricorn. This gives an admirable picture of his wonderful intelligence, introspective, philosophical, metaphysical.

More of the revolutionary phase of Uranus is found in the nativities of Gladstone and John Bright. The former has Capricorn rising, and Saturn is conjoined with Neptune, within two degrees, and with Venus within nine degrees. It is easy to see that the interest must be mainly human and political, for Jupiter trines this conjunction, and is in Aries, near the cusp of the third house.

The temperament is not very harmonious with the personality in Gladstone's case, though both are powerful; and in this diversity we see the possibility of trouble. In fact, his career was tumultuous, and he sometimes suddenly reversed his policy in an arbitrary, and, as some thought, an unwarrantable manner.

The career of John Bright, not so astoundingly successful, nor so tempestuous, was simpler and clearer in its astrologic particulars. Here Cancer is rising; the Moon is conjoined with Venus, close to Neptune, and Uranus is in conjunction with the Sun. Cancer and Scorpio being friendly signs, the man was always himself, and attained the highest reputation for suavity and for integrity.

We might also pair Charles Dickens and Alfred Tennyson. The former has Uranus rising in Scorpio, sextile to Mercury. Mars is squared by Saturn, making the temperament stronger than the personality. Hence, the man's work was more important than he himself.

Tennyson, with Gemini rising, and its lord, Mercury, suffering severely from the square of Jupiter, was of a coldly intellectual, almost priggish type. Uranus, too, is in conjunction with Mars. But Venus is rising, sextile to Jupiter, which is in the eleventh house, and so it is easy to understand that these influences counted more than the significators of either the personality or the temperament. The high honors paid Tennyson were due more to his adroitness in pleasing his sovereign than to any other quality inherent in himself or even the excellence of his poetry.

Another Victorian example is Sir Isaac Pitman, with Libra rising; Venus is not especially strong in any way, but is on the cusp of the third house, within which is Mercury. The inventive genius, therefore, turns naturally to seeking ease in matters connected with writing; in other words, to the construction of the system of shorthand which is associated with his name.

Before we proceed to the domain of art, let us look for a moment at the nativity of Cæsar Borgia. Virgo is rising, with Mercury on the cusp of the Ascendant, giving a cold, shrewd personality. Uranus, on the cusp of the third house, is opposed by the Moon, both of these being squared by Mars and Saturn in conjunction in Leo. From such a configuration we can picture to ourselves the oily, violent, sensual, and perfidious qualities of the man, while the Sun rising, trine to Jupiter and sextile to Mars and Saturn, assures ambition, and success in attaining its ends.

Wagner has Gemini rising, which accounts for the literary quality in his work; Mercury is square to an opposition of Mars and Jupiter; which explains the violent and brilliant qualities of his nature and his music; Uranus is opposed by Venus, and the whole figure represents strife and turmoil. Venus close above the eastern horizon, in her own house, in conjunction with the Sun and sextile to Jupiter is, on the whole, the most important planet in the horoscope. Her aspects give the intense humanity, the marked dramatic and artistic feeling, especially for pictorial effect (for Wagner's music has always a visual value); and these assure success. Like Wagner, in his own art, is Michael Angelo. Here Pisces is rising, Mercury and Venus are conjoined on the cusp, with the Sun not far below them. They are trine to Uranus and the Moon. Pisces and Scorpio are friendly; it is the ideal harmony which permitted the man to turn out apparently unlimited quantities of the finest work.

For a final example, Alfred de Musset offers himself as a contrast. Here Aquarius is rising, Saturn is in conjunction with the Sun and Mercury in the tenth house, with Neptune only nine degrees away. The personality goes well with the temperament though, Venus being in Capricorn, her hated house, and Jupiter close to the opposition of Uranus, the whole make-up is bound to be one of cynicism and disappointment, to which the square of Mars and Venus adds some violence of ill-regulated passion. In spite of brilliancy of talent, even genius, in spite of great achievement, one can only rank him sadly among those who are not quite immortals.

The following well known persons were born with Uranus in the sign Scorpio:

Dean Cornwell
Horace Greeley
P. T. Barnum
Michael Angelo
Sir Isaac Pitman
Chopin

For the benefit of those who are not in possession of Raphael's Ephemeris, or who are not able to interpret the symbols contained therein, the years when Uranus is in the sign Scorpio are as follows:

From	December	10th	1890	through	April	4th	1891
	September	26th	1891	"	December	1st	1897
	July	4th		"	September	10th	1898

URANUS IN SAGITTARIUS

In the sign of Sagittarius lies much of the nature of the horse and of the deer; timid, delicate, proud, courageous, and swift. Only the suddenness of its action in any way resembles the typical Uranus force; but the sign itself, if its lord, Jupiter, be happily aspected, may have much power to overcome that which seems hard and cold in the planet. Cold, for the cruelty of Uranus is calculated and deliberate, for the achievement of spiritual good to the native, while that of Mars is the hot cruelty of far more human passion. But Sagittarius never fails to give liveliness to the temperament; it is as Celtic on the Ascendant as Leo or Pisces; more so, in fact, than the latter; therefore, we here find in the planet what one might whimsically call a "reformed" Uranus; etherealized and sublimized. But, of course, bad aspects and an inharmonious Ascendant will weaken and corrupt these qualities.

For example, the horoscope of Queen Victoria shows arrogance and petulance; impatience of contradiction. Gemini is rising, the opposition sign of Sagittarius, and Neptune in the eighth house, within five degrees of Uranus in the seventh house. Saturn squares both; but, fortunately, Venus is trine, otherwise her temperament would have been impossible. Mercury is in the twelfth house, and not particularly strong; it is very evident that the temperament plays a much larger part than the personality.

George Eliot has Scorpio in the Ascendant, and the Sun, Venus, Mercury, Uranus, and Neptune all in the east, not far below the horizon. Uranus in conjunction with Neptune is squared by Saturn. Mars is in Leo, trine to Venus, but opposed by Jupiter and the Moon. The result is naturally a highly confused problem, from which it is difficult to resolve one separate, true resultant. A stormy life, and a mixed career of joy, sorrow, failure, and triumph are the visible effects of this complicated chain of causes.

Now, let us consider the horoscope of Shakespeare, with Virgo rising. Mercury, lord of the Ascendant, is in Aries, trine to Uranus and sextile to Neptune. There is no planet ascending; Uranus is in the fourth house in opposition to Neptune and Venus, a tremendous aspect; and Venus is also sextile to a conjunction of Saturn and Jupiter. Here, then, we see a wonderful temperament, and a negligible personality.

Another master-mind is that of Herbert Spencer. Uranus is on the exact cusp of the Ascendant, twenty-eight degrees of Sagittarius, with Neptune in close conjunction, again a tremendous aspect. Hence the epoch-making character of his philosophy. The man himself was retiring (Jupiter, the lord of the Ascendant being in Pisces softened by the square of Venus), but there is no conflict of any kind indicated between the temperament and the personality. He was, therefore, free to work out the splendid promise of his remarkable horoscope.

Bismarck has the Sun, lord of his Ascendant Leo, squared by the Moon and in trine to Uranus, who is himself trine to the Ascendant. Here is, again, an excellent harmony, save that the Moon in Capricorn gives some brusquerie. On the whole, it is a disposition certain to afford the best results, from the standpoint of a career.

Still more earth-shaking is the colossal Luther. Leo is rising once more, this sign, of course, being in trine to Sagittarius and therefore sympathetic with it. The Sun, Saturn and Mercury are in conjunction, sextile to the Moon and semi-sextile to Neptune; Uranus is sextile to a conjunction of Venus, Mars and Jupiter. Thus both personality and temperament are exceedingly strong, and harmonize one with the other. The result we know.

A far calmer figure is that of Cornelius Agrippa. Virgo is rising, and Mercury, its lord, is not especially strong in the second house. Uranus is near the square of the Sun, and within nine degrees of the opposition of Mars. Here we find indicated scholarship and deep thought, without any greater manifestation than some books, more curious than revolutionary, and the acquisition of a great, if not very well-deserved, reputation as a magician.

An interesting example of temperament stronger than personality is seen in Nell Gwyn, with Capricorn rising and its lord Saturn afflicted. But Uranus is exactly conjoined with Neptune on the cusp of the eleventh house, giving the temperament an extraordinary force to work through favoritism. As the Lord of the Ascendant, Saturn, is trine to the Sun, she had also the force of character to make use of her power mainly for good. Courtesan though she was, she was probably the best influence in the life of Charles II and a consistent friend to the common people.

William III of England has the Moon rising in Leo, trine to Mercury, with the Sun in conjunction with Jupiter. Uranus and Neptune are exactly conjoined—this, by the way, often stands for great and unexpected opportunities, as is seen, indeed, in the preceding case, and the whole figure is very favorable, so that, from a petty princeling of another country, he became King of England, through the apparent accident of the abdication of his wife's father. Mars is square to the Neptune-Uranus position, a testimony that it was through no charm of temperament that he came to win such a position.

The following well known persons were born with Uranus in the sign Sagittarius:

John Ruskin
Shakespeare
Gloria Swanson
Lord Tennyson
Queen Victoria
George Washington
Martin Luther
Cornelius Agrippa

For the benefit of those who are not in possession of Raphael's Ephemeris, or who are not able to interpret the symbols contained therein, the years when Uranus is in the sign Sagittarius are as follows:

From December 2nd 1897	through	July	3rd 1898
September 11th 1898	"	December	19th 1904

URANUS IN CAPRICORN

In Capricorn, Saturn's constricting restraint directs the explosive force of Uranus, just as the binding walls of the cannon intensify the effect of the discharge. With Uranus in this sign we get "an he-goat also, against whom there is no rising up." The native of this position is, in Kipling's phrase, "a first-class fighting man." The examples of this quality are so convincing that they need only to be mentioned. The power evoked is so great that no afflictions to the personality appear to daunt it, unless they are extraordinarily evil. The Magical Will of the Man, his Mission in the World, is everything to him.

We have, to begin with, Charles Baudelaire, who despite all persecutions, revolutionized French thought, and, by inspiring Swinburne as his spiritual first-born son, revolutionized English thought as well. We have Louis Pasteur, who revolutionized surgery in the teeth of the deadliest opposition; Huxley, who battled for science against orthodox religion, the most Homeric and spectacular combat of the Victorian period; Alfred Russell Wallace, one of his principal colleagues in the fight; Kruger, who broke the power of the British Empire, and "staggered humanity" by the dour fight that his handful of burghers put up against overwhelming hosts; Grant, who crushed Lee; Burton, the most desperate antagonist in private and in public life that England ever bore; and Tolstoi, who went out into the snow of a Russian winter to die in a wayside railway station so bitter, even in extreme old age, with the hand of death upon his shoulder, was his hatred of "home" and "comfort" and the normal life of man.

Then we have Rosa Bonheur, whose life was one long battle

against her own femininity; and, finally, George III (whom we must regard merely as a symbol of the race which he ruled), who broke, with dogged courage and endurance, the power of Napoleon. Even in the mad King himself we can see the fighting quality; it was his obstinate, bull-dog stupidity that lost to his crown these United States of America.

The following well known persons were born with Uranus in the sign Capricorn:

U. S. Grant
Tolstoi
Archbishop Laud
Mary Baker Eddy
Dion Boucicault
Louis Pasteur

For the benefit of those who are not in possession of Raphael's Ephemeris, or who are not able to interpret the symbols contained therein, the years when Uranus is in the sign Capricorn are as follows:

From	December 20th 1904	through	January 30th 1912
	September 5th	"	November 11th 1912

URANUS IN AQUARIUS

In this sign, Uranus appears most clearly as the emancipator. It has been generally claimed that Uranus has a very special affinity with the sign Aquarius, and the sign is so harmonious with the planet that the native who possesses an easy-going personality will probably be little more than commonplace. Some special excitement of adversity, which tries the soul, is necessary to make the possibilities of the sign operative to the full extent; and to produce a really great emancipator.

Thus, in the cases of the Emperor Maximilian, and of Lords Roberts and Wolseley, we find no marked revolutionary impulse. Roberts has Pisces rising, with Jupiter just under the cusp, in opposition to Saturn and Mercury. Uranus is "in prison," just within the twelfth house, with little help anywhere. There is, therefore, nothing sufficient to arouse those deeper and stronger spiritual forces to which we have learned to look for the revolutionary ideas which sway mankind.

Wolseley has Aquarius rising, with Saturn in Virgo not particularly strong. Uranus is near the cusp of the Ascendant, giving him the peculiar personality which, harmonizing so well with the temperament, brought him so much honor; for Uranus was close to the sextile of Jupiter. Once again, however, there is no deeper force at work; the career was conventional.

The unhappy Emperor Maximilian is an example of feebleness and lack of unity. The Sun and Mercury are rising in Cancer, and Jupiter is in the Mid-heaven; but the Moon is in the fifth house, in opposition to Mars. Uranus, too, receives no help. This is a fine illustration of how mere good fortune, unaided by personal strength, may fail to keep a man out of difficulties.

There are two humorists with this position, Du Maurier and Lewis Carroll. The former has Uranus on the cusp of the Ascendant, with nothing better than a semi-sextile of the Moon to assist him; Saturn is in opposition to Mercury. The latter, on the other hand, has Sagittarius rising, and Jupiter is close to Uranus near the cusp of the third house. He has the benefit of a semi-sextile of Neptune—here is the subtle yet sacred character of the humor—while Venus and Mars rising in conjunction lend passion and power to the personality. The Sun, too, is only eight degrees from Uranus. It is a most fortunate figure, on the whole; but, at the same time, nothing revolutionary is to be found in it.

President Garfield has Virgo rising, with Mercury not very strong but in the third house. Jupiter is in conjunction with Uranus; Saturn has just risen. There is evidence here of a clever, even nature, likely to move harmoniously enough; but without that quality which overturns faiths and empires.

General Gordon is a stronger type. Aries is rising, with Mars sextile to Jupiter. Uranus is only ten degrees from the Sun, well above the eastern horizon. One can understand the impetuous, romantic, adventurous disposition; there are also indications of great emancipatory ideas. But there is hardly sufficient force to carry them out, as Uranus is hampered by his position in the twelfth house.

Compare with these the nativity of Joan of Arc. Scorpio is rising, and Mars, its lord, is semi-sextile to Jupiter, trine to Saturn, and trine to Venus. Uranus, trined by Jupiter and the Moon, is square to the Ascendant. Here is an all-conquering personality; Uranus giving the revolutionary idea, which is fired with religious zeal for the freeing of the people of her country.

Consider a true empire builder, Franz Josef of Austria, who, from an ill-assorted conglomeration of races who detested each other, developed a nation which surprised the world by its unexpected internal strength in the shock of the greatest war in history. Libra is rising, giving the even judgment and sound balance necessary for such work, and Venus, in her beloved sign, Cancer, and in the tenth house, has the semi-sextile of a conjunction of the Sun, the Moon and Saturn, ensuring the affectionate devotion of all his subjects of whatever race. She is opposed by Neptune in the fourth house, which led to the domestic tragedies in his life, but failed to injure his popularity. Uranus trine to the Ascendant has the sextile of Mars. To this planet, so strong in Aquarius, we must look for the revolutionary awakening of his mind which led him from a beginning of repressive absolutism to become the most sincere constitutional monarch of Europe, devoted to the best interests of all his people.

A very different type of emancipator is Goethe, with Scorpio rising and Mars exalted in Capricorn, trine to Mercury and the Sun. Uranus has the square of Saturn, which is on the cusp of the Ascendant. It is a most harmonious picture, and a great one; for with such a sign rising, and such large planets involved, there must always be big things on the carpet. With this, compare Rossetti, a similar mind, but less original and far less cosmic. Gemini is rising, Mercury is with the Moon in the twelfth house, sextile to Venus and square to Uranus, and Venus is trine to Jupiter. All this is quite as harmonious as Goethe's figure, but not nearly so big. The forces involved are more conventional and so commonplace.

Another great mind was that of Mme. Blavatsky, with Cancer rising and the Moon trine to the conjunction of Jupiter and Uranus, the latter being opposed by the Sun. The Sun is rising (near the cusp of the second house) promising success; but the other combination gives the real force of the character, the receptiveness, the religious enthusiasm, and the occult impulse all working together.

Her chief of staff, Colonel Olcott, has a similar temperament. Libra is rising, and Venus is conjoined with the Sun; and the square of Mars to both contributes magnetism. Uranus is in opposition to the Sun. Naturally, such a figure promises the sympathetic service which his work manifested. The trine of Mars to Saturn gives further efficiency, and he did his work right well.

The great sage and mystic of antiquity, Proclus, the neo-Platonist, has Uranus in conjunction with the Sun and Venus; Saturn and Jupiter are square to them. Aries is rising, Mars, its lord, being in Capricorn in his exaltation. Here, once more, is the double gift of the Gods, the preoccupation with great things and the power to execute them.

The following well known persons were born with Uranus in the sign Aquarius:

Andrew Carnegie
Frank H. Dodd
Bishop Fallows
Cardinal Gibbons
Mark Twain
Alexander Agassiz
Dr. S. Weir Mitchell
Lord Roberts

For the benefit of those who are not in possession of Raphael's Ephemeris, or who are not able to interpret the symbols contained therein, the years when Uranus is in the sign Aquarius are as follows:

From	January	31st	through	September	4th	1912
	November	12th 1912	"	March	31st	1919
	August	17th 1919	"	January	21st	1920

URANUS IN PISCES

Pisces is an exceptionally receptive sign, altogether passive; there is no driving force in it. It is the precise antithesis of the aggressiveness of Uranus. There is, of course, a great deal of subtlety in Pisces, but this is of a different quality from that of Uranus. We shall, consequently, not expect to find very many men of the first class with this position.

Occasionally, however, the positions of the other planets may be such that Uranus is so completely blended with the sign that his occult influence finds its best expression through the fine menstruum of Pisces. There is, fortunately, one example of this in its perfection —William Blake. Here Cancer is rising with the Moon, its lady, just above the Ascendant, semi-sextile to Neptune and trine to Uranus, but in opposition to Venus, which is sextile to Uranus. It should be remembered that the effect of the opposition of two planets is very much mitigated by the presence of a third, trine to one and sextile to the other. The personality is here, therefore, extremely well-suited to the temperament. The general influence, is, of course, watery, and, Uranus being in the ninth house, it is only natural that religion—and particularly that extremely personal and true religion which takes the form of direct vision—should be the key-note of the poet's career. It is interesting to note that Swinburne, who discovered Blake and introduced him to his own blind countrymen, has the same position of Uranus. Cancer is again rising, and Uranus is in the ninth house.

We may now consider two writers, singularly sympathetic to each other, Alphonse Daudet and Thomas Hardy. Daudet has Scorpio rising with its lord, Mars, in his detriment in Taurus in the seventh house, in conjunction with the Sun. Uranus, on the other hand, has a square of Saturn, which is one of the better aspects of these planets, and he is near the cusp of the fifth house. The temperament is consequently very powerful and expresses itself naturally in an artistic form. Thomas Hardy has Libra rising with Venus in Taurus, near the conjunction of Mercury and Mars, but otherwise not particularly strong; nor is the ninth house altogether a desirable place for her. As with Daudet, Uranus has the square of Saturn; this aspect will here be taken to indicate the deep philosophical insight which permeates the realism in the works of both authors.

We shall now proceed to a consideration of the nativities of a pair of very clever and successful politicians, one born to ascend a throne and the other to own a screw factory; Edward VII and Joseph Chamberlain.

The late king of England has 28 degrees of Sagittarius rising, with Jupiter just touching the cusp of the Ascendant. Uranus is squared by the Ascendant, but has a trine of the Sun, while Jupiter has a sextile of Venus, all of which make for success. The subtlety and astuteness with which Edward engineered the Triple Entente and isolated Germany will long be remembered in history.

In the horoscope of Joseph Chamberlain, on the other hand, while we find indications of statesmanship we note that he changed his politics frequently, doubtless due to Uranus in the tenth, but did it so successfully, that, in spite of the distrust with which he was regarded by the more intellectual classes of his countrymen, he always managed to be on the side of the majority. Cancer is rising, with the Sun on the cusp of the second house, approaching a conjunction of Jupiter; Mercury is trine to Uranus and is exactly on the cusp of the Ascendant. From the whole figure, we see an extraordinary degree of concentration and political skill.

Our next pair, Jay Gould and the late J. Pierpont Morgan, should prove exceedingly instructive. Here the influence flows through a purely financial channel. Gould has Gemini rising with Mercury just below the cusp of the Ascendant, very strong in his own house, and with a trine of the Moon and Saturn. This is a very cold combination. There is no warmth from any source; the Sun himself is imprisoned in the twelfth house, and forms a square with Uranus. It is the very picture of a greedy, calculating, cold-blooded financier. Venus and Jupiter being in the second house turn the affections toward money, and assure its gain. The affliction of Uranus by the Sun in the tenth house shows that the financier could not escape the reprobation of his fellow men.

Morgan has Leo rising and its lord, the Sun, in close conjunction with Mercury, is exalted in Aries and is culminating, all of which renders him extremely powerful. Uranus is in trine to Saturn and opposed by the Moon. The personality is far finer and nobler than that of our last example, not nearly so concentrated upon pure gain and in no way inhibited from undertaking constructive work.

General Boulanger has Cancer rising with its lady, the Moon in Aquarius, within nine degrees of the conjunction of Uranus, which is on the cusp of the tenth house. Beyond a sextile of the Sun and Venus to the Ascendant (Cancer), and approaching semi-sextile of Neptune to the Moon and Uranus, but applying more to Uranus, there is no particular assistance to the Ascendant qualities. We find in fact, that it was the personality of the man which failed him, since at the critical moment he wavered and broke down. Contrast with him, the great Gambetta who has Scorpio rising and Mars in his own house, Aries, quite close to the conjunction of the Sun and Mercury. Saturn is rising within seven degrees of the trine to Mars. Uranus is in conjunction with Venus in her exaltation, but is opposed by Jupiter. The personality appears extraordinarily forceful, the temperament not markedly so. In fact his work was mainly that of rallying the French in the hour of their defeat, and idea which might have occurred to any patriot. The amazing energy and success with which he carried out his task are due to the great power of the Ascendant and the good aspects of its lord. It will be noted, of course, that the affliction of Uranus in the fourth house led to its logical manifestation upon the material plane, in his tragic death.

The last of our group is Robespierre. Here Aquarius is rising, Saturn just under the cusp of the Ascendant and Uranus a little below him. Saturn has the semi-sextile of Venus and the square of Mercury, which indicates a successful and plausible lawyer with a sense of reality, but no load of scruple sufficient to hinder his march toward power. Uranus squared by Jupiter receives only the doubtful assistance of a semi-sextile of the Moon; and, though Jupiter is in the tenth, in his own house, Sagittarius, trined by Mars, this cannot offset so powerful an affliction as that of Uranus, although it added executive force to the ambition. Here is a clinical picture of a cold, harsh, overbearing, ambitious, unscrupulous man, the only relief to which appears in the rising Venus, which is approaching a conjunction with Uranus; and this curiously reflects the contradictory strain of gentleness in his private home life. So, again, as in all the cases that we have been considering, we find the clearest possible witness of history through the truth of Astrology.

The following well known persons were born with Uranus in the sign Pisces:

Admiral Dewey
J. J. Hill
John B. Herreshoff
Joseph G. Cannon
Grover Cleveland
Sir Henry Irving
George F. Baker
John Burroughs
The late J. P. Morgan

For the benefit of those who are not in possession of Raphael's Ephemeris, or who are not able to interpret the symbols contained therein, the years when Uranus is in the sign Pisces are as follows:

From	February	11th	1836	through	April	18th	1843
	October	2nd	1843	"	February	9th	1844
	April	1st		"	August	16th	1919
	January	22nd	1920	"	March	30th	1927
	November	5th	1927	"	January	12th	1928

NEPTUNE SYMBOLICALLY CONSIDERED

The Mind of the Father said "Into Three!" and immediately all things were so divided.

This Oracle, attributed to Zoroaster, refers secondarily to the division of Nature into the three active elements of fire, air, and water. Earth is but a mixture of these three in divers proportions. In this division according to mythology, the kingdom of fire fell to Hades or Pluto, that of air to Zeus or Jupiter, and that of water to Poseidon or Neptune.

Neptune is therefore the lord of Ocean, and especially of that Oceanus the great river that girdles the whole earth. One is not wise to laugh, as the shallow laugh, at the supposed absurdities of old geography. The earth is not a flat plate, but the solar system is;

and on the rim of this plate is that lovely sphere, Neptune, the outpost of the fortress of the Sun. So that it was a most happy accident that this planet was called by the name of the Lord of Oceanus.

Such is the far-off base, in the wise and true dreamland of the philosophers, of the palace of our knowledge. Let us see how their strange symbols have been hints of truth, how from the root of poetry has grown the tree of prose.

First, consider Neptune as a lonely sentinel patrolling the confines of our camp. Think of the solitude and darkness of that mysterious and eternal journey, what thoughts must bloom. Mystic, austere, romantic, will they not be? What messenger comet may approach from utmost space? The spirit of adventure thrills the blood, frosted as it is by that contact with a space of icy nothingness, save (it may be) meteors and dark stars. Neptune is always starlit; at its distance from the Sun, our Father is hardly bigger than any other star. So Neptune gallops through a night always starlit, with his source of heat and motion too remote to cheer him, but with hope, faith, and love.

How spiritual, how star-pure, must then be the secret thoughts of such a one! The hermit of the solar system! How indomitable, how lonely, how refined must be his moods!

Yet there is something in solitude that sets men dreaming. Not always is that dream the starry aspiration of the Knight vowed to some inaccessible lady; often there steals through the faerie window a glint of some fantastic mirth. In lighter moments there is something of the Troubadour, and even of the Pierrot, in his melancholy, craving for the inaccessible. For it is not in the Neptunian nature to reach harbor. He longs for love and friendship; did he gain them, he would retire. For nothing can satisfy that thirst for things infinite; there is no goal attainable. Neptune is man's boundless spirit; heaven itself is too narrow for his desires. So, into his nature comes the fay coquettishness; he becomes conscious of his own anguish; and this is externalized as a love of masquerade. He knows that love is unattainable; and so he plays at love. He knows that happiness is beyond his reach; and so he seeks it by a violation of the limits of existence. His true nature, thrilled through by the wisdom of the stars, with whom he holds such raptured communings in the centuries of that tireless vigil, leads him to mystic trances, to visions of deity, to mysterious marriages with elements beyond our system. For he, the Ishmael of planets, never turns his face toward the Sun.

But if he is not steeled to endure exile, to attain the snowy summits of omniscience and bliss by the means of the wise eremite, then the false nature mocks the true. In revels fantastic and fond, in comedies bitter at the core, in the use of strange drugs or of perverse delights, in soulless and neurotic waking dreams, he seeks to satisfy his soul.

Ah, Neptune is the soul! And does not this fit the sea? Is not the sea at once infinitely calm and infinitely air-hungered? Does not the sea take strange shapes, break up the light into a myriad fantastically-colored flaws? Illusion, and art, chameleon and dragon, that is the sea! Is not the sea now tender and adorable, sun-kissed; now terrible in its torment, a whirl of insatiable desires? Did not Sappho fling herself into the sea, and did not Undine draw thence the bitter joy of her veins? Are not the seas' depths unstirred, unplumbed, and do they not harbor monsters more terrible than the fancy of antiquity ever invented? Ay! take the ocean of Ulysses and of Jason, of de Mandeville and of Swinburne; let the romance and the terror, the mystery and the unearthly joy of all the artists of the world direct your glance; look upon the sea through their eyes, and draw into your soul the wonder and the wantonness of it. Then understand how proper is the Ocean as an image of the soul, how proper is Neptune to be the ruler of the ocean. The soul!

Yes, there is the word! Neptune is the soul, with all its naked nerves played upon by rays of alien systems, malicious, capricious, faerie, or else like harp-strings swept by some Player from beyond, too subtle and too divine for His melodies to reach the ears of mortals.

Only that sympathy, that yearning, that other-worldliness, in ourselves, that influence of Neptune in our own horoscopes, enables us to catch a far-away echo of that lyre—faint, silvery music of the Psyche of our inmost beings.

NEPTUNE IN THE SIGNS

Not by accident are the planets named for the gods of Greek and Roman mythology. In early times the sea was not navigable in our modern sense. The voyage of Ulysses, from one end of the Mediterranean to the other, was considered worthy of celebration in the greatest poem transmitted to us from antiquity. To the Ancients, the sea, unknown and terrible, swarming with fabulous and appalling monsters, personified the Unknown; and the great river Oceanus which girdled the earth was to them bounded on the other side by the gloomy shores of Hades. The dwellers upon the coasts of Greece and Italy, however—many of them living in islands—knew the sea in its playful moods, as many gracious legends of Neptune attest.

They knew, too, its masquerade of still waters over cruel rock, the treachery of its whirlpool sucking into a vortex of destruction whatever ventured too near its outer sweep; they knew how currents are denied by surface tide; they had heard the "measurcless laughter of the loud sounding sea" and had been deafened by its storm, insatiable, murderous, pitiless.

And so the Ancients named that far, strange planet, which girdles the firmament as the salt sea girdles the earth, Neptune. Not by accident—but mindful of the ways of the sea—and of the symbolism of the god that rules the sea.

To arrive at the true valuation of Neptune's influence in the signs of the Zodiac and upon the native as he comes under the dominion of the signs, the reader must constantly bear in mind the peculiar nature of the planet as distinguished from other planets.

Whereas Mars, Jupiter, Venus, Mercury and Saturn exert their influences chiefly upon man in his mundane capacities, his evolutionary life, Neptune exerts a spiritual influence upon man in the midst of the latter's mundane existence, for Neptune is the planet of spiritual forces, of the revolutionary spirit itself.

Neptune's influence upon a life dominated wholly or chiefly by physical or materialistic interests is likely to be wholly bad or malefic, while this same influence, stressed upon a life already under a spiritual leading, will be wholly good or benefic.

It is the Neptune influence that gives the wings of vision to humanity in its long struggle out of darkness into the light of eternity.

Materialistic persons can think only in relative values of a day, a month, a year at most; intellectually developed persons think in values of a lifetime; but those of our sphere who are spiritually conscious think and work in terms of the eternal; to these a century is as a year, a cycle as a life; they are the true Neptunians. The materialistic astrologer classes Neptune "malefic, sinister, obscure," but the enlightened astrologian thoroughly understands that Neptune causes upon this earth and upon its natives the influx of a spiritual element unrelated to strictly earthly affairs. While the other planets are commensurable and deal with the relative, Neptune is incommensurable; he intrudes the absolute. In other words, for those developed spiritually Neptune is wholly "good," for others he seems wholly "bad." Neptune stirs the soul to aspiration toward the infinite; the result is that a humanitarian influence is projected by the native for the benefit of humanity's advance as a whole. On the other hand, for those whose desires cause them to plunge and wallow in the troughs of mere material delights and satisfactions, the Neptune influence is as a lightning bolt that shatters their temples of materialism to the very foundations.

Neptune's orbit, being the outer circle of our known universe, is so vast, the effect of his movement upon the earth is so slow, that we may best consider his influence as negative upon our physical life, and as positive upon our spiritual impulses. He is as an indication of the tendency of the period, the planet of the new era, a barometer of the latter-day Universe.

Neptune requires approximately fourteen years to move through a single sign. To give an account of his effects upon humanity would be to write the history of the world.

One can gauge him, to some extent, by considering certain events of comparatively recent times. Matters requiring wisdom are usually directed by men of between forty-five and fifty-five years, and the consensus of their influence may be divined from the place of Neptune at their birth.

Thus the Revolution of 1848 was brought about by men influenced by Neptune in Libra; they struggled for freedom and justice, but their policy lacked virility, while their methods failed because of indirectness. Similarly, the French Revolution was begun by people influenced by Neptune in Leo, but the generations of preparation toward that event involved people with that planet in Cancer or Gemini. Cromwell's Neptune was also in Leo.

The recent Great War was doubtless due to the influence of people born with Neptune in Aries; while the rebuilding of civilization has fallen upon those laborious and initiative men and women for whom Neptune works through Taurus and Gemini.

The scientific advance of the Nineteenth Century was due to pioneers stimulated by Neptune in Capricorn; and the fruits of their labors were gathered by men born with Neptune in Aquarius. Neptune was in Pisces, influencing the artistic, psychic decadent generation of the Nineties.

Times when skeptical thought attacks tradition by purely intellectual methods and makes constructive work possible are those influenced by Neptune in Gemini. Immanuel Kant, who destroyed the old philosophy, Voltaire, who destroyed the old religion, and their contemporaries were of such a generation.

Neptune, being the planet of spiritual forces, is always revolutionary. Forever he quickens the old life and increases the new life; the principle is the same; only the material varies according to the signs through which he moves.

Because of the character of Neptune and the long period of time it requires to pass through a single sign, its influence upon the individual is very dependent upon its position and aspect to other planets. It is, therefore, obviously unnecessary to go into a lengthy account of its effect upon the indivdual in the twelve signs.

NEPTUNE IN ARIES

People having Neptune in Aries are inclined to favor new religious and philosophical teachings; they have a great desire to teach humanity to aspire to higher ideals.

Aries is too militant, too martial, too efficient, temporal, and material for so purely spiritual a force as Neptune to express his vibrations sympathetically. His power lies more in revolution than in evolution, in the destruction of the wrong and the upheaval of the conservative. The position is spiritually radical and inclines the spiritual energies to be more dominantly mental and energetic than deep, emotional and cosmic. This is well illustrated by the religious diversity, as well as the theological skepticism, among the men and women of the Neptune in Aries generation. No two of them seem to hold the same ideas on any higher matters or on political or social matters. It has produced an age of diversity and unrest, not an age of cohesion and peace—an age in which more old dogmas are destroyed than new truths advanced.

When this planet is afflicted in Aries, it lends energy and independence to all its turbid forces for evil, while its mental quality adds initiative and a certain intelligence. It then tends to make one fanatical, Bolshevistic and revolutionary.

John Wesley, King George V, Mary, Queen of Scots, Benjamin Franklin, Cervantes, Samuel Johnson, Thomas Moore, Maeterlinck, Kipling, Yeats, Richard Strauss, Lord Northcliffe, Don Carlos of Portugal, Houdini, Charles H. Sabin, Alfred W. Smith, Ex-President Coolidge, are notable examples of people born with Neptune in Aries.

For the benefit of those who are not in possession of Raphael's Ephemeris, or who are not able to interpret the symbols contained therein, the years when Neptune is in the sign Aries are as follows:

From	April	16th	through	October	3rd 1861
	February	16th 1862	"	June	6th 1874
	October	1st 1874	"	April	6th 1875

NEPTUNE IN TAURUS

Those having Neptune in Taurus are emotional, responsive, and romantic. They are not dogmatic; and, while not irreligious, they are certainly not conspicuously ecclesiastical. They are well described by the generation born between 1876 and 1890. It has been a generation of builders, whose practical impulses have stood for solidity and endurance. Under it has come our great material development, our great buildings, our vast mechanical progress, our advance in industry and commerce.

On the other hand, the passage of Neptune through the signs of Venus, Taurus and Libra, seems to have attended most of the artistic and creative waves of time. The great Elizabethan period came during its passage through Taurus, though it did not reach its fulfillment until it entered Gemini, and a mental and linguistic urge had been added to the artistic and creative impulse.

When this planet is afflicted in Taurus, it inclines to sex perversion, chaotic emotions, illicit amours and lurid obsessions. Its malefic reactions are almost always of a sex nature when in a Venus sign.

Queen Wilhelmina of Holland, Christabel Pankhurst, Henry III, Samuel Adams, Francis Bacon, David Hume, Maria Theresa, Ex-Crown Prince of Germany, Sir Joshua Reynolds, Mussolini, Will Levington Comfort, are outstanding examples of persons born with Neptune in Taurus.

For the benefit of those who are not in possession of Raphael's Ephemeris, or who are not able to interpret the symbols contained therein, the years when Neptune is in the sign Taurus are as follows:

From	June	7th		through	September	30th	1874
	April	7th	1875	"	August	15th	1887
	September	22nd	1887	"	May	27th	1888
	December	28th	1888	"	March	21st	1889

NEPTUNE IN GEMINI

People who have Neptune in the sign Gemini have great capacity for intellectual brilliance, but also a tendency to mental chaos and diffusion. It adds inspiration, quickness of perception, breadth of vision, great versatility, and a tendency to study spiritualism. An afflicted Neptune in Gemini tends to cause absent-mindedness, restlessness and craftiness. It is necessary that those having Neptune in this sign, badly aspected, should concentrate on some constructive and definite line of thought and not indulge in morbid fears or obsessions.

Since Shakespeare had his Neptune in Gemini, it is quite possible that, in the figure of Hamlet, he painted a picture of his own inner nature and melancholic reactions. Hamlet, in his swiftness of mind, in his psychic, ghost-seeing power, in his broad observation and intellectual command, is a living picture of the finer inspirations and higher impulses of this Neptune position. Again, in his morbid brooding, in his chaotic imagination and neurotic emotion (if not actual madness), he is voicing Neptune in Gemini in its turbid, contradictory expression.

Proclus, John Adams, Catherine II of Russia, Voltaire, Kant, Shakespeare, George III, Mesmer, Moses, Mendelssohn, James Watt, Kepler, Galileo, Dean Cornwell, are some of the people of note who have Neptune in Gemini.

For the benefit of those who are not in possession of Raphael's Ephemeris, or who are not able to interpret the symbols contained therein, the years when Neptune is in the sign Gemini are as follows:

From	August	16th		through	September	21st	1887
	May	28th		"	December	27th	1888
	March	22nd	1889	"	July	19th	1901
	December	26th	1901	"	May	20th	1902

NEPTUNE IN CANCER

Those having Neptune in Cancer have a tendency to be too passive, too negative, too sympathetic and too affectionate. The position is not one conducive to greatness of action. There are far fewer great men all through history born with Neptune in Cancer than at any other period. It does not seem to empower the spiritual will in an expressive, positive manner. Rather it creates a susceptibility to impression and often psychic and mystical capacities.

Thus, Joan of Arc was born with this position, and it may explain, in part, the "voices" she heard; whereas the great astronomer Kepler, who, unlike so many merely mathematical and narrowly focused astronomers of recent years, knew and practised astrology as well.

A malefic Neptune in this position is necessarily particularly evil, causing those having it to be melancholy, conceited and self-indulgent. They must avoid being too romantic or giving way to self-pity.

Cardinal Richelieu, Wallenstein, Joan of Arc, Hannah Moore, Du Barry, Robert Peel, Goethe, are notable examples of people having Neptune in the sign Cancer.

For the benefit of those who are not in possession of Raphael's

Ephemeris, or who are not able to interpret the symbols contained therein, the years when Neptune is in the sign Cancer are as follows:

From July	20th		through	December 25th	1901
May	21st	1902	"	September 22nd	1914
December	15th	1914	"	July 18th	1915
March	20th		"	May 1st	1916

NEPTUNE IN LEO

Persons who were born with Neptune in the sign Leo are inclined to be moral, spiritually-minded, sociable and kind-hearted. Such persons will have power through their emotions and sympathies rather than through the intellect. Thus we find that most of the "Fathers of our Country," some signers of the Declaration of Independence, and many of the soldiers of the American Revolution were men with Neptune in this position. Indeed, we might almost maintain that we of America owe our very existence to this practical force and sound rationality, for Christopher Columbus also had this position, and it had much to do with his sane and sure determination to make good Galileo's theories.

The general influence of Neptune in Leo is to give a firm and commanding edge to the inner forces of the will, to make it less psychic, less typically spiritual, more concrete and materially practical.

The majority of the Neptune and Leo people turn their spiritual impulses to tangible things; thus Hahnemann founded homeopathy, McAdam constructed roads, Cromwell fought revolutionary battles, built and commanded a Protectorate, Robespierre cut off heads until his own followed suit. Indeed, the rank and file of the leaders of the French Revolution were men with Neptune in Leo—even as were the soldiers of our own Revolution, while the formation of the English Revolution was also due to men with Neptune in Leo. The same was true of those who fought in Italy in the days of Dante's banishment. It is a distinctly aggressive, commanding, radical and revolutionary position.

An afflicted Neptune in Leo makes for sensuality, cowardliness, tyranny and egotism.

Robespierre, Dante, Charles I, Marie Antoinette, William Blake, Thomas Chatterton, Aaron Burr, Nathan Hale, Cromwell, Columbus, Mozart, McAdam, Louis XVI, Hahnemann, Pope Alexander VI, are some of the people of note having Neptune in this sign.

For the benefit of those who are not in possession of Raphael's Ephemeris, or who are not able to interpret the symbols contained therein, the years when Neptune is in the sign Leo are as follows:

From	September 23rd		through	December	14th	1914
	July	19th 1915	"	March	19th	1916
	May	2nd 1916	"	September	20th	1928
	February	20th	"	July	23rd	1929

NEPTUNE IN VIRGO

THOSE having Neptune in Virgo have a tense, almost occult, critical power and ability to visualize and measure accurately events, substances and forces not then before the physical eye. This clairvoyant materialism is a tremendously active force in strong nativities; it gives the man almost uncanny knowledge of material events.

This was the major power of Napoleon's mind; he had this position of Neptune. It endowed him with marvelous physical foresight and an almost psychic knowledge of men and events. It gave him, as well, a practical, sound, law-giving wisdom, out of which grew some of the most potent forces of France. Yet, because of this very power of occult materialism and lack of spiritual vision, he doubtless met his downfall. He lost that higher guidance which alone gives enduring success and enduring wisdom.

Neptune in Virgo is a good position for the artist and scientist, since it gives such wonderful penetration into matter. Thus Humbolt and Humphrey Davy, owe much of their keen, rational perception to this position, while J. M. W. Turner, Coleridge and Beethoven are exemplifications of its power in the arts.

An afflicted Neptune in Virgo gives a cunning will, and lack of conscience and makes one destructively critical.

Alexander I of Russia, Humboldt, John Quincy Adams, Bolivar, Jane Austen, Beethoven, Humphrey Davy, Lord Brougham, Napoleon, Turner, Coleridge and Wordsworth, are all examples of persons of note who had Neptune in this position.

For the benefit of those who are not in possession of Raphael's Ephemeris, or who are not able to interpret the symbols contained therein, the years when Neptune is in the sign Virgo are as follows:

From	September 21st 1928	through	February 19th	1929
	July 24th 1929	"	November	1941
	February	"	September	1942
	June	"	July	1943

NEPTUNE IN LIBRA

Those having Neptune in the sign Libra are idealistic, humanitarian and with strong convictions of the rights and the welfare of mankind. It is a position of high purposes and fine spiritual ideals. This position of Neptune gives an impulse to creative idealism in art, music, literature, philosophy and social reform, rather than in the accomplishment of physical, political and mechanical advancement. The whole impetus of the great Italian Renaissance came during the passage of Neptune in Libra, while at a later period the wave of English art and poetry followed its passage through this same tabernacle of Venus.

In general, this position inclines to a genuine, but often uncertain and at times impractical idealism. The poet Shelley is an excellent illustration of this urge of altruism. So, too, is Byron in greater degree, and with them the whole of their school. Out of the observations and teachings of the men in Libra grew the Revolution of 1848, but their example lacks the passionate certainty of Neptune in Leo or the critical sagacity of Neptune in Virgo.

An afflicted Neptune in Libra lacks will power and practicality, and it inclines to sex perversions.

Rossini, Byron, Shelley, De Quincey, Cooper, Picus de Mirandola, David Wilkie, Haydn, Tom Moore, Maria Louisa, Buchanan, Daniel Webster, are outstanding examples of those having Neptune in Libra.

For the benefit of those who are not in possession of Raphael's

Ephemeris, or who are not able to interpret the symbols contained therein, the years when Neptune is in the sign Libra are as follows:

From	December	1941	through	January	1942
	October	1942	"	May	1943
	August	1943	"	December	1955
	March		"	October	1956
	May		"	August	1957

NEPTUNE IN SCORPIO

People who have Neptune in Scorpio are in danger of being too critical, skeptical and sarcastic. It is a distinctly malefic, reactive and materialistic position for this planet. It tends to exert a destructive influence in the lives of those having it so placed. A power so spiritual as Neptune finds scant opportunity for expression in so militant, physical and harsh a sign as Scorpio.

Thus, although we find major minds with Neptune in this position, we find few that are free from a strong hint of perversity. Even Michael Angelo, majestic figure that he was, was no angel; he possessed strong material passions, a proud, almost arrogant will, and a fierce temper. Yet were his energy, determination and courage those of a Hercules—endowments in which this position of Neptune played no small part.

In general, we must remember that those born with Neptune in Scorpio have never been born save in a time of war, pestilence and unrest. Peace seems not to attend the passage of Neptune through the scorpion. Thus, while the mature generals who assisted Napoleon and Wellington were men with Neptune in Leo or Virgo, the young soldiers who composed the bulk of their armies were men with Neptune in Scorpio.

When Neptune in Scorpio is afflicted, it arouses the vilest impulses, obsessions and neurotic perversions that man is heir to. During the last passage of Neptune through Scorpio, so many criminals of a brutal fierceness were at large that England maintained a regular series of criminal ships to Australia, while France built up the African provinces in the same way.

Joseph Smith, Brigham Young, Disraeli, George Sand, Michael Angelo, Victor Hugo, Dürer, Dumas, Sir William Hamilton, Copernicus, Cæsar Borgia, Thiers, Keats, Macaulay, Balzac, Lord Lytton, Emerson, Carlyle, John Brown, are notable examples of those having Neptune in Scorpio.

Obviously from the list of famous figures, the position of this planet in Scorpio is one of power.

For the benefit of those who are not in possession of Raphael's Ephemeris, or who are not able to interpret the symbols contained therein, the years when Neptune is in the sign Scorpio are as follows:

From	January		through	February	1956
	November	1956	"	April	1957
	September	1957	"	December	1970
	July		"	October	1971

NEPTUNE IN SAGITTARIUS

Those having Neptune in Sagittarius enjoy all the finer inspirational forces of Neptune, and are humanitarian and altruistic. All of these forces of Neptune are brought out by this position. Abraham Lincoln is a perfect picture of the high, spiritual and humane nature produced by Neptune in Sagittarius. His deep sincerity, his high purposes and broad spiritual vision, his wealth of brotherly love, together with a consuming desire for liberty and truth, may be in part attributed to Neptune in this sign.

The position is thus primarily one of spiritual and altruistic force, yet it endows with such power of conception and originality of vision that intellectual command is the result. The intellect, however, is not the critical intellect of Virgo, neither is it the acid intellect of Scorpio. It is rather that mental sweep which must inevitably follow consuming idealism and broad vision. Lincoln's speech at Gettysburg is not the painstaking product of a close, analytical or exact, scholastic mind. It is the result of compassionate feeling and dynamic inspiration from his overflowing heart and high spiritual impulse.

Thus, Neptune in Sagittarius, while its emphasis is upon the ideal and the humane, has also produced major minds of great philosophic and scientific penetration, creative geniuses and religious leaders whose force has changed civilization.

Even when Neptune in Sagittarius is afflicted, it is yet capable of little evil influence.

Abraham Lincoln, Walt Whitman, Tennyson, Bryant, Oliver Wendell Holmes, Whittier, Longfellow, Browning, Lowell, Poe, Dickens, Ruskin, George Eliot, De Musset, Wagner, Louis Agassiz, Chopin, Schumann, Isaac Newton, Pitman, Bismarck, Gladstone, Queen Victoria, Levi Morton, Stephen Douglas, Cornelius Agrippa, William Penn, Martin Luther, Sir Richard Quain, Nell Gwyn, Mendelssohn, are noteworthy examples of those having Neptune in this sign.

For the benefit of those who are not in possession of Raphael's Ephemeris, or who are not able to interpret the symbols contained therein, the years when Neptune is in the sign Sagittarius are as follows:

From	January		through	June	1971
	November	1971	"	February	1984
	June		"	December	1984
	September		"	October	1985

NEPTUNE IN CAPRICORN

People having Neptune in the sign Capricorn have painstaking exactness and comprehensive thoroughness, but they lack idealism or inspiration. The cold, practical, conservative qualities of Capricorn do not lend themselves well to the spiritual and impressionable planet Neptune. Neptune, when in Capricorn, gives an almost clairvoyant materialism, a penetrating perception into matter that, in strong nativities or when well aspected, is nothing short of brilliance.

There is no position more capable of producing great scientific minds in the realms of chemistry, physics, medicine, surgery, mechanics and the other material sciences. The comprehensive thoroughness, the painstaking exactness, the patient depth to the will is almost Herculean in its power. Such minds cannot see, beyond the matter, the realm of substance which, in itself, they see so thoroughly. They can picture nothing which the physical eye has not beheld and the material hand has not touched. Their souls usually lack the mystic sense. Intuition is, to most of them, impossible, and inspiration is a thing beyond their comprehension. God is more commonly in this vernacular an "essence" of utterly impersonal power, and man the mere evolution of a tadpole. Such is the basic impulse of this type of man, which, unless modified by some dominant aspects of Jupiter and the Sun, comes out in a vision of astounding limitations. When benefically aspected, this position may be considerably improved, particularly by aspects from Jupiter.

When malefically aspected in Capricorn, however, no power in a nativity will successfully save it from some degree of reaction and evil. Indeed, unless there are really tremendous forces to balance this weight of evil, criminal tendencies, blatant materialism, sullen will obsessions, perversions, will result. There is no more degrading force in a nativity than a truly malefic Neptune in Capricorn.

Huxley, Herbert Spencer, Lord Roberts, Pasteur, Cardinal Wolsey, Max Muller, Tolstoi, Garfield, Lewis Carroll, Earl of Strafford, Maximilian of Mexico, Franz Josef, Paul Kruger, Rossetti, Rosa Bonheur, Richard Burton, are notable examples of people having Neptune in this sign. It is worthy of note that many of the famous people having this position of Neptune have transcended it.

For the benefit of those who are not in possession of Raphael's Ephemeris, or who are not able to interpret the symbols contained therein, the years when Neptune is in the sign Capricorn are as follows:

From	March		through	May	1984
	January		"	August	1985
	November	1985	"	March	1998
	August	1998	"	January	1999

NEPTUNE IN AQUARIUS

Those who are born with Neptune in Aquarius have spiritual courage, idealism and vision. It was this force which, more than any other, endowed the boys of the Civil War with their flame of high bravery and transcendent spirits. It gives that power which Emerson voices perfectly:

> "So nigh is grandeur to our dust,
> So near is God to man,
> When duty whispers, 'Lo, thou must,'
> The youth replies 'I can.' "

This majestic force, so readily replying "I can," is the flame of conscience from Neptune in Aquarius.

This impulse of Neptune in Aquarius has had much to do with the practical fulfillment of the research of modern science. Indeed, we owe to this position our major advances of the last century—the practical development of steam, of electricity, of invention, and of mechanics in general.

This fine force had also much to do with endowing the leaders of the last French Revolution and the man who followed it. Gambetta had this position of Neptune. So, too, had Felix Faure and Sadi Carnot, and, curiously enough, that grand old figure who not only took part in the revolution which made France a republic, but lived to save her later in the Great War—Clémenceau, had this same position of Neptune. Indeed, since Neptune left Aquarius, it has no position endowing an equal force to the spiritual will—giving an equal idealism. Thus France owes much, not only to Clémenceau, but to his Aquarian inspiration and higher vision.

When malefically aspected in this position, the effect is more destinal than psychological, for the effects on character are not marked.

Thomas Hardy, Camille Flammarion, Ex-President Faure, Henry Irving, Wilson Barrett, Gambetta, Du Maurier, (the elder), Edison, Cleveland, Edward VII, J. J. Hill, Frances Willard, Bliss Carman, Carmen Sylva, Watteau, Catherine I of Russia, Jay Gould, J. P. Morgan, (the elder), Zola, Swinburne, Bret Harte, Carnot, Madame Patti, Cardinal Gibbons, John D. Rockefeller, Sr., Andrew Carnegie, Wm. H. Crane, Carl Henry Andrew Bjerregaard are examples of those having Neptune in Aquarius.

For the benefit of those who are not in possession of Raphael's Ephemeris, or who are not able to interpret the symbols contained therein, the years when Neptune is in the sign Aquarius are as follows:

From January	1st 1840	through	April	27th 1847
July	7th 1847	"	February	15th 1848
November	7th	"	November	18th 1848

NEPTUNE IN PISCES

PEOPLE who have Neptune in Pisces are psychic in the extreme, over-modest and reserved. As Neptune is the ruler of Pisces, it is the most propitious position which this planet can hold. Pisces is a distinctly passive sign, and this is a completely passive position for Neptune. Pisces is also not a sign of great active strength and assertive power; its forces are more negative, receptive, reflectively benefic.

Thus, while in its own sign, Neptune does not possess nearly so much power to affect the material plane as in either more active or more material signs. In fact, the very spirituality of the planet and the very psychic passivity of the sign inevitably do not make for strength of manifestation on a physical earth. Thus, as the materialistic Scorpio is the most powerful position of Neptune and the spiritual Sagittarius its next in force, so, the material Capricorn being the weakest position, the psychic Pisces is its next in weakness, viewed from a material standpoint. Otherwise, Pisces might be considered the most powerful position of Neptune.

In the individual nativity, this position of Neptune in Pisces does not, as a rule, make for singularly dynamic impulses of high, altruistic quality. Most people are too materially active for this passive, psychic force to exert its influence. Unlike the position in Sagittarius, so strongly active, this position has little effect upon the average man, while it may lend force to the extraordinary man.

A malefic Neptune in Pisces gives a craving for narcotics and strong liquor.

Professor Hyslop, W. T. Stead, Hodgson, Steiner, Lodge, Lily Langtry, Ellen Terry, General Booth, Marie Bashkirtseff, Mrs. Pankhurst, Havelock Ellis, George Bernard Shaw, Woodrow Wilson, Dr. Quackenbos, Robert Louis Stevenson, Dreyfus, John

Burns, Marshall P. Wilder, Oscar Wilde, de Maupassant, Ex-President Taft, Jane Addams, Lord Leverhulme, Queen Elizabeth, Handel, Charles Frohman, Woolworth, Emperor Wilhelm II, Theodore Roosevelt, Nordica, Asquith, Cecil Rhodes, Swedenborg, Balfour, Bryan, Seth Low, Elbert Hubbard, Andrew Mellon, Emile Coué, Clarence Darrow, John Drew, are noteworthy examples of those who have Neptune in Pisces.

For the benefit of those who are not in possession of Raphael's Ephemeris, or who are not able to interpret the symbols contained therein, the years when Neptune is in the sign Pisces are as follows:

From	April	28th		through	July	6th	1847
	February	16th		"	November	6th	1848
	November	19th	1848	"	April	15th	1861
	October	4th	1861	"	February	15th	1862

DISEASES OF NEPTUNE

Neptune causes diseases which come as the result of worry, and all illnesses of an insidious and wasting character. A general weakness and irritability of disposition may manifest itself in hysteria. Painful and intractable, though not dangerous, disorders may be the source of much discomfort. Those born strongly under Neptune should abstain from reading books on materia medica, as they are so susceptible to suggestion as to imagine that they evidence symptoms of every disease they read about. They should avoid dwelling on their ills, real or imaginary, and not form the habit of dosing themselves or taking patent medicines.

Neptune rules "the pineal glands, spinal cord, nerve fibre, telepathic and psychometric functions, those parts of the body which respond directly to superphysical impulses, as the chakras . . . occult action, Kundalini function, motion of chakras, flow of auric emanations."

Neptune causes "obscure diseases, such as comas, catalepsy, obsession, æsthetic ecstasy, somnambulism, hypochondriacism, trances, poison, drug habits.

"The misuse of mental and physical energies lays the native open to obsessions and diseases due to dabbling with occult forces."

Neptune is so intangible in its effects on the health that it is difficult to state with any degree of definiteness just what the effect will be in the twelve signs. The disorders caused by Neptune are mainly due to depleted nerves or psychic disturbances; the latter may be induced by inharmonious surroundings or uncongenial companions. It manifests itself in hysteria, nervous tumors and mental obsessions.

Obviously, when Neptune is in Aries, myopia, neuralgic headaches and exaggerated fears and false conceptions may result.

When in Taurus, irritation in the throat and nervous swellings of that organ may be suffered, as well as threat of goitre.

In Gemini, nervous coughs which may be an indication of a run-down nervous condition, could, if neglected, sometimes lead to tuberculosis.

When in Cancer, psychic indigestion is possible and a craving for narcotics and stimulants will be a danger to be avoided.

In Leo, nervous action of the heart, frequently incorrectly diagnosed as valvular, may be manifest.

In Virgo, psychic disturbances affecting the intestines, such as "colicky" pains and sensations which might suggest adhesions or even appendicitis, might be aggravated. These could be induced through the imagination or because they were suggested by the mind of another.

When in Libra there may be danger of hysteria, affecting the ovaries in a woman and the kidneys in both men and women, which may be caused by suppression or over-indulgence of sex, as well as sex perversions.

In Scorpio, nervous tumors, false conception and all irregularities of the sex organs may be caused by allowing the mind to dwell on sex pleasures.

When Neptune is in Sagittarius disturbances of the nervous system, resulting from religious mania and the abuse of the prophetic faculty, may be manifest.

When in Capricorn, there may be danger of melancholia, suicidal tendencies frequently caused by imaginary persecution or fear of being kidnapped, murdered etc.

In Aquarius, nervous toothache may result from fear of having teeth extracted, also there may be irritation of the skin and creepy sensations of the flesh.

When this planet is in Pisces, there may be itching or twitching of the feet, and general nervous debility which may be caused by lack of self-control and too great indulgence in the sensual emotions.

The eminent London surgeon, Dr. Schofield, in describing the various illnesses of a nervous or imaginary character, which baffle the most clever diagnosticians, states that a woman will frequently have all the symptoms of a tumor, with its attendant enlargement of the body, and still maintain the illusion, after an operation has been performed, unless the physician can substitute something which he has procured at a butcher shop to show her after she comes out of the anesthesia. These are the types of ailments which are of a strongly Neptunian nature and obviously the products of the imagination. He concludes by saying: "When a person is so ill as to be ill when he is not ill, he is very ill indeed."

THE PROBLEM OF DEATH

Astrologers have often been reproached with their comparatively frequent failures to predict the time of death. The reason has never been made clear; for the problem has never been properly understood.

Let us first consider how it has been treated. For example, the astrologer has looked at the Sun, or the Moon in the case of a woman, and at the eighth house, and the Lord of that house. From the radical afflictions of these, and from their afflictions by direction or transit, he has formulated his judgment.

Now the reason of his error is a fundamental one. Except in the case of violent death, by accident, suicide or assassination, death is not a single isolated phenomenon but the culmination and climax of a long series of phenomena. When St. Paul said "I die daily," he was speaking literal truth. All life involves metabolism, and the asymptote of the metabolic curve is called death. Death is the physiological goal; and pathology is only the history of short cuts upon the path.

Now when a child is born into the world, its hold on life is of the weakest. Very small accidents can cut short that life; and so frequently does this occur that until recently infant mortality was the standing shame of our race. But as a child grows, if it is healthy, this grip of life increases daily. It is well known what extremities of exposure, hunger and other trials may be endured by a strong man without the slightest permanent injury. Even self-inflicted wounds such as the drink and drug habits are borne by many for years before any visible damage to the physical constitution becomes apparent. In old age this hold again weakens, and is ultimately so tenuous that the cord snaps at an almost imperceptible strain.

The astrologers of the past have unaccountably neglected to make these considerations, obvious as they are. It is not the fault of the science. So slight a matter as the opposition of Mercury to the Moon may kill a girl baby outright; so serious an affair as the transit of Uranus over the Sun may leave the native apparently untouched. It is obvious that Mars either passes over the radical Sun, or squares him, or opposes him several times in every year. And what with the other malefics, and directions, and so on, one might well exclaim: "In the midst of life we are in death." Some of these attacks will be weak through being far out of parallel aspect; others will be mitigated by counterbalancing good aspects; but on the whole one may say that such caveats can only be entered against about one-half of the threats of life. It is moderate to say that, on the old astrological theories, it is a very good year when the native might not die at least three times. There is certainly never any difficulty in discovering why he did die after he is comfortably buried.

Then why are these aspects inoperative? How is it that a man can survive a series of bad afflictions to succumb later to a trifle? The answer is, first, that it depends on his general vitality, and, second, we deny the fact. Death itself does not occur visibly; but something in the nature of death may occur invisibly and insensibly in the organism. Who can say what is the true birth-hour of a cancer or diabetes? At what moment does that first degenerative change in the supra-renal capsules take place which is recognized much later, and always too late, as Addison's disease?

Such diseases, and there are very many such, have no symptoms discoverable (in the present state of medical knowledge) until the mischief is done. Here, then, astrology may render priceless service to the native. It can warn him of the time of the threat and its nature, so that at that particular time he may take some special precaution. The weak part of the body is indicated by the sign involved, and the type of disease threatened by the planet which menaces the mischief. The native can therefore take measures to obviate the peculiar risk to which his attention is thus drawn.

Forewarned is forearmed nowhere more than in astrology. The proper degree and quality of mental and moral action can take a most evil aspect and transmute its action, transform its character, and deflect its issue to a plane where all things visibly and unmistakably "work together for good to them that love God, and are called according to His purpose."

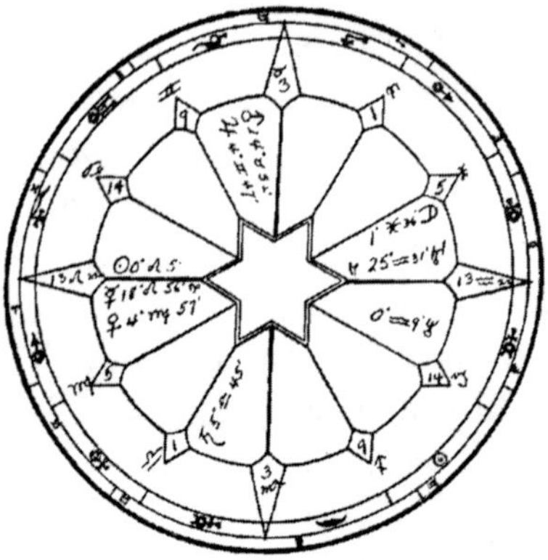

CARDINAL GIBBONS

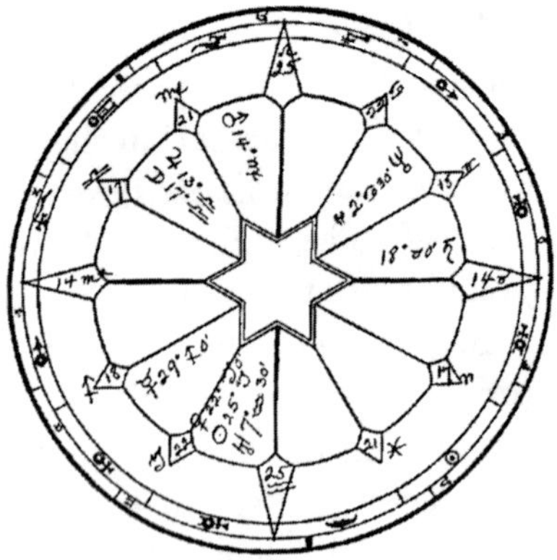

JOAN OF ARC

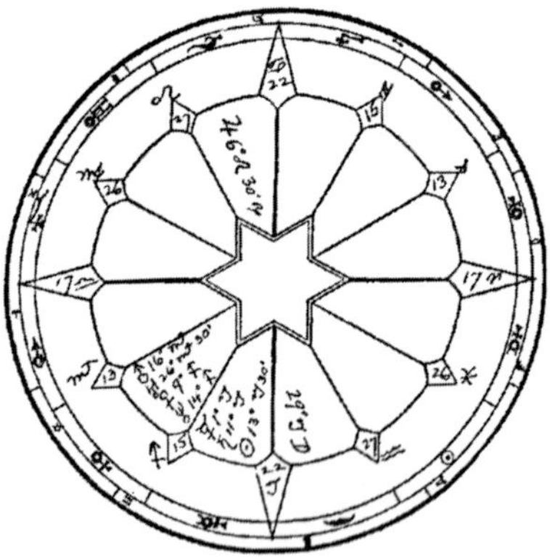

SIR ISAAC PITMAN

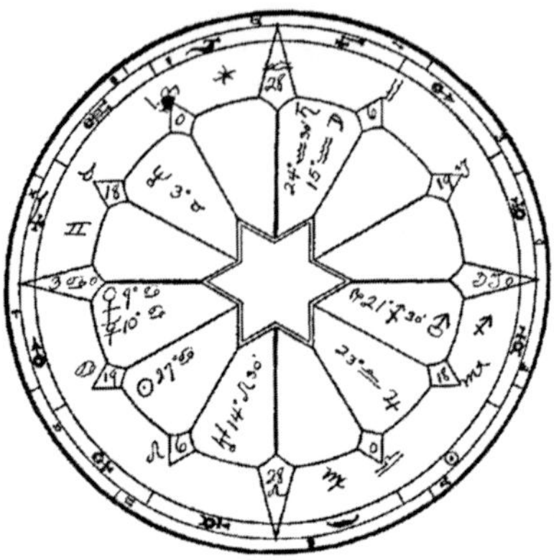

"DATAS" THE HUMAN ENCYCLOPAEDIA

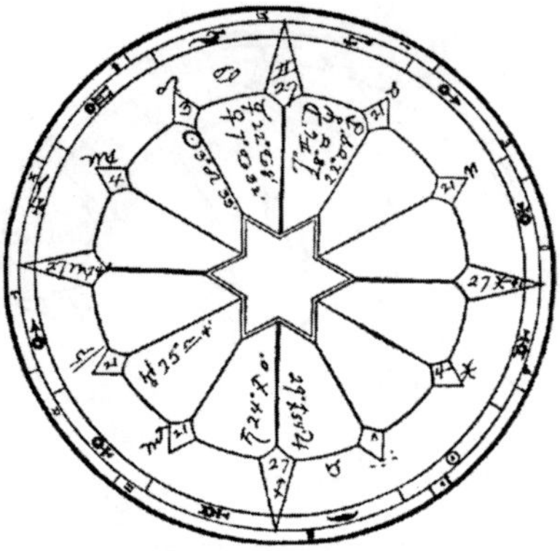

SIR JOSHUA REYNOLDS

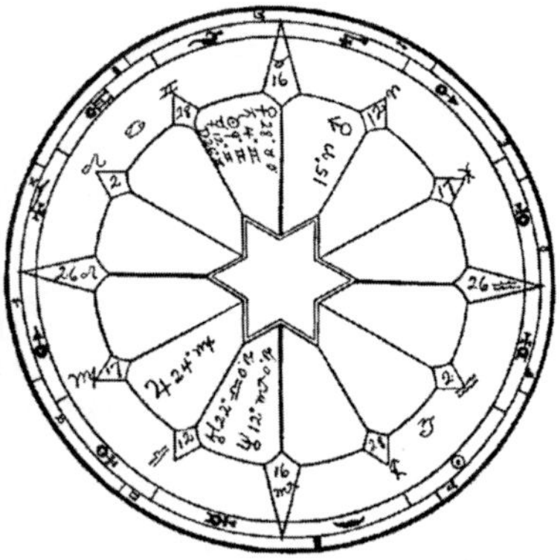

ALBRECHT DÜRER

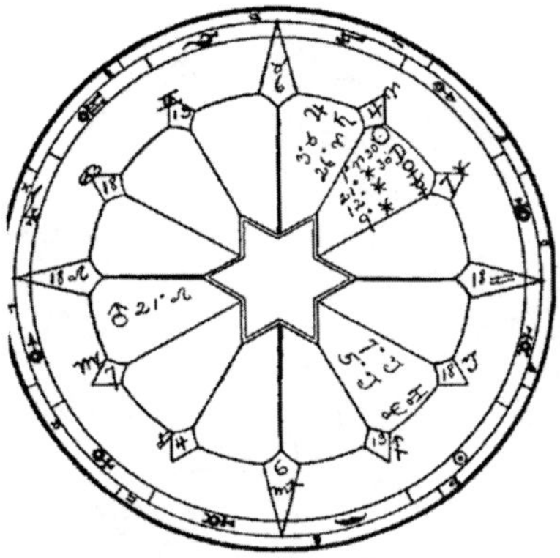

ROSA BONHEUR

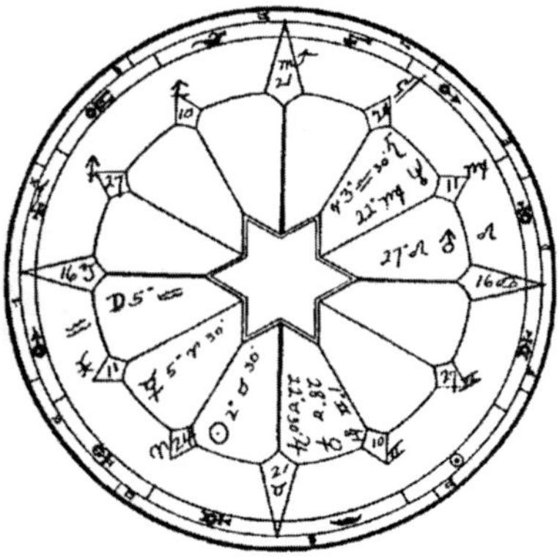

J. M. W. TURNER

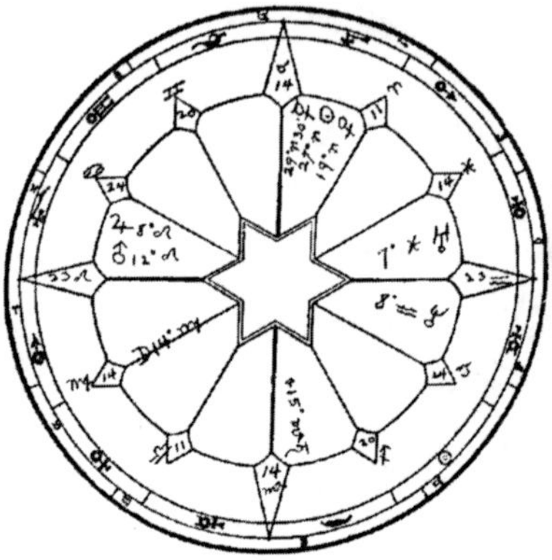

THE LATE J. P. MORGAN

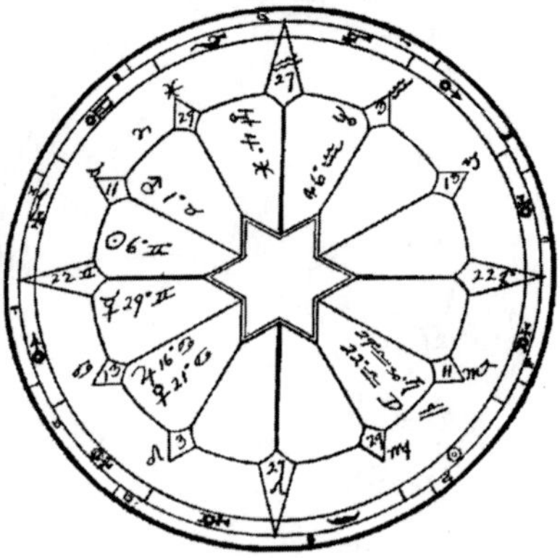

JAY GOULD

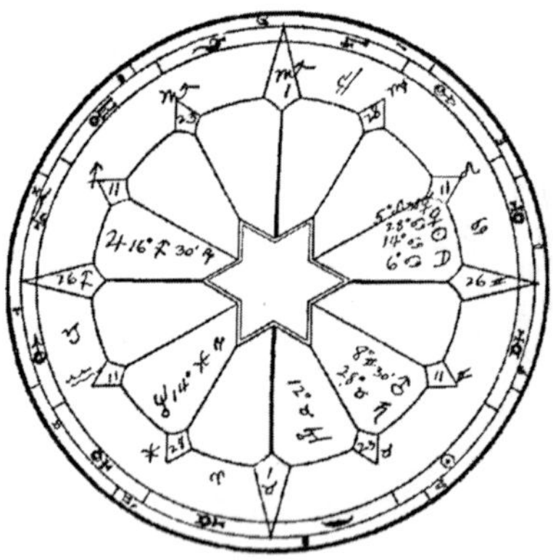

CECIL RHODES

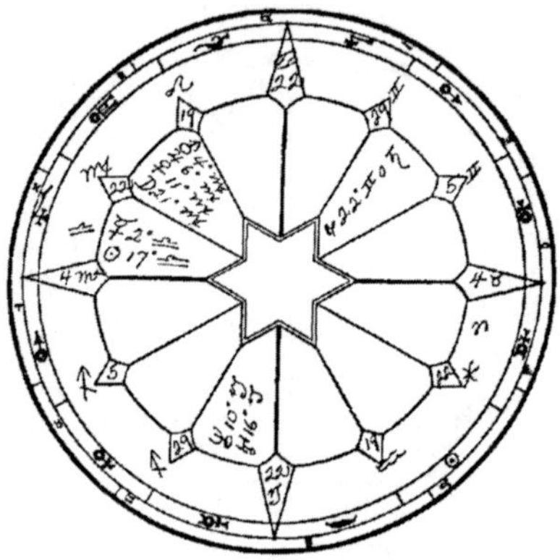

PAUL KRUGER

WILLIAM E. GLADSTONE

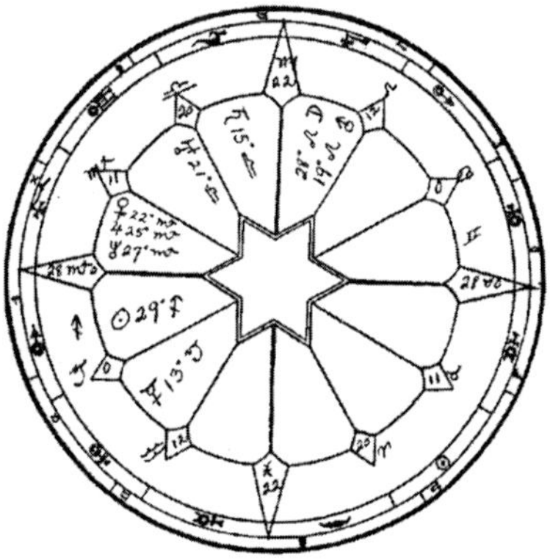

BENJAMIN DISRAELI (LORD BEACONSFIELD)

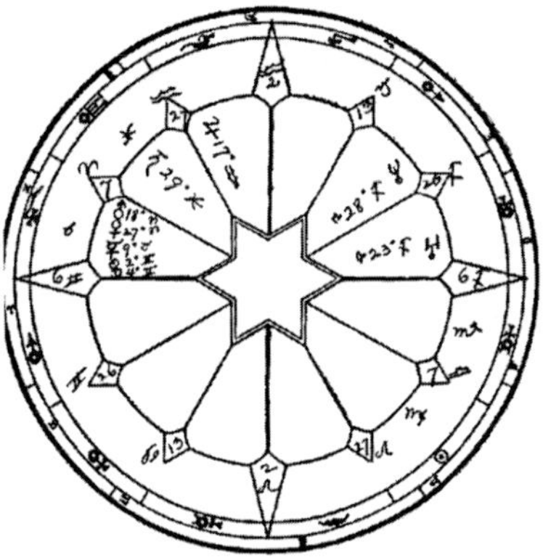

QUEEN VICTORIA

EDWARD VII OF ENGLAND

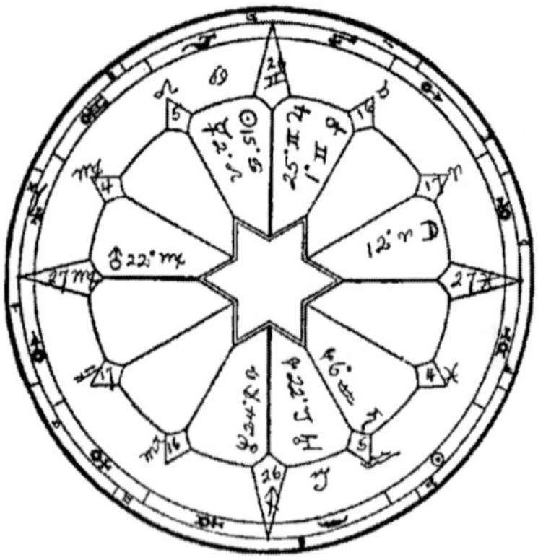

HENRY VIII OF ENGLAND

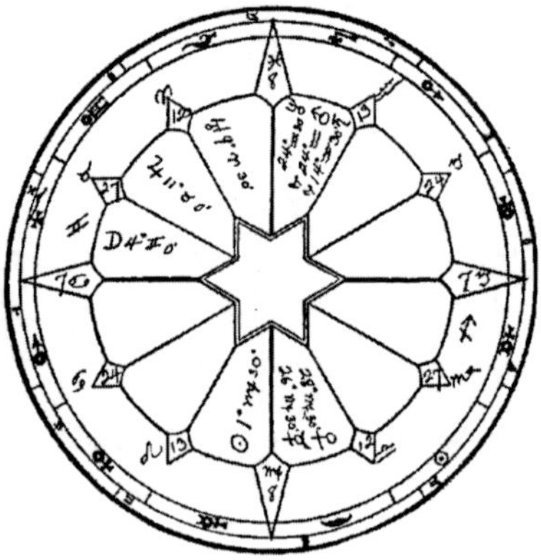

KING LUDWIG OF BAVARIA

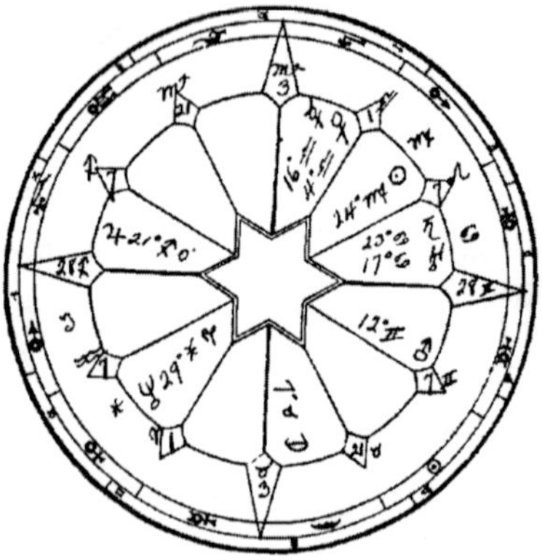

QUEEN ELIZABETH

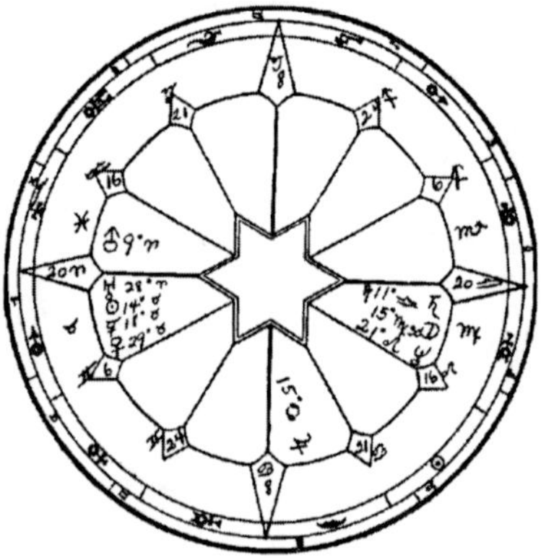

OLIVER CROMWELL

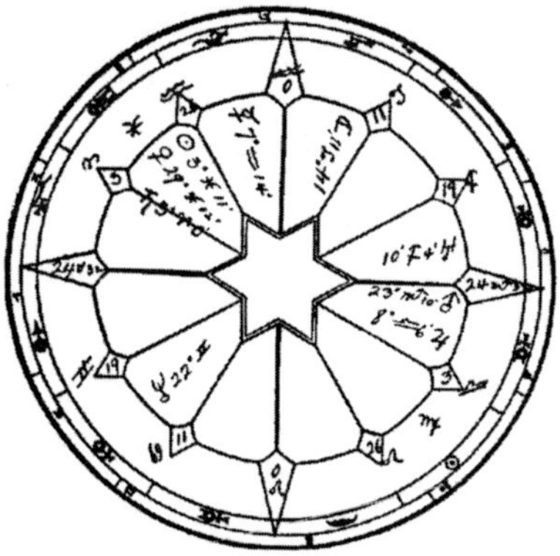

GEORGE WASHINGTON

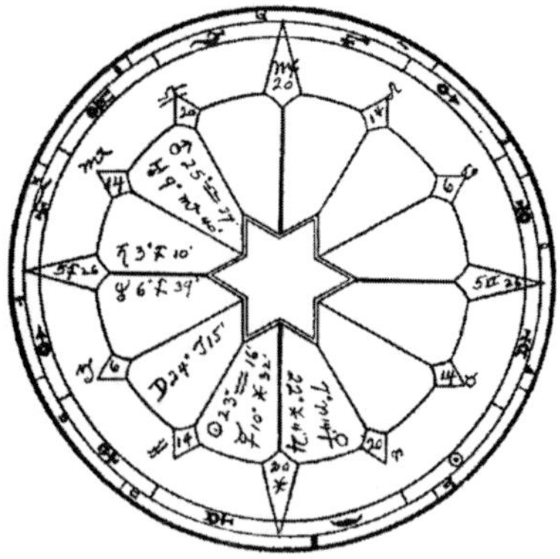

ABRAHAM LINCOLN

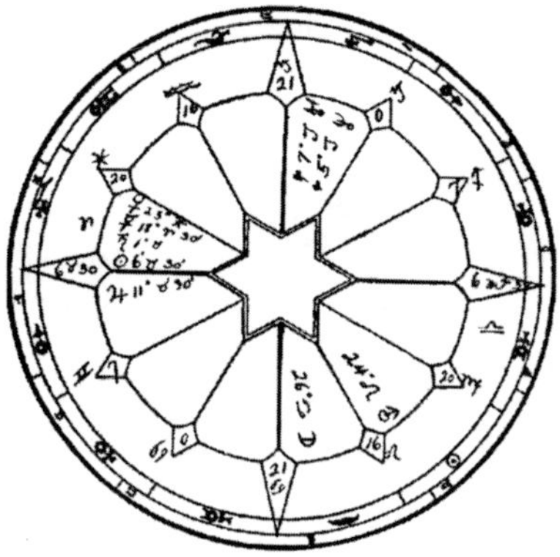

U. S. GRANT

JAMES A. GARFIELD

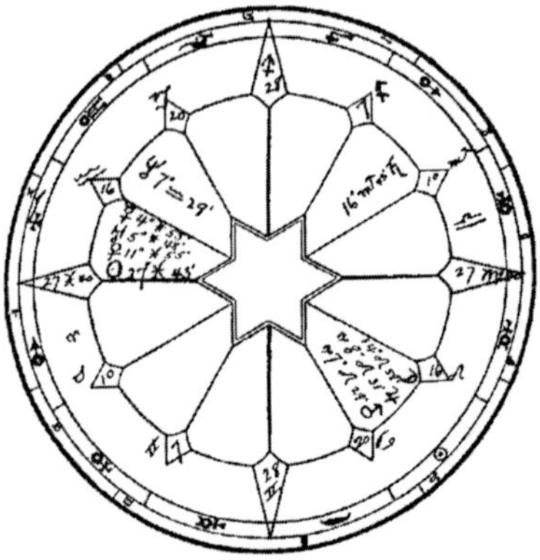

GROVER CLEVELAND

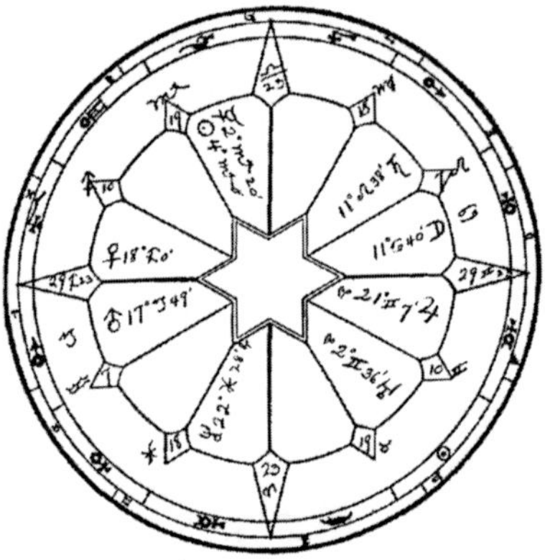

THEODORE ROOSEVELT

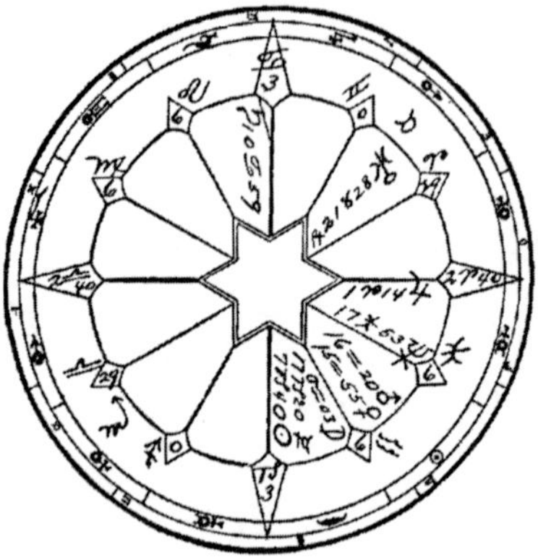

WOODROW WILSON

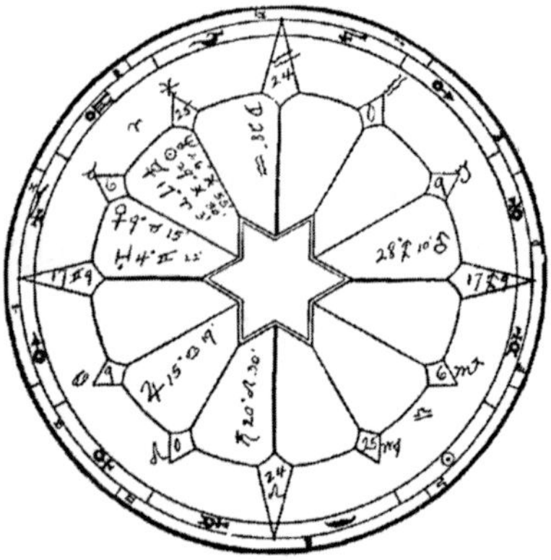

WILLIAM JENNINGS BRYAN

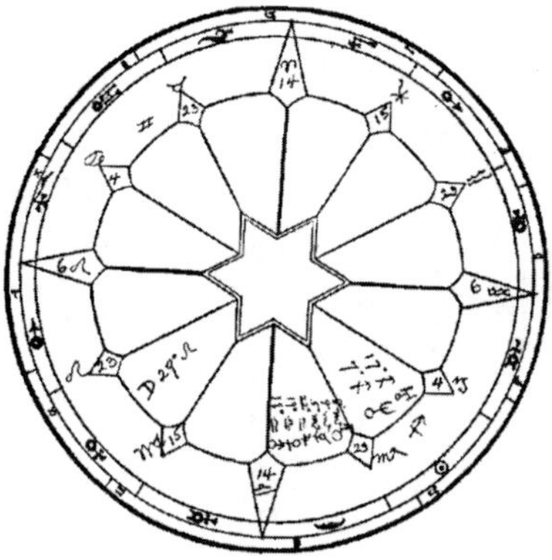

MARTIN LUTHER

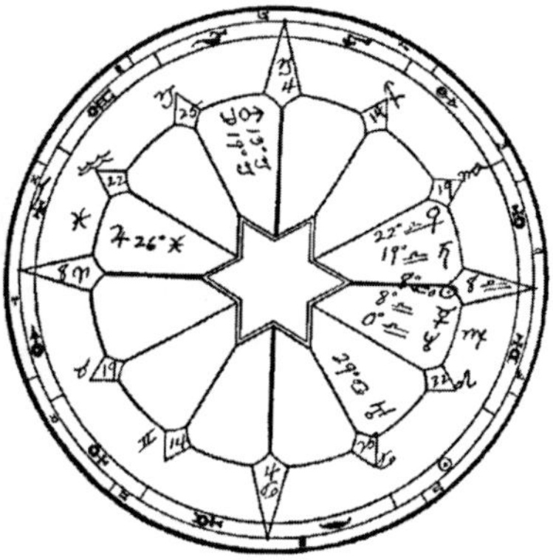

SAVONAROLA

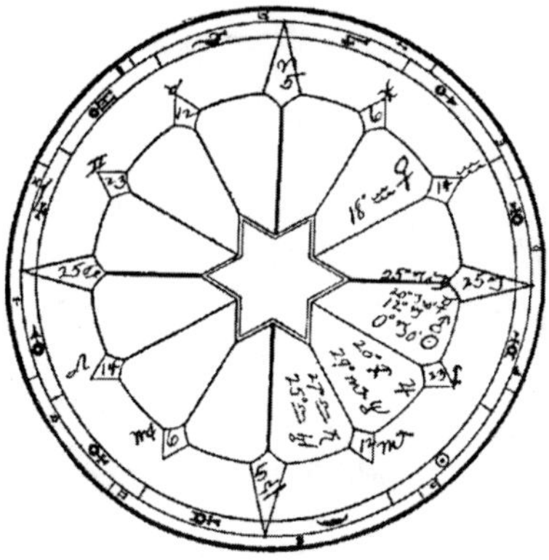

JOSEPH SMITH

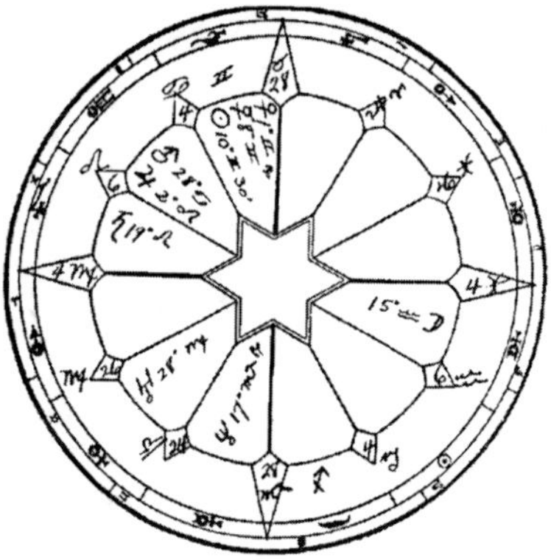

BRIGHAM YOUNG

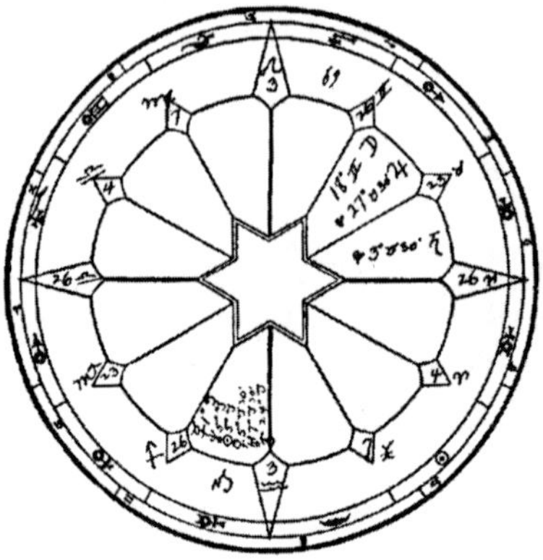

LOUIS PASTEUR

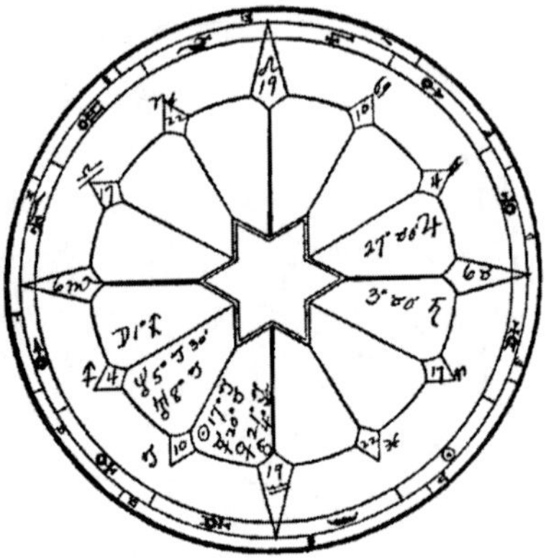

ALFRED RUSSEL WALLACE

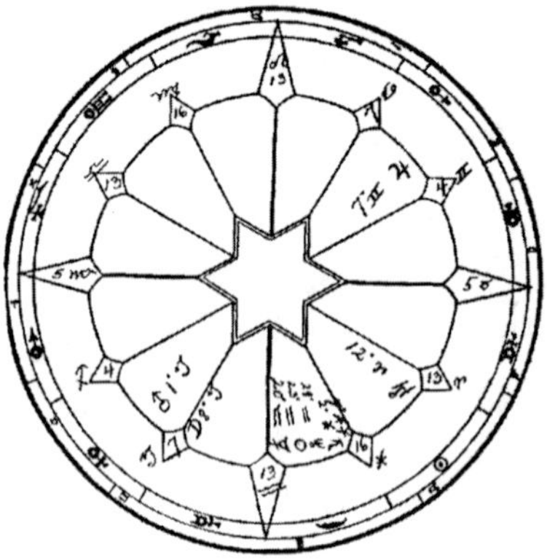

THOMAS EDISON

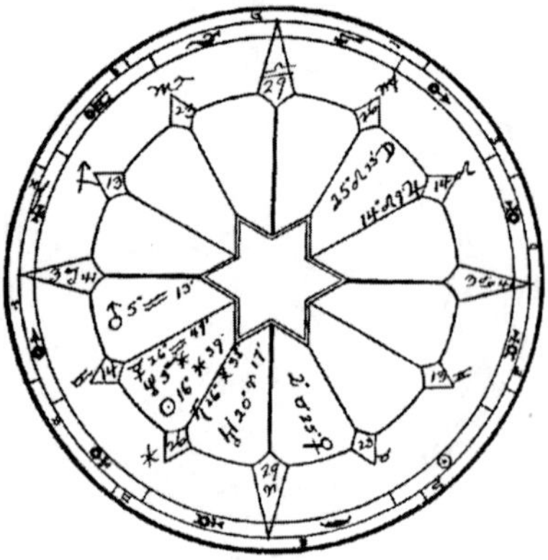

LUTHER BURBANK

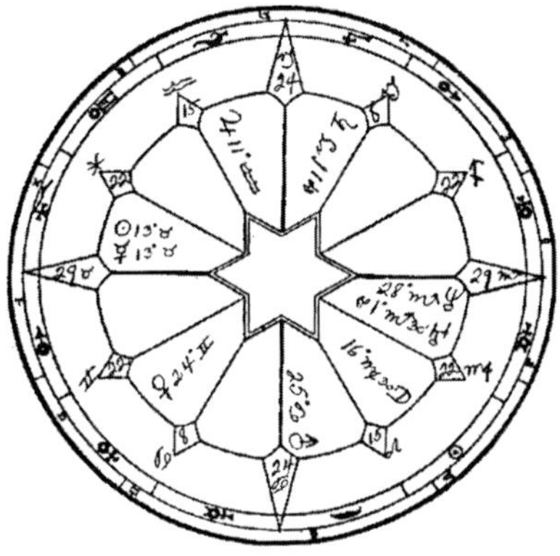

IMMANUEL KANT

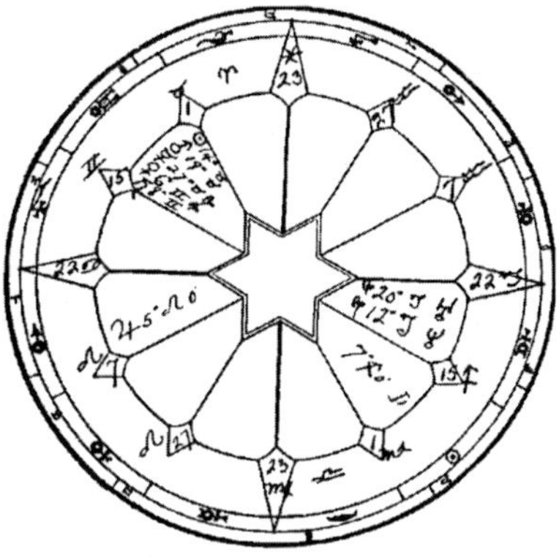

THOMAS HENRY HUXLEY

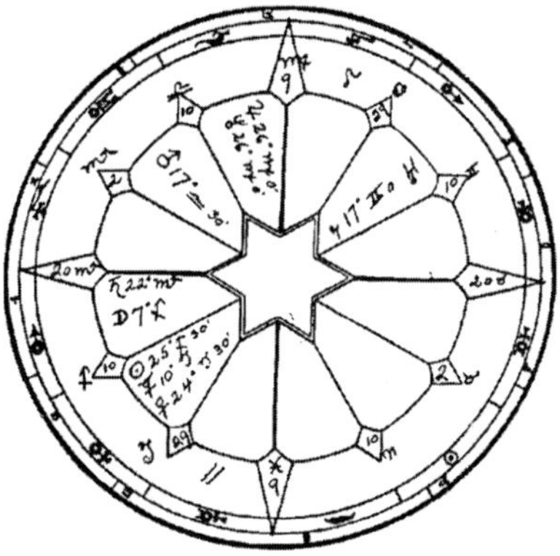

SIR HUMPHRY DAVY

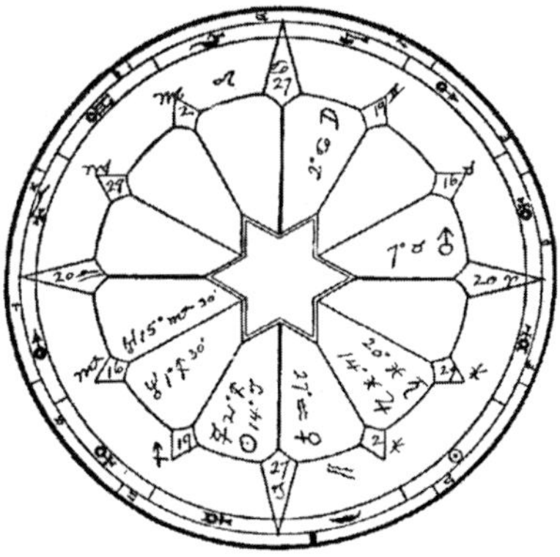

SIR ISAAC NEWTON

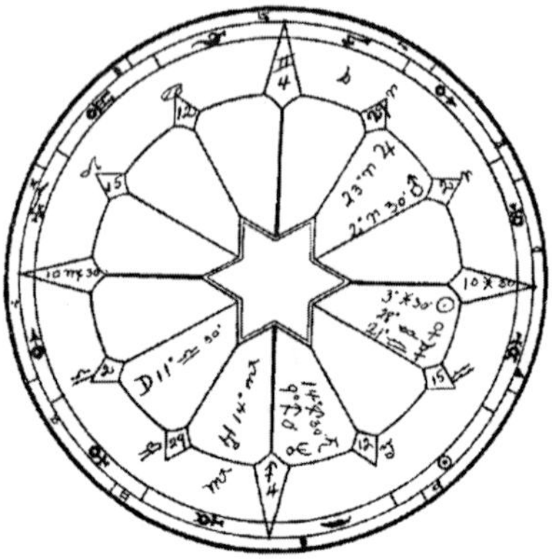

CHOPIN

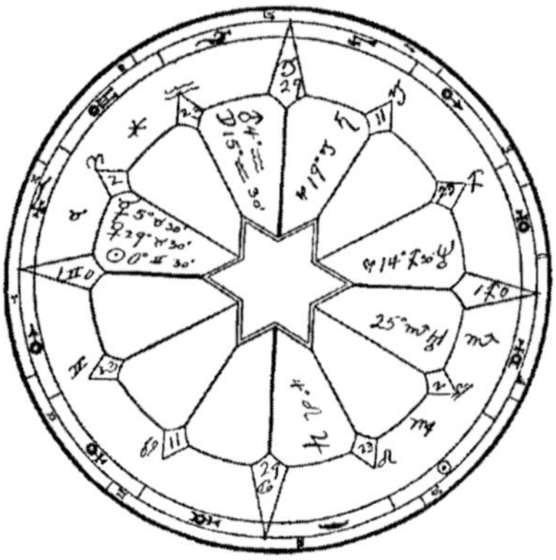

RICHARD WAGNER

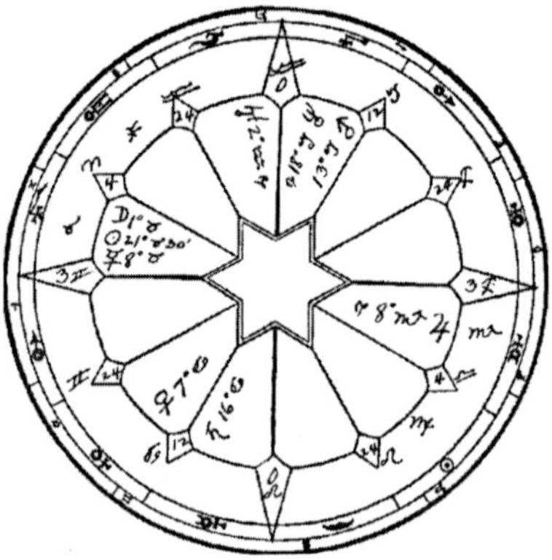

ROSSETTI

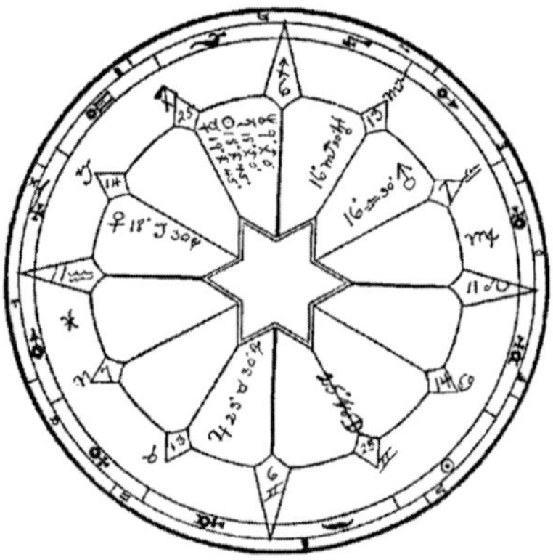

ALFRED DE MUSSET

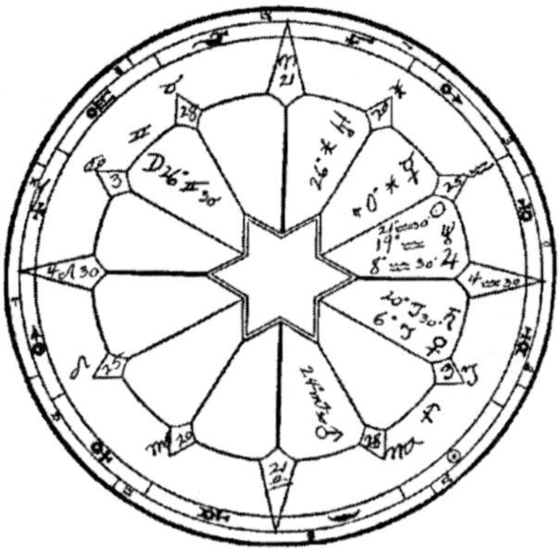

ADELINA PATTI

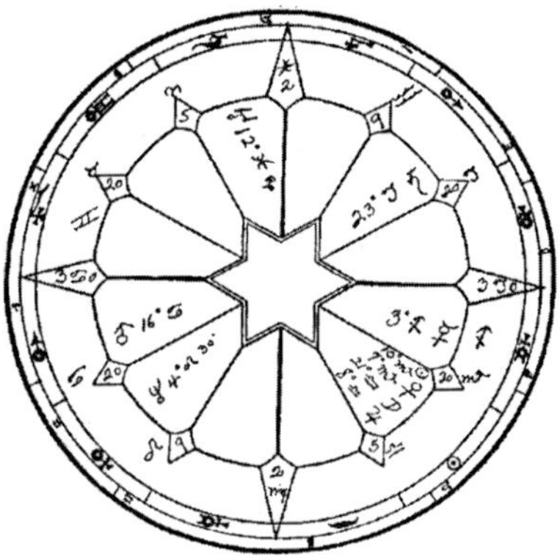

MARIE ANTOINETTE

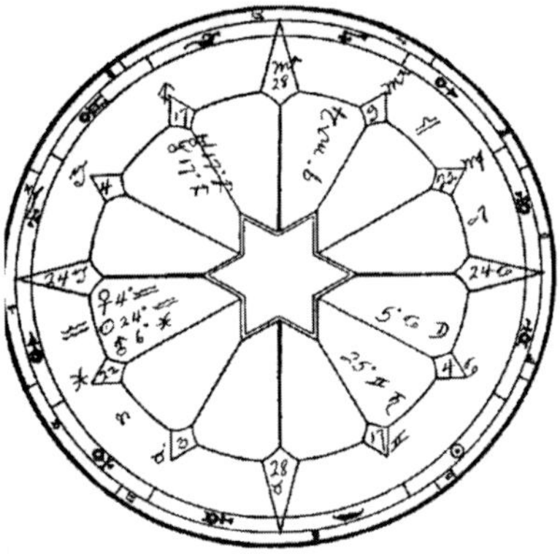

NELL GWYN

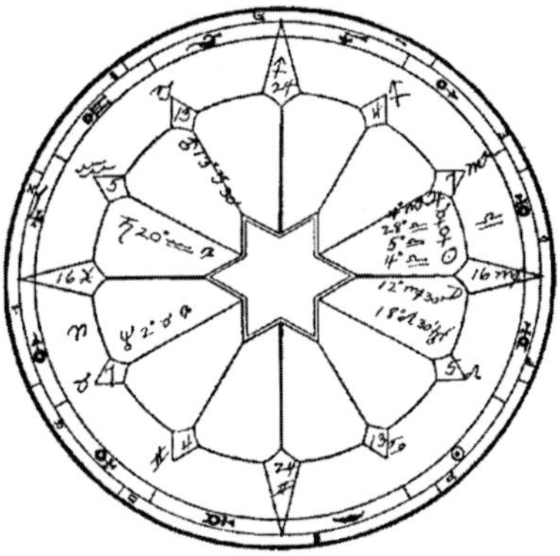

CLEO DE MÉRODE

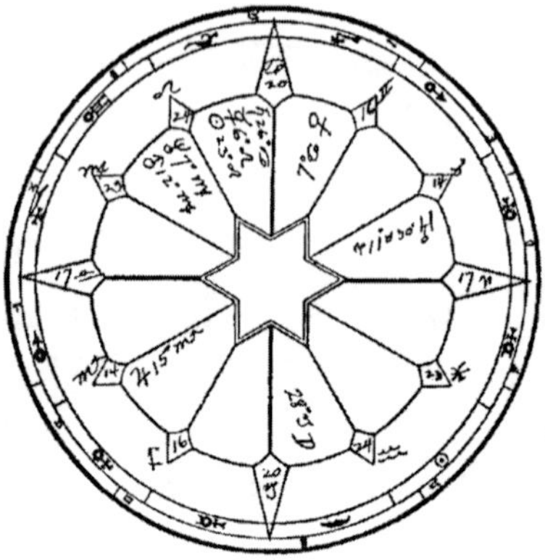

NAPOLEON

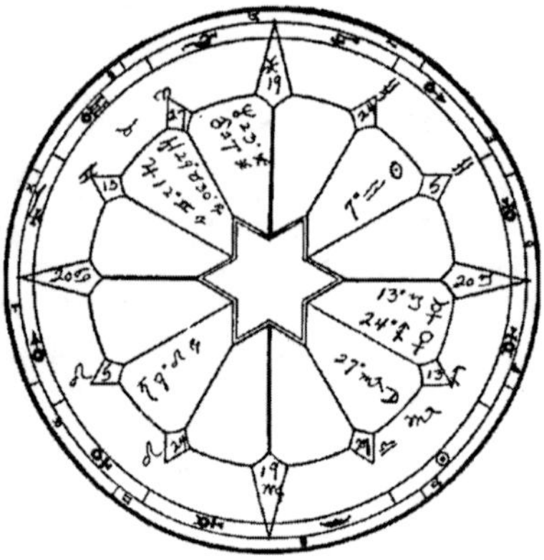

EX-KAISER WILLIAM II OF GERMANY

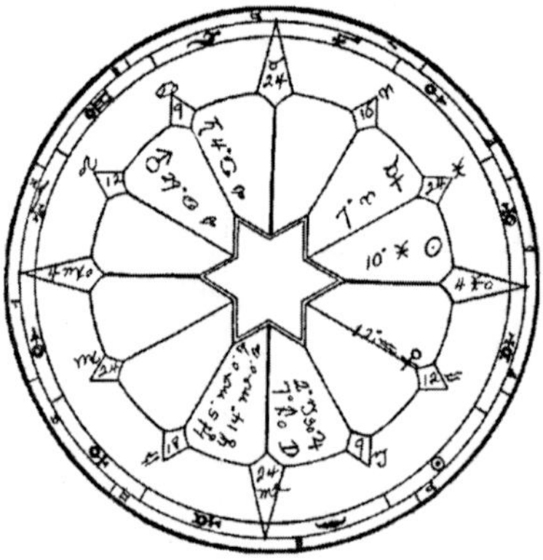

COPERNICUS

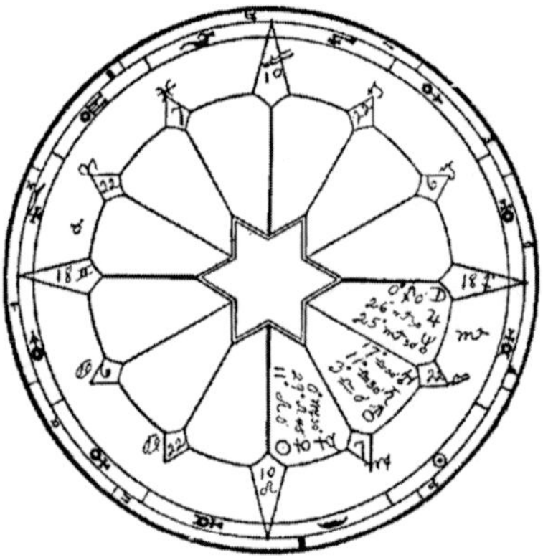

SIR WILLIAM HAMILTON

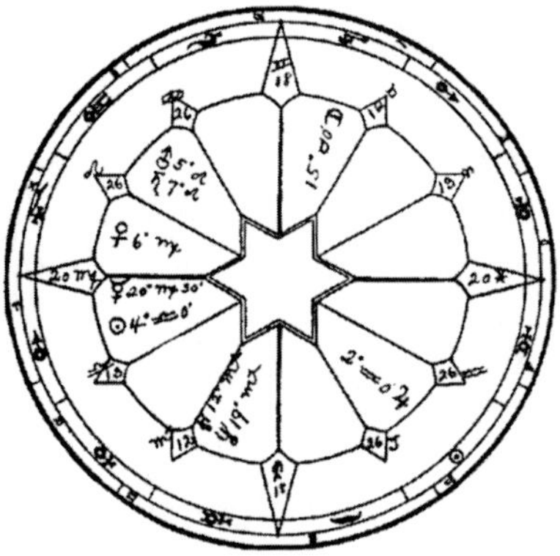

CÆSAR BORGIA

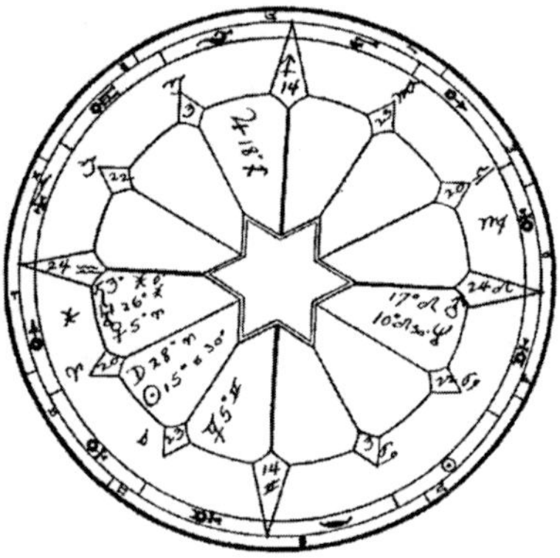

ROBESPIERRE

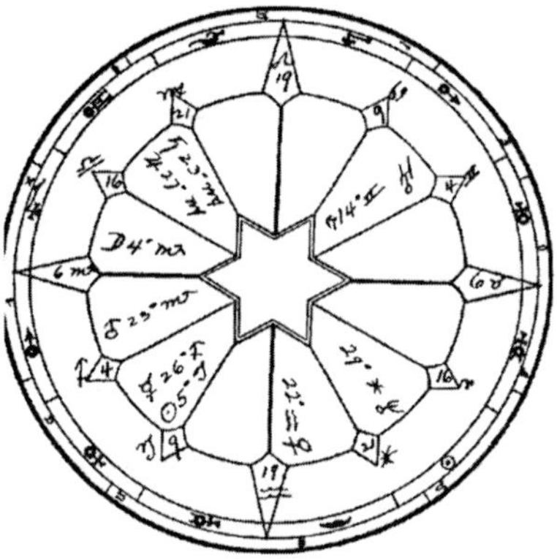

VAILLANT

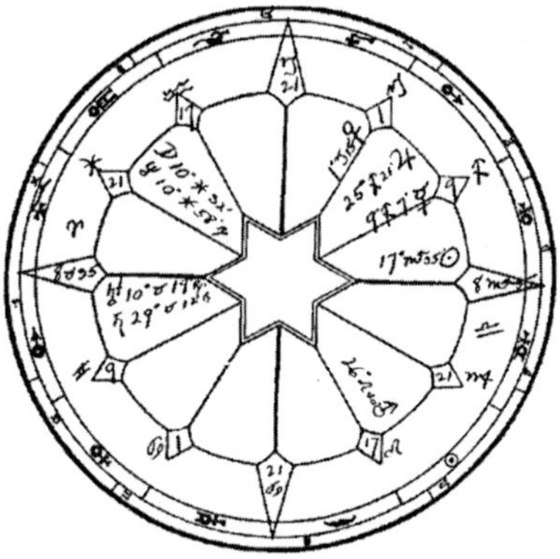

STANFORD WHITE

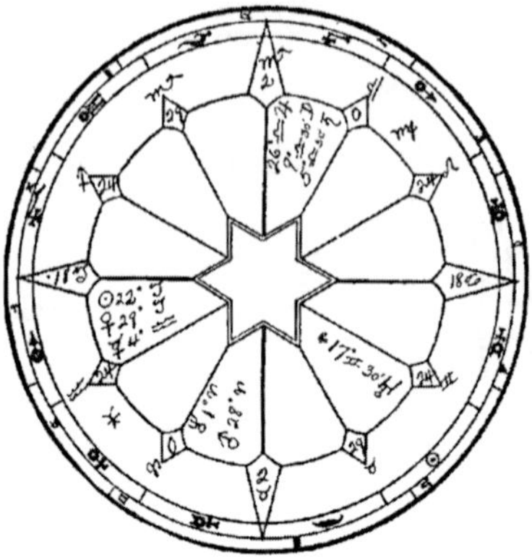

SWAMI VIVEKANANDA

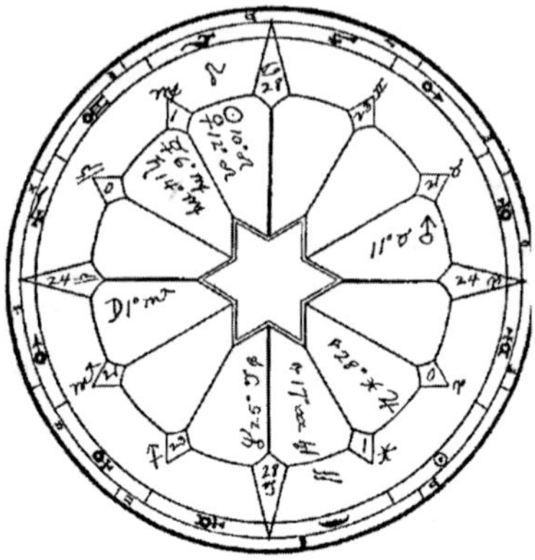

COLONEL OLCOTT

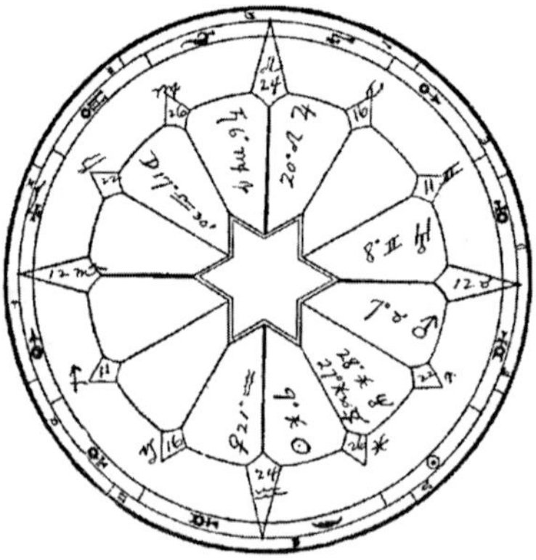

RUDOLPH STEINER

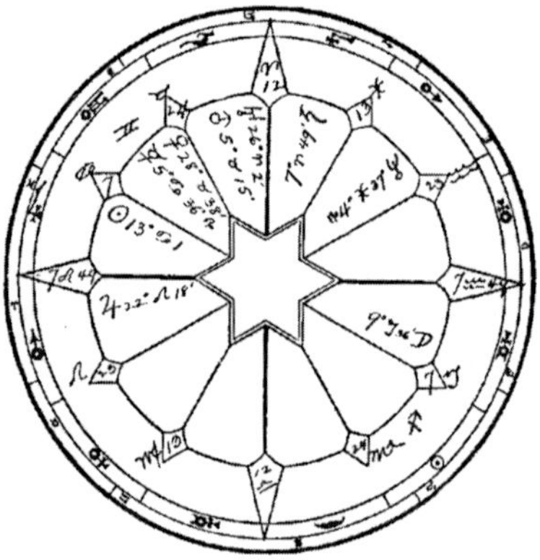

WILLIAM T. STEAD

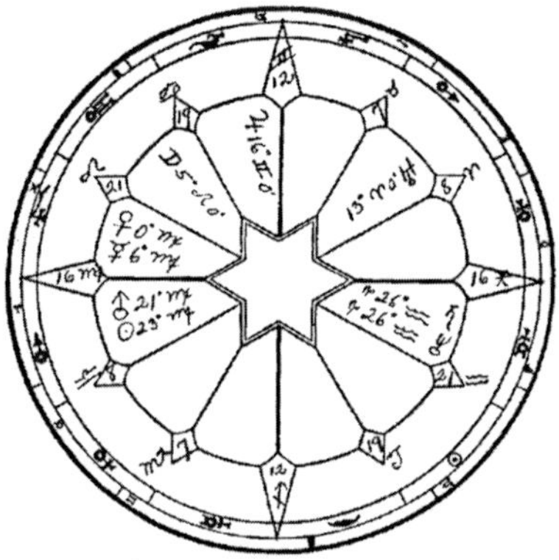

ANNA KINGSFORD

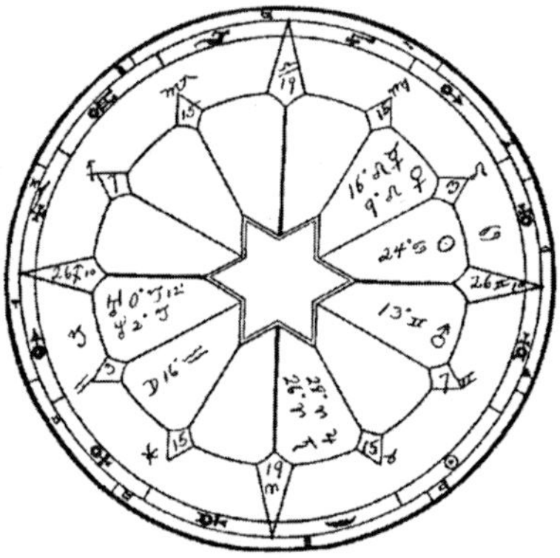

MARY BAKER EDDY

ANNIE BESANT

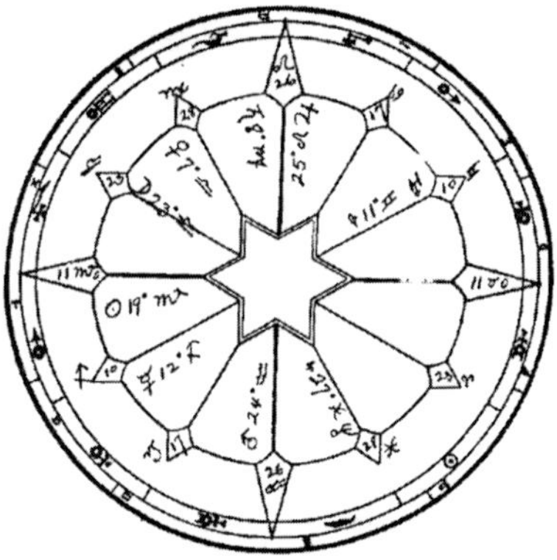

MARIE BASHKIRTSEFF

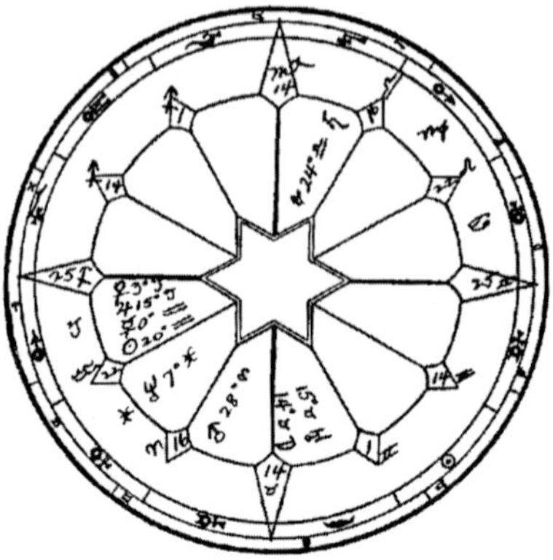

SWEDENBORG

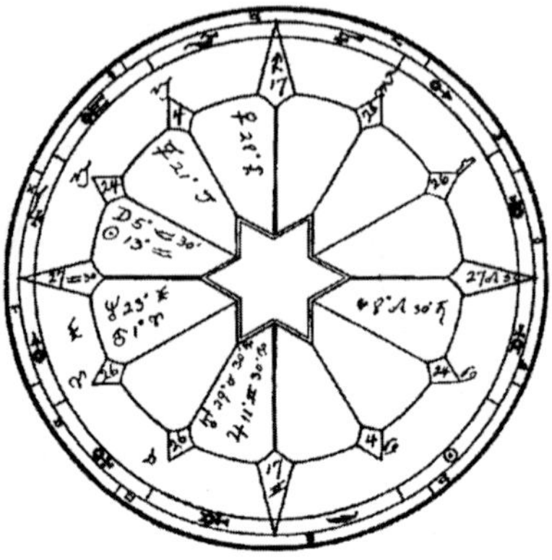

HAVELOCK ELLIS

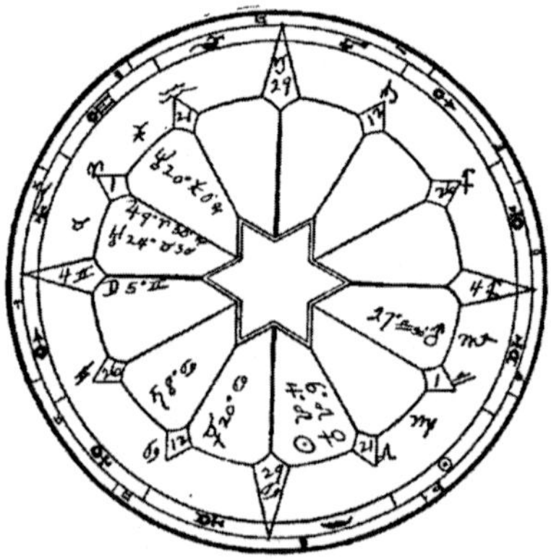

GEORGE BERNARD SHAW

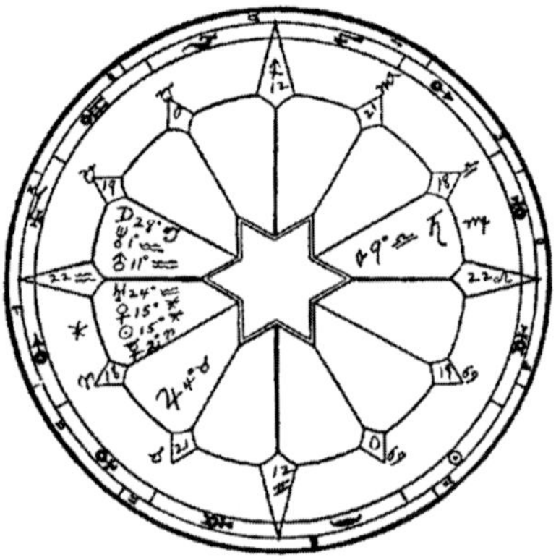

GEORGE DU MAURIER

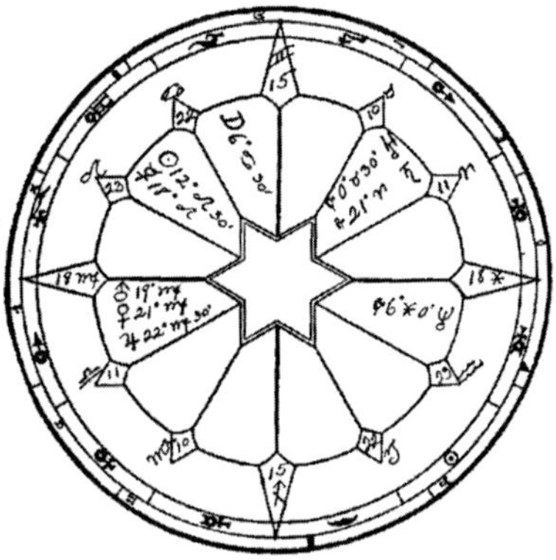

GUY DE MAUPASSANT

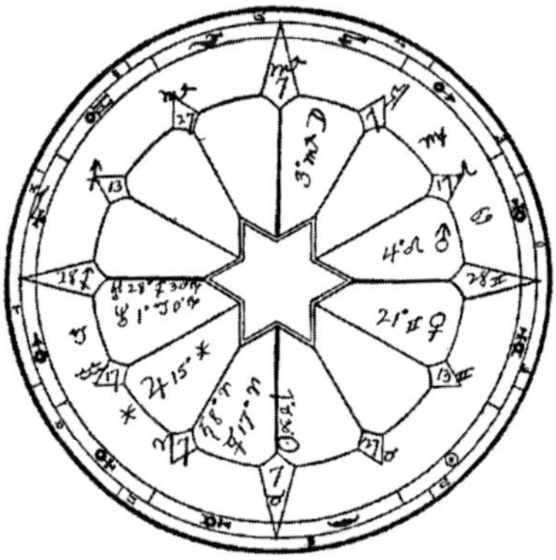

HERBERT SPENCER

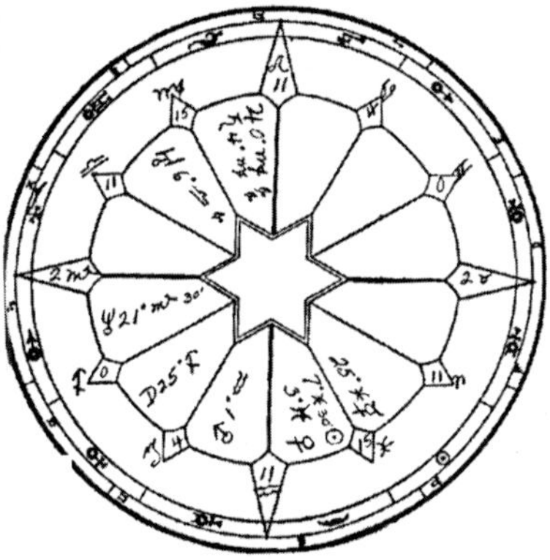

VICTOR HUGO

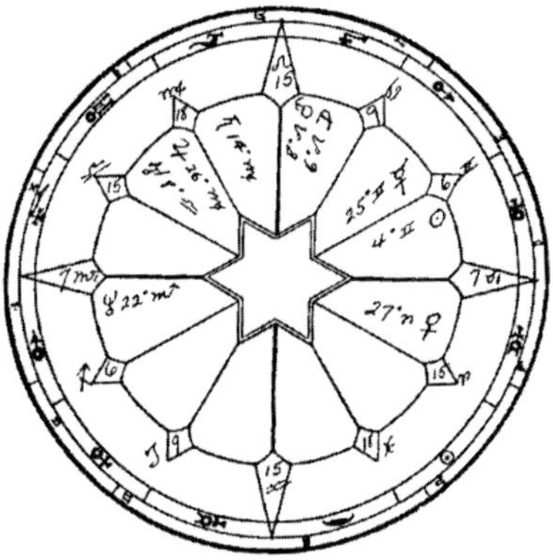

RALPH WALDO EMERSON

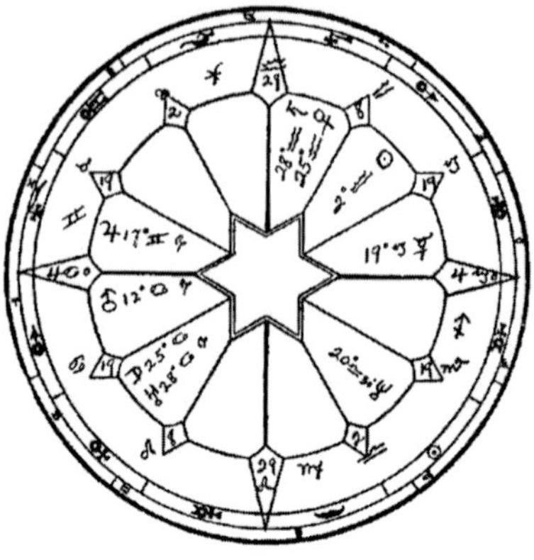

LORD BYRON

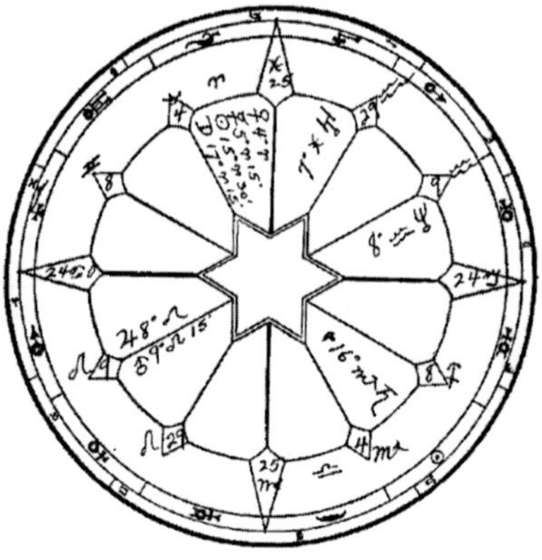

SWINBURNE

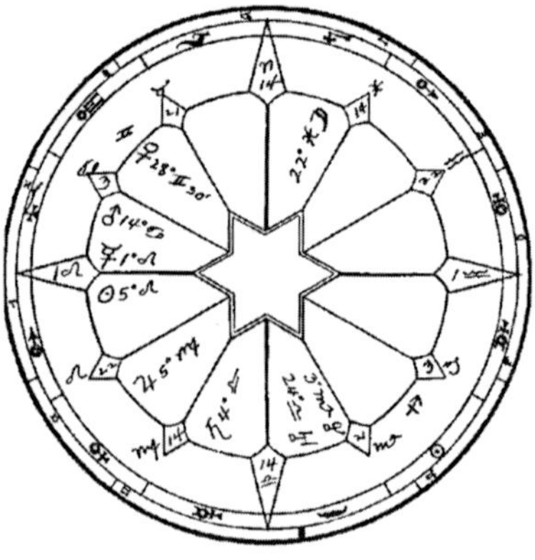

PETRARCH

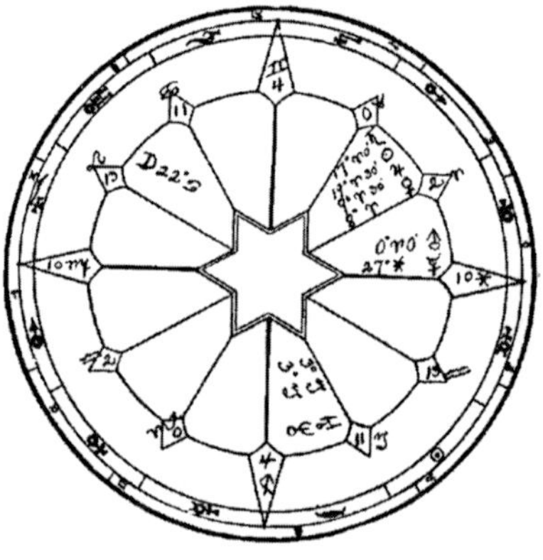

CHARLES BAUDELAIRE

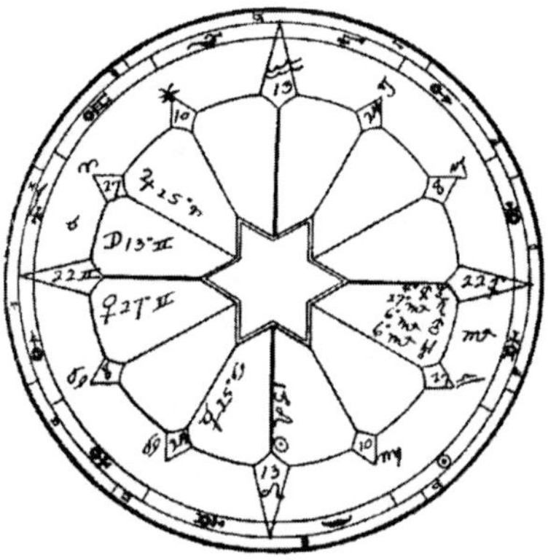

LORD ALFRED TENNYSON

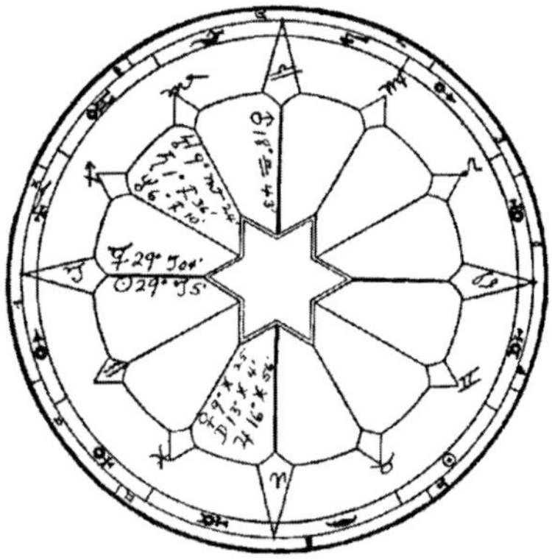

EDGAR ALLAN POE

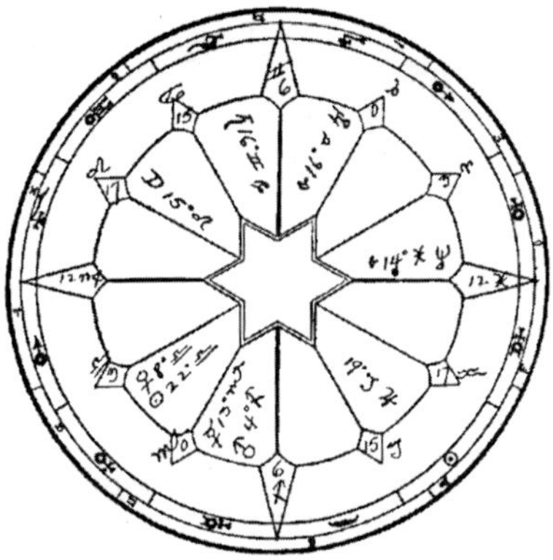

OSCAR WILDE

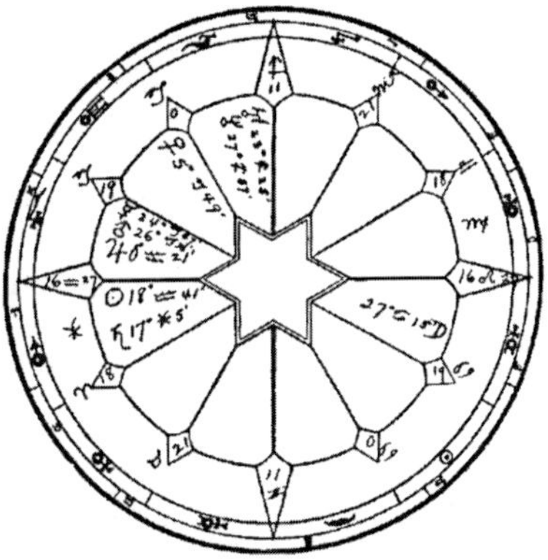

JOHN RUSKIN

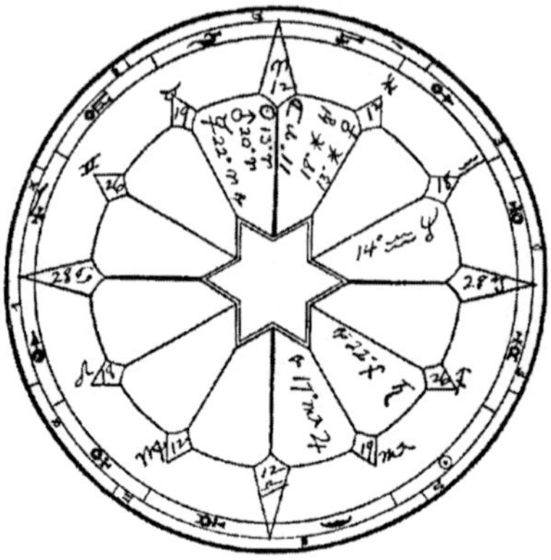

EMILE ZOLA

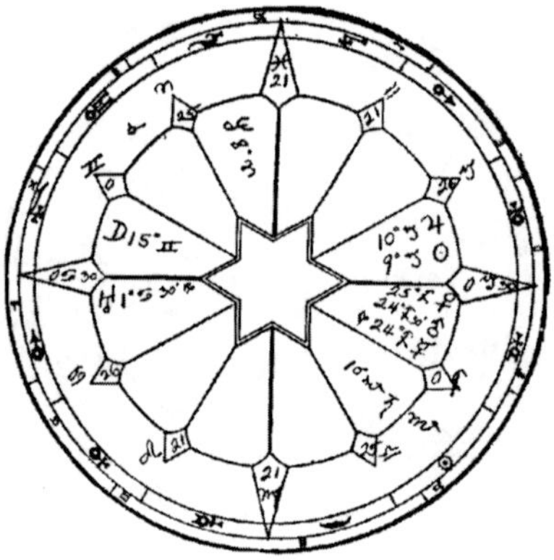

RUDYARD KIPLING

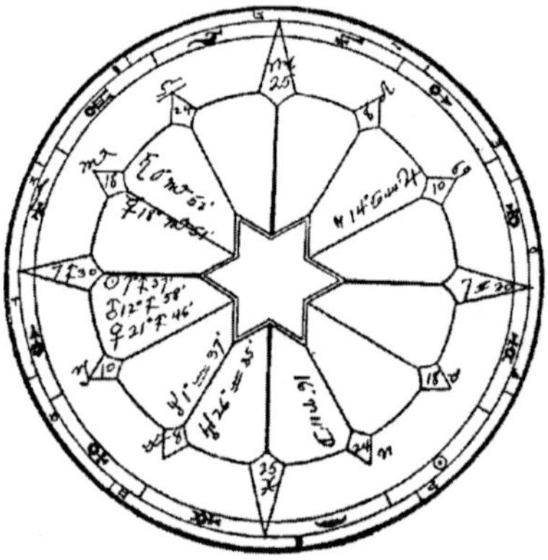

MARK TWAIN

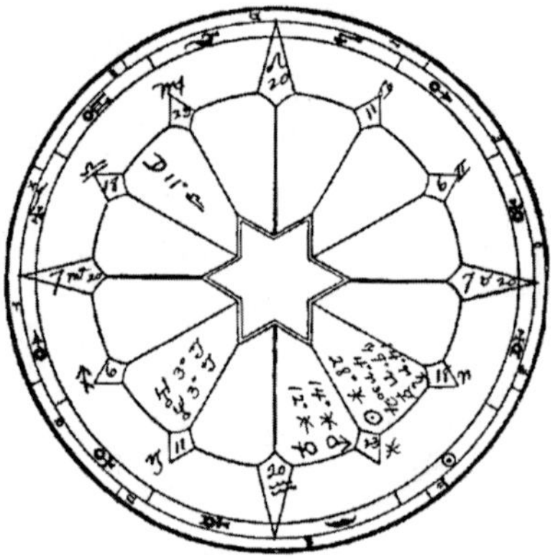

SIR RICHARD BURTON

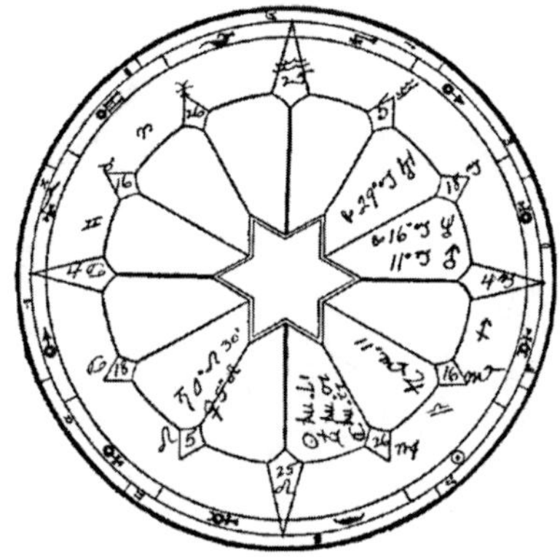

TOLSTOI

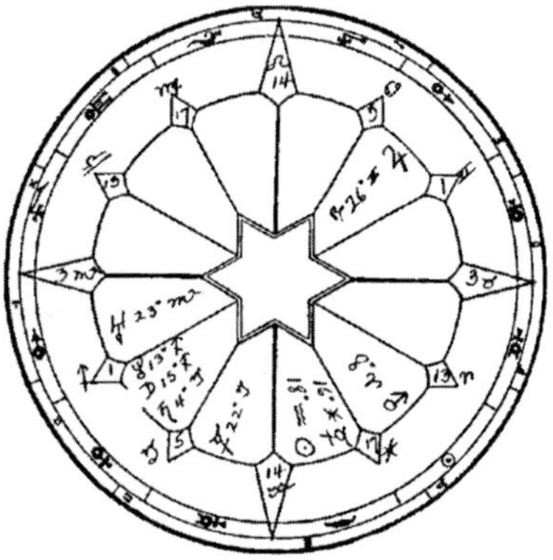

CHARLES DICKENS

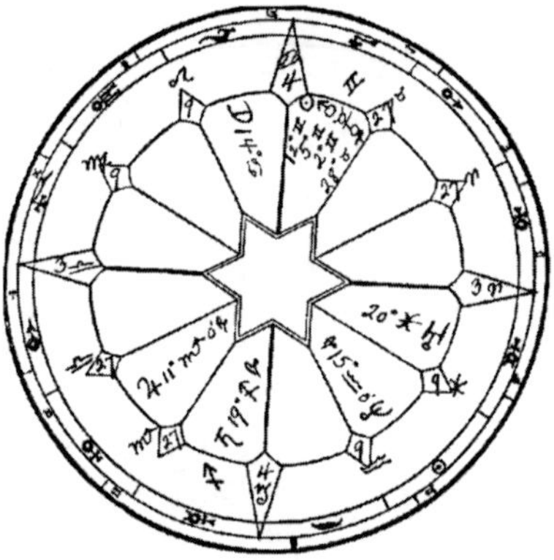

THOMAS HARDY

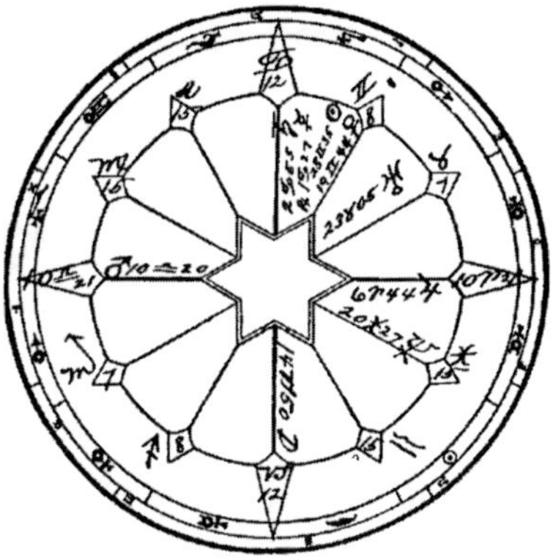

ELBERT HUBBARD

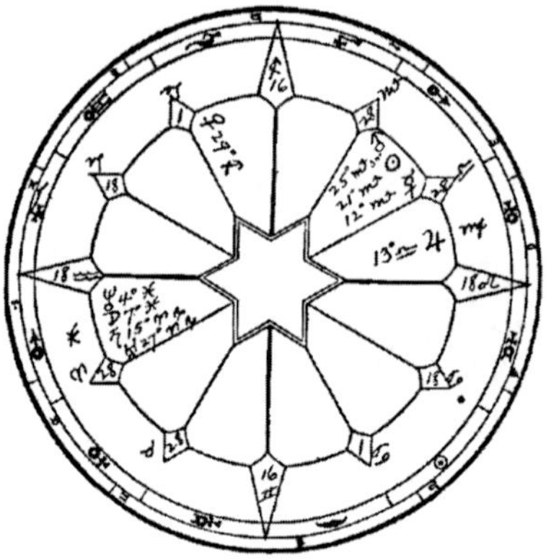

ROBERT LOUIS STEVENSON

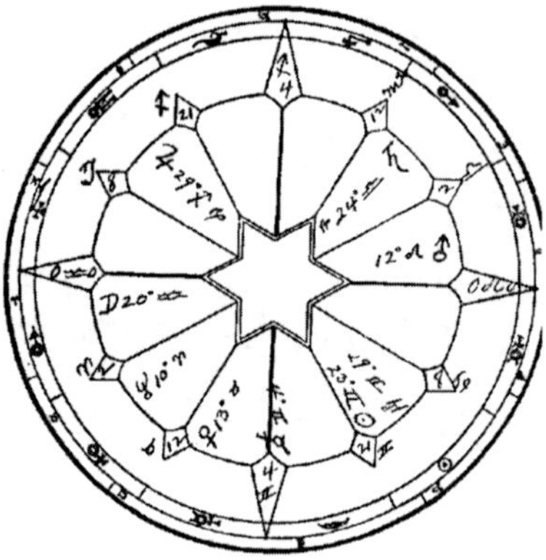

W. B. YEATS

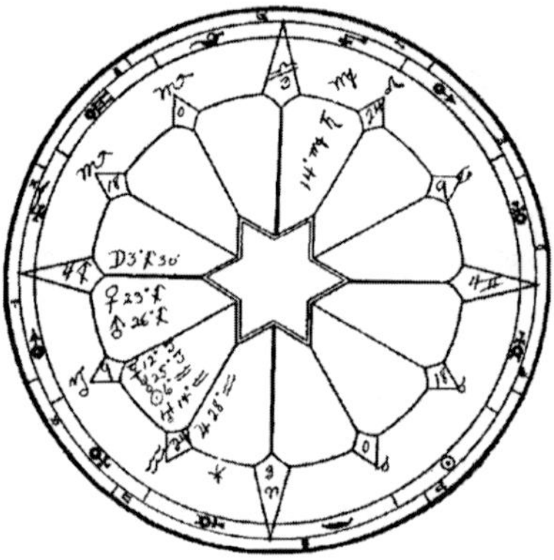

LEWIS CARROLL

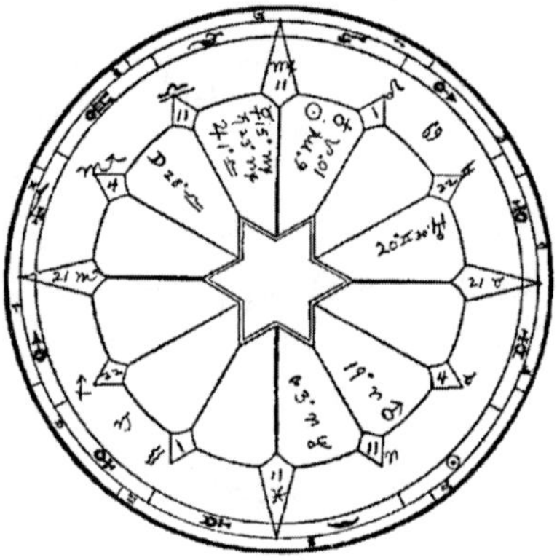

MAURICE MAETERLINCK

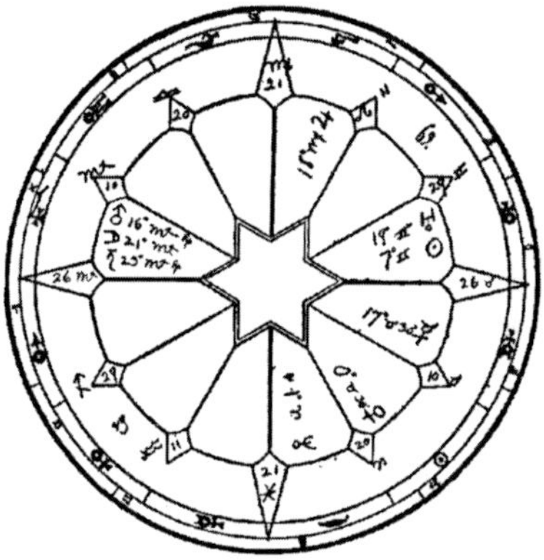

SIR THOMAS MOORE

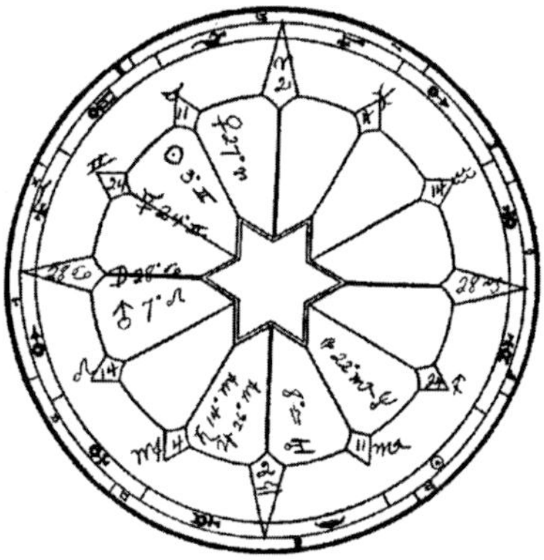

LORD LYTTON

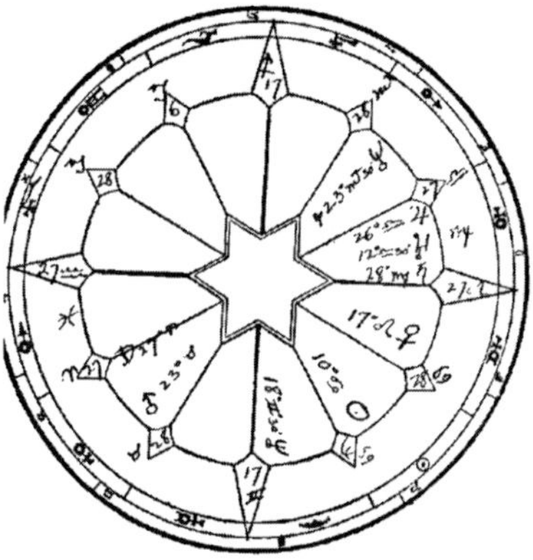

GEORGE SAND

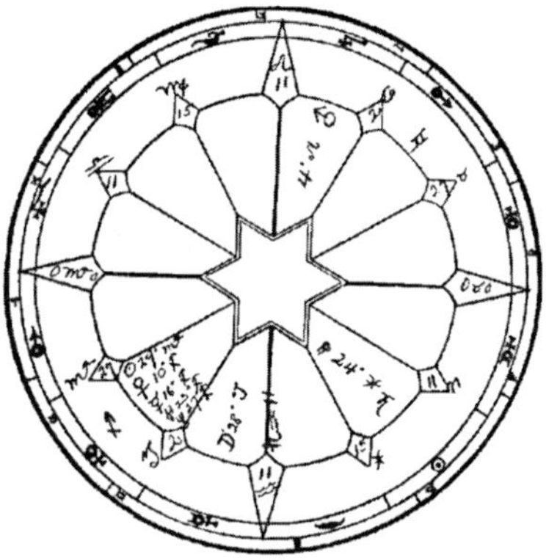

GEORGE ELIOT

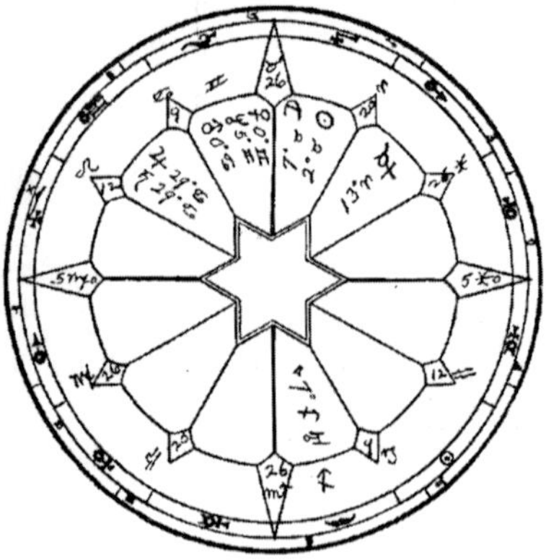

SHAKESPEARE

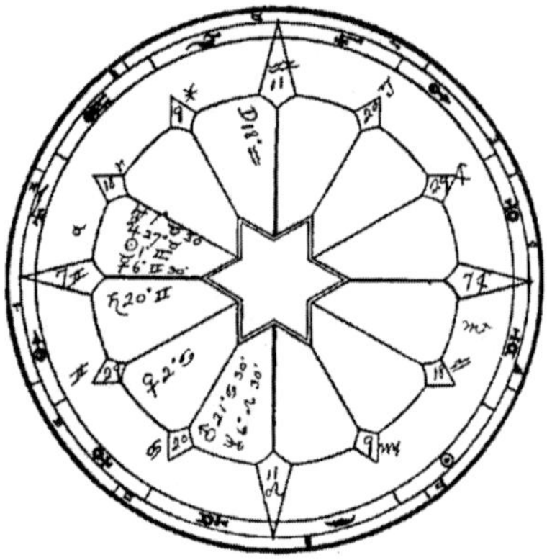

DANTE

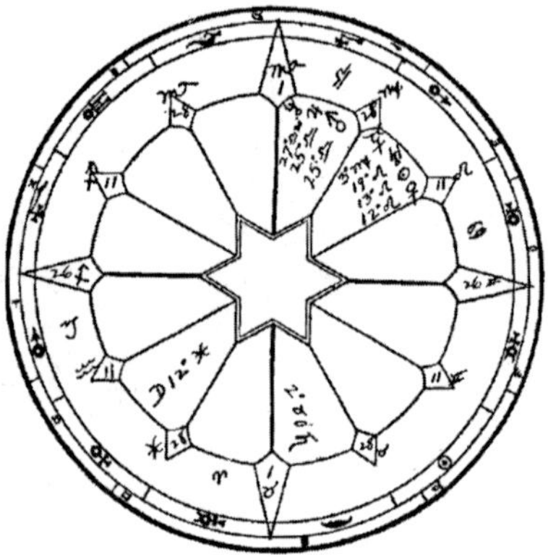

SHELLEY

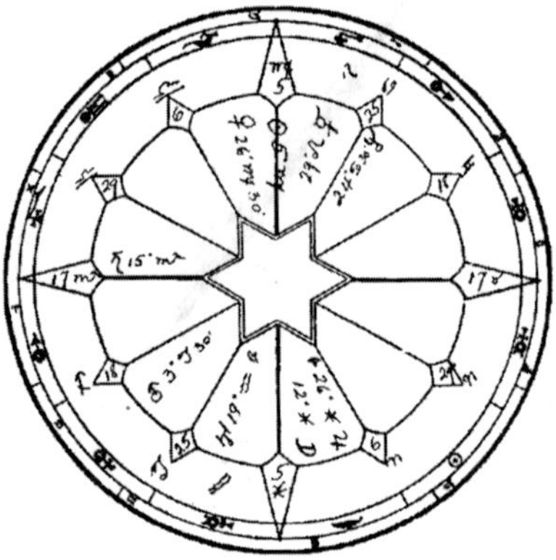

GOETHE